The Silence That Speaks

The Silence That Speaks

Short Stories by Indian Muslim Women

Edited by

HARIS QADEER

OXFORD
UNIVERSITY PRESS

OXFORD
UNIVERSITY PRESS

Oxford University Press is a department of the University of Oxford. It furthers the University's objective of excellence in research, scholarship, and education by publishing worldwide. Oxford is a registered trade mark of Oxford University Press in the UK and in certain other countries

Published in India by
Oxford University Press
22 Workspace, 2nd Floor, 1/22 Asaf Ali Road, New Delhi 110002, India

First Edition published in 2022

ISBN–13 (print edition): 978–0–19–013261–3
ISBN–10 (print edition): 0–19–013261–2

ISBN–13 (eBook): 978–9–35–497502–8
ISBN–10 (eBook): 9–35–497502–X

ISBN–13 (OSO): 978–9–35–497503–5
ISBN–10 (OSO): 9–35–497503–8

DOI: 10.1093/oso/9780190132613.001.0001

Typeset in Minion Pro 10/13
by Newgen KnowledgeWorks Pvt. Ltd.
Printed in India by Rakmo Press Pvt. Ltd.

For

Ammi

&

Muslim Women Across India

Contents

Foreword

Mehr Afshan Farooqi

The inordinate attention given to the alleged plight of "Muslim women" continues to grow along with the prejudiced notions of what constitutes "Islam" and the so-called Islamic world. The Muslim woman is stereotyped as a burqa clad, semi-literate, victim of triple talaq, and living in cloistered seclusion. The colonial fascination with the harem and subsequent discourses of veiling and unveiling have contributed and perpetuated this cynical view. The cataclysmic event of British India's partition also deepened the derisive view of Muslims as the "other." The massive literature that documents partition mostly bypasses women's role, especially Muslim women's participation in the freedom movement and their suffering in the wake of partition. Even feminist scholars have neglected the particular experience of Muslim women during partition.

The Silence That Speaks brings to us a collection of Thirty Eight short stories culled from over a century of fiction writing by Muslim women from India. The volume excavates stories from now-forgotten women's journals such as *Tehzeeb-e-Niswan* and *Saogat.* The editorial choices include stories from the rich terrain of regional languages and give space to both renowned and lesser known authors. This in itself is a complicated task which is compounded by the question of identity. What is Muslim identity? What does it mean to be an Indian Muslim woman? How is an Indian Muslim distinct from a Pakistani or Bangladeshi Muslim? The editor rightfully argues that identity is multifaceted: it is cultural and political rather than religious. It is influenced by class, education, region, and locale.

The choice to begin with Rokeya Sakhawat Hossain's classic story, "Sultana's Dream," is astute because it speaks to womanhood as an entity that is not splintered by sectarian or regional labels. Many stories in this path-breaking anthology engage with subjects that are relevant to the contemporary but also connect with the historical and cultural past. An unusual story that stands out from the bunch of fiction from the early part of the twentieth century is Mrs. Abdul Qadir's "The Tutor's Secret." This story is a truly fantastic narrative that builds on folk and mythic tales surrounding snakes. Mrs. Qadir was a prolific writer of horror stories, melodramas, and speculative fiction who published her first collection, *Lashon ke Shahr* in 1939. She, along with women authors of her generation such as Hijab Imtiaz Ali and Rashid Jahan, transcended stereotypes associated with women as writers.

Some powerful stories touch upon subjects that are symbiotic with what it means to be female. For example, Jeelani Bano's "A Day in the Labour Room," is a poignant yet forceful narration of what a woman undergoes during childbirth, abortion, or caesarian section. Shahjahana's Telugu story "Billiee" skilfully shows how the mistrust against a new neighbour is vented on a pet cat. There are stories in this volume that boldly tackle the communal boundaries that separate lovers, gender boundaries, and the politics of maligning the other with labels.

In curating a selection of stories from Assamese to Bengali, Hindi and Urdu to Tamil, Telugu, and Malayalam, the editor of this anthology challenges the stereotype of Muslim and Urdu. Indian Muslim women write in the regional languages from the length and breadth of India. They enrich and are enriched by the local culture to which they belong.

Mehr A Farooqi
University of Virginia

Acknowledgements

Anthologies of translated stories are almost always collaborative acts, and in an ambitious project such as this, which brings together stories from different Indian languages and cultures, one accrues many debts. This book would have not seen the light of the day without the generous support that I received from authors, translators, colleagues, family, and friends. A special thanks to all the authors and the translators: those who specially wrote stories for this collection, who translated stories, and who allowed me to use their published stories.

The idea of book was conceived a couple of years ago during one of the seminars of the MPhil course that I offer on the writings of Muslim women at the Department of English, University of Delhi. I thank all the faculty members and the students of the department for their encouragements and suggestions. An early draft of the introduction was written in Berlin, Germany, during my visit to Potsdam University, as a visiting faculty in 2019. I am deeply indebted to all the faculty members of the Department of English, Potsdam University, especially to Dirk Wiemann, Tanya Mayer, and Florian Schybilski—the trio was super-amazing hosts! I would also like to thank Rimli Bhattacharya and Jyoti Sabrawal who were caring, courteous, and tolerant during my stint at Germany (as they still are!).

Thanks are due to Prof. AR Kidwai, Prof. Supriya Chaudhri, Prof. Parvaiz Talib, Prof. Anisur Rehman, Dr. Rakhshanda Jalil, and Prof. Sukrita Paul for their constant encouragement and support. My PhD and MPhil scholars and the students of Masters deserve special thanks for the help that they extended at the different stages of the preparation of the manuscript. Thank you Abiral and Hiba for reading the draft of the introduction. Thank you Rafeeque, Archit, and Iqra for reading the drafts of various translations. Thank you Feba Rashid for helping with Sheeba's story and thank you Titas Bose for your archival assistance with Bengali stories. A special thanks to Zakia Mashadi for helping me to find the contact details of family members of Wajeda Tabassum and of Jeelani Bano.

I would like to thank Zakia Mashadi and Annie Zaidi for allowing me to use their published pieces for this collection. Zakia Mashadi's translation of Jeelani Bano's "A Day in the Labour Room" was first published in *Alien Home and Other Stories* (NBT, 2006) and Annie Zaidi's English story, Registered Post was published in *The Caravan* (2015)

A more general vote of thanks for supporting this project in myriad ways is due to Ananya Bhatia (ex-commissioning editor, OUP), Darshana Sarkar (commissioning editor, OUP), and the entire editorial team of the Oxford University Press, New Delhi, India. Darshana has been extremely prompt with her email replies and immensely helpful with her suggestions.

Over the years that the work of this anthology evolved, my family has been extremely helpful. I can't thank them enough for unconditional love and emotional support. Thank you my own motley group of friends: Asiya Zahoor, Bodhisattva Chattopadhyay, Ira Raja, Shad Naved, and Shweta Sachdeva Jha. Apart from all these names, many more people have assisted me directly or indirectly, though I can't thank each of them individually, they all are an indispensable part of the book.

Thank you everyone!

Introduction

Haris Qadeer

> "No one knew how many young minds these woman had inflamed by their action, by removing the idea of purdah from their mind."
>
> —Ismat Chughtai, *Kaghazi hai Pairahan*

> "If there is such a thing as a comparative degree of invisibility, Muslim women are even more invisible than are other Indian women."
>
> —Gail Minault, *Secluded Scholars*

In the preface to her travel book, *The Night of New Moon: Encounters with Muslim Women* (1992), Anees Jung, a journalist and an author, recalls an interesting remark by her European friend: "you don't look like a Muslim woman" (1992: 02). Baffled by the comment, Jung rethinks her status as a Muslim woman, ponders over the markers of her identity, and travels to different places in India in order to understand the diversity of lives and subjectivities of women of her religious community. Jung's book was one of the first texts that went beyond exploring the confines of stereotypical images of Indian Muslim women. Even though more than two decades have passed since the publication of the book, the discourses pertaining to the identity of Muslim women have not seen much change. Rakhshanda Jalil's recent book, *But You Don't Look Like A Muslim* (2019) demonstrates the construction of Muslim identity in the popular imagination. Analysing the problematics of representations of the Muslim community in literary and socio-political discourses, she writes how "the

Haris Qadeer, *Introduction* In: *The Silence That Speaks*. Edited by: Haris Qadeer, Oxford University Press. © Oxford University Press India 2022. DOI: 10.1093/oso/9780190132613.003.0001 entire Muslim community has suffered because of this steady infiltration of misconceptions and piling up of images and ideas" (2019: 08) and how she, often, meets people who are intrigued as she doesn't "conform to most people's idea of a Muslim woman" (2019: 01).

Most of the portrayals of economic and socio-political positioning of Muslim women are inhibited by the tropes of *purdah* and seclusion traditionally associated with Islam, and these tropes become visible indicators not only of Muslim women's identity but also of the deep-rooted problems with the community and the religion. Helen Watson expresses similar concern in *Women in the City of Dead.* She concurs: "the image of a veiled Muslim woman seems to be one of the most popular Western ways of representing the 'problems of Islam'" (1992: 153). Her observations reverberate contemporary socio-political discourses surrounding Muslim womanhood not only in America and Europe but also in Asian countries including India. The issues and debates pertaining to the portrayal of Muslim women seldom move beyond the "residual influence of colonial discourses of veiling and unveiling" (MacDonald, 2006: 07).

A Gaze of Her Own

There is no dearth of literature available on the representation of Muslim women on the world's literary map. Mohja Kahf traces the evolving Muslim woman archetype in Western literature in *Western Representation of Muslim Women: From Termagant to Odalisque*. She observes that the portrayal of Muslim women has undergone many changes, and "there is nothing essential or timeless behind Western representations of the Muslim woman; they are products of specific moments and developments in culture" (1999: 02). These representations range from the bold, powerful, and heroic queens in the medieval age to odalisques or concubines in the eighteen-century. She demonstrates how the emergence of "the subjugated Muslim woman concurred with the build-up of British and French empires in the nineteenth century, which, in subjugating whole Muslim societies, had a direct interest in viewing the Muslim woman as oppressed—even as their policies had oppressive effects on flesh-and-blood Muslim women" (1999: 06). Her reading of the emergence of the images of the "oppressed Muslim Women" during the colonial period resonates with the contemporary socio-political debates on the representations of Muslim women in different cultures and societies.

In an attempt to challenge the Western representations of monolithic narratives of Muslim women, several Muslim women authors in Europe, America, and Arab countries are publishing their own counternarratives. Lila Abu-Lughod's *Do Muslim Women Need Saving* (2013) is a remarkable intervention in this area. She describes the book as an "intellectual journey to make sense of the disjuncture" (2013: 04) between her experiences and the public attitudes towards Muslim women, and attempts to examine "the politics and the ethics of the international circulation of discourses about 'oppressed Muslim women'" (2013: 16). Mariam Khan, the author of *It's Not about Burqa*, counters the hegemonic representations by diversifying the narratives of Muslim women in the West. In her interview with Reuter, she explains her struggle to counter the Muslim women stereotypes: "Muslim female narratives are often co-opted by everyone who isn't a Muslim—rarely will you hear authentically, or in an unfiltered way from Muslim women, and it is really unfair" (Kanso, 2019: n.p.). In contemporary geopolitics, the stereotype of the subjugated Muslim women continues to dominate public discourses throughout the world, and as Abu-Lughod would put, "Muslim women's issues regularly stir up international debate in ways that concerns about women elsewhere in the world do not" (2013: 16).

Similar tropes of representation are also prevalent in India. Contemporary scholars such as Flavia Agnes, Zoya Hasan, Ritu Menon, Shahida Lateef, Ghazala Jamil, and Nida Kirmani examine various socio-political issues pertaining to Muslim women in different spheres of Indian societies. Kirmani elucidates the ways in which Muslim women are generally represented in socio-political discourses and discusses how they are often perceived as symbolic bearers of the identity of the Muslim community. She comments:

> The category of 'Muslim women in India' is constructed through various discursive channels including the (local, national and international) media, the state and academia, as well as in the discourse of religious groups and of leaders of national as well as transnational women's organisations. (2009: 48)

Hasan and Menon argue that in postcolonial India, it has become quite usual to view the Muslim community and Muslim women as a monolithic category. They critique the reductive approach of such generalisation which is based on "a complete misapprehension of Islamic history, culture and politics" (2005: 53) and propose the need to deconstruct cultural essentialism involved in imagining Muslim womanhood in relation to the tropes of multiple marriages, triple talaq, and purdah. Flavia Agnes, in her interesting article, "From Shah Bano to Kausar Bano: Contextualising the 'Muslim Woman' with a Communalised Polity," analyses the fixation of Indian media with Muslim women's victimhood and examines how "in order to fit the media formula Muslim women had to be portrayed as victims of sexist and obscurantist biases within community" (Agnes, 2012: 41). The hypervisibility of images of oppressed Muslim women in print and electronic media, to an extent, has resulted in the creation of Muslim stereotypes. In the loud rhetoric around the discourses and debates surrounding Muslims in India, experiences, efforts, and voices of Muslim women are, often, ignored. They become mute witnesses to the subject of endless discussions on various issues pertaining to Islam, identity, agency, and womanhood.

While the scholarship on Muslim women's writings is growing in the West, and there is a surge in publications of life writings, fiction, and poetry, in India, the field has received little attention. Scholars such as Gail Minault, Siobhan Lambert-Hurley, Rakhshanda Jalil, M Asaduddin, Priyamvada Gopal, and Barnita Bagchi should be credited for initiating much-needed academic discussions on Muslim women's writing in India.

A Literature of Their Own

Elaine Showalter, while analysing "The Female Tradition" in the women's literary history, draws upon John Gross's idea of "residual Great Traditionalism". She points out the limitation of focusing only on a few women novelists in English literary history:

> ... even theoretical studies of "the woman novelist" turn out to be endless recyclings and recombinations of insights about "indispensable Jane and George." Criticism of women novelists, while focusing on these happy few, has ignored those who are not "great," and left them out of anthologies, histories, text-books, and theories. Having lost sight

> of the minor novelists, who were the links in the chain that bound one generation to the next, we have not had a very clear understanding of the continuities in women's writing, nor any reliable information about the relationships between the writers' lives and the changes in the legal, economic, and social status of women. (Showalter, 1977: 07)

While exploring the writings by Muslim women authors in India, one may only come across "indispensable" Ismat and Rokeya. Curriculums of a few Indian universities have given spaces to these renowned authors, but "the links in the chain that bound one generation to the next" (Showalter, 1977: 07) need to be explored in order to have "a very clear understanding of the continuities" (07) in Muslim women's writing. Drawing attention to an important point in this connection, in the introduction to his translation of Chughtai's *Kaghazi hai Pairahan* (*A Life in Words*), Asaduddin writes, "accounts of Muslim women's resistance from behind the purdah have not been fully recognised" (2012: xiii). From the turn of the twentieth century, there were many Muslim women authors—purdah-observing and defiant—who, through their writings, vociferously critiqued patriarchy and orthodoxy in Muslim societies.

It is quite difficult to map the literary history of Muslim women authors in India as the geography and the idea of the nation have changed with times. This field of research, like any other study of genealogy, "requires patience and a knowledge of details, and it depends on a vast accumulation of source material" (Foucault 1977: 140). The earliest writing by a woman of Muslim ancestry could be traced back to Begum Gulbadan (1523–1603), who is considered to be the first woman from the Mughal court to have written a full-length account of the life of a Mughal ruler. Her memoirs, *Ahval-e-Humayun Padshah* (The Life of King Humayun), apart from giving details of the life of Emperor Humayun, presents glimpses of the *zenana* of the court as well as of her own life. Writing life narratives and poetry was common among the women from the Mughal royal court. Jahanara Begum (1614–1681), the princess who designed Chandni Chowk, was a poet and a hagiographer. She authored books such as *Sahibia,* a hagiography of Sufi saint Mulla Shah Badakshi, and *Munis-ul-Arwah,* a biographical account of Sufi Khwaja Moinuddin Chishti. Zeb-un-Nissa "Makhfi" (1702–1639), the eldest child of Mughal Emperor Aurangzeb, has a collection of Persian ghazals, titled *Diwan-e-Makhfi* to her credit. It won't be gainsaying that the Mughal era witnessed a significant amount of women's contribution to the development and sustenance of art and literature. Apart from the women from the Mughal court, one could also think of two other important early women poets: Habba Khatoon (1554–1609), the Nightingale of Kashmir, occupies an important place in Kashmiri literary history. She composed and sung poems in memory of her husband Yusuf Shah Chak, who died in prison after he was incarcerated by Emperor Akbar. The courtesan-poet, Mah Laqa Bai "Chanda" (1768–1824), who lived in Nizam-ruled Hyderabad, was the first woman poet to have a complete collection of Urdu *ghazals* to her credit. Her collection *Gulzar-e-Mahlaqa* was published posthumously.

The decline of Mughal sovereignty in India severely affected the tradition of writings by the women of the court, and it is extremely rare to come across any piece of women's writing during the period of the decline of the Mughal Empire. However, references to the presence of Muslim women in zenanas are found in various narratives by male authors and the English memsahibs who visited India. Mrs. Meer Hasan Ali, a British woman who married an elite Indian Muslim, wrote detailed accounts of the lives of Muslim women in her book *Observations on the Mussulmauns of India* (1852). An interesting book that outlines the "signs of progress in India" and deals with "a new era for Muslim women" is *Daylight in Harem* (1911) by Annie Von Sommer and Samuel M. Zwemer.

Networks of socio-political reforms among the Muslim communities in the later decades of the nineteenth century and the early decades of the twentieth century involved practical measures to promote women's education: the formation of Muslim women organisations (*Anjum-e-Khwateen*, Muslim Women Association, and others), publication of women's journals, and the establishment of girls' schools in different parts of India. Two strands of reform emerged among the Muslim community as Amina Yaqin notes, "The two camps of Aligarh and Deoband came to represent on the one hand a progressive strand which cooperated with colonial power and on the other an anti-colonial Islamic stance which rejected modernity wholesale as a Western construct" (2007: 383). The vision of religious reformers such as Maulana Ashraf Ali Thanvi (1863–1943), the author of *Bihishti Zewar*, was steeped in Islamic ideals, and modernist reformers such as Sir Syed Ahmad Khan, Nazir Ahmad, Altaf Hussain Hali, Sayyid Mumtaz Ali, and others were influenced by colonial modernity. These reformers, through their writings and efforts, persuaded the Muslim community to rethink the position of women in their contemporary society. Although Sir Syed Ahmad, according to some scholars, had an ambiguous position towards the modern education for women, he, in his article on "The Education of Mohammedan Girls," emphasised the importance of traditional and religious education for Muslim girls within the four walls of the *zenana* (De Souza, 2004: 170). Along with male reformers, many Muslim women participated in educational reforms by encouraging other women to understand the importance of female education. Contrary to the popular belief, Muslim women were not mute observers of changing cultural configurations, Moolji writes in *Forging the Ideal Educated Girl: The Production of Desirable Subjects in Muslim South Asia*:

> Muslim women were not silent objects of reform projects but actively engaged in them. Unlike their male counterparts, however, their work was often featured in periodicals, dairies, reformist literature, interviews, letters, and pamphlets—writing products that have not been considered worthy of preservation. These texts, however, give us important clues about the political and social culture of the period, as well as the dominant idioms in and through which life was lived and imagined. (2018: 34)

Waheed Jahan, along with her husband Miya Abdullah, established a school for girls in Aligarh; Iqbalunnissa Hussain, a twentieth-century novelist and essayist, founded a school in Bangalore; and Rokeya Sakhawat Hossain and Nazr Sajjad Hyder started girls' schools at Bhagalpur and Dehradun, respectively. The Begums of Bhopal established and supported many educational institutions across India. Such initiatives for female education were taken by Muslim intelligentsia across India.

In her study of the Muslim women in colonial Bengal, Mahua Sarkar demonstrates how "the phallocentric tendencies of normative historiographies that typically ignore women as historical subjects" (Sarkar, 2008: 01). Sarkar's comment appears to be valid for the history of reforms among Muslims in colonial India. The efforts for female education by women such as the Begums of Bhopal, Muhammadi Begum, Nazr Sajjad Hyder, Rokeya Sakhawat Hossain, and Waheed Jahan are rarely acknowledged.

Print culture played a crucial role in the role of reformist discourses of the Muslim community in the late colonial period. Many women and men from the *Ashraf* class began to get involved and contribute to the social reform debates, through their participation with the print media. Sayyid Mumtaz Ali and his wife Muhammadi Begum launched *Tehzeeb-e-Niswan*, a weekly women's journal in 1898. Although it was not the first journal in Urdu, it was the first to survive. Sayyid Mumtaz Ali (1860–1935) in his well-argued work, *Huquq-un-Niswan* (The Rights of Women), asserted that the position of women in "Islamic law was theoretically much higher than their contemporary status was" (Minault, 1990: 149). Maulana Hali depicted the status of Muslim women in his contemporary society in his women-centric poems such as *Chup ki Daad* and *Majlis un-Nissa*, and Nazir Ahmad wrote *Mirat al- Arus* (The Bride's Mirror), emphasising the need of female education and the crucial role of educated women in the family and the society. It can be speculated that the novel was written as demand for suitable literature for women emerged in the late nineteenth century. The demand was further strengthened by the colonial government's interest in female education. In "Prize Winning Adab: A Study of Five Books Written in Response to the Allahabad Government Gazette Notification " (1984), CM Naim mentions the details about the five novels that were submitted by different authors in response to a notification issued by the colonial government. The notification with the promise of reward of a cash prize persuaded many authors to produce "useful" and "suitable literature," specifically for women readers. The theme of female education was adopted by many early Muslim female authors. *Islah-un-Nissa* (1881), the very first Urdu novel by a woman author, was written in response to Nazir Ahmad's novel. In the preface to the novel, Rashidunnissa, the author of the novel, expresses her gratitude to Nazir Ahmad for his efforts towards female education.

The late colonial period witnessed a surge in the publication of a variety of writings: poetry, travel accounts, personal narratives, and fiction. In his article, 'Literary Notes: A History of Women's Urdu Periodicals'(2016), Parekh mentions Hakeem Faseehuddin Ranj Meruthi, the author of *Baharistan-e-Naz* (1864), who anthologised the names and samples of seventy Urdu women poets in his book. Lambert-Hurley and Sharma, in their fascinating study of travel accounts of Muslim women in the late colonial period, give details of journeys of women such as Atiya Faizi, Begum of Janjira, Ammat-ul-Ghani Noor al- Nissa, and Sultan Jahan, who traveled to different shores across the globe and have documented their travels. Many educated women from *Ashraf* Muslim families published their women-centric novels, essays, and life narratives from the turn of the twentieth century. Muhammadi Begum (1878–1908) published her Urdu novel *Saughar Beti* and a biographical account *Hayat-e-Ashraf*; Nazr Sajjad Hyder (1894–1967) became popular with her Urdu novels *Akhtarunnissa Begum* (1910), *Ah-i-Mazloom* (1913), *Suraiya* (1933), and *Najma* (1939); Rokeya Sakhawat Hossain wrote in English as well as Bengali. Her Bengali works such as *Padmarag* (1924), *Abarodhbasini* (1931), and other collections of writings made her a household name in Bengal. In *Women in Concert: An Anthology of Bengal Muslim Women's Writings (1904–1938),* Shaheen Akhtar and Moushumi Bhowmik bring together stories, essays, and interviews of Bengali Muslim women authors. Their writings not only illustrate Muslim women's negotiations with modernity but also debunk myths about their backwardness in colonial Bengal. It is interesting to note that there were Muslim women authors who were writing and publishing in English from the beginning of the twentieth century. Iqbalunnissa Hussain, born in 1897 in Bangalore, was one of the first women from a Muslim family to have earned a degree from the United Kingdom. Her essays were published as *Changing India: A Muslim Woman Speaks* (1940); her novel *Purdah and Polygamy* (1944) is a scathing critique of patriarchy in Muslim society. Zeenuth Futehally's *Zohra* (1951) is considered to be the first English novel written by a Muslim woman in post-partition India. Set in Hyderabad in the early twentieth century, Futehally's novel narrates the story of a girl from an aristocratic Muslim family. She is taught Urdu, Persian, and English literary and cultural traditions, yet forced to give up her intellectual and poetic aspirations and marry a man much older than her.

The cartographic cracking of 1947 partition of India and Pakistan redefined the identity of the Indian subcontinent. Feminist scholars such as Urvashi Butalia, Kamala Bhasin, and Ritu Menon have studied and documented the voices and experiences of women in partition history but the lives and the experiences of Muslim women in partition studies appear to be in "a realm of virtual anonymity" (Ali, 2009: 248). Lambert-Hurley also expresses a similar opinion. For her, in the discourses of partition, the experiences that are "often neglected were the particular experiences of Muslim women" (Lambert-Hurley, 2018: 117). However, Muslim women authors have dealt with the horror of partition in fiction as well as non-fiction. Mumtaz Shahnawaz's *The Heart Divided* and Attia Hossain's *Sunlight on a Broken Column* are among the first English novels on the theme of 1947 partition. Urdu narratives such as Khadija Mastur's *Aangan* (Women's Courtyard) and *Zameen* (Promised Land), Zahida Hina's *Junoon Raha Na Pari Rahi* (All Passion Spent), and Qurratualain Hyder's *Mere Bhi Sanamkhaane* (My Temples too), Begum Anis Kidwai's memoir *Azaadi ki Chaawon mein* (In the Shadow of Freedom), and Ismat Chughtai's *Jadien* (Roots) deal with the trauma and the madness of the partition of India.

Listening to the Silence

The Silence That Speaks: Short Stories by Indian Muslim Women brings together thirty-eight short stories by Indian Muslim women authors from different ethnic and linguistic backgrounds to reflect upon the diversity of imagined and lived experiences, to understand the intersectionality of various identities, and to examine voices and agencies of the Muslim women authors of the early twentieth century to contemporary time.

A project such as the present one also carries the danger of "validating the very category of 'Muslim women' that it seeks to unhinge" (Nagel 2005: 05). Though the focus of the anthology is on the Muslim identity of the women authors, the collection neither aims to explore the "Muslimness" of the authors nor attempts to read the stories from a nationalist perspective. The Muslim identity of the authors, referred to in the collection, is cultural and political rather than religious. The collection includes short stories by the authors who identify themselves as Muslims and also by the authors – such as Malika Amar Shaikh and others – who come from Muslim ancestry. More than often, the Muslim identity becomes an overarching identity in the discussions of their lives and works—especially in times of socio-political crisis. Explaining the importance of the category, Nagel opines:

> In the present political climate, in which Muslim women more than ever are subject to stereotypes, negative representations, and constant

> scrutiny within their own societies and by others, it becomes important to present more complicated readings of the Muslim woman category, even if this means, in a sense, legitimating the category itself. (2005:05)

Most of the short stories in the collection debunk the assumption that Muslim women in India constitute a silent and homogeneous constituency for their specific allegiances that derive from Islam. The stories also demonstrate how identities are framed by their specific socio-cultural context: class, education, geographical regions, and local cultures. They reflect upon how the authors navigate the world of voices and silences. Ranging from imaginary geographies of utopia to topographies of Muslim ghettos, most of these powerful short stories narrate the spaces that Muslim women inhabit.

The anthology is organised around the genre of the short story and its individual female authors. Although the stories do not follow a strict chronological order, the scope of the collection extends over generations of Muslim women writers in India. Providing a broad spectrum of short stories, the anthology includes different genres of stories by celebrated authors such as Rokeya Sakhawat Hossain, Jeelani Bano, Hijab Imtiaz Ali, and unconventional authors such as Mrs. Abdul Qadir and Wajeda Tabassum. It also includes contemporary emerging women authors who are writing and publishing in twenty-first-century India. The collection brings together authors from different states of India (both urban and rural areas) such as Bengal, Assam, Tamil Nadu, Andhra Pradesh, Kerela, Uttar Pradesh, Madhya Pradesh, Delhi, Maharashtra, Punjab, Rajasthan, Meghalaya, Telangana, Karnataka, Bihar, and Kashmir. Attempts have been made to cull representative stories from English as well as different regional languages, but there is an inevitable imbalance in the favour of authors who wrote in different dialects of Urdu as the body of work by Muslim women authors available in Urdu is incomparable to another regional language—many women authors from both northern as well as southern parts of India use Urdu as their medium of expression. Similarly, many contemporary Muslim women authors from cities publish in English.

The choice of the genre of short stories was determined by various factors: the very first was the preference of the genre by the women authors from the late colonial period. The publication of women's journals in colonial India provided avenues of publication for short pieces of writings—letters, personal narratives, and short stories. In her interesting article on three twentieth-century Urdu women's journals, Gail Minault (1998) explains how journals such as *Tehzeeb-e-Niswan*, *Khatun*, and *Ismat* published articles and stories which dealt with the issues of female education, the age of girl's marriage, and the importance of her consent in marriage, polygamy, and purdah. Bengali journals such as *Saogat*, *Bangiya Mussalman Sahitya Patrika*, and *Nabanoor* invited Muslim women to publish their articles, poems, and stories. Explaining the importance of the journals for Muslim women, Firdous Azim and Perween Hasan demonstrate how in the times when "the issue of modernity and the place of Islam within these" (2014: 03) were being debated in Bengal, "the editors of journals such as *Nabanoor* or *Saogat* appealed to women to come forward and write" (2014: 03).

In the present book, the opening story "Sultana's Dream" by Rokeya Sakhawat Hossain was first published in 1905 in *The Indian Ladies' Magazine*, one of the first women-edited journals to be published in colonial India. Written in English, the story is a satire on the gender segregation prevalent in Rokeya's contemporary society. She imagines Ladyland, a utopian society where gender norms are reversed—women are roaming freely on the streets, and men are imprisoned in the *zenana* (women's quarters). Apart from Rokeya Sakhawat Hossain's story, three more stories in the anthology have been selected from various women's journals published in the early twentieth century. The Bengali stories "Dear Naseem" and "Spartan Hearts" have been taken from *Saogat,* and the Urdu story "Husnara Begum" has been picked from *Tehzeeb-e-Niswan*. Unlike *The Indian Ladies' Magazine*, these journals published articles and stories in Indian languages. Hossain's Bengali story "Dear Naseem" and Begum's Urdu "Husnara Begum" adopt the intimate epistolary form to reflect upon the issues of love, marriage, and domesticity. The form of these stories are akin to the letters that were published in the early women's journals. The epistolary form of writing has been used by women across the world; it has been used by women in the West for a long time. Elizabeth C Goldsmith, in her reading of the genre, comments: "Newly educated women could easily learn to write letters, and, as epistolary theory became more adapted to worldly culture, women's letters began to be considered the best models of the genre" (1989: vii).

Through stories and articles published in women's journals, women formed different communities of readers and writers. In this regard, Asiya Alam notes, "Urdu women's magazines provided one of the most accessible print forums for Muslim women to express their ideas and publicly converse with other members of society in early twentieth-century India" (2015: 83). Begum's Urdu story ends with a question to "*Tehzeebi sisters*," a female community of contributors and readers of the Urdu journal, *Tehzeeb-e-Niswan.* The story deals with the issue of polygamy in a very discreet manner: the husband deserts his first wife Husnara and gets married to the daughter of a rich businessman. It is a narrative of the misery and struggles of an abandoned wife who decides to teach at a school to educate her daughter. The journey of this female protagonist from penury to prosperity delivers the radical message of women's empowerment. The eponymous protagonist of the story negotiates with the competing demands of respectability and economic precarity redefining the traditional concept of *sharafat* that seems to be threatened by the idea of women's economic independence. This story demolishes the stereotypes about Muslim women as mere victims of Muslim patriarchy and deprived of any agency. Hossain's story "Dear Naseem" questions the choices that men have in matters of marriage and companionship. Afzal, through his letter to Naseem, tries to communicate the reasons of his running away and not marrying Naseem's sister, Zubaida. While these two stories deal with themes of marriage and domesticity, Ahmad's fascinating story, "Spartan Hearts" demonstrates the author's knowledge of Greek mythology. The trans-Islamic framework of the story debunks various myths about knowledge and education in Muslim families in colonial India. The author of the story wants other women to be brave and courageous; she wants them to have "Spartan Hearts".

The purpose of anthologising the stories of lesser-known authors, along with the stories of canonical writers such as Rokeya Sakhawat Hossain and Jeelani Bano, is to think about the "missing links" in Muslim women's literary history, to rethink the presence of other Muslim women authors who have been lost in the pages of history, and to acknowledge the contribution of such authors in the growth and development of the genre of short stories in colonial and postcolonial India. One such author is Hijab Imtiaz Ali, who lived in Lahore (now in Pakistan). Most of her writings have not been translated into English, and hence, she is rarely acknowledged in the tradition of women's writings. She is counted among the first South Asian women pilots and is also regarded as one of the first women authors of romance and gothic fiction in Urdu. Her oeuvre has influenced generations of writers—Ismat Chughtai acknowledges Hijab's influence on her young mind in her memoir *Kaghazi Hai Pairahan*. In the present collection, Hijab Imtiaz Ali's story "The Blue Envelope," Mrs. Qadir's story "The Tutor's Secret," Seemin Hasan's "A Lady and her Husband," and BM Zuhara's "Azrael," are remarkable in their treatment of "mysterious" and "strange." Hijab Imtiaz's story deals with the mystery of blue envelops that were delivered to the narrator's house every Saturday; Mrs. Qadir's "TheTutor's Secret" was published in her famous 1939 collection, *Lashon ka Shehr* (*The City of Corpses*). It is a story with a double frame, set in a well-to-do, seemingly progressive household, which takes a plunge into a rural, apocryphal world through a fearful secret that the resident tutor harbors. A modern frame is set off with an evocative rendering of an older world steeped in the fearful, the sublime, and the occult. The story takes natural landscape as an important departure point, to weave a world which is both scintillating and unsettling in its lack of familiarity. Seemin Hasan's "A Lady and Her Husband" portrays the life of a convent-educated, elite Muslim woman who is married to a doctor from London. Rukhsar, the newly-wed bride tries to break a double curse at her in-laws' estate. Hasan's story vividly illustrates the culture of Muslim landowning class of North India. In Zuhara's "Azrael," Ayesha, a dutiful wife and a concerned mother, is bedridden at a hospital. However difficult it might be, she still wishes to go back to her routine life. Through the story, the author ponders over the crucial role that women play in society. Zuhara portrays the life of an average woman whose worries and dreams are etched within her domestic sphere.

The question of female agency occupies a central position in the debates on gender, society, and Islam. The following stories are interesting in the way they deal with the notion of female agency. While Sara Aboobacker's Kannada story "Chappals" deals with the agency of a purdah-observing woman, stories such as Wajeda Tabassum's "Zakat," Noor Zaheer's "The Smokers' Mazaar," and Tarannum Riyaz's "The Men and the Woman" deal with the question of agencies of women from the economically weaker sections. The absence of a husband in Aboobacker's "Chappals" empowers Samira, the protagonist of the story; she finds her strength in loneliness and solitude. She is a rebellious woman who challenges the patriarchal structures through her symbolic act of standing unveiled at the gates of her maternal house. Her confrontation could be read as the defiance of "the laws of threshold" (Lal, 05). Wajeda Tabassum's Urdu story "Zakat" captures the theme of gender, sexuality, and class exploitation. Tabassum, who is famous for her story "Uttran" (adapted into a film titled, *Kamasutra* by Meera Nair), has dealt boldly with the themes of female desires and sexualities in her writings. Ujjala, her protagonist in "Zakat," is an extremely beautiful young girl from a poor family who is forced to perform *mutah* – a temporary marriage with an old, womaniser Nawab. Noor Zaheer's "The Smokers' Mazaar" revolves around a mazaar (shrine). Though headed by Pir Baba, the old patriarch, the mazaar becomes a site of a momentary alliance between women of different classes and communities. The "sacred" and the "sacrilege" are brought together, and female bonding in the story is formed through the act of sharing cigarettes at the shrine. Riyaz's "The Men and the Woman" is an interesting story of Sundari, a tribal girl of Jharkhand, who works as a domestic help at Aasima's house and has physical relationships with male servants of the house. The story also deals with issues of abortion and adoption.

Most of the stories written by Zahra Rai and her sister Moghal Mahmood are set in a feudal Muslim haveli, which was their ancestral home. Rai's "Mango Blossoms" is a story of love and desire. Shami, a young beautiful girl from a Muslim family, is attracted to her brother's friends. Rai's depiction of the family shatters many stereotypes about the status of women within feudal Muslim societies. Mahmood's "The Will" conjures up a different image of feudal societies. The story is centred around realistic, identifiable characters, and their greed and needs. It deals with the drama that unfolds at Nishat Manzil after the death of Badi Begum.

The focus on the genre of short stories in the collection is also crucial as from the late colonial period. The forms of short story have undergone many mutations. In the early decades of the twentieth century, the form and usefulness of literature became the focus of discussions and deliberations in the Urdu and Hindi literary circles. The discussion gained momentum with the publication of a collection of short stories and a play titled, *Angaray* (1932) by a group of young and energetic authors from

Aligarh. The severe criticism of the book by the orthodox sections of the Muslim society and the subsequent banning of the book by the colonial government led to the formation of the Progressive Writers' Association (PWA) in 1936. The association emphasised rethinking the roles of literature as well as authors in society. Two twentieth-century authors included in the anthology were associated with the PWA at some point in their literary careers. The work of Progressives writers such as Rashid Jahan and Razia Sajjad Zaheer, as Priyamvada Gopal notes, "is inflected by the question of what it meant to 'become modern', not only as women, but as professionals, as middle class, as Muslim, as Indians and, particularly, as intellectuals with an investment in social change" (2005: 68). Rashid Jahan was one of the authors who contributed a short story and a play to *Angarey* (1932). Her short stories primarily deal with the plight of women of middle-class Muslims of northern India. "She" (*Woh*) is a story of Safiya, a school teacher and an unnamed social outcast woman whose body was decaying gradually. It was Rashid Jahan's writings that influenced the imagination of Ismat Chughtai. Rashid's realist stories persuaded young Ismat to move away from the world of romance.

Razia Sajjad Zaheer was a dedicated member of the Progressive Writers' Association; she was married to Sajjad Zaheer, one of the founding members of the association. Her story "Salt" is representative of the trauma and plight of the 1947 partition. The story narrates experiences of a woman who is traveling to Pakistan to meet her brothers, after partition. Sulema Khatun Kajol's "Sunset" and Mariam Karim's "Riding Raksh" are two more stories in the present book that deal with the cartographic cracking of the Indian subcontinent. Women's writings dealing with the partitions of the Indian subcontinent have been attracting attention in recent decades. The English translations of these stories will add to the growing body of literatures on the partitions of the Indian subcontinent.

Seven stories explore sensitive and crucial issues of communalism, violence, and intolerance in contemporary societies: Eli Ahmed's Assamese story "Rehmat's Red Calf Has Gone Missing," Husn Tabassum Nihan's Hindi story "Blue-Winged Girls," Shajahana's Telugu story "Billiee," Ather Zia's English story "Loving, Dying," Asma Khan's English story "Maina: Return of the Bowls," Sarwat Khan's Urdu story "People's Court," and Annie Zaidi's "Registered Post." Three of these stories focus on interfaith love relationships and outline the problems that interfaith

The anthology is a humble attempt to introduce global English readers to different aspects of Muslim women's short stories. Though it would be a sheer impossibility to cover the whole range of Muslim women's writing in a book, the collection brings together stories by many celebrated as well as emerging authors. There are many other prominent authors such as Ismat Chughtai, Attia Hosain, Qurratulain Hyder, and others who could not be included in the collection because of various logistical challenges. Besides any anthology reflects the interests and preferences of its editor and contributors. Written in different languages, modes, and forms, the stories deal with identity, culture, domesticity, religion, desires, love, rebellion, and freedom. Stories, in the collection, discreetly question the old values and gender relations and debunk the stereotyped identity of Muslim womanhood, thus creating refreshing and provocative images of Muslim women in India.

Works Cited

Abu-Lughod L (2013) *Do Muslim Women Need Saving?* USA: Harvard University Press.

Agnes F (2012) "From Shahbano to Kausar Bano: Contextualizing the 'Muslim Women' Within a Communalized Polity." In *South Asian Feminism*. Edited by A Loomba and RA Lukose, 33–51. New Delhi: Zubaan.

Akhtar S and Bhowmik M (2008) *Women in Concert: An Anthology of Bengali Women's Writings (1904–1938)*. Kolkatta: Stree.

Alam A (2015) "Interrupted Stories: Self Narratives of Nazr Sajjad Hyder." In *Speaking of the Self: Gender, Performance, and Autobiography in South Asia*. Edited by Anshu Malhotra and Siobhan Lambert-Hurley, 72–94. Durham, NC: Duke University Press.

Ali RU (2009) "Muslim Women and the Partition of India: A Historiographical Silence." *Islamic Studies*, Vol. 48, No. 3 (Autumn): 425–436.

Azim F and Hasan P (2014) "Language, Literature, Education and Community: The Bengali Muslim Woman in the Early Twentieth Century." *Women's Studies International Forum*, Vol. 45 (July–August):105–111.

Chughtai I (2012) *A Life in Words: Memoirs*. Translated by M. Asaduddin. New Delhi: Penguins.

De Souza E (2004) *Purdah: An Anthology*. New Delhi: OUP.

Foucault M (1977) *The History of Sexuality*. Vol. 1.Translated by Robert Hurley. New York: Pantheon.

Goldsmith EC (1989) *Writing the Female Voice: Essays on Epistolary Literatures*. Boston: Northeastern University Press.

Gopal P (2005) *Literary Radicalism in India: Gender, Nation and the Transition to Independence*. London: Routledge.

Hasan Z and R Menon (2005) "Reviewing Muslim Women and Marriage: A Preliminary Analysis of Survey Finding." In *Women in India: Colonial and Postcolonial Periods*. Edited by Bharati Ray, 53–81. New Delhi: Sage Publications Ltd.

Jalil R (2019) *But You Don't Look Like A Muslim*. Delhi: HarperCollins.

Jung A (1992) *The Night of New Moon: Encounters with Muslim Women*. New Delhi: Penguin.

Kahf M (1999) *Western Representation of Muslim Women: From Termagant to Odalisque*. Cambridge: Cambridge University Press.

Kanso H (2019) What does it mean to be a Muslim woman? New book challenges stereotypes. Available at http://news.trust.org/item/20190220215032-rciqa/

Kirmani N (2009) "Deconstructing and Reconstructing 'Muslim Women' through Women's Narratives." *Journal of Gender Studies*, Vol. 18. No. 1, 47–62.

Lal M (2000) *The Law of the Threshold: Women Writers in Indian English*. Shimla: IIAS.

Lambert-Hurley S and Sharma S (2010) *Atiya's Journey: A Muslim Women from Colonial Bombay to Edwardian Britain*. Delhi: Oxford University Press.

Lambert-Hurley S (2018) "Narrating Trauma, Constructing Binaries, Affirming Agency: Partition in Muslim Women's Autobiographical Writing." In *Partition and the Practise of Memory*. Edited by M Chrunjeet and M Anne, 115–136. Cham, Switzerland: Palgrave Macmillan.

Macdonald M (2006) "Muslim Women and the Veil: Problems of Image and Voice in Media Representation." *Feminist Media Studies*, Vol. 6: 7–23.

Moolji SK (2018) *Forging the Ideal Educated Girl: The Production of Desirable Subjects in Muslim South Asia*. California: University of California Press.

Minault G (1990) "Sayyid Mumtaz Ali and 'Huquq un-Niswan': An Advocate of Women's Rights in Islam in the Late Nineteenth Century." *Modern Asian Studies*, Vol. 24, No. 1 (February): 147–172.

Minault G (1998) *Secluded Scholars: Women's Education and Muslim Social Reform in Colonial India*. Delhi: Oxford University Press.

Nagel C (2005) "Introduction." In *Geographies of Muslim Women: Gender, Religion, and Space*. Edited by Ghazi-Walid Falah and Caroline Nagel, 1-15. London: Guilford Press.

Naim CM (1984) "Prize-Winning Adab: A Study of Five Books Written in Response to the Allahabad Government Gazette Notification." In *Moral Conduct and Authority: The Place of Adab in South Asian Islam*. Edited by Barbara D. Metcalf, 290–314. Berkeley: University of California Press.

Parekh R (2016) A History of Women's Urdu Periodicals. Available at https://www.dawn.com/news/1293303#:~:text=According%20to%20Dr%20Akhter%2C%20Rafeeq,Delhi%20on%20Aug%201%2C%201884.

Sarkar M (2008) *Visible Histories Disappearing Women: Producing Muslim Womanhood in Late Colonial Bengal*. New Delhi: Zubaan.

Showalter E (1977) *A Literature of Their Own—British Women Novelist: From Bronte to Lessing*. New Jersey: Princeton University Press.

Sommer AV and Zwemer SM (1911) *Daylight in Harem: A New Era for Moslem Women*. Edinburgh and London: Oliphant, Anderson & Ferrier.

Watson H (1992) *Women in the City of Dead*. Trenton, NJ: African World Press.

Yaqin A (2007) "Truth, Fiction and Autobiography in the Modern Urdu Narrative Tradition." *Comparative Critical Studies*, Vol. 4, No. 3: 379–402.

1

Sultana's Dream

Rokeya Sakhawat Hossain

One evening I was lounging in an easy chair in my bedroom and thinking lazily of the condition of Indian womanhood. I am not sure whether I dozed off or not. But, as far as I remember, I was wide awake. I saw the moonlit sky sparkling with thousands of diamond-like stars, very distinctly.

All on a sudden, a lady stood before me; how she came in, I do not know. I took her for my friend, Sister Sara.

"Good morning," said Sister Sara. I smiled inwardly as I knew it was not morning, but starry night. However, I replied to her, saying, "How do you do?"

"I am all right, thank you. Will you please come out and have a look at our garden?"

I looked again at the moon through the open window and thought there was no harm in going out at that time. The men servants outside were fast asleep just then, and I could have a pleasant walk with Sister Sara.

I used to have my walks with Sister Sara, when we were at Darjeeling. Many a time did we walk hand in hand and talk light-heartedly in the botanical gardens there. I fancied Sister Sara had probably come to take me to some such garden, and I readily accepted her offer and went out with her.

When walking I found to my surprise that it was a fine morning. The town was fully awake and the streets alive with bustling crowds. I was feeling very shy, thinking I was walking in the street in broad daylight, but there was not a single man visible.

Some of the passersby made jokes at me. Though I could not understand their language, yet I felt sure they were joking. I asked my friend, "What do they say?"

Rokeya Sakhawat Hossain, *Sultana's Dream* In: *The Silence That Speaks*. Edited by: Haris Qadeer, Oxford University Press. © Oxford University Press India 2022. DOI: 10.1093/oso/9780190132613.003.0002

"The women say that you look very mannish."

"Mannish?" said I. "What do they mean by that?"

"They mean that you are shy and timid like men."

"Shy and timid like men?" It was really a joke. I became very nervous, when I found that my companion was not Sister Sara, but a stranger. Oh, what a fool had I been to mistake this lady for my dear old friend, Sister Sara.

She felt my fingers tremble in her hand, as we were walking hand in hand.

"What is the matter, dear, dear?" she said affectionately.

"I feel somewhat awkward," I said in a rather apologizing tone, "as being a purdahnishin woman, I am not accustomed to walking about unveiled."

"You need not be afraid of coming across a man here. This is Ladyland, free from sin and harm. Virtue herself reigns here."

By and by I was enjoying the scenery. Really it was very grand. I mistook a patch of green grass for a velvet cushion. Feeling as if I were walking on a soft carpet, I looked down and found the path covered with moss and flowers.

"How nice it is!" said I.

"Do you like it?" asked Sister Sara. (I continued calling her "Sister Sara," and she kept calling me by my name.)

"Yes, very much; but I do not like to tread on the tender and sweet flowers."

"Never mind, dear Sultana. Your treading will not harm them; they are street flowers."

"The whole place looks like a garden," said I admiringly. "You have arranged every plant so skillfully."

"Your Calcutta could become a nicer garden than this if only your countrymen wanted to make it so."

"They would think it useless to give so much attention to horticulture, while they have so many other things to do."

"They could not find a better excuse," said she with [a] smile.

I became very curious to know where the men were. I met more than a hundred women while walking there, but not a single man.

"Where are the men?" I asked her.

"In their proper places, where they ought to be."

"Pray let me know what you mean by 'their proper places.'"

"O, I see my mistake, you cannot know our customs, as you were never here before. We shut our men indoors."

"Just as we are kept in the zenana?"

"Exactly so."

"How funny," I burst into a laugh. Sister Sara laughed too.

"But, dear Sultana, how unfair it is to shut in the harmless women and let loose the men."

"Why? It is not safe for us to come out of the zenana, as we are naturally weak."

"Yes, it is not safe so long as there are men about the streets, nor is it so when a wild animal enters a marketplace."

"Of course not."

"Suppose, some lunatics escape from the asylum and begin to do all sorts of mischief to men, horses and other creatures: in that case what will your countrymen do?"

"They will try to capture them and put them back into their asylum."

"Thank you! And you do not think it wise to keep sane people inside an asylum and let loose the insane?"

"Of course not!" said I laughing lightly.

"As a matter of fact, in your country, this very thing is done! Men, who do or at least are capable of doing no end of mischief, are let loose and the innocent women, shut up in the zenana! How can you trust those untrained men out of doors?"

"We have no hand or voice in the management of our social affairs. In India, man is lord and master; he has taken to himself all powers and privileges and shut up the women in the zenana."

"Why do you allow yourselves to be shut up?"

"Because it cannot be helped as they are stronger than women."

"A lion is stronger than a man, but it does not enable him to dominate the human race. You have neglected the duty you owe to yourselves and you have lost your natural rights by shutting your eyes to your own interests."

"But my dear Sister Sara, if we do everything by ourselves, what will the men do then?"

"They should not do anything, excuse me; they are fit for nothing. Only catch them and put them into the zenana."

"But would it be very easy to catch and put them inside the four walls?" said I. "And even if this were done, would all their business—political and commercial—also go with them into the zenana?"

Sister Sara made no reply. She only smiled sweetly. Perhaps she thought it useless to argue with one who was no better than a frog in a well.

By this time, we reached Sister Sara's house. It was situated in a beautiful heart-shaped garden. It was a bungalow with a corrugated iron roof. It was cooler and nicer than any of our rich buildings. I cannot describe how neat and how nicely furnished and how tastefully decorated it was.

We sat side by side. She brought out of the parlour a piece of embroidery work and began putting on a fresh design.

"Do you know knitting and needlework?"

"Yes; we have nothing else to do in our zenana."

"But we do not trust our zenana members with embroidery!" she said laughing, "as a man has not patience enough to pass thread through a needlehole even!"

"Have you done all this work yourself?" I asked her pointing to the various pieces of embroidered teapoy cloths.

"Yes."

"How can you find time to do all these? You have to do the office work as well? Have you not?"

"Yes. I do not stick to the laboratory all day long. I finish my work in two hours."

"In two hours! How do you manage? In our land, the officers—magistrates, for instance—work seven hours daily."

"I have seen some of them doing their work. Do you think they work all the seven hours?"

"Certainly, they do!"

"No, dear Sultana, they do not. They dawdle away their time in smoking. Some smoke two or three choroots during the office time. They talk much about their work, but do little. Suppose one choroot takes half an hour to burn off, and a man smokes twelve choroots daily; then, you see, he wastes six hours every day in sheer smoking."

We talked on various subjects; and I learned that they were not subject to any kind of epidemic disease, nor did they suffer from mosquito bites as we do. I was very much astonished to hear that in Ladyland no one died in youth except by rare accident.

"Will you care to see our kitchen?" she asked me.

"With pleasure," said I, and we went to see it. Of course, the men had been asked to clear off when I was going there. The kitchen was situated in a beautiful vegetable garden. Every creeper, every tomato plant, was itself an ornament. I found no smoke, nor any chimney either in the kitchen—it was clean and bright; the windows were decorated with flower gardens. There was no sign of coal or fire.

"How do you cook?" I asked.

"With solar heat," she said, at the same time showing me the pipe, through which passed the concentrated sunlight and heat. And she cooked something then and there to show me the process.

"How did you manage to gather and store up the sun-heat?" I asked her in amazement.

"Let me tell you a little of our past history then. Thirty years ago, when our present Queen was thirteen years old, she inherited the throne. She was Queen in name only, the Prime Minister really ruling the country.

"Our good Queen liked science very much. She circulated an order that all the women in her country should be educated. Accordingly, a number of girls' schools were founded and supported by the Government. Education was spread far and wide among women. And early marriage also was stopped. No woman was to be allowed to marry before she was twenty-one. I must tell you that, before this change, we had been kept in strict purdah."

"How the tables are turned," I interposed with a laugh.

"But the seclusion is the same," she said. "In a few years, we had separate universities, where no men were admitted."

"In the capital, where our Queen lives, there are two universities. One of these invented a wonderful balloon, to which they attached a number of pipes. By means of this captive balloon which they managed to keep afloat above the cloud-land, they could draw as much water from the atmosphere as they pleased. As the water was incessantly being drawn by the university people, no cloud gathered and the ingenious Lady Principal stopped rain and storms thereby."

"Really! Now I understand why there is no mud here!" said I. But I could not understand how it was possible to accumulate water in the pipes. She explained to me how it was done; but I was unable to understand her, as my scientific knowledge was very limited. However, she went on:

"When the other university came to know of this, they became exceedingly jealous and tried to do something more extraordinary still. They invented an instrument by which they could collect as much sun-heat as they wanted. And they kept the heat stored up to be distributed among others as required.

"While the women were engaged in scientific research, the men of this country were busy increasing their military power. When they came to know that the female universities were able to draw water from the atmosphere and collect heat from the sun, they only laughed at the members of the universities and called the whole thing 'a sentimental nightmare'!"

"Your achievements are very wonderful indeed! But tell me, how you managed to put the men of your country into the zenana. Did you entrap them first?"

"No."

"It is not likely that they would surrender their free and open air life of their own accord and confine themselves within the four walls of the zenana! They must have been overpowered."

"Yes, they have been!"

"By whom? By some lady-warriors, I suppose?"

"No, not by arms."

"Yes, it cannot be so. Men's arms are stronger than women's. Then?"

"By brain."

"Even their brains are bigger and heavier than women's. Are they not?"

"Yes, but what of that? An elephant also has got a bigger and heavier brain than a man has. Yet man can enchain elephants and employ them, according to their own wishes."

"Well said, but tell me please, how it all actually happened. I am dying to know it!"

"Women's brains are somewhat quicker than men's. Ten years ago, when the military officers called our scientific discoveries 'a sentimental nightmare', some of the young ladies wanted to say something in reply to those remarks. But both the Lady Principals restrained them and said, they should reply not by word, but by deed, if ever they got the opportunity. And they had not long to wait for that opportunity."

"How marvelous!" I heartily clapped my hands.

"And now the proud gentlemen are dreaming sentimental dreams themselves."

"Soon afterwards, certain persons came from a neighbouring country and took shelter in ours. They were in trouble having committed some political offense. The king who cared more for power than for good government asked our kind-hearted Queen to hand them over to his officers. She refused, as it was against her principle to turn out refugees. For this refusal, the king declared war against our country.

"Our military officers sprang to their feet at once and marched out to meet the enemy.

"The enemy, however, was too strong for them. Our soldiers fought bravely, no doubt. But in spite of all their bravery, the foreign army advanced step by step to invade our country.

"Nearly all the men had gone out to fight; even a boy of sixteen was not left home. Most of our warriors were killed, the rest driven back, and the enemy came within twenty-five miles of the capital.

"A meeting of a number of wise ladies was held at the Queen's palace to advise [as] to what should be done to save the land.

"Some proposed to fight like soldiers; others objected and said that women were not trained to fight with swords and guns, nor were they accustomed to fighting with any weapons. A third party regretfully remarked that they were hopelessly weak of body.

"If you cannot save your country for lack of physical strength," said the Queen, "try to do so by brain power."

"There was a dead silence for a few minutes." Her Royal Highness said again, "I must commit suicide if the land and my honour are lost."

"Then the Lady Principal of the second university (who had collected sun-heat), who had been silently thinking during the consultation, remarked that they were all but lost, and there was little hope left for them. There was, however, one plan which she would like to try, and this would be her first and last efforts; if she failed in this, there would be nothing left but to commit suicide. All present solemnly vowed that they would never allow themselves to be enslaved, no matter what happened.

"The Queen thanked them heartily, and asked the Lady Principal to try her plan.

"The Lady Principal rose again and said, 'Before we go out the men must enter the zenanas. I make this prayer for the sake of purdah.' 'Yes, of course,' replied Her Royal Highness.

"On the following day, the Queen called upon all men to retire into zenanas for the sake of honour and liberty.

"Wounded and tired as they were, they took that order rather for a boon! They bowed low and entered the zenanas without uttering a single word of protest. They were sure that there was no hope for this country at all.

"Then, the Lady Principal with her two thousand students marched to the battle field, and arriving there directed all the rays of the concentrated sunlight and heat towards the enemy.

"The heat and light were too much for them to bear. They all ran away panic-stricken, not knowing in their bewilderment how to counteract that scorching heat. When they fled away leaving their guns and other ammunitions of war, they were burnt down by means of the same sun-heat.

"Since then, no one has tried to invade our country anymore."

"And since then your countrymen never tried to come out of the zenana?"

"Yes, they wanted to be free. Some of the police commissioners and district magistrates sent word to the Queen to the effect that the military officers certainly deserved to be imprisoned for their failure; but they never neglected their duty and therefore they should not be punished and they prayed to be restored to their respective offices.

"Her Royal Highness sent them a circular letter intimating to them that if their services should ever be needed they would be sent for and that in the meanwhile they should remain where they were.

"Now that they are accustomed to the purdah system and have ceased to grumble at their seclusion, we call the system *mardana* instead of zenana."

"But how do you manage," I asked Sister Sara, "to do without the police or magistrates in case of theft or murder?"

"Since the mardana system has been established, there has been no more crime or sin; therefore we do not require a policeman to find out a culprit, nor do we want a magistrate to try a criminal case."

"That is very good, indeed. I suppose if there was any dishonest person, you could very easily chastise her. As you gained a decisive victory without shedding a single drop of blood, you could drive off crime and criminals too without much difficulty!"

"Now, dear Sultana, will you sit here or come to my parlour?" she asked me.

"Your kitchen is not inferior to a queen's boudoir!" I replied with a pleasant smile, "but we must leave it now; for the gentlemen may be cursing me for keeping them away from their duties in the kitchen so long." We both laughed heartily.

"How my friends at home will be amused and amazed, when I go back and tell them that in the far-off Ladyland, ladies rule over the country and control all social matters, while gentlemen are kept in the mardanas to mind babies, to cook, and to do all sorts of domestic work; and that cooking is so easy a thing that it is simply a pleasure to cook!"

"Yes, tell them about all that you see here."

"Please let me know, how you carry on land cultivation and how you plough the land and do other hard manual work."

"Our fields are tilled by means of electricity, which supplies motive power for other hard work as well, and we employ it for our aerial conveyances too. We have no rail road nor any paved streets here."

"Therefore, neither street nor railway accidents occur here," said I. "Do not you ever suffer from want of rainwater?" I asked.

"Never since the 'water balloon' has been set up. You see the big balloon and pipes attached thereto. By their aid, we can draw as much rainwater as we require. Nor do we ever suffer from flood or thunderstorms. We are all very busy making nature yield as much as she can. We do not find time to quarrel with one another as we never sit idle. Our noble Queen is exceedingly fond of botany; it is her ambition to convert the whole country into one grand garden."

"The idea is excellent. What is your chief food?"

"Fruits."

"How do you keep your country cool in hot weather? We regard the rainfall in summer as a blessing from heaven."

"When the heat becomes unbearable, we sprinkle the ground with plentiful showers drawn from the artificial fountains. And in cold weather, we keep our room warm with sun-heat."

She showed me her bathroom, the roof of which was removable. She could enjoy a shower bath whenever she liked, by simply removing the roof (which was like the lid of a box) and turning on the tap of the shower pipe.

"You are a lucky people!" ejaculated I. "You know no want. What is your religion, may I ask?"

"Our religion is based on Love and Truth. It is our religious duty to love one another and to be absolutely truthful. If any person lies, she or he is . . . "

"Punished with death?"

"No, not with death. We do not take pleasure in killing a creature of God, especially a human being. The liar is asked to leave this land for good and never to come to it again."

"Is an offender never forgiven?"

"Yes, if that person repents sincerely."

"Are you not allowed to see any man, except your own relations?"

"No one except sacred relations."

"Our circle of sacred relations is very limited; even first cousins are not sacred."

"But ours is very large; a distant cousin is as sacred as a brother."

"That is very good. I see purity itself reigns over your land. I should like to see the good Queen, who is so sagacious and far-sighted and who has made all these rules."

"All right," said Sister Sara.

Then, she screwed a couple of seats onto a square piece of plank. To this plank, she attached two smooth and well-polished balls. When I asked her what the balls were for, she said they were hydrogen balls and they were used to overcome the force of gravity. The balls were of different capacities to be used according to the different weights desired to be overcome. She then fastened to the air-car two wing-like blades, which, she said, were worked by electricity. After we were comfortably seated, she touched a knob and the blades began to whirl, moving faster and faster every moment. At first, we were raised to the height of about six or seven feet and then off we flew. And before I could realize that we had commenced moving, we reached the garden of the Queen.

My friend lowered the air-car by reversing the action of the machine, and when the car touched the ground, the machine was stopped and we got out.

I had seen from the air-car the Queen walking on a garden path with her little daughter (who was four years old) and her maids of honour.

"Halloo! You here!" cried the Queen addressing Sister Sara. I was introduced to Her Royal Highness and was received by her cordially without any ceremony.

I was very much delighted to make her acquaintance. In the course of the conversation I had with her, the Queen told me that she had no objection to permitting her subjects to trade with other countries. "But," she continued, "no trade was possible with countries where the women were kept in the zenanas and so unable to come and trade with us. Men, we find, are rather of lower morals and so we do not like dealing with them. We do not covet other people's land, we do not fight for a piece of diamond though it may be a thousand-fold brighter than the Koh-i-Noor, nor do we grudge a ruler his Peacock Throne. We dive deep into the ocean of knowledge and try to find out the precious gems, which nature has kept in store for us. We enjoy nature's gifts as much as we can."

After taking leave of the Queen, I visited the famous universities and was shown some of their manufactories, laboratories, and observatories.

After visiting the above places of interest, we got again into the air-car, but as soon as it began moving, I somehow slipped down and the fall startled me out of my dream. And on opening my eyes, I found myself in my own bedroom still lounging in the easy chair!

First published in *Indian Ladies Magazine* (1905).

2

Dear Naseem

Begum Sufia Hossain

Naseem,

I received your letter. Yes, I ran away from home, but did I have much of a choice? I had tried to make you see reason, but you were unyielding. I am grateful for the gift of your friendship, and for the love of our families. I shall remain indebted to my mother, to your father, to Zubeida, and to you. Yet, I had no option but to leave. You are still mad at me because you probably do not understand why it was imperative for me to go. I wanted to get married, but not to Zubeida. You are not right in assuming that I do not consider Zubeida to be worthy of my love. That is not true, Naseem! Zubeida can light up the dark with her beauty, and you know that as well as I do. She is your sister, Naseem, and she is like a sister to me too. I have never had romantic thoughts about her. I will always continue to love her and pray for her. I hope she finds a groom like Amaan Ullah. I hope she gets married to someone who deserves her. I wish her joy and peace.

I have a lot to say to you. Why did I leave even after committing to get married? I owe you an explanation, Naseem.

"The sun lights up our world, but if there were more than one sun, the earth would be reduced to ashes." Do you remember the revolutionary poet who had once said this? I had to run away from that place before I got burnt down to ashes. You were about to consume me whole: Zubeida, you, and your entire family. I was also struck by another premonition: what if Zubeida truly loves me? What if she thinks of me as more than just her brother's friend? I do not have it in me to break her dear heart. The floral wreaths you were weaving for me felt like adamantine chains around my neck. I had to get away from it all to save myself and, in the process, I think, I saved Zubeida too.

Begum Sufia Hossain, *Dear Naseem* In: *The Silence That Speaks*. Edited by: Haris Qadeer, Oxford University Press.
 DOI: 10.1093/oso/9780190132613.003.0003

I fell in love with a girl when I was twenty-six. I am thirty-three now, and I still yearn for her every day, daily. I have not been able to forget her. You know nothing about her. Seven years ago, you had probably figured out that I was attracted to a young woman. Yet, you never realized the extent of my passion. One day, you assumed that my heart had stopped longing for her and that I was ready to devote myself to Zubeida. You wanted me to marry your beloved sister. You had faith in me. Do you realize what that has led to, my friend?

That girl was my first love, Naseem. I have never wanted anyone as much as I want her. How can I ever forget her? I do not want to keep you in the dark anymore, and so, I will come clean today.

The girl's name is Sara. You have never met her, but I'm certain you know of her. You might frown at my choice, and that's quite alright! However, my life revolves around her today, and therefore, you must know more about her. Be patient with me, my friend. Is she pretty? I do not know. My judgement is biased. In my eyes, she is the most beautiful person in this universe. My heart is so full! I cannot take my mind off her. When I first saw Sara, she was ailing. They had called on me to prescribe some medication for her. She was lying on her bed like a bouquet of withering night jasmines, frail and tender. Her body was burning with fever, her cheeks were flushed, her eyes moist. I noticed the little black mole above her left brow. She raised her feeble, henna-stained hand to her forehead and greeted me. I held a lamp close to her face and looked at her. She was beautiful! Oh, she was exquisite! I knew I would have to save her—somehow—anyhow. I heard a voice in the deep recesses of my heart whisper to me, "She is yours! She belongs to you! Rescue her!" I knew if she died, a part of me would die with her. Therefore, without further ado, I went to the city. There was no time to be wasted. I consulted senior doctors there. They assured me her condition was completely curable. She came into my life like a gift from god. Allah seemed to have answered my prayers. The thought of spending the rest of my life without her was torture. However, she recovered. When the colour returned to her deathly white face, she looked at me gratefully, smiled, and said, "Thank you for saving my life." I replied, "You need some fresh air now. I recommend a vacation. That will make you feel better soon." She stared at me for a while, her brows furrowed. The smile disappeared from her countenance. Her eyes darkened, and she whispered, "I'll be fine. I don't need a vacation."

Cutting her short, I said, "You need to take care of yourself. Don't be stubborn now. Where would you like to go? I shall arrange for a vacation for you." She looked into my eyes, and replied, "Why should I take care of myself? Where will I go anyway? Where should I go . . . ?" She could not complete her sentence. She broke into tears while I stood there helplessly. I said, "Why are you crying? Don't be a child now! We shan't force you to go anywhere if you do not have the heart to leave this place." Sara tried to muffle the sound of her tears, and answered, "Thank you for your kindness, but you may leave now. I shall talk to you another time." I was flabbergasted. What could I have told Sara? What should I have said? A part of me wanted her to know what she meant to me, but I was afraid of how she would respond to my undying love for her, especially since we had known each other for just about a week. Would she be willing to alter the course of her life and embrace me? Would the free bird in her consider my love to be a cage, a trap? Little did I know then that Sara was in love with me too. I walked out of her room, quietly, without confessing to her the secrets of my heart.

Gradually, Sara showed remarkable improvement. I would pay her a visit once every day, whenever I could make time from work. I was drawn to her in ways I cannot explain. I had imagined I would find a beeline of worshippers outside Sara's house. She was, after all, extremely beautiful, and an acclaimed singer. When I realized Sara had no gentlemen callers waiting on her, I felt a strange sense of relief. I had been mistaken about Sara: she was a celebrated singer, but she did not have the airs of a celebrity. I tried to confess my feelings to her on many occasions, but I failed. What could I have said? Sara, you are the reigning queen of my heart! Sara, I wish to make you mine forever! Would those words suffice? I always ended up tongue-tied in her presence.

One day, I requested her to sing a song for me. She blushed, and said, "I don't sound like I used to before. Why do you want to hear me sing?" I was unrelenting. I replied, "As your doctor I am well aware that you are not well. We are in the privacy of your room. Why can't you hum a couple of lines for me? I wasn't asking for a public performance." I might have crossed a line with those words. She looked at me sharply, and said, "Very well. I shall sing for you some other time, kindly excuse me today." I sat in front of her stupefied. I did not know what I could say to make light of the situation. She giggled after a while, and told me, "You needn't look so sombre. This gravitas is not becoming of you! What's bothering you? Are you worried about the next patient you will have to rescue from the clutches of death? I hear that people don't fall ill frequently anymore. Are the doctors going out of business?" I laughed, and said, "I appreciate the faith you have in me! Do you really think that I'm out of business?"

"Indeed!" she replied. "You sit at my feet all day long. How do you make time for other patients? This is no way to run a business!"

"Oh, well, I'm not too bothered about my business. But do you think I spend too much time with you?"

"Don't you?"

"I see no harm in that! Do you?"

"You could have invested this time better! You could have treated other patients instead of sitting here with me."

"We'll worry about my other patients later. But if you are not comfortable with me being around, do let me know. I shall not make my presence felt in this house anymore."

"This isn't about me, it's about you. You are wasting your time here. You really could use it better elsewhere."

"Alright! I'll be gone then. Good bye. But don't hesitate to let me know if you need anything. I'll come over."

As I stood up to leave, she stared at me with disbelieving eyes. When I stepped out of her door, I wondered if she had entirely misread me. Did she have no idea of my feelings for her? Why did her face light up each time she saw me? Should I have left so hastily? Should I not have told her of my confused adoration? I was mad at myself for behaving so recklessly. I had sworn not to go back to her house until she called for me, but I could not keep my word.

I showed up at her doorstep before going to work the next day. I was told she was not at home. I also saw her attendant cleaning her musical instruments and notebooks. They had been lying in a neglected corner of the house gathering dust for a while. Was Sara planning on going back to her old ways? I spent a restless, fretful day in the hospital. On my way back from work, I stopped by her house once more. It was late in the evening. She had not returned. I was livid. I did not check on her for three days. On the fourth day, when I returned home from work late in the afternoon, I found a card lying on my desk. It was from Sara: "Come over when you can. I have some work with you." I had been waiting for her missives with bated breath. I had a quick meal, and then rushed to her place. I saw the clear autumn sky, and felt hopeful. The time was ripe. I was ready to let Sara know about my feelings for her.

When I arrived at her house, I was asked to wait in the visitor's room. Sara was taking a bath. "At this hour?" I asked the attendant. "She wasn't home all day," I was told. Sara stepped into the room soon after that. Her face was glowing. I thought she looked ethereal. She had fresh henna stains on the palms of her hands and her feet. She was wearing a saree with a bright scarlet border. The loose end of her saree caressed her feet gently as she walked towards me. I focused on the tiny beads of water on her lashes and her brows. Her wet hair was wrapped in a soft cotton towel. Her body smelled of fresh flowers and perfumes. I sighed. She smiled, and said, "You've caught me at an indelicate moment! Had I known you would come so early, I would have prepared myself for it!"

"I believe you returned home a little while ago," I replied. "What made you consider taking a bath so late in the afternoon? Do you fancy falling ill again? Have you eaten anything? Why did you send for me?"

"My work took longer than I had anticipated. I sent for you because I want to sing for you."

"Why were you out of the house all day?"

"I had to get some work done."

"What kind of work?"

"I found myself a job with the Music Society."

"Ah, I see. That explains why your instruments needed cleaning. How hubristic of me to have imagined that it was all for me! Anyway, are you really in need of that job?"

"Of course. How else can I afford my expenses? Everyone needs a job."

"How did you manage to survive without one for so long?"

"Let bygones be bygones," she replied, her eyes cold and distant. "I want to take charge of my life now, and I will do things differently, henceforth. You wanted to hear me sing. You saved my life. I owe you a song. However, this is no hour to sing. Perhaps you will come back another day, when the time is more opportune!"

"I am not going anywhere today. I will stay right here. I have things to say to you, but after you've had your lunch."

"The lunch can wait," she said, sitting in front of me, making herself comfortable.

"No, I need you to eat something first! Get some food, I will wait for you."

She got up quietly and left the room. I flipped through the pages of one of the notebooks in which she had written down the lyrics of several songs. She returned in less than five minutes. She was carrying betel leaves in her hands. When she offered one to me, I declined politely, and said, "Sit here, and look into my eyes. I want to ask you something. Please be honest with me."

"What if I am not?" She pursed her ruby lips to suppress a smile.

"In that case, consider this to be our final conversation. I shall not get in touch with you again."

"Go on . . . ," she said, looking at me patiently.

"I will not bring up the past, but did you really need to find a job to support yourself at this point in time? Are you really so lonely and helpless?"

"Yes."

"Was there no other way out?"

"I couldn't think of one."

"What if someone else wants to take care of you and support you?"

"Why would anyone want to do that?"

"Why not?"

"I don't know. I can't think of a person like that."

"What if I tell you the name of one such person?"

"There is no one."

"There is."

"There can't be. Given my past, who would want me?"

"There is someone. He knows everything about you. He has seen you, and he likes you just the way you are."

"He must be a fool!"

"Well, he could be foolish, but how do you feel about him?"

"Oh, be done with it! This is madness, and I do not want to incite it any further! This conversation is over. Did you have anything else to say to me?"

The colour rose to her cheeks. Every pore on her body appeared tense. I was quiet for a while, then said, "I have been coming to your house for over a month now. We did not have occasion to know each other before that. But in these last few days have I given you any reason to doubt my sanity? Do I come across as a madman? Do I look like a fool to you?"

She stared at me for a few minutes, transfixed. The conversation had taken a turn she had not anticipated. Her face was flushed; she went hot behind her ears. Lowering her eyes, she said to me, at last, "No. But why would you say that?"

"Good, so you do not think I am crazy. What if I were to say I am that person? What if I want to take care of you and support you? Will you allow me to do as much?"

Her lips trembled. She stared at me silently.

"Answer me, Sara!"

"What do you want from me? Are you not aware of my past? Have they not told you who I am?"

"I know who you are, and I want you, Sara. I want you from the very core of my being. I do not pity you. I do not want to gain control over you. I love you with all my heart. There is a big vacuum in me. I need you to complete me as a person. Will you be mine, Sara? If there's someone else who loves you as much as I do, or if there's someone you love with this kind of intensity, feel free to choose that person over me. I want you to be happy. I want you to feel loved and desired."

Sara broke into tears. Her body was trembling. Someone had unlocked the sluice gate of her heart. I sat there looking at her, wanting to reach out to her beautiful, broken, bruised soul. My hands felt paralysed. I could not embrace or comfort her. When she was unwell, I had touched her soft skin with my fingers so many times. However, I had chosen to maintain a professional distance since she recovered and had watched her from afar. I could not, somehow, reach out to her in that moment when she was probably most in need of me. Emotions flooded her heart like waves breaking on the shore. She stood up after a long time, her body still trembling. Her face was pale, but still so beautiful! So exquisitely beautiful! I stood up, walked to her, and whispered, "Have I hurt you in any way, Sara?" She shook her head; or it might have been a nod, I couldn't quite understand. I held her elegant, trembling hands in mine, and inched closer to her. Choking on her tears, she pulled away from me and rushed to the door. She turned back to look at me once, as I saw the towel falling off her head and freeing her long, dark, wet tresses. "Don't go away, Sara," I pleaded with her. "Hear me out, please." She stopped in her tracks. "Have I hurt you, Sara? Tell me, have I hurt you?"

She fell at my feet like a wounded animal, and cried, "No! No! You've not hurt me! You've saved me! But I cannot do this to you. This is not right. I cannot allow this to happen."

I was delirious with joy! Sara loved me too! I finally knew her answer! Her life was in shambles. Our society, traditionally, has ostracized women like Sara, but for me, she was no less than divinity. She was beautiful, smart, educated, and accomplished. My joy knew no bounds! I drew her close to my bosom. She pulled away from my embrace, and said, "Go away! I do not deserve such kindness! I do not deserve to be so happy! Don't come back to me again!" She walked out of the room like a flash of lightning, and slammed the door on my face. Her servants came out to check on us. I was stunned into silence. I could still hear her crying bitterly behind that closed door. What could I have done to make things better for her? How could I have helped her? An elderly woman who worked for Sara, and was the closest to her, said to me, "Sir, you should perhaps go home now. That girl is quite headstrong. I don't think she's going to step out of her room anytime soon. And that really is the only flaw in her character—no matter what people say. She can be quite pigheaded. I've known her since she was a child. And you've known her for a while now. The fault is in her stars—not in her. She was born on such an ill-fated day that she had to choose this miserable way of life for herself. But she is such a … " The old woman could not finish her sentence. She started weeping inconsolably. I sighed, and walked out of Sara's house. I swore I would never go back there.

A little less than a month from that fateful day, I heard from my bosses that I would be transferred to another workplace. I felt restless. How could I have left the town without letting her know? Yet, she had made no effort to establish contact with me since our last encounter. Did she really love me? If not, why did surrender herself to me for a moment, no matter how brief? Why did she lie at my feet, crying? Is that how she rejected all her other suitors? Was she ever rude? Or, was she always so graceful? Why did she say that I saved her? How did I save her? What did I save her from? Her words seemed so earnest. Why then did she turn me away? Why did she not allow me to embrace her? A woman's heart is, indeed, a deep ocean of secrets. It is almost impossible to lift the veil and see through that impregnable layer of mist.

I went to her house in the afternoon. I was aware that she was busy at work during the day and in the evenings. As I stood outside her door, I heard her mellifluous voice. She was singing a mournful song about darkening clouds. Why had she refused to sing to me? I waited patiently at the door, allowing her music to envelope my being. She sang with so much heart, and so much passion! Her doorman came out suddenly and greeted me, jerking me back to reality from the heaven I had momentarily been transported to by her soulful melody. She seemed delighted to see me. She stood smiling, without saying a word. She had grown frail. I broke the ice, and said, "You look weak. Were you unwell?"

"Yes. But what took you so long to come and see me?"

"Why did you not send for me when you were ailing?"

"I knew you would come looking for me some day."

"You seem to know everything! Why are you giving me such a hard time then?"

"No! My stars seem to be giving me a hard time!"

"This has nothing to do with your stars. You are willful and stubborn."

"Stubborn?"

"Yes, indeed. Not only are you depriving yourself of happiness but you are also denying me peace. Why are you being so reckless, Sara? Is this fair?"

"I can hardly tell fair from foul. I am in no position to judge this situation."

"Fair enough! But do you at least know that time and tide wait for none? Today you probably value your thoughts and your ego over everything else, but you might have to regret this decision in the future. The opportunity waiting for you now might not be knocking at your door then."

"I am a fatalistic person. I believe in Destiny. If this is what is meant to be, it will be. I cannot sit and brood over my losses. If I deserve this happiness, it will be mine, someday, somewhere, and that will be the most auspicious day in my life. I will not have to go out of my way to make it happen."

Her eyes grew dark, her voice sombre. Was she not aware of the ways of the world? Why was she being so adamant? How could I explain to her the gravity of the situation? How could I tell her that she was making a mistake? Did my eyes not speak for me? Could I not somehow convey to her the deepest feelings of my heart? I could not argue with her. If Sara were a man, I would have tried to win her over with logic. But how can you reason things out with a woman? And so, I remained quiet. She was silent too. After a while, she asked, "Are you mad at me?"

I sighed, and replied, "No, I am not angry. I am sad. You failed to understand me. You do not trust me. You have no faith in me. And that makes me infinitely sad."

She lowered her eyes, and said, "Well, there are things you value today, but what if you change your mind tomorrow? What if these things are no longer worthy of your love in the future? What if they are no longer beautiful and true in your eyes? How are you ever going to get rid of those things then? How will you cleanse your life of that dirt?"

"Never mind the future. Here's what I have to say to you now, Sara: if you say a yes to me, I shall take you with me and try to build a new, happy nest for us. We shall live in peace. However, I cannot keep returning to your doorstep, humbling myself like a beggar, and putting you through this ordeal."

There was fire in her eyes. She protested, "When have I ever asked anyone to stoop low for me? How can I ever be so daring? What have I got that can make me so vain?"

I grew impatient, and said, "This is not the time to discuss what you possess and what you don't. I shall take your leave now. I shan't come back to bother you. If you ever need me, call for me. I have received a transfer-order. I'm going away from here to work in a different place. Here's my new address."

She looked at me with frenzied, incredulous eyes, but then said rather calmly, "You're lying! This is a lie!"

"Have I ever lied to you, Sara? I am, indeed, leaving this town. This is my last week here. In case you change your mind in the meanwhile, do let me know. I'll take your leave today."

I did not look back at her; I had made up my mind.

Naseem, there are moments in our lives when we feel strong and invincible. There were times when I felt like Superman too. I felt as though I could direct the winds and rule the earth. I thought I could challenge the universe and let it know that I exist, that I am powerful and unstoppable. However, that one encounter with Sara made me realize how mistaken I was, Naseem! I did not know the limits of my own strength. That woman, that frail, fragile, delicate woman, managed to turn all my dreams to ashes. We are strange creatures! The absence of a woman was enough to shatter my heart to bits. I felt broken and dejected! Lost! Defeated! I have been writing this letter for two days now, yet, I cannot seem to convey all that I want to say. I cannot seem to give words to the intense feelings in my heart. Still, I must write to you. It has been seven years since that day. There may be some loose strands in my narrative, but I shall try my best to tell you everything. My unuttered words are spilling onto the page now, not only because I owe you an explanation, but also because I want to re-live my pain once again.

I returned from Sara's house that day and went to the hospital later in the evening. I was on call that night. On my way back home after work, Sudhir, my batchmate and assistant, said, "I've heard you've been transferred. There's something I'd like to tell you, if you don't mind."

I was, as you now know, preoccupied with other thoughts. I said casually, "Go ahead! Be done with the formalities!"

Sudhir hesitated before asking, "Will you be going to the city alone? Or, um, are you taking a partner along?"

I was taken aback by his question. I replied, "Well, I do not have a partner to take with me."

"Oh, correct me if I'm wrong, but the grapevine has been abuzz with strange news of late. Begum Sara is rumoured to be accompanying you to the city as the mistress of your house and your heart. We, of course, took the news with a pinch of s—"

"I do not want to talk about this any further. Anyway, be informed that if Sara were indeed prepared to marry me, I would be the happiest man on earth. Who is spreading such gossip?"

"These rumours are in the wind, but I don't think I am in a position to name any names tonight. However, now that I have all this information from the horse's mouth what more can I say? So, has the begum said a no to your proposal?"

They say love, fire, and the essence of flowers can't be hidden. They are too strong to be suppressed. Too potent. Too present. I replied, "Well, I cannot comment on her decision right away. Yet, I want to assure you that no matter what the world thinks of her she is no less qualified than any other woman to be my wife. In fact, she's far more accomplished than most others. Unfortunately, her stars have so aligned themselves that today she doesn't even have the confidence to recognize her own worth."

I dropped Sudhir off at his place, then rode away on my motorbike. The distant, dark fields were awash in silver moonlight. The roads were deserted, shyly becoming one with the black horizon. Our rural town was asleep. I heard the crickets crying in the tranquility of that autumn night. I was overcome with emotions. Sara! What was Sara up to? Was she asleep? Was she awake? Was she thinking about me, just like her thoughts haunted the daylight out of me? Was she feeling as uneasy as I felt? I slowed down my bike. I wanted to go to Sara's place desperately. The moon smiled a brilliant silver light at me. The wind was restless. Won't Sara respond to urges of my fitful heart on a night so wild? Won't she take charge of my wasteful, lonely, meaningless life? However, I was not the kind of person who, in a moment of weakness, would take undue advantage of a woman. I decided to wait for her instead of forcing my love on her. I will wait until eternity for her to accept my love and embrace me. I returned home that night, devastated. I had never felt so lonely and helpless before.

I moved to the new city in a week. I sent her a letter before leaving:

"I'm off! The lord knows how hard it has been for me to not show up at your door before leaving this town. But your heart is made of stone! You'll never understand what I've been through. I hope it is not too late for us by the time you realize what a beautiful life we could have had together.

"I wanted you to be mine: with all your hopes and your fears. Yet, you chose to deny yourself that joy, and deliberately kept me away from this bliss. I do not think I can ever be truly happy again. However, deep in my heart, I want you to win this game. I hope I can disappear from your life completely and leave behind no dirty traces. I hope you can start a new life. Farewell! I've said this before, and I'll reiterate it now: reach out to me should you need me. I'll never be too far away. For now, I'm going to a place which is about eight hours from here. Yet, it feels like I'll be lightyears away from you."

Three days after relocating, I received a letter from Sara at my new address. Her words were like poetry to me. I remember every syllable of it. I can reproduce her letter for you, in verbatim. She wrote:

"I received your letter. It was like a missive from god, brightening my dark life. Your words brought me so much joy that I can forget all my pains, all my sorrows. They complete my broken, fragmented existence.

"I was just a young girl, an adolescent when I realized that my Fate has betrayed me, that this society has rejected me, and that my people have cheated on me. There were no kind words to comfort me that day. My heart was filled with bitterness. I hated my life. I wanted to end it. I did not kill myself because I wanted to avenge the wrongs done to me. I was too naïve to realize that the world doesn't work like that. I lived a wretched life, drawing sadistic pleasure from denying favours to men who were charmed by my physical beauty. There weren't too many suitors though! How long can someone live such an empty, barren life? You walked into my life when I was severely ill. You came unasked, uninvited. I did not send for you, yet you came to me in this all-consuming way, like a saviour, a messiah. You came like a flood but after I had already lived through my desert days. You are like an innocent flower, your touch healed me. But soon, you spread your beggar's bowl in front of me, looking for alms from me. What could I have given you? I was reminded of my bleak, desolate days once again. I had never realized how empty my life was until you asked me to complete yours. I would derive a strange sense of fulfillment from denying all the suitors who had queued outside my door once upon a time. But when you knocked at my door, I saw the hollowness within me, dearest. This world, no matter how beautiful, how bountiful, has robbed me of my very essence, has taken away from me my everything! I had nothing to offer you but my emptiness.

"You appeared at my door looking lost and helpless. I could not stand it! I'm glad you did not come to me before leaving. What if I had surrendered to you in that moment? What if my heart had broken free from its constraints, lured by the greed of happiness and your love? What if I had erred, and in an unguarded moment stained your honourable, blameless life with my guilt-ridden existence? Thank you for not coming to me before leaving. You've saved me, once again.

"It is not that I do not love you. I do. You are mistaken in thinking otherwise. Should I have allowed you to continue to harbour that misconception? That probably would have been for the best. But I had to write to you to convey to you my heartfelt gratitude, and my best wishes for you. The sun shines in the faraway sky. Many a flower is born to worship it from a distance. My body might be bruised and broken, but my heart is still so full of love. My heart feels blessed to have found you, to love and worship from afar. You want me! That knowledge fills me with endless pride! I feel whole again! My body and my soul no longer have to live separate lives. I do not deserve to be your wife—do not make such a request again, please! You are an angel, a giver, but how will I live the rest of my life under the painfully heavy burden of your gift? I will never be able to repay your kindness, your donation! You want me just the way I am. You want me despite knowing who I am. Yet, I said a no to your proposal. And so, you went away from here, probably hurt and angry. But think about it—no one can ever be an impediment to our love after this. There is no wrong in this kind of love. However, the relationship we would have birthed, the legacy we would have left behind, had I said a yes to you, would have been a tainted, poisonous one. I am not a good girl. Our children would have had to carry my foul blood in their veins. They would have had to pay for the sins of my body. It gives me shudders to imagine such a life for them. Your love has fulfilled me. I want nothing more from life. You, however, feel rejected and incomplete. You would probably have enjoyed your life with me—that is how desire works. Yet, beloved, if my denial can save your family and your future, your legacy and your lineage, so be it!

"You wanted to live with me for the rest of forever. You longed for a simple, happy life with me. And that thought brings me so much joy! I feel like I have found you, and you can now be mine in this profound, unspeakable, indescribable way. I have denied you joy but found my happiness in the process. Allow me to embrace the pain of this moment. I have given birth to this pain. It is mine, all mine, mine. I have not been able to give you anything. I haven't been able to fulfil any of your desires. And so, like a meteor turning to dust, I want to be able to disappear from your life; that is my sincere prayer. Please try your best to forget me. May you find a partner who deserves you, a wife who will make your life beautiful. Let me remain like the thorn to your flower. Yet, I feel truly blessed today. Yours, Sara."

I did not send a reply to her letter. It was a deliberate decision. I wanted to see how long she would continue to remain so sweet and loving and polite, yet distant and cold. I also wanted to test the strength of my love for her. There was so much I wanted to say to her, but I chose to wait. The earth went into hibernation that winter following a cruel autumn. Spring blossomed into summer after that. The monsoons brought the world alive again. Seasons changed, and I kept waiting for Sara.

In the new city, I got involved in various activities to keep my mind and my body occupied. It was painful to think, so I postponed all thoughts. I returned home late one afternoon. I took a shower and was preparing to go to the hospital. As soon as I sat down to eat my meal, I felt a strange sense of inertia take over my limbs. Within half an hour, my body started burning with fever. I lay in bed feeling paralysed. I lived in my house with Kalu Khan, my cook, my attendant, my man Friday. He took great care of me. Kalu called up the hospital as soon as he realized that I was unwell. In the evening, a senior doctor came over to my place with an intern. However, I wanted to be left alone. So, Kalu managed to send them away after a while. Many people came over to see me the next day. I had managed to make several friends in the city. But when I was delirious with fever, the only faces I wanted to see in that sea of people were yours and Sara's. You were far, far away. And Sara—well, Sara was the queen of my heart but, physically, she was nowhere close to me.

By the next afternoon, Kalu started fretting about my deteriorating health. I soon began to lose consciousness and eventually went into a comatose state. I was later told that I remained in that condition for about five days. The suffering, however, brought me boundless joy. Let me write to you how Fate shined on me in those grey times.

When I opened my eyes after days in the dark, everything around me was quiet. It was probably midnight. I felt the coolness of a bag of ice on my forehead. I tried to move my body but I was too weak. The silver moonlight, entering my room through the window, lay next to my bed curled in a ball. The world around me was dim and blue. I felt soft fingers on my brows. I assumed there was a nurse sitting by my bedside, attending to me. I tried to remove the quilt covering my legs, stretched out my hands, and asked her what hour of the night it was. The ball of moonlight lying next to my bed rose, then came and stood next to me. Bliss! Ah, what bliss! I saw Sara staring at me! It was Sara, indeed! Was my feverish brain playing tricks with me? I called out her name repeatedly: Sara! Sara! She did not reply. She came closer and lay down next to me, her head resting on my chest. Every pore on my skin was alive. I felt Sara's love coursing through my blood and reviving me in that sweet, sweet moment of union. I felt blessed, I felt complete. I had nothing else left to ask for from Life. She was the answer to all my fears, hopes, dreams, and prayers. I must have done something good in my previous birth.

The lord was merciful! I pressed her face with my hands and brought her mouth close to mine. My eyes were watering with joy! Sara's eyes were moist too, as though the floodgates of the seven oceans trapped in her heart had broken free at last! We held each in an embrace and cried together. I thought of the words of our poet:

"Beloved, there is nothing left to fear,
We're bound to one another now by our tears."

My weary body, my broken soul had found a home at last. I fell asleep in peace.

When I woke up the next morning, my eyes immediately started looking for Sara. She was not in the room. Was it a dream then? A mere figment of my imagination? I rubbed my eyes and tried to sit up. Kalu rushed to my bed. "How are you feeling now?" he asked. He looked relieved. I asked him, "Were you not in my room last night?" Pushing a stool close to my bed, Kalu replied, "I was here. We were all here. Come, let me help you wash your face. You need to have some medicines now." I protested, "My head feels like lead, I don't have the strength to sit up; go away!" Kalu realized that I was angry. He left the room quietly. I felt shattered, I wanted to cry.

A little later, someone pushed open the door of my room. Sara stood there in front of me. It was broad daylight. My eyes were not deceiving me. Her face looked tired. Her shy eyes were lowered. She wore a white mark between her brows, on her forehead. She was carrying a goblet in her hands. She looked divine. I thought the Iranian damsel from Hafez Khaiyyam's poem had lost her way and miraculously ended up in my house. She turned her coy face away from my transfixed eyes, and said, "Your temperature has gone down now. I checked earlier in the morning. Shall I help you wash your face?" I nodded. I couldn't speak; I had lost all my words.

She stayed with me for eleven days, Naseem! Eleven priceless, unforgettable days! And then, she left just as she had arrived—suddenly, without a word. I don't think I would have been able to bid her farewell; I'm glad she did not give me that chance. You must be wondering how she showed up at my place, and why. She later told me she would sometimes visit my workplace to look at me from a distance. I never got to see her, but she always enquired after me. She came to the city when I was down with fever—perhaps, on the third day. And then, she stayed with me for eleven days, the reigning queen of my heart. She took care of me, making me fall more hopelessly in love with her. Like a fleeting deer, like a beautiful nightingale, she added colour, music, and warmth to my dry, hay-like days, and showed me who she truly was. I can never describe in words what she means to me. You might take offence at it anyway. She disappeared, taking away with her all my happiness, but she left behind this strange sense of contentment. That is what I live with now. I've visited her a couple of times since then. She has been careful to maintain her distance from me. She is mine, Naseem, truly mine, but we are destined to live like the two banks of a river. If you look hard enough, if you look deep enough, you will realize that there is nothing separating the banks really. In essence, the two banks are one. They are the same soil. They are a continuous body. The river flows down the bed of this soil, dividing it into two shores. The shores look at each other longingly, all day long, all night long. They are complete in their own ways, replete with treasures, yet they wait for one another. Someday, somewhere, we will meet. Maybe a tempest or a flood will unite us again. Our relationship has no name. Sara is happy, she is happy because she knows I love her and she loves me. This realization is enough for her, but my selfish heart weeps to be one with her every now and then. I want her to be mine completely. Perhaps, my love is weak. Perhaps, I do not love her like she loves me. And that is probably why my sickly heart longs for her with such an intensity. When I told her about my feelings, she asked me to find myself a suitable bride. Sara was serious. I could see the earnestness in her voice. I, however, was joking when I told you that it's time for me to look for a suitable bride. You misread my humour and gave rise to such a chain of events that I was forced to run away from home and live in exile!

Your friend,
Azam.

First published as "Satyikar" in *Saogat*, vol 11 in 1934. Translated from Bengali by Somitra Ganguly.

3

She

Rashid Jahan

I met her for the first time at the clinic. Like me, she was there to get her medicines. As soon as they saw her, all the women kept their distance. Even the doctor made her displeasure known by wincing her eyes. Despite my disgust, I somehow managed to look towards her and smile, which she returned. Or at the very least, she tried to. Her face lacked a nose, and instead had two gaping red holes in its place. She was also missing an eye and had trouble seeing from the remaining one without craning her neck.

After a short while, I ran into her once again at the medicine counter. She asked politely—"Where have you come from?" I told her so, and she took her medicine and left. As soon as she was gone, the compounder launched into his own unprovoked tirade—"She is not a good woman. A whore! A filthy whore slowly rotting to her death. Now she has come for her treatment, and the doctor has lost her marbles, writing her prescriptions and what not. The bitch should be thrown out!"

I was a teacher in a girl's school at the time. Freshly graduated from college, I thought the world was at my feet, and the future lay before me like a garden full of roses and jasmines. The world resembled a cool moonlit night with a happily flowing stream, sometimes gurgling along merrily, and at other times, it became a magnificent waterfall. In this happy state, I did not know of sadness and pain. Teaching was nothing but a pastime. The entirety of existence was nothing but the eager wait of possibilities before me.

The bamboo curtain parted, and "she" entered my office. Puzzled, I stood up and out of habit, politely asked her to take a seat. At first, she hesitated, but sat down eventually. She held a *motia* flower in her hand, which she placed in front of me. I felt a quiver of disgust while picking it

Rashid Jahan, *She* In: *The Silence That Speaks*. Edited by: Haris Qadeer, Oxford University Press. © Oxford University Press India 2022. DOI: 10.1093/oso/9780190132613.003.0004 up, but somehow, I forced myself to overcome the feeling and placed the flower in my hair. She smiled, got up, and left the room.

This became a daily routine. Every day, she would enter my office after school hours. I would politely ask her to sit, and she would place a flower on my desk. My peers made fun of me. No one would sit on the chair that she had been sitting on. After all, she was really disgusting to look at. Even I would not touch the chair. Naseeban, the old cleaning lady, would also grumble after she left, "This new teacher is a strange one, getting chummy with that piece of scum. Why should I have to dust that chair?"

The principal would also furrow her brow and remark "Why do you call her to the school? The parents will surely ask us why a prostitute comes here." And the next day, she would come again, and I would politely ask her to sit. Gradually, she started staying for longer, staring at me the whole time. We never spoke. Did she think that I don't know her truth? And she would keep staring with her one crooked eye and that nose-less, ugly face. Sometimes, I suspected that her eyes were brimming with tears. What was she thinking? I often wanted to ask her, but where would I even start?

Many times, it would so happen that as soon as she would come, my colleagues would get up and leave immediately while taunting me in English "Safiya, 'she' has come, let's go to the library, look at her cursed face!" Some would say "Safiya, after looking at her, I find it difficult to eat, I feel like vomiting"

"She has picked a damn fine specimen! *Numero uno* amongst you all, I say."

"She should keep herself veiled," the old hag who taught religion would grumble.

I would keep working while she stared at me. It made me feel uneasy. Why does she keep staring? What are her thoughts? Once upon a time, was she also like me? I would often get goosebumps at the thought.

Why does she keep on coming? Doesn't she know that people hate her and are disgusted by her very sight? Her snot kept dripping down those red holed nostrils. Every day, I would think of mustering up the will to forbid her from coming in the future. The principal was right after all, and the girls have also started gossiping. The teachers vomit at her very sight. In spite of all this, whenever she would come, I would involuntarily blurt out "Please take a seat."

Does she not have a mirror? Does she not realize that she is paying for her sins? Why doesn't anyone tell her? Does she even have someone? Where does she live? Where does she come from? Does she realize that I think of her as a scourge? I am the laughingstock of the school. In fact, I have become an object of ridicule. However, as soon as she would keep a flower in front of me, I would put it in my hair, and she would smile that ghastly smile.

Why does she keep staring? Who is she? Who was she? Where was she born and how did she become like this? Does she feel at ease when she meets me, or is she pained?

One day, when she got out of my room, she blew her nose and wiped the snot on the wall. Naseeban, who was putting a fresh coat of fowler's earth on the slates of younger pupils burst forth with agility of a much younger woman. She smacked her on the back with a slate. The woman was shaken up. Forgetting all the etiquette that she had picked up at the school over the past twenty years and which she used to insist upon while interacting with students, the "Naseeban of the street" emerged. "You ill-bred whore! You dare to sit on the chair! You used to sit on the market square till yesterday. Now that your skin is peeling off, you have adopted the airs of a lady?"

One kick, then another one, and finally a punch.

I ran out and caught hold of Naseeban. "What are you doing," I yelled at her, as girls crowded around us. The teachers also rushed towards the scene. Naseeban was seething with anger.

"You have made her the frigging Queen of the World! This piece of filth whom you have picked from the sewer has ruined the wall! I have served this place for twenty years and have never seen whores come to the school. I won't stay here for a goddamn second, hire someone else who can." Naseeban charged towards her once again but was restrained by the crowd.

I bent forward and helped the woman get up. She was sobbing. I took her towards the gate. Blood was oozing from the side of her head, but she didn't seem to be particularly aware of it. Hiding her tears from me, she mumbled "Well, now you know," and left.

First published as "*Woh*." Translated from Urdu by Amit Julka.

4
Mango Blossoms

Zahra Rai

I'd open the door myself whenever someone knocked. His way of knocking was different from anyone else's, but I felt pleasurably excited to think that it might be him. This happened every time there was a knock. In the time that it took me to get to the door, I thought about how I'd greet him if he was there. Would I smile or put on a sad face? Would I ask him where he'd been all this while or not? I also went to the door at the slightest sound because I was always waiting for him, every minute of the day; I thought about him all the time. My fear was that if a servant announced his arrival, Bi Amma, who'd be sitting right there, would send word that Bhaiyaji wasn't home, and he'd go away without coming inside or giving me a chance to set eyes on him. But if I brought him inside, she wouldn't be able to say very much, and we could chat a little in Bhaijan's study.

I'd be disappointed even though I knew it wasn't him, and for a while, I could not study or do anything else. Then, I'd go and lie down in my room and think of all the possible reasons that could have kept him from coming.

Bi Amma was my grandmother, and she was very fond of me. We too loved her because apart from her affectionate and trusting nature, she did not try to exercise undue control over us. She didn't mind my sitting around in the company of young men, flirting and playing cards with them, but when visitors asking after me looked embarrassed at seeing me surrounded by young men, she'd get worried too and once in a while tick me off. She did not approve of Bhaijan's friends coming inside the house in his absence, and how could I tell her that it was not Bhaijan that all of his friends came to see?

People at home had already begun to talk. They'd try their best to figure out what was going on, to see if they could read the story of my heart

Zahra Rai, *Mango Blossoms* In: *The Silence That Speaks*. Edited by: Haris Qadeer, Oxford University Press. © Oxford University Press India 2022. DOI: 10.1093/oso/9780190132613.003.0005 from my face. And I'd do my best to keep them guessing by treating all of Bhaijan's friends the same way. I was attracted to quite a few of them. To tell the truth, I was attracted to all young men. What after all was there in a young man for a girl to dislike? If I liked one for his masculine good looks, I liked another for the interesting things he said, and a third for his attractive voice. Each time I heard his voice, a shiver went through me, and I wanted him to speak again and again so that I could experience the whole thing once more. There were other men I liked for their big American cars or television sets and refrigerators, and here age was no bar, nor looks—I didn't care if they had three chins. The only ones I disliked were those who remained indifferent to my blossoming youth and my beauty. The fact was that I liked all of Bhaijan's friends for all of them were crazy about me. I too, at least on the surface, gave none cause to despair. I'd sit in their midst like a doll and my presence added such charm to the evening that it was two in the morning even before we knew it. Card games would be in full swing when Bi Amma called out—"Shami, come and sleep now, it's late." But I went to my room only when the game had finished and everyone had left. I'd wake feeling pleasantly languorous, the spell of the previous evening still upon me. I didn't feel like going to the university and attending lectures, but if all of a sudden, he happened to turn up my lassitude would disappear and I'd be a changed person, as though I'd become someone else. I found myself unable to walk slowly or speak without laughing; I felt as if I was flying. I had no need of anyone else when he was around; I was content to be with him. I knew that Bhaijan did not approve of the way I'd bet and play cards with him because he was a good player and won each time. He'd provoke me into betting large sums; I'd lose and keep emptying out Bhaijan's pockets. But I felt happy when I slid the pile of coins that I'd lost over to him, for it seemed to form a connection between us. And when he gathered up the money I felt grateful, my heart softening even more towards him. It pleased me to lose against him.

I noticed that he didn't like me playing cards with anyone else, though he never said as much. He'd take my place at the game and ask me for some coffee. There'd be other times when he looked bored and started wandering about the room, scrutinizing the knickknacks. He'd view the painting on the wall or go up to the books cupboard, rest a knee on the carpet, and look at the books. He'd fiddle with some fat books, but it was quite obvious from his distracted manner that he was simply turning the pages. He had a wheatish complexion, and with his thick hair falling over his forehead, he looked even more handsome. I loved the way he knelt down, dressed in his tightly fitting clothes.

"You're reading very seriously!" I teased him.

"Who's winning?" he asked, changing the subject.

I told him happily that I was, for I didn't like losing against anyone else. I became dejected too if he looked off-colour; he probably didn't know that I played with others simply to get an excuse to be where he was, not because I was interested in them. I completed my deck of cards in rummy and smiled at Sohail.

"What, done already?" he asked.

"Well, what do you think!"

"Show me the sequence first."

I showed him the sequence, then the run and the trail and got up.

"I'll go get some coffee," I said and left.

I put on the kettle and stood in front of the mirror. I was wearing a light lipstick. My face looked radiant, my eyes shone as though I'd just woken from a bewitching dream. My fine silken hair curled on my brow. I'm quite beautiful! I thought. He too must have seen my enticing lips, my shining eyes, and my alluring smile. It was as if his lips came close to mine and I trembled, my ears began to burn, and I had an intense desire to touch him.

Just then, the lid of the kettle began to rattle, startling me. The water had boiled. I poured it into the long-necked golden teapot that Bhaijan had brought from Japan, which was my favourite. It had a covering of rough wool and the long neck of the teapot had an opening at the top. The knob of the lid and the three legs of the pot were made of ivory. I took out this teapot only when I had a special guest.

I was relieved to find that Sohail had left when I entered the study with the jar of Nescafe and the other items on a tray. Rohit seemed to be dozing, bent forward on the writing desk. He opened his eyes when he heard me come in and looked at me without blinking—a long stare in which I read many things and again I felt a shiver go through me. I lowered my eyes, embarrassed. He kept looking at me. I thought about how I must look to him as I went about fixing the coffee. He must have seen my slender hands and my shapely arms, I became aware that the deep purple blouse was tight on my arms and that my breathing had become rapid—was it possible for him to read my heart in my eyes? I felt a little worried.

Suddenly I heard him say—"Will you come to the music conference at Rana's?"

"Alone?" I asked and at once became self-conscious. What would he have thought? Had I offended him? Surely, there was no harm in going with him alone.

"No, your brother will also come, there's nothing to be afraid of," he said and smiled.

Feeling like a fool, I tried to save the situation—"Who said I was afraid?"

"Then why did you ask if you'd have to come alone?" he asked with a hurt smile.

"Oh, I didn't mean to upset you! I just wanted to know if Bhaijan would come too. Isn't this your friend Rana who has a big house in Neelkanth Gali?"

"Yes, it's the same Rana who has a big house in Neelkanth Gali," he mockingly imitated me and laughed.

"I've heard people say that Neelkanth Gali isn't safe!" I said.

"Well, it's true that the Gali is a dangerous place … ," he teased me. "Shami, just now you look like that frightened little schoolgirl whom the ruffians carried off from the same Neelkanth Gali."

I thought just then of the bird that flits restlessly for a safe uninhabited and quiet place to build a nest in spring.

The prospect of going to the performance shut away in a carriage, listening all the while to the sound of horses trotting was not my idea of a romantic outing. I've always despised the sound of hoofbeats and have never been fond of horses anyway.

I wanted to go on a rickshaw, for I could cuddle up to him on it—but of course I couldn't tell him this.

"What time will the program begin? Shall I ask them to have the carriage ready?" Bhaijan asked and my heart sank, but I kept quiet.

"Why, aren't you coming? Why are you still lying down?"

"No yaar, I have a headache. Who knows how long the performance will go on for."

"It could go on till 4 a.m. It'll be appropriate for him to close with an early morning Bhairavi—he'll probably sing his dadra "*chalo kahe ko jhuti banao batiyaan …* " You think the audience will let him leave without listening to this special piece of his?"

"Then, the two of you had better go without me. Do ask for the carriage."

"Two of you?" Again, a shiver went through me.

The lane was too narrow for a carriage, he told Bhaijan. Even a rickshaw could only go up till Kunj Gali and then we'd have to walk. But what I wanted to know was whether he wanted to go on a rickshaw because he didn't have a choice or was it something else …

He hailed a rickshaw. It was Basant Panchami, the festival of spring, and in the excitement of listening to Raag Basant, I decided to wear a bright yellow sari that I thought would be appropriate for the occasion. It had turned cold; I put on a black cardigan. I stood in front of the full-length mirror when I had finished dressing. I don't know if my face was flushed because of the cold or was it the turmoil in my heart? I drew a thin line of kajal in my eyes, extending the line a little beyond its corners, and darkened my lipstick to enhance the colour. The cardigan, with the buttons fastened, emphasized the contours of my figure. I thought I looked ravishing. He was waiting for me outside, and when he saw me, he said delightedly—"Ah! So, this really is a serious celebration of Basant!" I smiled and pretended to look shy as I climbed onto the rickshaw.

We'd come quite a long way. The wind was strong, and my hand brushed against his.

"Your hands are so cold! Why, are you scared?"

"Not at all, do you take me for a coward?"

He didn't reply but spread out his heavy overcoat over my knees and beneath it he pressed my hand.

"I'll soon warm them up," he said familiarly. He held my hand in a firm grip and so affectionately that I did not have the heart to take it away. He might get offended if I did so, and I never could bear the idea of annoying him. It was as if he'd cast a spell on me. I began to tremble, and my voice seemed to be sinking. "It's very cold," I said in a low voice.

He nestled closer, and now we could feel the warmth of each other's bodies. My head dropped by itself onto his shoulder, and I felt my heart flutter as I got the intoxicating smell of his aftershave.

We had reached Neelkanth Gali. We got off the rickshaw and walked to Rana's place. Rohit kept getting pushed against me in the crowd and each time he'd catch hold of my shoulders. The music hall was on an upper storey that was reached by climbing a narrow staircase. Guarding me like something precious, he escorted me upstairs.

The hall was full, so we had to sit close up against each other. I was still mesmerized. It felt so good to be sitting right next to him I quite forgot that the hall was full of people. I was aware only of him.

Soon, Ustad Hafiz Ali Khan struck the first note on his sarod and I sat up. I wanted to soak in the music, each limpid note clear, like water. He started an alap in Raag Basant Bahar. The intricate interweaving of Raag Basant and Bahar was so melodious that the audience was enraptured. After playing for an hour, a thin stream of tears flowed out from the ustad's eyes. The melancholy of spring pervaded the atmosphere. The spirit of the raag came alive, and it was as if mango blossoms were raining down from the strings of the sarod. I wasn't sure what it was that kept twisting and throbbing within me. My imagination had become active, and it was as if I saw miles upon miles of yellow mustard fields blooming. The hall seemed to be fragrant with mango blossoms. It was strange. I wondered at the deep connection of Indian classical music with the seasons; without a pre-written score or theme, the music seemed to contain the whole universe.

Right after the sarod, when Faiyaz Khan started on a lively Jaijaiwanti, the mood of the audience changed and faces lit up. What a raag he'd chosen! It seemed to consist of those very emotions that we felt then; it certainly echoed mine. I could feel my fists clenching as the music scaled a peak. The vibrant notes seemed to shake up my nerves which tingled with excitement at the surprises slowly revealed by the music. After singing for an hour, he doubled the tempo and started on "*nadan ankhiyaan lagin*" playing around with the rhythm in his characteristic manner. Our heightened emotions became quieter, and I found that Rohit was leaning so close onto my shoulder that I could feel his warm breath on my face. The ustad kept up a steady display of his wizardry with rhythm and the performance ended at 4 a.m. with Raag Bhairavi.

I felt drunk on the music I'd heard—the sadness of Basant Bahar and the restless Jaijaiwanti that was infused with the longing of separated lovers. We climbed down the stairs into the lane which was pitch dark but for a light that glimmered in the distance. He took my hand again, and I did not try to free it. I had no energy left after listening to the music.

We got into the rickshaw and as it picked up speed, the air of that spring evening seemed to me to be steeped in sorrow. The music had filled me with a sweet pain, and I felt a lump in my throat; it was as if there were tears and not blood flowing in my veins. This was probably because of the proximity of Rohit, the few priceless moments that I'd got with him.

There was a blast of cold wind, and he wrapped a big woollen shawl around both of us. It seemed quite natural for us to be covered with the same shawl, and I felt carried away by the romance of it. I'd been brought up on conservative values, so the thrill that I felt on being so close to him was tempered by an anxious hesitation, though I could hardly tell him all this. Encouraged by my silence, he slipped his arm around my waist. I did not object. We were getting close to home. He cupped my face in both his hands and planted his lips on mine, which immediately felt crushed, burnt.

The rickshaw had reached the compound of the house and we alighted. I still felt intoxicated, and my body seemed to be on fire. He looked serious and a little troubled. He glanced casually at my face, trying to read what I felt. I said nothing.

"What on earth came over you?" I asked, breaking the silence.

"Please forgive me, I should not have behaved as I did," he said, anxiously running a hand over his forehead. I felt a stab of disappointment. Forgive? What was there to forgive? This wasn't at all what I was expecting. I felt like telling him "You're an idiot. You haven't the least idea what a girl wants, have you?" But I couldn't bring myself to say this and he left.

I went to my room and collapsed on the bed. I don't know when I fell asleep, wondering whether he'd come again or had been frightened away by the encouragement offered by my ardent body.

First published in *Dharmyug*, October 1969 and subsequently collected in *Mahalsara ka Ek Khel aur Anya Kahaniyaan* ed. Sara Rai, Vani Prakashan 2020. Translated from Hindi by Sara Rai.

5

The Tutor's Secret

Mrs. Abdul Qadir

Hasan was employed as the academic tutor to my children—he would teach them with a lot of hard work and commitment. Like other tutors, he didn't have any pride or selfishness, even in name. This was the reason why he very quickly became loved by everyone in our family. He was around forty years old. He was a thin, tall man, with a yellowish complexion, like mustard blossoms. The features of his face, which at some point, must have been well-proportioned and attractive, had now gone to ruins—his cheeks were hollowed out, and his eyes had sunk into his face. Due to his leanness, his forehead appeared unusually broad and his ears too long. Despite all these faults, his face was definitely somewhat agreeable—the children loved him dearly, and he too loved them with all his heart. While he had all these qualities, he also had a flaw, which was that for each lunar month, he would take the last three or four days as holidays and go away.

When he would come back after spending the holidays, his condition would be much worse. His face and appearance would also become quite scary. We would be surprised at this strange habit of his, and at his deteriorated condition.

It was the first month of monsoon rains. Early morning, my attendant went to the tap outside to perform ablutions. She saw that a black-tongued snake is crawling away from under an ivy creeper. The attendant screamed to raise alarm. On hearing her, all other servants arrived on the spot, armed with sticks, but in this while, the snake moved ahead of the servants' quarters and towards Hassan's room, and entered the room by way of a window. Hassan's room was locked, since it was only the second day of his usual holidays. But letting the snake be would have been very dangerous, and therefore we decided to break the lock and kill the snake.

Mrs. Abdul Qadir, *The Tutor's Secret* In: *The Silence That Speaks.* Edited by: Haris Qadeer, Oxford University Press.
 DOI: 10.1093/oso/9780190132613.003.0006

When the servants entered the room after breaking the lock, their shock had no limits. Hassan lay face down on the bed. Tears were rolling down from his shut eyes. He was frothing at his mouth. His right hand limply hung downwards, as if the snake had just bit him.

The snake was killed, and Hassan was admitted to the hospital. We were all worried about him, but he recovered very soon. Finally, like usual, he presented himself at his room's doorstep. As soon as people saw him, they attacked him with many kinds of questions, but he didn't answer a single one of them. However, when I asked him, very worried and wanting to know the secret, he said that he cannot relate that terrible tale in front of children, because they might get scared, and start hating him after knowing his secret.

2

It was night. Perched on the mango tree, the cuckoo bird was singing in her painful voice. Sitting on a bench, Hassan was narrating his tale.

My name is Husnat Ahmad, and I hail from Akhnoor in the Province of Jammu. My grandfather was the Chowdhary of a village, and our farming used to happen on a vast scale. My father passed away when I was still a child. My grandfather was the only security for my widowed mother and me. My uncle was a *tehsildar*. My grandfather loved my father dearly and adored me as his image. My uncle had a daughter named Sakina. She was four years younger to me. Our house was located around one and a half kilometers from Akhnoor, in a heaven-like refuge, around which we owned several acres of land. Our house was very expansive, built in royal, stately style. It had several rooms, many doorsteps, servant quarters, bow windows, and peculiarly shaped rooms.

A spectacular garden which spread over several acres surrounded our house. This garden was dotted by several canals, which had been cut from a nearby hilly river. Beyond the garden, in a spectacular piece of land, to the point that human gaze could perceive, one could see fields of saffron and rice rippling in the wind. On one's right and left, beautiful trees extended for miles. Towards the rear end of the plot, near the river bank, my grandfather had a few bamboo trees planted. However, the trees had become so dense that the small piece of land had been transformed into an entire forest of bamboo.

Sakina and I were the only children in the household who, away from the rigors of the world, were being brought up in this peaceful and calm abode. Sakina and I loved each other dearly. A tutor had been employed for our education. I was sixteen years old when I went to Jammu to write my high school exams. When the results came out, I stood first among all other boys. Consequently, my uncle's opinion was that I should be sent to Jammu to pursue further education.

The preparations for my departure had begun. I intensely disliked being separated from my near and dear ones, especially Sakina. Unknown to everyone, my heart was slowly sinking at the thought of leaving. Sakina too appeared grief-stricken. Our condition was inexpressible. She was crying that she would not let her brother go. My grandfather was trying to console her through this. But I conducted myself with strength and though it wasn't my heart's desire, I took their leave.

3

Two years passed. I went home for several vacations but could never meet Sakina, because coincidentally, whenever I used to go home, she would either be at her maternal grandparents' house, or with her father in Udhampur.

Finally, after I had taken my matric examinations and was back home, Sakina too was there. On seeing her, my heart suddenly sank. I was in a state of shock. In a brief period of those two years, she had completely transformed. Now, instead of the innocent and playful child that I had known, she had become a demure and bashful young girl. She was now a fully blooming flower of beauty and comeliness. There was an unbelievable magic in her doe-like eyes. Her features tugged one's heart. One would often confuse her playful locks for a thick black snake. Her shrub-like height and a robust, healthy built would wreak havoc all around. Her incomparable beauty had a magnetic charm, which had me bewitched, and I couldn't dare address her directly.

She was sitting silently, with her eyes cast down, but sometimes look at me through sideward glances. She seemed very happy. Whenever she would try and talk to me, her cheeks would redden. But despite several attempts, I couldn't make get any words out. After a few days, our awkwardness disappeared, and I felt that Sakina was entering the depths of my heart.

One afternoon, I was sleeping in the men's quarters of the house. I woke up and saw that my grandfather and uncle were sitting in a corner, deep in conversation.

Grandfather: Son, I am very old now. Who knows how soon I will meet my destiny? My desire is to see Husnat in his wedding attire.

Uncle: Father, I plan to provide a good education to Husnat. If he gets married now, he will have to forsake his education. Secondly, Sakina is immature now. Three or four years are not a big deal.

My marriage with Sakina? A wave of happiness ran through me, but I remained glued to my bed, eyes shut. My grandfather and uncle continued their conversation on this topic.

Days of happiness whoosh past in the blink of an eye. After I passed my Entrance Exams, I was sent to Aligarh. Now, Sakina and I had a continuous, uninterrupted correspondence through letters. However, after a few months, her letters began arriving late, and then slowly, they stopped altogether.

4

When I came back home for the summer break, I met her, but found her rather cold. I was very surprised at her aloofness but couldn't find any reason for it.

The day was over, and the moon was rising. Redness had spread over the sky, and the last traces of sunlight were falling on night jasmine trees, because of which the entire forest seemed to be aflame. Sakina stood at the edge of the garden near a wall. The orange-tinged shadows of the night jasmine threw a strange beauty across Sakina's face. She was fully absorbed in gazing at the beautiful vista of the forest. She had a fawn in her lap, who she fed milk through a glass bottle.

At that moment, her beauty would have put heavenly virgins to shame. I couldn't control myself anymore and softly walked and stood next to her: "Sakina," I said.

Sakina (without looking at me)—Hassan, look how beautiful everything is today!

Me: But not as beautiful as you!

Sakina: I don't like such indecency one bit.

Me: I have noticed that you are being very distant with me.

Sakina: No, this is just your misunderstanding.

Me: No, before this, you loved me.

Sakina: Who says no to love? Blood relations always inspire love, but you are trying to give this a different meaning.

I was pained to hear these words from Sakina's lips, to the extent that I didn't have dinner that night, and only lay on my bed. It was a moonlit night. Soft and pleasant bursts of wind were providing some relief. Every leaf of the garden was drenched in this perfume. The entire world was lost in dreams. But how could I sleep? I was restlessly turning on my bed.

Around twelve o' clock, I heard the creaking of the door. I raised myself a little and saw a shadow behind a short, dense bush. I was shocked to think that someone wanted to go out of the house at this hour. I got up to figure out who it was, and hid behind some trees.

The person was walking very slowly. When I reached closer the person, I realized it was Sakina. She walked to the edge of the bamboo thicket and then stopped- I hid behind a tree to look at her. By this time, the bamboo trees parted a little and a young man emerged, whose beauty would have made the moon look insipid. He came and stood next to her and started speaking.

The Man: Ah Sakina! We meet today after so long.

Sakina: Rafiq, I have to come to meet you for the last time today.

The Man: Sakina, for god's sake, don't say this. I can't live without you.

Sakina: I am helpless, because I am being forcefully married off to my uncle's son, and that is my parents' will.

The Man: My dear Sakina, please don't let your tongue say such painful things. Tell me, don't you love me?

Sakina: If I didn't love you, why would I come to such a place at this hour?

Saying this, she started crying inconsolably. On seeing her condition, the blood in my veins began boiling. Finally, after some time, she came back to the house.

I bore true love for Sakina. Therefore, I swore that I will not let her happiness be sacrificed for my desires.

Consequently, I went back to my room and wrote a letter addressed to my grandfather:

"I have heard that I am going to get married to Sakina. To avoid this, I am leaving the house. I am not one to toe the line and ruin my life by getting married to an unrefined, village lass, just to please your conservative minds.

Raqam Husnat Ahmad."

I put this letter in an envelope, placed it on my bed, and left to live with an old friend in Peshawar, where he found me a job as a caretaker to an old Pathan's familial estate at 20 rupees a month.

I worked very hard for one month. Sardar Sahab was very kind to me. I had decided to continue my education. He gave me permission to study and took the expense of fees etcetera upon himself. Consequently, I resumed my education while also managing my duties on the estate.

5

Four years had elapsed since this incident. I had now completed my B.A. It was evening, and I was passing through the Qissa Khwabi Bazaar, when someone called out my name. I turned to see that it was someone from my village. I asked him about the health and well-being of my family, and then found out that my uncle had died, and it had been four years since Sakina got married to a rich young man named Rafiq, who was living an exiled life close to Akhnoor.

He told me that my grandfather's health had deteriorated and that he often cries remembering me. I was in utter shock at hearing of my uncle's death, and on hearing about my grandfather's precarious state, I couldn't control myself and left for home.

On seeing me, my grandfather became full of life, as if anew. When he asked the reason for my wanderings, I narrated to him the entire story of Sakina and Rafiq. He was very happy to hear of my mature and kind-hearted behavior. He pointed out Sakina's magnificent palatial home which stood in the middle of the forest of night-flowering jasmine trees, as if tall enough to touch the sky.

The news of my arrival spread far and wide very quickly. People started flocking to the house to meet me. Sometime in the afternoon, Sakina also arrived. My heart sank when I saw her, her golden complexion had dwindled to a sickly yellowish hue, there were dark circles around her eyes, and she had been reduced a skeletal frame.

"Ah Sakina! What happened to you?" I blurted out.

She didn't really answer, but I saw two fat teardrops sliding down her yellowed cheeks, which got me worried. I thought perhaps Rafiq behaves badly with her, but everyone was all praises for Rafiq.

The second day, I was invited to Sakina's home. I complained to my grandfather that Rafiq hadn't even come to meet me, that perhaps he still thinks of him as his rival, and that I won't go to their house. My grandfather said, "That makes no sense. Rafiq is a very reclusive man and almost never steps out of the four walls of his house."

In the evening, my grandfather and I set out for Sakina's house. Sakina's house had been constructed in the middle of such a beautiful garden that its very sight would steal your heart. The courtyard of the house opened into the garden. Pine trees stood tall in their majestic stature, proud of their own grandeur and splendor. The landscaping of the garden was a testament to the craftsman's skill. One could see several fountains rising up from multiple reservoirs. Along the railings, dense beds of roses blossomed. The garden was chock full of flowers. The house, with its unique manner of construction, expensive furniture and several other adornments, seemed nothing short of a royal citadel. Sakina showed every inch of her house to me, and then I finally got to meet Rafiq.

Rafiq preferred solitariness, and except for a few men, didn't meet with anyone else. Then for his flaws. The first was that he bore strong hatred for music. Secondly, he hated any and all wise men and sages. But this second flaw too wasn't important enough to hurt Sakina. I often thought that perhaps Sakina is grief-stricken because of her separation from me.

6

It was the time of winters. The glowing celestial boat of stars had reached the very middle of deep blue sea of the night sky. Owing to its generous bounty, each bit of the universe seemed drenched in light. Seeing this bountiful and nourishing atmosphere, the clogged streets of the heart had opened up on their own. Only Rafiq had no fondness for this beautiful atmosphere. He was steadily sitting on a sofa near the fireplace in his ceremonially arranged room. In front of him, several books lay spread on a black, ebony table, and Rafiq would often be lost in the contemplation of these books. Sakina and I were walking around in the garden. A snake charmer was walking down the thin clearing through the fields. Sakina expressed her wish to see the snake in action. The snake charmer had only begun playing his pipe when Rafiq came into the scene running and drove the snake charmer away, beating him mercilessly. I was embarrassed at my mistake, but Sakina felt very bad.

Sakina: Rafiq, what you did was terrible. What right did you have to interrupt me when we were just amusing ourselves? Perhaps you don't like such things—but I really enjoy these little shows and performances. Everyone has their own disposition.

Rafiq: "My dear! These people are very dangerous—they steal the beauty of beautiful ones, make a young person old, suck off the blood of the brave, and ruin the lives of lovers. What do you know? Their magic is bewitching." Saying all this, he kept looking at both of us intently. Suddenly, I felt that my heart on its own was succumbing to him. Sakina too began to feel ashamed at her own behaviour. She helpless swayed into his control. Rafiq took her in his arms with deep affection, and then took us both inside, where he continued offering advice to us very softly.

In the evening, when I set out to go back home, I felt as if I was recovering from the hangover of some intoxication. My body felt drained with deadening exhaustion. I crashed on my bed and began thinking of my predicament of how inflamed Sakina seemed at Rafiq's untimely strictness, and how I myself was irritated. But when he gazed at us with that intensity, our hearts melted as if made of wax. Perhaps he knew some strange sorcery. Or his gaze has some satanic power.

After this incident, I developed a deep hatred for Rafiq. However, whenever I would go in front of him, my heart would brim over with love for him, and, like a pet dog, I would start following each and every small wish of his.

One day, I was taking a walk in my garden when I saw someone walking towards me. He had tied a thick cloth on his forehead so that his face could not be seen. As soon as he reached, he began saying: "Sir, I have a plea. Please hear me out in a secluded place."

He demanded this in such a way that I couldn't say no to him and took him to the edge of the bamboo forest. Now, the man took off the cloth from his face, and I immediately recognized him. He was that snake charmer who Rafiq had insulted and beaten the other day.

Snake charmer: Sir, I want to acquire some important information about that sir from the other day. I hope that I won't be disappointed in this.

Me: I only know this much that he is a rich exile from Iran and that my uncle's daughter is married to him.

Snake charmer: I have heard this from the people around already. But have you also witnessed some natural power of his?

Me: Yes, there is some deep pull in his eyes for sure.

Snake charmer: Does he blink his eyes at all or not?

Me: I am not sure about that, because I never really paid any attention to this. But what is your suspicion about him? Do you think that he is a magician?

Snake charmer (with laughter): No, in fact much more than a magician. Okay, inspect his eyes carefully today. I will come back again in the evening.

7

It was ten o'clock. Gusts of a cold breeze were wreaking havoc. Walking at a fast pace, I entered Sakina's house. Coincidentally, no servant saw me entering the house. Walking very quietly, I went into Rafiq's room and hid myself behind a curtain.

At that moment, Rafiq was sitting on a sofa and was smoking a cigar. Sakina was sitting on a low stool next to an open window and was knitting something with a pair of needles. She was wearing completely plain and white clothes. The cold breeze was irreverently playing with the long, beautiful tresses of Sakina, spreading them all over her face.

Although it seemed that Rafiq was fully rapt in smoking his cigar, his gaze was fixed intently on Sakina's face. I kept looking at his eyes very carefully for a long time and eventually found out that Rafiq never really blinked. I felt a fear taking hold of me. I looked at Sakina very carefully. She was sitting in a drugged and drowsy state. While her hands gripped the knitting needles, her fingers were motionless. Stupefied, I quietly went out of the room.

Around the evening, the snake charmer met me again and said: "Sir, tell me? Did you manage to find out anything?"

Me: "Yes, I found out today that he never blinks. What do we do now?"

Snake charmer: Sir, I want to read out an incantation. If we can get a room with a strong door in that house, I will show you the wonders of my sagacity. We only need that space- even if it is a separate quarter outside the house, as long as it is close enough for my voice to reach his ears.

Me: We can find such a room easily in the house of some servant.

Snake charmer: But then we might get interrupted by the servants.

Me: Don't worry. There is a wedding tomorrow in Akhnoor, and all servants are planning on going there.

The snake charmer was very happy to hear this, and after promising to come on the next night, took his leave. I went to Sakina's very early in the morning. They were all still in bed. I went and carefully looked at all the servants' quarters. One quarter particularly fit the snake charmer's specifications; it had no windows or ventilation, and the door was also very strong. After this, I came back home.

At night, the snake charmer was waiting for me in the bamboo forest. Both of us together set off from there for Sakina's house. It was the 27th night of the lunar month. The darkness was so intense that it was hard to tell anything apart. Due to the sheer cold, the place was nearly frozen all over. But my forehead was drenched in fearful sweat.

Although, to be on the safe side, I had kept a loaded pistol in my pocket, my feet still shook and trembled with fear. However, I somehow managed to reach Sakina's house. Here, it was completely silent. In the quiet of the night, that house looked terribly scary and dreadful. Quietness and sadness pervaded all around the house, near and far, although at some points, one could faintly hear dogs barking in a far off village. Both of us entered the quarters. The snake charmer latched the door from the inside. He then took out an earthen lamp from his bag and lit it. He also plastered the floor in the center of the room with loose soil, drew a circle around it, and then both of us sat within that circle.

I sat very quietly and observed his activities. After all this, he lit up a fragment *masala*, and then, in a strange tune, started singing something in some special tongue. He kept on humming this melody for the next fifteen or twenty minutes. All of a sudden, something banged against the door, and at the same time, we heard Rafiq's tormented voice. "What wretched fellow is raising hell in here? Open the door, quickly!"

I quaked with fear, but the snake charmer did not care. He was lost in his work. Rafiq was banging the door very loudly, while also cursing at the top of his voice now. He seemed to be going mad with rage. When he couldn't break down the door, he was agitated, and began saying: "If you don't open the door, I will set the quarters on fire! And you will burn down to ashes!"

Even that threat had no effect on the snake charmer. However, he stopped his incantation and picked up the pipe and began playing it. When Rafiq realized that his harshness was of no use, he started begging: "For God's sake, have mercy on me!"

But the snake charmer refused to budge. Disappointed with our stubbornness, Rafiq started running to and fro. It sounded like a horse race was underway outside. After doing this for a few minutes, he again came and stood at the door and began saying, "You cruel one! What will you get out of my destruction?"

Saying this, he started screaming in pain. The snake charmer continued playing the pipe with gusto. Slowly and slowly, Rafiq's voice died down.

Suddenly, I saw that from behind the snake charmer's back, an extremely fat, hissing snake had entered the room through a sewer. Seeing the snake, I froze with fear, but then immediately strengthened my heart and fired the pistol at the snake. The snake charmer stood stupefied, as if a grave error had been made. The pipe dropped out of his hands, and he stared at me through his wide open, aghast eyes. I gestured towards the snake. The snake charmer then turned, only to see the boa fading away.

Snake charmer (hastily): Ah! You have acted cruelly!

Me: Is this your pet snake?

Snake charmer: This was Rafiq Sahab. Ah! He met a terrible end!

Me (quaking): What, Rafiq! How is this?

Snake charmer (in a mournful voice): "When a snake reaches the age of a hundred, he acquires the power to change his hide." At this strangest of revelations, I stared at the snake in utter shock, and after a while, slowly inched towards it. It suddenly opened its darkened eyes and looked at me, and lifting its wounded head, tried to lung at me. But it couldn't reach me because it was very weak, and drooping down at that same spot, died. The thin stream of blood that flowed from its head came and touched me.

8

The next day, the news that Rafiq had gone missing spread like wild fire. My grandfather sent out many people to look for him, but to no effect. Finally, he brought Sakina back to his house, and her house was locked up. She was completely unaware of Rafiq's secret, since because of the magic of Rafiq's gaze, she would often sleep in a drugged fashion throughout the night. Only some time had elapsed since this incident when god knows how, Sakina's house caught fire. The flames from the fire leapt up to the sky. We spent every moment trying to douse the fire, but to avail. By the evening, the house along with the garden and the forest of night jasmine burnt down completely.

Sakina was in a state of shock at the destruction of her life, and her health dissipated fast. When the *hakims* of Akhnoor proved ineffectual, I had to go to Jammu to fetch a trained doctor.

It was the 27th night of the lunar month. It had been a month since Rafiq had met his end. That night, I slept at the house of a friend of my grandfather at Jammu. I had to go back in the morning with the doctor. Suddenly, a fragrance began emanating from my arm, and it made me squeamish. I tried hard to make myself feel better, but then suddenly I vomited uncontrollably. Bent on the headboard of my bent, I was throwing up. As my arm bent a little, I felt a sharp pain shoot through it. I was writhing with pain. I looked to see that my arm was bleeding. Eventually, my arm started throbbing with intense pain. I sat up restlessly. I suddenly looked at the floor of the room to see several snakes crawling on it. I was terrified, a sharp scream let out from my lips and I fainted.

My treatment went on for two or three days. When there was finally some relief, I came back home along with the doctor. When my grandfather asked me the reason for the delay, I made up some excuse and avoided the conversation. After a month, when it was again the 27th night of the lunar month, a fragrance again rose from my arm and I fainted with pain. The next day, I learnt that I had again been bitten by a snake.

When my grandfather learnt that this has been going continuously for two months, he became very worried.

Many doctors and sages tried to cure me but nothing changed. Now, each month on the 27th night, a snake would bite me. For Sakina, she had first of all the pain of seeing her household destroyed. On top of that, my unique illness pained her too and made her health worse day by day. Finally, within six months, that unhappy and unlucky soul passed away from this earth.

Sakina's death and my illness broke my grandfather, and with this sadness weighing on him, he too passed away within two months. Now in that huge house, it was just me and my mother. Although I had no interest in the world anymore, care for my mother made me take up the role of the new landowner.

For the first year, the crop was very good. But in the second year, a peculiar kind of locusts gripped the fields which ate up the entire crop like termites. I had to bear severe losses that year and only after a lot of effort could drive away that evil from the fields. The next year, when the crop was ready, the same problem appeared again. That year the losses were so high that my the estate was affected and I went into debt.

After that, every year, some similar calamity would descend on my fields. Quickly, my situation became so bad that I had to declare myself bankrupt, and along with my mother, shifted to Jammu, where I started working as a school teacher. However, people started becoming hesitant on hearing of my strange illness. Some of them would want to touch my hands, or even talk to me. Finally, several parents complained that such a terrifying person did not deserve to be a teacher. Consequently, I lost my job, and I began undertaking physical labour to make a living for myself and my mother.

It has been two years since my mother passed away, and since I left my home. Fortunately, I managed to find a job with you. Now every final night of the lunar month, I take leave, but actually, I lock my room from the outside, enter it again through the window, and keep myself restricted in the room for three or four days. Till I become better again, I simply lay low in the room.

First published as "Mualim ka Raaz" in 1939. Translated from Urdu by Jaideep Pandey.

6

The Blue Envelope

Hijab Imtiaz Ali

(1)

For several weeks, something strange had been taking place at the dining table every Saturday.

Although many years have passed since those events transpired, yet I remember the frightening events and those disturbing incidents as if they happened just yesterday. I'm telling you the truth. I don't believe in telling tall tales, but what can you do when someone's own life assumes the shape of a protracted tale.

I remember that we generally ate lunch at about 12 or 12.30 p.m., and this was also the time the mail arrived. Recently, Chacha Jaffar had started waiting somewhat impatiently for the mail on Saturdays. No sooner did the mail arrive than he frantically set down his fork and knife on his plate and pushing back his chair, stood up. The fact of the matter was that a blue envelope from the port of Shune had been regularly arriving for him in the Saturday mail and for some days now, the sight of it would make him turn pale. No one paid much attention when the envelope arrived the very first time. When he received the envelope next, we thought it was a joke and still didn't give it any thought. Then, the envelope started coming every Saturday without fail, and the situation became somewhat serious. Now when poor Chacha laid eyes on the envelope, an agitated look would appear on his face. It became obvious that it was not in his power to solve this mystery. By chance I was visiting Chacha as his guest in those days and soon I developed a deep interest in this puzzle.

Hijab Imtiaz Ali, *The Blue Envelope* In: *The Silence That Speaks*. Edited by: Haris Qadeer, Oxford University Press.
 DOI: 10.1093/oso/9780190132613.003.0007

(2)

It was Saturday. Chacha had invited old Doctor Gaar to lunch so that he could discuss the matter of the mysterious blue envelope with him as well. So we three were at the dining table, eating. Dressed in his blue coat of stylish design and seated at the far end of the table, Doctor Gaar was sprinkling black pepper on a slice of potato and relishing it. As usual, I was on the other side of the table, feeling a little apprehensive as I squeezed lemon on the rice in my plate. Suddenly, Chacha became agitated and turned around to look at the old Arab.

"Ahmed, the mail hasn't arrived yet?"

"It has, Sir," Ahmed, the cook said.

"Is it there?" Doctor Gaar said, quickly swallowing the morsel of potato in his mouth.

"Good Heavens!" I exclaimed involuntarily. "For God's sake, Doctor Gaar, take the envelope and run to the library or else poor Chacha will be sick with worry and . . . "

Hearing this, Doctor Gaar extended his hand took the envelope and was about to slip it into his pant pocket when Chacha interrupted us.

"No, Roohi!" Roohi is the name I use for my stories. "Don't stop the Doctor," Chacha continued. "The unpleasantness and concern that we were expecting have already occurred. I know what's inside this envelope. Then, what's the use of looking at it after lunch. I would like Doctor Gaar to look at it now. Doctor, please bring your chair closer to mine."

Doctor Gaar hastily wiped his mouth with his napkin, drank some water, and then eagerly pulled his chair close. Chacha ripped open the envelope.

> "Here . . . " Chacha said. He pulled out the letter. "Do you see Doctor? It's the map of a room. What does it mean Doctor? Oh my God!"

Doctor Gaar took the letter from him gingerly and going to the window, holding it up to the light, closely examined the markings on it. "I'm surprised what this strange matter is and why it's happening to you. It defies reasoning. Daughter Roohi, would you run and get my spectacles please, they will be on a table in the library."

Such requests from Doctor Gaar had irritated me since I was a child. Leaving his snuffbox on the arm of the chair and then requesting me to look for it, putting his spectacles on a table somewhere and then asking me to run and get them—these were old habits. But because Chacha was present, I remained silent and ran and got his spectacles. Turning it around this way and that, Doctor Gaar continued examining intently the map of the room for a while. Then, he looked up at Chacha and said, "Sir Jaffar, if I'm not mistaken, this . . . this . . . !"

He paused and returned his gaze to the map again. The way he spoke with long sentences and pauses in his speech had also always annoyed me. I would start getting exasperated. I became frustrated.

"Well, Sir, what do you think," I finally said irritably.

"I'll tell you Daughter, be patient. Yes, Sir Jaffar, if I'm not mistaken this map is of the room which is located on the second storey of your bungalow in Shune (Shune is the name of a city). Am I wrong? Look at this carefully."

Chacha took the paper from him and observed it with interest. "Which Shune bungalow? The one that's on the banks of the river? Which room? What does this mean?"

I also leaned over Chacha's shoulders from behind to see what he was talking about.

"What do you think daughter Roohi?" Doctor Gaar said, tapping the snuffbox with his finger. "Do you remember the upstairs room in the Shune bungalow, the side overlooking all those oak and Deodar trees?"

I was absorbed in examining the map. "Yes, I remember," I said. Ahh . . . this is so strange, dear Chacha. That's correct, Chacha! The doctor is absolutely right. This is the room in your Shune bungalow. Oh God, what a coincidence. There's a small picture next to the door on the map Doctor Gaar . . . what happened is that this summer I brought Chacha's full-length picture and hung it in this room by the door. The picture is also marked on this map. Dear God, how strange, how strange this is."

Chacha looked surprised. "Do you people really think this is the room in my bungalow on the river?"

"Yes Chacha, yes," I said emphatically.

"Then, why didn't you say so my Daughter, you've been looking at it from the very beginning?"

I felt a little embarrassed. "But Chacha . . . " I stammered and then looked around disconcertingly. Truth of the matter was that I had not at all imagined this could be a room in Chacha's own bungalow.

Doctor Gaar looked thoughtful and then he said, “Is there a tenant in this bungalow of yours or is it vacant?”

Chacha looked at me. “Daughter, is there a tenant living there?”

I said, “Yes, there is. At least that’s what I think Chacha.”

“Who lives there?” Doctor Gaar asked.

“That I don’t know. Chacha’s agent should know. But the problem is that the agent is away on sick leave.”

“Why do you ask Doctor?” Chacha said anxiously. “What does all this mean?”

“No doubt this is all the doing of a devil or some jinn,” I exclaimed instantly.

“Don’t be silly child,” Chacha said. “The stories of *Alif Laila* have turned your thoughts. So, Doctor, what were you saying?”

The Doctor said, “Was it something about this room? Sir Jaffar what did you use this room for?”

“I didn’t use this room. It stayed locked up or was only opened up for a guest.”

We continued to exchange views on this subject until evening fell. Chacha looked quite nervous. Doctor Gaar was deep in thought and I was feeling somewhat scared but scrutinizing this secret with great interest at the same time.

(3)

One afternoon, we were sitting on a bench in the garden talking about this subject when Doctor Gaar said, “Sir Jaffar, I think we should go to the Shune bungalow and see what is going on there.”

Chacha looked petrified when he heard this. “Oh no Doctor, what are you saying? What if some disaster befalls us there?”

“What kind of disaster do you mean?” Doctor Gaar asked.

Chacha said hesitatingly, “Like … like murder … or some other accident … something like that must have happened … we’ll take someone along to help.”

“Don’t worry, Sir Jaffar, I’m with you. Believe me we won’t need any help, neither police nor friends.”

“And I’ll come along as well Chacha,” I said.

"As you like. I'm very worried these days," Chacha said, anxiously puffing away on his cigar.

"No reason to be so worried, Sir Jaffar," Doctor Gaar said. "God willing, just as other problems have been resolved, this too will be resolved. All right, so Daughter Roohi, we'll leave next Saturday evening."

"Yes, I'm ready," I said, and breaking off a leaf from a plant nearby I began rubbing it between my fingers and then, inhaling its fragrance, said, "Why wait until next Saturday? It's Saturday today, we'll check the mail and then leave in the morning tomorrow."

"Well, that's a possibility," Doctor Gaar said.

Chacha said, unhappily, "So our journey begins tomorrow."

"Of course," the Doctor said.

Just then the mail arrived. The envelope was there as usual. Chacha hastily ripped it open. We were all filled with dread. This time there was a note along with the map, addressed to Doctor Gaar, Chacha, and I. It said,

> "Come to this room once. Why have you never come this way? My name is 'M.'"

"God help us . . ." Chacha said, gazing up at the sky.

Doctor Gaar said consolingly, "My dear Sir Jaffar, don't worry at all. Roohi is here and I'm at your service. We three will leave tomorrow morning and will be in Shune by about nine at night. Whatever takes place there, we'll deal with it. At least the mystery will be solved and this constant anxiety will end."

"You still want to travel to Shune Doctor? Even after seeing this note?" Chacha Jaffar asked in surprise.

"Of course. I'm more determined than before," Doctor Gaar said confidently.

I too was completely ready. Finally, we left for Shune the next morning.

(4)

What transpired in Shune is something that even today, if I think about it, after so many years, overwhelms me with strange feelings, and my heart sinks.

It was night. We travelled in a rented carriage from the station to Chacha's river bungalow. The carriage was advancing slowly on the path that ran alongside the garden. In the still of the night and on the isolated road, the continuous clip-clopping of the horses' hooves created a feeling of terror. On both sides of the road, the tall box-trees stood silently like enchanted giants. The weather was warm and pleasant, the sky was cloudless, and the moonlight seemed to be swooning over the lawn. Through the unmoving leaves of the trees, one could see glimpses of the high white walls of the bungalow.

Finally, our carriage stopped in the porch of the bungalow. The bungalow was engulfed in silence. There seemed to be no one around.

"Hunh? There's no one here," Chacha said, surprised. "Is the bungalow vacant?"

"I'm sure," I said. "Let's take a walk around the bungalow once and we'll find out."

I fearfully clutched a corner of Chacha's coat and jumped off the carriage. I was panting like a frightened cat. I had wrapped myself in a blue shawl with a flowered print. The three of us examined different parts of the bungalow from the outside, but saw no one. Finally, we strode off towards the servants' quarters and found them all locked up as well, after which we went to the stables and the car garages and discovered they were all vacant too. In the end, when exhausted from all this walking, we had just turned in the direction of our carriage and we suddenly heard the sounds of doors being opened and shut rapidly. It seemed as though someone was struggling to force open a door.

"Sir Jaffer, did you hear anything?" Doctor Gaar, who was about to get in the carriage stopped and asked. He turned to look at us.

"Yes Doctor," Chacha replied. "Someone is trying to open the door from the inside."

"For God's sake, let's take off from here Doctor," I said, cowering as I squeezed myself into the backseat of the carriage. "Naturally it's some ancient jinn. Dear Chacha please come on."

Chacha climbed into the carriage and sat down.

"Oh no, what are you doing?" Doctor Gaar said. "You're trying to leave just when we finally have something? Daughter Roohi, get down, let's sneak a look through the glass panes and see what is going on."

"I don't think I can do it," I said irately. "Forgive me, but if you are interested in peeking through the window panes to see what's going on, you can." I felt weak with terror and wrapped inside my blue shawl I looked as yellow as the flame of a candle. Even today when I recall that horrifying night of my life, I turn pale with dread just as one would on be during a nightmare. Absolute silence reigned all around us. The trees in the garden stood erect mutely like corpses. A macabre and eerie hush prevailed, everything looked sinister. The quiet was such that something had happened even to the bats, which screech noisily on moonlit nights but were completely silent at this time.

All of a sudden, we heard the door opening with force.

"Here," Chacha said. "The door we could hear being forced is now open. Now let's see who comes out."

"You stay here, I want to go to the other side and look in through the door in the verandah," Doctor Gaar said and walked hurriedly towards the verandah door. For two minutes, he gazed through the door and then, quickly, he shrank back fearfully and rushed to us.

"Sir Jaffar, Sir Jaffar" he said, "come here for a minute, there's a very strange scene inside, a man is crawling on the floor."

"Crawling? Dear God protect us! What has happened to him?" Chacha said in amazement.

"God is all knowing," Doctor Gaar said, keeping his eyes on the door.

My hair stood on end. "It's not an evil spirit, is it? Oh God, what is this horrible catastrophe that has befallen us!"

Just then arose the most horrible sounds, sometimes consisting of a shrill whistling sound, sometimes like a voice coming through a gramophone horn, and then the sound of someone knocking on the door nearby.

Doctor Gaar said, "What? This door is locked from the outside."

"Chacha said, "So the evil spirit is locked up inside."

"And what will happen if it comes outside?" I clung to Chacha fearfully.

Suddenly through the window pane we glimpsed eyes staring at us, wide open and filled with terror. All three of us saw those eyes at the same time. In all my years, this was the first time I had seen the devil.

Chacha said, "It's a man, not some jinn as Roohi thinks. We should talk to him."

The moment this strange man's gaze fell upon Doctor Gaar, he began to scream. In a rage, he began cursing heavily and was also crying at the same time.

Chacha was inside the carriage. I was still clinging to him. But Doctor Gaar was on the stairs, staring at this man.

"What is the matter, young man," Doctor Gaar finally addressed the man. "What are you suffering from, what are you doing here?"

He screamed in response. "I'm imprisoned here ... there are people who have shut me up here, cruel, heartless people have imprisoned me, I have been punished wrongfully, I'm innocent ... for God's sake, open the door."

"But," Doctor Gaar said, "the door is padlocked and I don't have the key. Tell me your story. Perhaps I'll be able to help you. Who imprisoned you here?"

But the man stared angrily at him. "You won't open the door either! All right then, I'll break it down and come out and ... and ... and then I'll do what I please ... I'm imprisoned here but wait until I'm out."

Saying this, he started beating down the door forcefully.

"Let's run away from here, Doctor, for God's sake," I whispered. I had not completed my sentence when suddenly a glass pane shattered in splinters of flying glass.

He was now trying to smash the second pane. Doctor Gaar looked very worried and Chacha was feeling very nervous, and I felt as if I was about to die from fright.

"My girl, this is undoubtedly the same man who was writing the letters and signing them with 'M.' He's being held captive in this room."

"Of course, Chacha. Do you have any doubt that this is the same devil?"

Suddenly more glass was splintered.

Doctor Gaar said agitatedly, "Dear man, what are you doing? We don't understand your strategy at all. What exactly do you want?"

"I ... I want to come out." Saying this he started banging on the door.

"The door will break," Doctor Gaar said wearily.

"Let it break ... if I had my way I would smash people's heads." With that he started violently pushing against the door.

But when the door didn't yield despite all his efforts, he gave up or perhaps had some other thought and went inside. We became apprehensive when we heard a loud bang and what do we see but that the man had jumped down from the porthole and was now walking swiftly towards Doctor Gaar.

Seeing this, Chacha quickly alighted from the carriage. No sooner had Chacha got down than all hell broke loose. Like an arrow this man sprang on poor Chacha as if he was going to swallow him like a cobra. He screamed and said, "This is the man, by God, this is the man … murderer, murderer … ruffian … today he's here to kill me … I won't let him go now."

As he was saying this, he tackled Chacha. My eyes closed of their own accord and I started gasping for air. I wanted to scream, but I couldn't. Doctor Gaar used all his strength and pulled him away from Chacha with his arm around his waist. Chacha was also dragged along with him. Oh, poor Chacha.

Oh God! I too was in a terrible state. My head was filled with the most horrifying thoughts. What if this man spots me? Will he pick me up and throw me into the river? I quickly hid in the back seat of the carriage. The old carriage driver was even more frightened than I and he cowered in a corner of the carriage. I slowly and cautiously opened my eyes. The scene before me was appalling. The stranger was wrapped around Chacha and Doctor Gaar had his arms around the stranger … and the stranger kept shouting, "You're a murderer, a murderer … a despicable man!"

In the silence of the night, the horrible shouts of "Murderer! Murderer!" filled the atmosphere with a sense of horror. I cringed. But I couldn't scream. I was afraid the devil might catch sight of me.

With great difficulty, Doctor Gaar separated him from Chacha and then pinioned him with both his arms and asked, "What exactly do you mean? What do you want?"

"I want to …" he screamed, "I want to drink this man's blood, this man who murdered my Zulofia, he didn't reply to my letters, he stayed in my room all the time, isn't he the same man? It is he, the wretch!"

"You lunatic, you've lost your mind. This respectable man is Sir Jaffar, who do you think he is? And who is Zulofia? Who murdered her? When did you start living in this bungalow?"

"Sir Jaffar!" the man shouted. "Yes, I know this respectable man; in my last letter, I told him to come, and now he's here. Now I will suck his blood, my name is Mansoor, I've been in search of my Zulofia's murderer for a long time, his vile picture is in my room; today, he's before me in the flesh, now he won't escape from my clutches."

Saying this, he sprang up and tried to seize the poor man. Chacha was struggling to get out of his grasp, but it was useless. Dr. Gaar was punching this man . . . but . . . he was a strong young man. How could these two overpower him.

I could see death before me. Suddenly, I looked up and saw that the horrible man had pushed Chacha back. I let out a scream. "Oh, Chacha . . . Doctor!" I shrieked.

The moment I screamed the man turned around to look at me. I felt I was about to faint. Tightening the shawl around my shoulders, I sat back. I was trembling; it seemed my heart would stop beating any minute. For a few seconds, he observed me carefully and then, shouting, he ran towards me. "Who is inside the shawl . . . Zulofia . . . is this my Zulofia? Certainly, the wicked old man has hid her here."

"Oh God, where is my death . . . " I jumped from the carriage and dashed towards the Doctor. The man followed me with the speed of an arrow. Chacha and Doctor Gaar became frantic. Oh God, what was to be my fate in the hands of this tyrant!

Doctor Gaar got hold of him with much difficulty while Chacha placed himself in front of me. I was praying for death.

Just then, the clock struck the hour of midnight, and the atmosphere became even more frightening. Suddenly, a small black car entered the compound and stopped right where the wrestling was in progress. A tall thin man wearing a night hat got off.

"Uff! What is happening? Mansoor, Mansoor! Who are all these people? Where are the servants? Have they all gone to the cinema? What's going on? What . . . ?"

But who had the presence of mind to pay any attention to him. The three were embroiled in a tussle. I slipped from behind Chacha. "O Sir, please, control this wild beast. This is my uncle Sir Jaffar, and this is his doctor. A man escaped from inside the house and he's beating them both up."

"This is Sir Jaffar?" the stranger said and turned to look at him and then, shouting, "Mansoor, Mansoor," he went towards them. Mansoor was startled when he heard his name. He saw the stranger; his face grew pale. He quickly went up the stairs, hid behind the door, and then peeked at everyone from there.

"Sir Jaffar, I'm so sorry you've been treated so badly. But how did this lunatic come out?"

"He's a lunatic?"

"Completely mad. He's my patient."

"Your patient?" Chacha asked in astonishment. "So you're a psychiatrist? You live here in this bungalow?"

"Yes," the psychiatrist said. "But how did all this happen?" Why are you people here? Where are the servants? How did Mansoor get out? I'm really very sorry. Please come in and rest. I want to know everything."

Chacha and the Doctor turned to go with him, but I wasn't going to budge from my place. "Chacha Jaan, don't go in, the wretch will devour us."

"No, young lady," the psychiatrist said. "He won't dare do anything in my presence. Please come inside."

We all went in. Cowering, I stayed close to them as we walked in.

"Please sit down and be comfortable. Would you like a cigarette? Now tell me, what are you here for? This has all been very distressful for you."

"Yes indeed, it has," Chacha said and then proceeded to recount the entire story of the blue envelope to the psychiatrist.

The psychiatrist was dumbfounded. "I'm so sorry. The mistake I made was to leave your picture hanging on the wall. He often talked to your picture. By chance your address is on the back of the picture and he must have used that to communicate with you. His story is tragic. He was in love with a young woman whose name he mentions sometimes. Zulf, or Zulfia. She died in an accident. The incident had a horrible effect on his mind, and he went mad. He was brought to me for treatment, and I gave him an airy room upstairs to stay. Your picture was on the wall and that being the only human face he saw, he began talking to it. I left it there to keep him engaged. Gradually, he developed the idea that the man in the picture had murdered his beloved. He also mentioned it to me several times, but I didn't pay any attention to what he was saying. I had no idea what he was secretly up to."

We were looking at each other as if we had all lost our minds. Chacha was massaging his sore knee.

First published as *Neela Lifafa* (1935). Translated from Urdu by Tahira Naqvi.

7
The Will

Moghal Mahmood

Tahira had heard so much about Nishat Manzil that when she thought about it now her mind conjured up scenes of beauty and happiness. She was sure that the cheer of the place must once have been such as to make it seem like heaven. Along with this thought came another, that the deaths there would have been grand too. And as soon as she thought about death, her face would glow with joy.

Badi Begum was the most important person at Nishat Manzil. She had grown old and very weak. People dreaded even her minor indispositions.

This time she was seriously ill. The medicines that usually helped her fever were proving ineffective. Hakeem Sahib tired of turning the pages of his books but she did not recover. Even the best medicines did her no good. Tahira had always come to see her whenever she heard that the Begum was sick. She came this time too and slowly she understood what was behind the silence that lay over Nishat Manzil. The trees seemed to be asleep in their deep shadows. A cold sadness was everywhere. She could not take her eyes off the Begum's pure innocent face. She felt that the Begum was shedding the green clothes of life and becoming denuded. In the glittering valuable tops that she wore in her ears, she saw the last flicker of the morning star and the ring with the large gem that she wore on a finger of her right hand seemed to have lost its lustre, as though no longer belonging to it. A shiver would go through her when she saw the stamp of death on the Begum's face and she'd smile to herself.

The night was dark and terrible. The atmosphere became even more ominous and frightening because of the sound of the street dogs howling. Tahira sat in her hovel, thinking. She had raised the wick of the lantern

Moghal Mahmood, *The Will* In: *The Silence That Speaks*. Edited by: Haris Qadeer, Oxford University Press. © Oxford University Press India 2022. DOI: 10.1093/oso/9780190132613.003.0008 with its blackened chimney. She could feel her heart beating in her chest. A blast of freezing wind set all the dogs howling together and Tahira hastily shut the door. The chain of her thoughts was unbroken. She thought—this time if Allah heard her prayers, she'd be able to do her duty by her daughter. The Begum Sahib was rich; alms would be distributed at her death. She'd be able to change the door of her hut; it was broken and she stayed apprehensive all through the night. The thought startled her. It was as if she was cursing the Begum, praying for her to die. But everyone had to die; there were so many desires in her heart that could only be fulfilled if someone were to die.

She lay awake through the night. She'd go out with the lantern at the slightest noise and then come back inside.

It must have been four o'clock in the morning when she heard someone calling out.

"Is Tahira Begum there?" She started up and came to the door holding the lantern with the blackened chimney.

"Who is it?"

The visitor said, "I've come from Nishat Manzil." He spoke haltingly, his voice choked with tears, "Begum Sahib is dead. You've been summoned."

Tahira gave him an appropriate reply and sent him off; then she lay there waiting for it to be morning, filled with pleasing dreams.

It was almost daybreak when Tahira left home, the city still asleep. Young, healthy looking sweeper-women were out early, cleaning the streets. Doors were shut against the intense cold.

Tahira walked towards Nishat Manzil with long strides, wearing a black burqa. Her face bore that look of terrible calm which made people weep, for they knew what it meant. Her heart wanted to celebrate. She'd got the chance to work in a rich home after a long time. She could hear lamenting voices as she reached the big gate and she got the familiar smell of incense. She took off her burqa as soon as she came inside, decorously covered her head and moved to where the sounds were coming from. The crying voices settled on her soul like music.

Nishat Manzil looked desolate, burnt out and ashen. Despite the noisy lamentations of so many people, you could feel the silence. The Begum Sahib's daughters and other relatives were the loudest, creating quite a commotion. The doors of the Begum's room had been opened, and she lay in eternal sleep on her high *niwar* bed with its soft mattress, covered with a sheet white as snow. There was a stream of mourners. Soon, each corner of Nishat Manzil was crowded with people.

Tahira was sitting on the threshold, by the foot of the bed where the corpse lay. She'd covered her head with her white sari and held her face in both hands. At short intervals, she'd speak out in measured tones "May Allah's name remain" and then she'd start examining the state of things around her. Sitting on a chair by the head of the corpse was a middle-aged woman with a divine expression on her face, reading aloud verses from the Koran. Her voice was thin and tuneful, her manner of rendering the Koran so affecting that the old women listening swayed to the rhythm and the arrested tears of the Begum's daughters began to flow again. A servant standing by swung a flywhisk over the body to make sure no flies settled on it. Tahira would occasionally take some incense glue from the box and put it in the fire and then she'd cover her face with both hands and listen to the Koran recitation. There was a rose water sprinkler and some flowers on a stool and the woman who was reading would now and again sprinkle some rose water on the corpse.

Tahira remembered the incident a few days ago when she told her mother about the corpse she'd recently bathed that was so ghastly she couldn't get it out of her mind. She'd held both her ears and asked Allah's forgiveness for her sins. She imagined she saw that corpse again, lying on the ground. The big black ants in the ears and nose, the horrific blue face, the swollen stomach, as though it would burst the moment she touched it. "Ya Allah forgive me" she said in a loud voice and her heart began to pound at the thought that she might be misunderstood. There was no way she could stop her thoughts. Ants came out each time she poured water on the face. She'd bathed innumerable corpses, it was nothing new for her, but she'd never seen one corpse so different from another. She kept thinking about the dreadful corpse she'd bathed recently and compared it to this one. The Begum Sahib's deeds were such that it seemed the doors of heaven were already open for her.

After weeping for long, the Begum's older daughter wiped her tears, swallowed a pill for energy along with a gulp of glucose, then looked at her sister and said, "Sister, you'll kill yourself crying. Who will then do all the work that remains? Come on, pull yourself together. Saidani needs help with all the arrangements to be made. It's the last thing we'll be doing for our mother."

The younger sister's tears started flowing again and Saidani, going to the corpse, set up cries of "Oh my Sarkar, oh my lady" loud enough to make the sky tremble, and the whole household began to shriek again.

Tahira got up and asked Saidani to be calm and then she began to fill water for the bath and for washing the requisite utensils. She couldn't get that other corpse out of her mind, after which she'd seemed to see shadows of death in her own home. It all comes down to your deeds, she thought. Flowers rain down on the blessed when they die. What a sweet smell there was in the atmosphere. It was written in the books that the places visited by the angels of mercy become perfumed like this. The dead woman looked splendid, as if she was sleeping and seeing beautiful dreams.

They'd filled a lot of water. Several large pots made of tin-plated copper were full, and there were the bowls and *lotas* also made of copper and similarly gilded with tin. Gram flour and jujube leaf paste had been kept at hand. No one except for Tahira and Saidani was allowed to touch the water, for none knew the intricacies of the last rites. This was the Begum's final bath and Allah would have to be answered to if standards of cleanliness and purity fell short.

Then, Saidani wiped her tears and brought out the box in which the Begum had kept her shroud years ago. She'd written something on a piece of paper and kept that in the box too. For the past twenty years, she'd been taking care of this shroud. Each time she fell ill, she'd tell her daughters and Saidani—"Look, before you begin my last rites, do open the box that has my shroud and read the paper I've put there, which is my will." And during this illness in particular, she'd told them, "I'm not going to survive; don't forget what I said about the paper in the box."

And everyone had spoken in one voice, "God forbid! Why do you talk like this?" But the Begum closed her eyes and said—"Death is inevitable. There is no escape from it."

Saidani remembered her words in the midst of all the crying, but the cold was so intense that her hands wouldn't move. And one feels even more cold in the presence of a corpse. Saidani produced the box only when the sun had come out and its light had spread everywhere.

Tahira's heart was pounding. A new mourner had come and when the Begum's face was uncovered at her request, Tahira too went and stood there. She'd been anxious to scrutinize the body in the light of day. Those tops in the Begum's ears were still there. Her hands rested on her breast and the gem-studded ring on her finger glittered brightly. That was a relief. Tahira felt she was really lucky. What a woman the Begum was! Look at the arrangements she'd made before dying. It was only the pure-spirited who arranged for things after they were gone. Tears of happiness welled up in her eyes and she wiped them, trying to give the impression that she'd burst into tears on seeing the Begum's face.

Saidani opened the box. The shroud had been folded carefully and wrapped in a water-proof wax cloth. There was a closed envelope on top, on which was written in big letters—"Read this first."

Saidani brought the envelope to the daughters and spoke with the kindliness of an elder, "Be patient dear ones, she was lucky that she had the two of you to leave behind in the world. Allah gave her no sorrows. Everyone has to die one day, but she was really fortunate that she suffered no torments while she was alive."

Keeping up her narration, Saidani said, "Here, read this first and then get started on the work. It'll be evening by the time we're done with the preparations. It's cold, the day is short and our Sarkar has a long way to go."

The girls began to cry again. Saidani lovingly said, "Come on, stop crying and get on with your duty; this is the day for which one has children."

News came in that Maulana had come. The bustle of the house increased. Tahira rolled up the sleeves of her old but warm jacket to her elbows. She tidied her hair, tightening it into a small plait and was ready, sari wrapped around her waist. She'd been in a similar state of preparedness to bathe corpses many times in her life. But she'd never before felt such an eagerness to begin work.

Outside, Maulana said a prayer for the dead woman, talked a little about her and sent word inside that they should hurry with the essential work.

When the older daughter got up and took the warm shawl off her head, many silver strands shone out from her thick beautiful hair. She cast a glance at the gathering and holding out the envelope to the woman who'd been reading the Koran, she said, "Please read this out loudly so that everyone may hear."

The woman opened the envelope and began to read aloud. Everyone fell silent and listened.

1) That if there is sunshine available, my shroud should be spread out in the sun for a while.
2) That the twenty-five gold coins kept in the shroud should be used for my last rites and no other money should be used.

Vah! Vah! There were approving noises. Such wisdom! No ordinary mind can think of these subtleties. People had their eyes fixed on the reader. Tahira's anxiety was growing. The woman read on:

3) That whoever bathes me should be given the jewellery on my body and my bed, along with the bedding.

The woman put down the paper and now that they'd heard the will, the daughters stopped weeping. There was no particular effect on Saidani, but energy shot through Tahira's body like a current and her face began to shine.

Saidani got up and spread the shroud on a white sheet in the sun. She put away the wax cloth in the empty box, counted the twenty-five gold coins and handed them over to the older daughter.

There were long quotations from the Koran written in beautiful letters with saffron ink on the shroud. Some of the women who'd come picked up their children and moved away.

Setting out the things needed for the bath, Tahira made a mental estimate of the ring and the ear-tops. She'd be able to make the best arrangements for her daughter's wedding with so much money. Allah willing, she'd discharge her duty this year itself. It was not good to keep a grown daughter at home. May Allah grant the Begum Sahib heaven; it was so kind of her to have left a will. A curse would befall those who ignored the wishes of the dead. It was her beneficence that lit up the dead face, as though there were a lamp shining within her.

The water containers were being moved around, the gram flour and camphor mixed in bowls. Between Tahira and Saidani on one side and the two sisters on the other, they placed the Begum's body, graceful even in death, on the wooden bed. This led to another burst of crying and some people stepped away. Saidani and Tahira readied themselves to begin.

Just then, the older sister thought of something. She called out to the younger sister and said to Saidani, "Saidani wait, don't touch her yet. We're going to do this last service for her by our own hands. It's not as if we're going to get another chance. Come sister, there's nothing to cry about, it's your duty."

Tahira felt the ground slide from beneath her feet and a darkness came over her. Those dreams she'd nurtured for so long, what would become of them? And what of her daughter? All her plans had turned to ash, her desires washed away.

The sisters touched a dead body for the first time in their lives with trembling heart. They'd never even seen a corpse from so close. The younger one kept crying throughout. The ring and the tops were taken off carefully, the rites completed. The white shroud, elegantly inscribed with saffron ink seemed to heighten the glow on the Begum's face.

There was such a commotion when the Begum was given her last farewell that earth and sky seemed to quake.

Tahira got one copper *lota*, one bowl, the Begum's bedding, a quilt, and ten rupees, Saidani the other *lota* and bowl, the *niwar* bed, a warm shawl and ten rupees.

It was ten o'clock when Tahira came home, and incredibly cold. It was one of the last nights of the moon. There was deep darkness and from far away came the sound of dogs howling.

Tahira reeked of camphor. Her hair was loose. The door was opened when she knocked and she sat down on the floor in a corner of the hut, trembling with cold and grief.

Tahira's old mother was sitting on the bed dozing, and a girl of fifteen or sixteen slept beside her. The mother gave Tahira a subdued look, for she knew what the strong smell of camphor meant. She drew a blanket over the girl and dozed off again.

Tahira did not speak to her mother. She glanced at her sleeping daughter and closed her eyes. Her pale face looked even more yellow. It was as if there were ants crawling inside her head. She seemed to see spectres of death in the terrible loneliness of the night. The dogs, frozen in the cold, would soon begin to howl. There was a raw wind blowing; she felt benumbed, paralysed.

First published in *Kahani,* January 1961 and subsequently collected in *Mahalsara ka Ek Khel aur Anya Kahaniyaan* ed. Sara Rai, Vani Prakashan 2020. Translated from Hindi by Sara Rai.

8
Salt

Razia Sajjad Zaheer

Safia was filled with wonder as she looked at the Sikh lady—how much she resembled her late mother! The same heavy build, small, shining eyes radiating with love, kindness, and tenderness; the same broad, round face, clear and transparent like an open book; and a white *dupatta* of fine, delicate muslin—so like the one her mother would cover her head with for the *Muharram* gatherings.

When Safia glanced at her a few times with love and affection, the Sikh Lady enquired about her from the daughter-in-law of the house. She was told that Safia was a Muslim and that she would be going to Lahore next morning to meet her brothers whom she had not seen for many years now. Lahore!—she came and sat near Safia and began telling her what a lovely city her Lahore is; how beautiful the people who live there, how fond of delicious food and in love with attractive clothes, seekers of pleasure in outings and tours, the very picture of open-hearted jollity ... *Kirtan*, the devotional singing continued and she went on talking in a low voice. A couple of times, Safia interjected—"Mata ji, it must be many years now since you came here?"

"Yes dear child, we came when India was partitioned—now, though, here too we have a large house of our own. We are in business, all is well, but Lahore—oh, how often I remember Lahore, my child, because Lahore, after all, is our homeland." A few stars dropped from her eyes and were absorbed in the hem of that milky *dupatta*. The conversation would move on but then come back to the same theme—our Lahore!

The *Kirtan* came to an end at around eleven. As she got up to leave with *prasaad* (the holy offering) in hand, Safia said in a low voice—"If you wish to have me bring anything special for you from Lahore, please do not

Razia Sajjad Zaheer, *Salt* In: *The Silence That Speaks*. Edited by: Haris Qadeer, Oxford University Press. © Oxford University Press India 2022. DOI: 10.1093/oso/9780190132613.003.0009 hesitate to ask me." She was standing, leaning by the door. Very hesitantly, in a slow, low voice she said, "If you can, bring a handful of Lahori salt."

A fortnight whizzed past: the evenings at the gymkhana, the love and affection of friends, the warm hospitality of brothers who seemed unable to fulfil their desire to lay the heaven at the feet of their separated, foreign sister. Friends, near and dear ones, came laden with gifts: where to keep them, how to pack them all for the journey back? And most important of all was a small, light-brown paper-packet containing just about five hundred grams of Lahori salt.

She asked her brother, a prominent police officer, "Bhai, is one allowed to take salt across the border?"

Surprised, he said, "Salt? No, salt can't be taken across. Doing so would be illegal and … and why do you need salt? You have got a much larger share of salt than us." Piqued, she said, "I am not talking of what share came to whom—I need the salt of Lahore; that is what my mother has asked for."

The brother couldn't understand anything. Mother? His mother and Safia's had passed years before Partition. Softly, trying to make her understand, he said, "Look Apa, you have to pass through the Customs, and if they find even a single thing that is not in order, they'll search and rummage through all your luggage, the law … "

Angrily, she asked, "Find! What do you mean find? Will I hide it? Carry it on the sly? Why would I conceal it? I'll take it openly—I shall declare and carry it."

"That will be very wrong if you do that … The law—"

"You go on talking about the law … are all laws always of the State? … Are there no laws of love and affection, of humanity and generosity? … After all, those at the Customs too are men, not machines!"

"True they are not machines but I can assure you, neither are they poets; they are bound by duty."

"So when am I saying that they should not do their duty … it's just a gift, worth no more than a few *paise*—they are welcome to have a look; it is not gold or silver, not something being smuggled, or something from the black market!"

"It is useless arguing with you Apa. You are, after all, a writer—and all writers are a bit crazy. Let me tell you, though, you won't be able to take it across the border. And imagine the disgrace that will come with it! What, after all, do you writers know of the Customs?" She retorted in anger, "Maybe we know nothing about the Customs, but we do know a bit about human beings. And as to our craziness, the world would be a lot better place to live in, were a larger number of people a bit crank like us writers ..." Her eyes now overflowed with tears of rage. Shaking his head, the brother sat silent.

It was late night by the time this argument came to an end. She was to depart the next day at two in the afternoon. She had a very busy schedule for the morning and so had to complete the packing at night. She closed the door and set to work—everything scattered here and there was gradually adjusted in the suitcase and the hold-all. All that was left were two items: a small basket of *kinnoos* gifted by a dear friend—a fruit that is a hybrid of the orange and the grapefruit: lush and sweet like the grapefruit, delicate and juicy like an orange, elegant and graceful like an Anglo-Indian girl ... and—the small paper-packet containing the salt.

Safia's anger had subsided by now. Emotion and sentiment gave way to reason—she had to take it along, but how? What if she kept it handy and presented it first before the Customs? But what if they refused permission to carry it?—well then, there was no help for it, I'll have to leave it there. But then what about my promise to my Mother? I have always prided myself in keeping my word, how can I go back on it? The promise has to be fulfilled even at the cost of my life—but how? How about placing it at the bottom of the basket of *kinnoos*? No one is likely to see it under so much fruit. But what if it *is* noticed? How can it be—the baskets of fruits were not being checked on the way in—bananas from that side, *kinnoos* from this, were being brought and taken across. Yes, that's right—we'll do that and if it is caught then we'll cross the bridge when we come to it.

Safia emptied the basket of *kinnoos* on the carpet and placed the packet of salt at the bottom of the basket. She glanced at it for a moment and felt as if she had lowered someone very dear into the dark depths of a grave. She squatted and continued looking at it for some time—she recalled the stories she had heard from her mother in her childhood, how a prince would incise his thigh, conceal a diamond in it, and effortlessly pass by terrifying ghosts and demons. No such trick was possible in this age—or she would have split open her heart and concealed that packet of salt there.

One by one, she started placing the *kinnows* in the basket—here, there, on the sides and above the packet, ultimately concealing it completely. Satisfied, she dusted her hands, slid the suitcase beneath the bed, picked up the basket to place it near the head of the bed, lay down, and covered herself with a sheet.

It was about half past one in the night. The pleasant, March-end breeze blew in through the lattice-window. In the clear, cool moonlight, the shadow of the dense *champa's* leaves by the window fell on the wall opposite. Now and then, from the servant-quarters came the sound of a muffled cough, the sound of a dog barking or howling afar, the whistle of the *chowkidar*—and then, dead silence. This was Pakistan, where she had three brothers, born of her mother; countless, ever so loving friends; here, was her father's grave; here lived her little nephews and nieces who in all innocence had ask her, "*Phoophijaan*, why do you live in India where we cannot come?"—and between her and them was the border, and a jungle of many pointed iron rods, known as the Customs . . .

Tomorrow she would be leaving Lahore. May be she would come back in a year's time. She could definitely not be able to come back before a year had passed—and it was quite possible that she would be unable to come back ever again.

Gradually, she was overcome by sleep. Then, she saw the undulating hem of a milky white *dupatta*, stars shining on it here and there.

"Yes many years have passed since we came from there, we have a large house here, business too; we are now settled here but Lahore is homeland." In the vision arose the Iqbal tomb, the Fort of Lahore in its backdrop; behind the Fort, the setting sun's rays; the rising-swelling darkness around, soft breeze flowing in this colourful darkness; the breeze imbued with the fragrance of the *Molsiri*—and, on the steps of the tomb, two beings sitting with their heads bowed, silent and sad like two static, lifeless shadows . . .

"So, you'll be going tomorrow?"

"Yes."

"When will you come now?"

"Don't know, may be next year, may be never again." Then, a milky white *dupatta* began waving over the darkness—"Our homeland, our native place is Lahore . . . "

All of a sudden she woke up. She had plucked a blade of grass covered by cold, frozen dew, just below the stairs of the tomb ... No, turning over in sleep, her hand had touched the basketful of *kinnoos* ... sweet, luscious, cool *kinnoos*—her friend, as he handed them to her, had said, "This is the fruit of Indo-Pakistan friendship."

Time as is its habit passed quickly. Safia was sitting in the First Class Waiting Room. The fare to Delhi had been paid by her brother. Ticket held tight in his hand, he was walking up and down the platform. And she, a cup of tea in her hands, was looking intently at the basket of *kinnoos*—acutely aware that of all those present here, she alone knew of the packet of salt in the base of this basket.

But when her luggage was on its way for the Customs, she felt a bit of a shiver run down her body and at once decided that this gift of love would not go across like hidden stolen goods. She would declare the salt to the Customs. She quickly took the packet out and kept it in the largish handbag containing her purse and passport, etc. When the luggage moved towards the train from the Customs, she approached a Customs Officer—most of the tables were now free, there was a bit of a luggage on one or two, and that's where the officer was standing—tall, slim, silver-streaked hair, spectacles that seemed to have been thrust on those eyes before time. He was in uniform; yet it did not seem to go with his personality.

With a touch of hesitation, Safia said, "I wish to ask you something." He looked hard and long at her, and said, "Yes, please." His manner of speech gave her courage, and she asked, "You ... you ... where are you from?"

A bit surprised, he again looked at her attentively, "My homeland is Delhi. You too seem to be from our parts, must have come to meet your near and dear ones."

"Yes, I am from Lucknow. I had come to meet my brothers; they've been here since the Partition. You ... you ... too have perhaps been ... ?"

"Yes, we came over just when Pakistan came into existence, but then our homeland is Delhi."

Safia placed the handbag on the table and put the packet of salt before him—and then, slowly, falteringly, told him everything.

Gradually, he began moving the packet towards himself—when Safia had had her say, he picked it up in both his hands, wrapped it up good and proper, and put it in her bag. He picked up the bag, gave it to Safia, and said, "Love goes past the Customs with such effortless ease that Law is left standing aghast."

Just as she was about to move, he stood up and said, "Please pay my obeisance to the steps of the of Jama Masjid staircase and when you give the salt to the lady, tell her on my behalf—if Lahore is still her homeland and Delhi is mine ... then with the passage of time everything else will be alright."

Safia exited from the Customs railing, reached the second platform—and moved to her coach.

On the platform were many of her friends, brothers, dear relations. The train moved on towards the border, leaving behind eyes full of longing, flowing tears, cold sighs, and clenched lips. At Attari, the Pakistani Police got down and the Indian Police boarded the train. One could not tell where Pakistan was and where India, who was from India and who from Pakistan, where Lahore ended and where Amritsar began—the land was one, one the language; same were the facial features and attire; nor was there a difference in the tone and tenor of speech—and the streets in which they were exchanging courtesies full of warmth and affection, too, were the same. The only problem was that both had loaded guns in their hands.

At Amritsar, the luggage of the First Class passengers was to go through Customs right in front of their bogey. When her luggage had been inspected, she addressed herself to the young Customs Officer who, going by his demeanour and appearance, looked like a Bengali—"I have salt, a bit of it." She then opened her handbag and in words that came out slow and hesitant, related the whole story as she moved the packet towards him. Even as she was speaking, he lowered his head, now and then raising it to look attentively at her—and continued listening to her in silence. At the very end she said, "If you like please withhold everything of my baggage but let me take this packet of salt."

When she was over with all that she had to say, he again looked at her, top to toe, and said slowly, "Come, please." As he moved away, he said to another officer, "Look after her luggage." At the other end of the platform was a room, looking a bit like clerks' room. He entered it; Safia hesitated. He smiled, and said, "Come, come please." He brought out a pocket handkerchief and dusted an old, shaky chair placed near an ink-stained table and said, "Be seated, please." Safia put the packet and the bag on the table and sat on the chair. He looked out and gestured to a policeman. Safia's heart sank and she felt the ground slipping under her feet—what now?

"Two cups of tea, the special one." The policeman went away, staring at Safia. The Customs Officer pulled the drawer of the table, extricated a book from its depths, dusted it clean, and opening its first page placed it before Safia—on the left was a photograph of Nazrul Islam and on the title-page, some hazy, blurred words in English—"For Sunil, with love from Shamsur-Rahman. Dhaka 1946."

"Are you from East Bengal?"

"Yes, my homeland, is Dhaka," he responded with great pride.

"When did you come here?"

"We came at the time of the partition, but our homeland is Dhaka. I was then no more than twelve or thirteen, but we read Nazrul and Tagore right from childhood. Exactly a year before the day we came over, my most intimate, oldest childhood friend had given me this book. It was my birthday. Thereafter, we lived in Calcutta. I completed my studies and got a job. We did, though, continue to visit our homeland."

"Homeland?" Safia asked, a bit surprised.

Somewhat displeased, he said—"I just told you, my homeland is Dhaka."

"Oh, yes, yes," Safia said, quickly.

"Earlier Customs was just on this side, now it is on the other side as well . . . "

He pushed the cup of tea towards Safia and, taking a large sip from his cup, said—"Green coconut is, of course, available in Calcutta too, just as salt is—but the taste of green coconut in our parts is of another level; our land, our water—the joy and the pleasure thereof is a class apart."

As he got up, he put the packet back in Safia's bag and carrying it himself, he moved ahead. Safia followed him. As she was ascending the bridge that descended into Amritsar, he stood silent at the foot of the stairs, his head bowed. And Safia was constantly thinking—whose homeland is where? The one who is this side of the Customs or the one who is on the other side?

First published as "Namak." Translated from Hindi by Noor Zaheer.

9

Zakat

Wajeda Tabassum

The Moon was not shining in the sky but on the earth! Nawab Zain Yar Jung was reminded of the words of a song he had heard at someone's wedding. It was sung along the beats of a *dholak* by *mirasins,* the traditional singers:

How insane are people of this world, Mother!
Why do they go up to the terrace, Mother?
Keep your eyes open; do not pry.
Look in your courtyard, mother . . .
How the stupid moon is all bedecked.

He was truly insane! And if not this, then, what else could be called insanity! He had been living in that *haveli* for a long time and until now, was unaware that the moon could shine not only in the sky but even on earth.

It was the eve of Eid celebrations, and people of the *haveli* had been on the terrace even yesterday to sight the moon. Nawab Sahab was at an age that he had a special concession granted by Allah from fasting and praying. The real happiness on sighting the moon is felt by those who observe fasts during the month of Ramdhan Ramadan with dedication. Why would he, then, go up to the terrace? But today everyone insisted. Even the Maulvi sahib of the *haveli* said that to witness the moon in such an auspicious month improves one's eyesight, and one is showered with blessings. More than receiving blessings, it was the temptation to improve his eyesight that persuaded him to go up to the terrace, as his eyesight had been weakening. He was around forty or forty-two years old and had not reached the stage when he could be accused of not acting his age. But he had been squandering away his youth since the dawn of it that by now

Wajeda Tabassum, *Zakat* In: *The Silence That Speaks*. Edited by: Haris Qadeer, Oxford University Press. © Oxford University Press India 2022. DOI: 10.1093/oso/9780190132613.003.0010 he had nearly lost half of his manly strength. But he considered himself to be a very strong young man. Nevertheless, his special attendants—experienced women coming out of his bedroom—would hide their faces behind their *dupattas*, laughing, and share the details of their nights, and while doing so would also reveal the reality of his virility, in a hushed manner.

"I did not even get to know there when the night got over … "

"Why?" someone asked. "Were you awake the whole night?"

"Awake?" she laughed and said, "I slept and continued to sleep … What is the point of saying anything here."

If one of the women moved around without any care, another would incite and say, "Have you not taken a bath? I went to the *hamaam* (bathhouse) and the water is still hot; it hasn't been used."

Annoyed, she would respond, "If a man would sleep away like a father and a brother, then of what use these baths and this purity?" These incidents had, in no way, raised questions on Nawab Sahab's youth? Of what use was Hakim Sahib anyway! According to Hakim Sahib, Nawab Sahab should be around adolescent girls. This would give him a lot of strength as well as keep him young for days to come.

Nevertheless, Nawab Sahab's plan to go upstairs had no wrong intentions behind it. He had really gone up to the terrace to witness the moon. He followed people's directions in sighting the moon; on his own, he could never sight one. And he would fix his gaze in that direction. Suddenly standing on the terrace of his *haveli*, his eyes glided down and were fixed on the courtyard of a poor man's hut. His eyesight was indeed weak; obviously, he could not see the crescent of the first day of the month, but if the glowing full moon is in front of one's eye, then even the eyes of weak-sighted man will shine all by itself.

"How stupid was I? Years have passed but I did not do anything to find out about my own neighbourhood."

Diwan ji was standing in front of him full of remorse.

"You never told me about such a ravishing beauty in our neighbourhood."

"Yes … yes … My lord I never noticed."

"You don't have to reflect on this but bring this girl to me by any means possible. That is all you have to do."

Diwan ji turned to go while Nawab Sahab opened the drawer and took out a purse full of money and threw it at the feet of Diwan.

"I do not take anything for free. If the girl protests or if the parents object, give them this money … It is enough to last them a lifetime."

But the next day, Diwan ji was standing in the same manner. He kept the empty purse on the table.

"My lord … " He was stammering: "They … they … "

"Why are you stammering?" The lord was annoyed. "Speak up; did nothing happen? or what?"

"My lord, they turned out to be extremely decent are very honest people." They said, "We do not sell our daughters for money. We are honest and god-fearing people. We will bid farewell to our daughter through proper wedding ceremonies and rituals as laid down by Allah. And … and … My lord, they threw this heavy purse on my face."

Nawab Sahab was grinding his teeth: "So, are you an offspring of a human ? " Then, he asked, "Will they marry her off to me?"

Diwan ji was shaking in fear. When Nawab Sahab used to get extremely angry, he would, instead of hurling abuses, question the origins of one's lineage – which was the worst of abuses.

"I did ask my lord."

"And what did they say?"

"They said … said that my lord is very old and our daughter is very young."

On hearing the words "*very young*", Nawab Sahab was furious. Enraged he asked, "Do I look that old?"

The sycophant Diwan responded—"No, my Lord! … you are not at all old. Such type of women you have … " and then out of respect and politeness, he did not complete the sentence but Nawab Sahab was extremely happy on hearing this, he smiled, "That is what I was saying as well … " And he became serious. "But I want that girl at any cost."

"You are wise my lord … we are poor and less intelligent ones. Will follow your instructions."

"Find out how many people are there in that family."

"That I have already found out my lord" and he quickly added, "Mother, a sick father, and a grandmother who cannot move around. And three to four younger siblings … Ujaala is the eldest."

Nawab Sahab was beaming with happiness. "Ujaala ... Such a beautiful name!" Agitated, he said, "The name suits her face."

"Yes, my lord she lives up to her name. If she sat in a dark room; it would light up."

"Silent! Do not sing praises of her," a jealous Nawab Sahab responded. "Now you go and inform them that Nawab Sahab is getting all the nearby lanes demolished and making a compound. Tell them to vacate their house by tomorrow evening."

Diwan ji was happy to hear this solution, "Yes, my lord! What a bright idea, my lord! Where will these miserable ones go along with their large family ... They will have to bow down to you."

On the day of Eid, the husband and the wife stood in the presence of Nawab Sahab, wailing.

"My lord, we have spent our lives under your patronage. Now where would we go? Our old mother cannot even get up and sit without any help. My husband has not been keeping well for a long time. Our children are small. Please tell my lord ... Where would we go? ... " Sakina Bi was weeping bitterly.

"We have a lot of space in our servant quarters, you can shift here." Nawab Sahab suggested in a gentle voice.

Looking at her ill husband, her courage failed.

"Your beneficence on us my Lord ... I say with honesty that your generosity is bestowed upon this entire estate."

And it was true that there was no other Nawab, in Hyderabad who like Nawab Zain Yar Jung, was generous and large-hearted. He immensely disliked taking anything from anyone. He never accepted any gifts from his relatives or his loved ones. His hands were always raised but only to provide. In giving, he had reached such a limit that if anything fell from his hands, he would never bend and pick it up. His servants would be told to pick it up and it would be given away as *baksheesh* to them.

A family of traders had ruled over Hyderabad for a long time. But how did they amass so much wealth? Once as a child, a pouch full of gold coins fell from his hands. Generosity had been ingrained in him since childhood, and he had never learnt to bow down. A servant was called for to pick it up and as he tried to give it to him, Nawab Sahab was furious, "Uncouth! Trying to give me dropped goods ... Get out of my *haveli* right now and take that purse of money with you!" Good fortune came attached with this purse for him. Some say that he started his business and began to lead a life like those of Nawabs. Just think if he was like this as a child; once grown up, it is these habits that mature and become firmly entrenched as one grows old.

The servant quarters of the *haveli* were nothing like their name would suggest. One of the best residences was bestowed upon these unfortunates. However, there remained a hesitation in one's heart regarding the price that will be asked by Nawab Sahab for his kindness and benevolence. But what could Nawab Sahab ask for; when he was always used to giving.

Crushed under the burden of favours, Sakina Bi would have given her life as an offering to Nawab Sahab. *In some way, I should be of use to my master.* She would send her small children to Nawab Sahab's room to press his feet since she could not think of anything more.

One day, the master smiled and said, "How will these small children press my feet well enough; if you want then send for your eldest one."

Sakina Bi looked at him in fright. She remembered that he was the one who had sent over money to buy her daughter. When she did not sell her daughter for money then how ... How could she send her daughter alone to a room with closed doors? The master read her thoughts in one glance.

"I know what you are thinking. But think this that if I wanted, I could have gotten your girl by force. Who could have stopped me?"

"My lord you should marry her ... " Moved to tears, helpless Sakina Bi suggested. "A young girl's honour is like that of a glass vessel. It is fragile!"

"Marriage?" Nawab Sahab's voice was a mix of anger and astonishment. "Marriage is a lifelong responsibility and if there are any offsprings then property-related quarrels come up. Have you lost your mind?"

Fearing, Sakina spoke, "But my lord when your *shervani* and high *topi* clad servant had come that day then he mentioned that you ... " She became silent.

Nawab Sahab agreed and said, "I did say that but I did not mean that. I was thinking of doing a *mutah* (temporary marriage)."

"*Mut ... mut ... muta..*" Sakina was stammering. "What does that mean my lord?"

The master told her clearly, "Recently I went for two weeks on a visit to the estate. How could one live without a woman for that long? And so

I got married to a girl there. And when I was about to return, I divorced her. I mean to say that it was a marriage for a short duration. Don't be afraid. In the name of *mehr*, I will give so much money that your next two generations will remain self-sufficient. It all depends on when I am completely satisfied and ready to divorce her. But hear this that I have done several *mutas* but whenever I noticed symptoms of any low and vile woman getting impregnated then my *hakim* would give that woman medicine to abort the child."

"This is forbidden, my lord! This desire is *haram*!" Every bit of Sakina's body was screaming out loud against it, but she did not have the courage nor the strength to either agree or disagree with it. She sat there with her mouth open and Nawab Sahab continued to pass decrees. "I have legally married only one woman who is known as Bade Paasha. Although I have only learnt to give, and for this purpose only these women live with me, and I perform *Muta* then divorce them … In the end, the poor should be given a means of livelihood. If I don't give then what will happen to them?"

This was all about that twilight when Nawab Sahab was standing on his terrace; looking through the haze of darkness sighted a moon that was shining at a distance. That distance and this vicinity.

Today, he learned what Ujaala was all about. Allah had generously bestowed beautiful long hair upon these poor Hyderabadi women! Nothing left to say regarding that, but the colour of her skin!

What colour! As if silver had dissolved into her skin and was coursing through her veins. Wine or intoxication of any kind was useless in comparison to her eyes. These eyes were solely created to intoxicate whosoever they looked at. Regarding her figure … in Arabic poetry, a woman's beauty has been praised by suggesting that if a sheet of cloth covers a woman's body, from head to toe, then that sheet should slightly touch upon two places — one on her bosom and another on her hips. The rest of the sheet should crave to touch the body. Ujaala was the mistress of such a body that makes the sheets crave for it. Those beautiful rose-coloured lips were the biggest highlight of Ujaala's beauty. Nawab Sahib was so intoxicated and euphoric that he was not able to save himself from the silent, sharp, and lightly satirical smile of those lips.

What surprised Nawab Sahab was that not once did he require the help of the *hakim*. She who was herself a concoction of pearls, gold-silver, and precious jewels, in her presence of what use were any other medications! The moments that she gifted Nawab Sahab made him feel that his life till now had been all but a waste and a ruined existence.

Each day spent with her felt as if it had been spent in heaven. Everything was there, but Ujaala never spoke to him. It was not that he felt that loss, but at times, felt that these two globules of wine; this calamity; this mischief of a woman should create magic through her lips. On any talk, she would just smile slowly and sharply and lower her head. Just a little movement of her neck would be an answer from her side.

"Are you happy with me, Ujaala?"

As a reply, she would just smile . . . a slight satirical smile.

"Do you like something very much? I can give you anything but still, is there anything?"

By the movement of her neck, she would say her no.

"Then, why don't you talk to me Ujaala. You are so beautiful! Your voice will also be as beautiful as you are; at least speak to me."

That same smile—slightly murderous, slightly innocent, a little sharp, with satirical undertones—but it was a slight smile.

The gatherings at Nawab Sahab's place were the talk of the town. Dancing, singing, free-flowing wine, and women. He was a very generous man. At such gatherings if any friend of Nawab Sahab's took a liking to the woman that Nawab Sahab had done *Muta* with, then Nawab Sahab would instantly divorce that woman and gift her to that friend. This was a small example of his large-hearted and generous nature. This was a usual practice amongst his Nawab friends, but he had never accepted a gift like this from anyone. He was made only to give and there was no question of taking from anyone.

That night another gathering of such mind-numbing kinds had been set. Hot *kebabs* were being served; gold-coloured glasses adorned with silver bells with gold and silver work on them filled with wine were being served; and on Nawab Sahab's special orders, dressed in red with gold work all over, came Ujaala like the wine that was being served. People were stunned by her beauty!

The proud Nawab looked around. He was doubly intoxicated. One because of the wine, while the other was to be in possession of such a matchless beauty. He was looking at everyone with pride. In response, people were slowly coming back to their senses.

"This is what we call Beauty," said one admiringly.

"And this is how one should walk."

"Have heard about the maidens of heaven. Now I have seen one in this world."

"Now even if Nawab Sahab is sent to hell! So what? He has seen heaven on this earth and experienced it."

"But for how much did you buy this precious diamond?"

Nawab Sahab looked around with pride and had no idea of what he was about to say when for the first time in his life spent with Ujaala, for the very first time, he heard the beautiful voice of Ujaala like a tune from a flute that crashed against his ears. The question that had been posed to Nawab Saheb was now being addressed by her in a satirical manner:

"You people only know that Nawab Zain Yar Jung is a very prominent Nawab. A very generous Nawab. All he does is give but never takes from anyone … But let me tell you this poor girl from a poor family of Hyderabad is not any less generous. In his entire lifetime, the one who never took anything from anyone; asked for my beauty and I gave the *Zakat* of my beauty to that one beggar in the long queue of beggars and *fakirs* who had been hankering for my attention. And it was him; your Nawab Zain Yar Jung. I had heard that he was such a big-hearted man that he never accepted anyone's gift; only gave … I ask that how did he accept the *Zakat* of my beauty? Of what social standing is he to buy my beauty? I made him a beggar."

He who always wanted to hear her voice; today, he heard her voice, but it was like everything had been melted and poured into his ears so that he could never hear anything else. His glass of wine slipped from his hands and with that he swayed towards the ground, never to get up.

Translated from Urdu by Semeen Ali.

One of the five pillars of Islam, *Zakat* is a form of obligatory charity for the followers of Islam who meet the necessary criteria of wealth.

10
Spartan Hearts

Mrs. K Ahmad

The women of Sparta had sturdy, adamantine hearts: unbreakable, imperishable. When their husbands and sons went out to war, they bade farewell to their men with these words: "You must come back victorious, or you must die fighting." This is a clear indication of what tough materials their hearts were made of! They had no patience for the weak, no mercy for the vanquished. Defeat was shameful, patriotism a matter of glory. They were willing to lay their lives down for their fatherland. They ostracized the men who lost wars. It was a person's duty to put up a brave fight and not run away from the battlefield like a coward.

In the Battle of Leuctra, fought in 371 BC, the Greeks defeated the Spartans.

Three hundred Spartan soldiers walked homewards, heads bowed low. Most of their comrades had died. The people of Sparta were filled with loathing for the men who were marching back. They did not shed tears for the lives lost; instead, they spat in anger at those who had managed to escape alive. When the news of defeat reached the court of Sparta, the ephors conveyed the message to the families of the deceased.

However, the women were not allowed to indulge in the luxury of grief. They could not cry for the departed souls. Eucrates was one of the many Spartan soldiers who had died. His mother started weeping when she received the news. The rest of Sparta reprimanded her for mourning the death of her son. Her neighbours said, "Why is this woman lamenting? She has no reason or right to cry. Her son, Eucrates, has died in the war like a hero."

When an elderly man called Phaedon paid the old mother a visit, he found her actively engaged in household chores to keep her mind off her dead son. Her eyes, however, told a different story. Phaedon was a true

Mrs. K Ahmad, *Spartan Hearts* In: *The Silence That Speaks*. Edited by: Haris Qadeer, Oxford University Press.
 DOI: 10.1093/oso/9780190132613.003.0011

Spartan at heart. He addressed the old woman brusquely, "Aeon, it is extremely wrong on your part to lament the death of your son. You do not have the permission to cry. You do not have the right to mourn. Your son died like a valiant warrior. My weakling of a grandson, on the other hand, is returning home from the battlefield alive. I have every reason to cry. You do not. Once upon a time, my son had made me proud with his selfless sacrifice for our land. My head is now bowed in shame because of the inefficacy of my son's son. I cannot bring myself to look at his dishonourable face. Aeon, my son's birth was a matter of immense pride for me. He never let me down during his lifetime, but my grandson, Calais, has today managed to tarnish the reputation we had built for ourselves. He is spineless. The gods have been unkind to me. Why are they punishing an old man? Were they jealous of me?"

Aeon realized her mistake. She wiped her tears and tried to comfort the miserable Phaedon. Eucrates and Calais had grown up in each other's company, playing games and learning lessons together. As children they had been inseparable, and their friendship continued to blossom in beautiful ways when they matured. They would stand next to each other on the battlefield whenever they went out to war. Why did the two not embrace death together then?

Aeon told Phaedon, "We do not know the ways of the gods. Perhaps, Calais is meant for bigger things. Maybe the gods have saved him today because tomorrow he is destined to script history by slaying the Greeks."

Phaedon had no such confidence in Calais and, therefore, Aeon's words brought him no solace.

After some days, when Phaedon seemed resigned to his fate, Aeon requested him to forgive Calais. She said, "The boy is alive because Fate has other plans for him. Forgive him, Phaedon. He will bring home honour and glory someday. Sparta will be proud of him."

Phaedon got agitated, and replied, "Do not mention his ill-fated name to me ever again, Aeon. I can never forgive Calais."

Aeon lost hope. Even the gods could not sway a resilient, hardened Spartan heart.

One night, Aeon woke up from a strange dream. The king of Sparta had asked the survivors of the Battle of Leuctra to assemble in his court. He wanted to pardon them on behalf of the people of Sparta. However, Phaedon put his foot down, and said, "My grandson escaped from that battlefield and came home alive. Sparta might be ready to pardon him but I shall never forgive Calais. Never."

Aeon recounted her dream to Phaedon the next day. Her heart was torn by the look of remorse on Calais's face. The news of her son's death had been less painful than seeing Calais's grief-stricken eyes haunting her in the dark of the night. She pleaded with Phaedon, "Show him some mercy! Forgive him, Phaedon!"

Phaedon was moved by Aeon's dream, but he was firm on his word. He said, "It is not easy to shake my resolve. You might be right, Aeon, in assuming that Calais is meant to achieve bigger things in life. By the grace of the Gods, if he returns home triumphant someday, I will perhaps forgive him; but not now. It breaks my heart to even think of it."

Aeon's dream was probably a prophecy from the gods. In two days, the king officially pardoned the men who had escaped from the battlefield, much to the chagrin and surprise of the people of Sparta. Men like them were usually treated poorly and constantly reminded of their failures. However, these men were so many in number that it might have been difficult for the king to punish them at large after the Battle of Leuctra.

Phaedon grew increasingly impatient to see his grandson. He said, "Aeon, you were, indeed, right. I probably should forgive him. If our king has pardoned him, if our people have accepted him, who am I to torture him thus? Yet, it is true that I would have been happier if he had sacrificed his life in that battle. I would have been proud of Calais."

At long last, the soldiers who had escaped from the battlefield after hearing the news of their defeat returned to Sparta. Their families were ecstatic to see them alive. They embraced the broken, bruised warriors, and hoped the men would be able to serve their kingdom better in the future. Thus, within a few days, things took quite a different turn in Sparta.

Aeon heard the news, but she did not go out to greet the wounded warriors. She sat in a corner of her house, weaving. Her tears had dried. Her heart was strangely at peace. She felt proud of her son's sacrifice. She did not want to be a part of the public jubilation, choosing instead to remain by herself in the quiet of her room. She was hungry for some tranquility and isolation.

Phaedon suddenly knocked on her door and walked into her room. He said to Aeon in a frenzy, "Calais has not come back. He is not there with the others, Aeon. I asked those boys about Calais, but no one had any information on him. Does that mean . . . ? Is he . . . ?"

Aeon's neighbour, Timotheus, knocked on her door. He walked into the room, greeted Aeon, and said, "I was at Leuctra. When the battle was in full swing, Eucrates did his best to slow down our enemies. Eventually, he was slain by one of the Greeks. I saw him die. I also saw another young man lay down his life—he was standing right next to Eucrates and fighting as bravely. The two friends lived, fought, and died together."

"Who was that other young man?" Aeon asked. She pressed her hands to her heart and started keening. Her face was pale but her eyes were dry.

"His name was Calais," Timotheus replied. "I need to inform his grandfather, and so, I shall now take your leave, Aeon."

Phaedon, who was standing behind the door, overhearing the conversation, stepped out of the shadow, and said, "You need not go to Calais's grandfather. He has already heard everything. He is thanking the gods for showing him mercy. He would have liked to see his grandson once more, but he accepts what the gods have in store for him."

Turning to Aeon, he said, "We can finally be at ease. Eucrates and Calais have made us proud. We can now celebrate their death together."

"Indeed, we can finally celebrate their death together," Aeon replied. Her tone was reserved. The face of her dead son haunted her, but she did not let it show on her countenance.

She was, after all, a Spartan. Her heart was not meant to be easily broken.

The Spartans never accepted defeat. They were full of hope and aspirations. As long as they were alive, they were prepared to fight. They were unafraid to take on any challenge.

Can we not be like them?

First published as "Spartan Hriday" in *Saogat*, Vol. 10 in 1933. Translated from Bengali by Somrita Ganguly.

11

Husnara Begum

Jamila Begum

Little Husnara was barely five years old when her father left home in search of livelihood abandoning his young wife and small daughter. Although Husnara's mother was old-fashioned, she had a good command over Persian and Arabic. She was also well-versed in stitching. But unfortunately, she was married to a person who was not only bereft of learning but also did not value things related to it. Owing to his worthlessness, when the husband could not find any means of livelihood in his own country, he decided to try his fortune out abroad. At the time of departure, his virtuous and faithful wife cried for justice in the name of God and his prophet. "Don't forget your poor wife and keep communicating to me the news of your safety." At the time of parting, the husband consoled his wife and took away whatever little money she had earned from stitching work.

The penurious and helpless wife did not eat anything that day. Only bread worth one paisa was brought from the market for Husnara. The wife began to live in poverty. It had been two years and ten months since the husband left her. In the beginning, she received two letters mentioning the address of the shop where he was employed. He was untraceable after that. Notwithstanding, these two women led a respectable existence. The destitute wife, who was wasting away by the lack of her husband's affection, began to teach some girls of the neighbourhood and undertook various laborious jobs to eke out a living. The helpless woman had no support of relatives or of dear ones. Due to her straitened circumstances, her kith and kin too turned their back on her.

Whatever learning and skill Husnara's mother could teach her daughter, she did. Since God had endowed Husnara with qualities of intelligence and enterprise, she acquired great skills within a short period

Jamila Begum, *Husnara Begum* In: *The Silence That Speaks.* Edited by: Haris Qadeer, Oxford University Press.
 DOI: 10.1093/oso/9780190132613.003.0012

of time. In this manner, the mother–daughter duo spent eight years, encountering many difficulties and suffering many misfortunes. One day, a stranger came and knocked on the door asking, "Does Mirza Saadat Ali live here?" His wife sent the answer that her husband has not come back for eight years. The stranger said, "If Begham Sahiba permits me, I want to convey a message from behind the veil." Begham stood behind the veil to listen to his message. The gentleman told her that after his departure from home, Mirza Sahib served in a factory for a long time. Mirza was gradually promoted to the position of a manager by the owner. Having earned a lot of money, he left for Rangoon (Burma), where he has been staying for the last four years. He is a big factory owner and trades with European countries, Japan, America, and other nations. And listen! He has married the daughter of an affluent trader. She is a wealthy widow. Your husband has sent you this message: "Fend for yourself, and I have nothing to do with you."

The helpless wife fainted on hearing this. After many efforts, she recovered her senses. Husnara, who was only thirteen or fourteen years old now, got deeply worried. Till now they had been hoping against hope, but now all their hopes came to an end. What will happen now?

Sometimes, this gentleman would come and give good counsel to the oppressed mother and daughter. One day, he said, "Follow my advice. Enrol Husnara in a 'training' school and you teach pupils of lower grade in the same institution." Husnara's mother accepted his suggestions and admitted Husnara in the school. And she herself opened an elementary school.

With God's grace, there was satisfactory success and progress in this enterprise. Husnara too became educated and capable.

Now, their circumstances improved. Their house was well-decorated, which also served as a school. Servants were also employed according to their resources. That is how the duo were spending their life.

One day, Husnara said to her mother, "Did you notice mother? How much progress can be made if people work with an honest intention and resign to the will of God! God has filled our life with prosperity. Yesterday, I read in a newspaper that Mirza Saadat Ali's house and factory caught fire and his entire stock burnt down. Fire department was immediately telephoned. But everything had been reduced to ashes by the time the 'engine' arrived. It is written that since the factory had not been insured, the owner suffered a huge loss. The estimated damage is around one and half or two lacs." Mother replied, "Beti, we should thank God that He helped us in penury and made us opulent. Husnara! The prayers of the destitute never go unanswered. Still I am pained to hear the news of your father's distress. Whatever God has willed for us is the best."

When these things were being discussed, a postman came. Maidservant placed two letters in the wife's hand. She immediately opened one of the letters and began to read:

> Calcutta
>
> Janab aunty Sahiba. My compliments to you. You may have forgotten your humble servant. But if you remember the events of fifteen years ago, you will recall that I am the same Ahmad who used to frequent your old house accompanied by Amma Jan. I referred to Mirza Sahab as uncle. My sister Ruqaiya studies at your school. My mother and my father, Maulavi Mohammed Sahab Khan Bahadur, Inspector of Schools, left for heavenly abode a long time ago. I am left with only one sister, who is receiving education under your protection. I have returned from abroad with the degree of a barrister and I am practising here these days. Since you already know the particulars of my family and relatives, it will be futile to write about them. The purpose of writing this humble petition is to request you to accept me as your son-in law, though *my* sending of this marriage proposal is against the practice of our country and the customs and traditions of our society. But I am constrained to do so as there are no elders alive in my family. And I would not like to involve my friends in this matter. I will definitely present myself before you tomorrow. Your humble servant,
>
> Ahmad, M.A. Barrister, Law.

The mother was absolutely pleased with herself after reading this letter. Guessing the subject of the letter by her mother's countenance, Husnara excused herself and left from there.

The author of the second letter was Husnara' uncle, in which he had profusely requested the mother and had sent his son's marriage proposal for Husnara. Husnara's mother sent an instant reply to this letter: "We have no relation with you. You deserted us in our time of need and now you write to us as it serves your own interest."

Barrister Sahib came from Calcutta next day, and he himself settled all things regarding marriage respecting the custom of purdah. And within a period of 7 to 10 days, his marriage was solemnized. Barrister not only gratified his own wishes but also fulfilled all the expectations of the poor woman. He left no stone unturned to make his wedding a grand affair.

Barrister looked exultant in his wedding robe at having married such a worthy partner. Husnara was also happy that God had elevated her to such an exalted rank that she was wedded to a highly educated barrister.

Tehzibi sisters! Pay attention and tell me was it possible for Mirza Sahib's wife in straitened circumstances to earn a good reputation and lead a life of comfort and contentment if she had not put in great effort, had not worked with such exemplary determination and courage, and had not educated her daughter? All these qualities are derived from education. Imagine if she was illiterate, what options could she have except for adopting the profession of a maidservant or an attendant in women's apartment? And in what misery the daughter would have spent her life? May God create in all women the spirit of resoluteness and enterprise and let them benefit from the priceless blessings of education. Amen.

First published in *Tehzeeb-e-Niswan* (1915). Translated from Urdu by Mohammed Afzal.

12

The Smokers' Mazaar

Noor Zaheer

When Zohra had visited the plot of land for the housing society where she had booked a flat, there was a huge dump of sacks of cement, piles of bricks, sand, and grit on one side and a clump of neem, guava, date, and mulberry trees on the other. Near the grove she had noticed a mound earth, a bit longish in shape. Presuming that it must be a heap of mud from a newly dug up drain, she observed that there was a cluster of huts near the trees, somewhat like the temporary shelters of migratory labourers. A year and a half later when she arrived with the key of the flat to take possession of her first ever permanent home, she discovered that the mound had turned into a *Mazaar*, with a proper red platform, a grave made of bathroom tiles which was about three metres long and was called "*Nau gaja Pir*" or the nine-yard-long saint. Zohra had seen innumerable graves of nine-yard-long saints in her fifty year long life. The temporary huts also seemed to have been perked up. The neem, guava, date, and mulberry trees were still there and created a green canopy around the shrine. Beyond the trees was a low wall that served both as a protective demarcation and on which people would sit to rest. In this endless concrete jungle, this patch of green granted a soothing break to the heart, mind, and eye.

Zohra had tried to find out when and how this Mazaar had come into being. She learnt that Ghaziabad Development Authority had sold away the entire piece of land to Jagat Singh, the builder. There was no Mazaar on the land then; when the design for the residential colony had been submitted and passed, there was no mention of any such shrine nor had the plan any land marked for it. When the caretakers of the Mazaar approached Jagat Singh to lay claim on the piece of land, he refused to budge. Thirty-two flats had been planned on this bit of land; why would

Noor Zaheer, *The Smokers' Mazaar* In: *The Silence That Speaks*. Edited by: Haris Qadeer, Oxford University Press.
 DOI: 10.1093/oso/9780190132613.003.0013

he let go so much money? The caretakers and inheritors also summoned their relatives, friends, and well-wishers. Some Hindus also collected since a Mazaar is considered to be a secular space and then who would not want an open green space bang opposite their suffocating flats? Jagat Singh came to know of the sit in protest and arrived bellowing like a bull; a hollering contest took place. After all he was a Jat; his first lesson had been: "Land which is not bequeathed, has to be seized." He threatened, warned, and before leaving kicked the Mazaar which was still a mound of mud and said, "Let us see how you can harm me. Tomorrow morning, the bulldozer shall roll and it shall be you or me left standing!"

Next morning, he was found dead on his bed.

Before one could say "Jack Robinson," the grave had been cemented, the low surrounding parapet built and incense was being burnt every Thursday. Most ardent devotee was Jagat Singhs son, Mohit Singh. Whether he was really frightened or satisfied at suddenly finding himself the owner of such a big construction company is of course another debate. Every son believes that he can be a better administrator of the kingdom he father had founded. Fathers always ignore the opinion and advice of their sons; rare is the son who prays for the long life of his father.

The Mazaar was not only paved and tiled, the steps leading to it also encroached half of the road, multicoloured flags were hung around the grave, and tinsel and ribbons adorned its tin roof. The Mazaar was covered with a green silk sheet and a locked tin box proclaiming "donations" in Urdu and Hindi was to be found at the head of the grave. A white-haired old man was the caretaker of the shrine. He lived in the two-roomed hut with his two wives and four of the five daughters. The fifth daughter, the eldest one, was married and lived in Meerut. At nine every night, the main light at the Mazaar would be switched off, the donation box put away. The old man, now reverently called Pir Baba would appear wobbling, loudly singing some vulgar song, and take a round of his empire. He had quivering legs because of his age, but this was a wobbling of a different kind that had an elation and joy of a distinctive kind.

Although Pir Baba had a number of failings, his voice was so loud and reverberating that it's echo caused a tremble in the walls across several blocks. With the support of this voice, the domestic helps in the flats of the colony would sit down near the Mazaar to rest. There was the cool shade of the thick trees; in this lonely spot, the older ones would take a nap, and the younger ones would repair the nail polish damaged in washing clothes and utensils, take out sticks of bubble gum or a pinch of tobacco and mimicking their mistresses would lighten the stress of back breaking, underpaid labour.

No man would dare to act fresh with these women. These women themselves were quite capable of giving tit for tat to such men. Most of them had been working for long stretches in unfamiliar households. They were familiar with flirtatious masters and could deal with pestering drivers, guards, and cooks. They were quite self-reliant as far as their personal security was concerned. But Pir Baba never let things reach that stage where these women had to defend themselves. If some man so much as dared to step towards the clump of the trees, he would holler from the head of the grave, "Why there? Why that side? The water hand pump is this side, here is the Mazaar, this is me, and by me is the donation box, incense sticks, and match box! What are you stepping that side for? Come here! Are you stone deaf? I said come this way! The poor fellow's condition would be that of a street dog receiving a tongue lashing on daring to extend its nose towards a pedigree bitch. With his tail between his legs, he would run for his life.

Among these women some were fond of good things of life. Or maybe they were more tormented by life. Just gossiping, chewing gum, or straightening their backs on a bit of cardboard did not give them the relief they required. It is also possible that they wished to move with the times and getting up every few minutes to spit tobacco juice seemed uncouth to them. Whatever be the reason, six or seven of these women found relief in a few draws of a cigarette. Usually just one cigarette would be lighted and passed around. With its price touching the sky, who could dare to smoke a whole cigarette alone? And then, this way the sense of relief could be shared and extended. Caste and clan would be so side-lined that even a Muslim woman was part of the group.

These women took care to cover their heads and see that they were well-hidden by the trees, but they would be invariably caught in passing the cigarette from one to the other. Care for equal sharing and concern for the other's need would expose them and Pir baba would yell from the Mazar, "*Lahaul-e-vila qoovat*!" Curse be on the womankind! Is this the only place you could find to commit this impious act. Ill-fated ones, don't you dare, don't you even think about committing this filthy sin! I shall kick you out of this compound, I swear by the Mazaar of the Pir!" The women embarrassed at being caught, would giggle and smirk awkwardly, quickly snuff out the cigarette, would get up grumbling and complaining under their breath and walk away to their left over work. No one would argue with the old man; God forbid, he might curse them and with the blood of the Pir in his veins, the curse just might bear fruit!

The old man himself would get his hookah filled four or five times in the day. He would sit at the head of the Mazaar, with his back resting on the right side wall and call out, "Hookah!" His younger wife, with her head demurely covered would appear with the tobacco-filled hookah, with one of the daughters carrying a red hot ember held in iron tongs and place it over the hookah. The old man would pull quickly three or four times making the water gurgle, nod his head, and say "*hunh*." Both the wife and daughter would disappear.

On one such day, the eldest daughter arrived from her in laws. She carried the blight of "divorced" on her forehead and a four-year-old son in her arms. When she was done with weeping and repeatedly cursing her fate, she began to help in the upkeep of the Mazaar. She bought two earthen pots, filled them from the hand pump, and put them on the low parapet so that anyone passing by could quench their thirst from the Mazaar. Every morning she would collect flowers from the houses around and decorate the grave; from somewhere, she got hold of an old CD player and began playing *qawwali* and *Naat* every Thursday. Her son could be seen jumping and dancing at the beat of the music. It was she who began talking to the domestic helps resting under the trees. When the old man tried to object, she countered and said, "So? Are they not human? They work hard and earn their livelihood; they are neither thieves, nor murderers!"

The condition of the Mazaar was improving. It was clear that donations were generous. Both the rooms now had some comforts; a second hand cooler, a gas cylinder in place of the wooden chulah, four or five chairs, and an old generator that noisily provided electricity to the Mazaar in the long nights of load shedding. The old man would ask the CD player to begin playing every Thursday evening. Naturally, there was no Urs nor were there any qawwalis for such an unknown Pir, so songs in praise of Nizamuddin Auliya and Khwaja Moinuddin Chishti held sway.

The old fellow, faced with logic had shut up but was on the lookout of an opportunity. One day, at dusk, the eldest daughter was narrating her story. When she began describing the tortures she had to bear from her husband and his family, she broke down and began weeping. Perhaps, in manner of showing sympathy, or to provide some kind of a consolation, one of the women extended a lighted cigarette to her. Before she could accept it, the old man's voice admonished, booming from the Mazaar, "Don't you dare! Sharks! Whores! You commit all kinds of sins yourself and on top of it harbor the desire of destroying others! I have been watching you immoral group and noting your wicked designs! Get up! Get up this very minute and don't dare show your face at this pious shrine or I shall not answer for the consequences! Illiterate, corrupt, evil womankind! Get lost from here!"

He dragged the eldest daughter and pushed her inside one of the rooms; rest of the women moved away, guilt and remorse etched on their faces. The old man turned out to be true to his words. Women would look longingly at the cool green shade on hot afternoons, one or two of them fearfully asked his pardon and promised never to commit the crime of smoking near the shrine, but the old man's legs might have been tottering, his decision was unwavering. He did not budge.

Improvement in the financial conditions had led to the increase of his liquor intake. One night swaying and wobbling after a few drinks, he tottered over the steps, slipped and collapsed on the road, and then never got up. The Mazaar was suddenly orphaned. The domestic helps saw the desolate shrine and talked among themselves; some of the brave ones began sitting on the low wall. The doors of the rooms would be closed from inside; if one of them opened suddenly, the women would jump down and run for their lives. Some weeks later, a few of the older ones knocked on one of the doors of the hut. The door opened just an inch and then more when the inner ones saw it was only women outside.

"Listen! How long are you going to keep the door shut and yourself inside? Come out and take cognizance of Pir Baba, sweep the Mazaar, fill up the water pitchers, put the donation box in place . . . !"

A discussion followed between the women of the Mazaar and the domestic helps. It does not require a lot of sense to decipher that the seven women of the Mazaar had no other source of income except the shrine. Next Thursday, three of the younger girls washed the grave and covered it with a green sheet; the donation box was placed near the epitaph. The second daughter washed the pitchers and filled them with water, and the eldest daughter placed a brass pot near the feet of the grave. The elder wife spread a small mat near the grave and sat with her rosary, and the younger one sat with an open Quran, rocking and mumbling. Word soon spread that the brass pot had sugar-coated puffed rice, and children began collecting around the Mazaar every Thursday.

Such a large open space, right in the centre of a middle-class residential complex and no one else would have an eye on it! Unthinkable! A couple of Mullahs had begun visiting the Mazaar while the old man was alive. Now they became bold and fearless. One among them began to plan his future and with this design one day he grabbed the hand of the second daughter at the hand pump.

The girl screamed, and before her mother or sisters could emerge from the hut, a dozen women ran out from the houses nearby. Some carried a broom, some a cloth-beater, others had a washing brush or floor mop in their hand. Maulvi Sahib was not only given a good beating, he was also warned to keep away. The fellow ran for his life.

The women washed the face of the frightened, weeping girl, made her drink some water, and calmed her down. As they were leaving for work, the younger of the wives said, "Listen! You women used to rest here in the afternoons! Do continue that."

One of the women replied, "Just a few days before his death, Pir Baba had stopped us. We don't wish to hurt his soul, so we stay away."

"No, No! It is not that way at all. Tired and aching bodies need rest. Come and rest when you like."

As the women began to move, the older wife said, "And you can smoke a cigarette or *beedi*. No one say anything."

The place became alive again. Women could be seen resting, talking, and often sharing a cigarette at the Mazaar. The women living in the hut would also finish their household work and join these women. Sometimes they would sing film songs, at others words of dialects such as Bhojhuri, Avadhi, and Haryanvi would ride on folk tunes and spread the yearning of a lost motherland. Often Adil, the son of the eldest daughter, would be found dancing like a little Krishna between the women. All women doted on him. A daughter of one of the women was learning stitching, and she made a green kurta pajama for him; another wove golden beads into a crochet cap for him. Every Thursday, five-year-old Adil could be seen wearing the green suit and golden-beaded cap, distributing the sugar-coated rice. Most devotees would place a few rupees in his hands; some would place his hand on their heads in blessing from the inheritor of Pir Baba.

Not a believer in the hocus focus of pilgrimages and Mazaars, yet Zohra would feel a sense of relief passing by the shrine. Perhaps it was the generosity of these women, maybe it was their friendship and sisterhood, their desire to touch a few moments of happiness in a life laden with difficulties. All of this together had made this shrine a human place; its humanity would leave a mark even on the casual passer-by, and they would feel a sense of serenity, an elimination of tension and stress.

After a while, some jovial people renamed the Mazaar that anyway did not have a proper name and began calling it "The Smokers' Mazaar."

Five years passed as if in the blink of an eye. Not as if these five years didn't bring any change. Most of the domestic helps acquired a mobile phone. Women at the Mazaar also managed to procure one and began instructing the devotees on what to bring with the "*chader*," the time for "*sehri*" and "*iftar*" during the month of Ramzan, the dates of festivals from the Hijri or Islamic calendar, the cost of an amulet and the manner in which it had to be worn.

All the women had become somewhat self-reliant and fearless. They would sit without caring for the dupatta that often lay in their lap. One of them firmly refused to marry the man selected by her parents. When the older women from the Mazaar tried to persuade her, she replied, "Why? When I have to live it, I should be the one to decide it. From the age of seven, I have been working in such flats, earning and feeding the family, not to be pushed blindly into any damn well of their choice." She said this so loudly and clearly that it was audible even in the nearby apartments. These women also began to refuse to accept old clothes; they would open and turn them this way and that, and if any was torn or discoloured, they would point blank refuse to accept them, leaving the donor embarrassed and shamefaced.

But the one to change the most was Adil. He was now a boy of ten, good looking but of a strange obstinate nature. He had a weird stubbornness and would insist on being called "*huzoor*." If he was addressed by name, he would refuse to answer; he would just turn a deaf ear till he was addressed as "*huzoor*." The devotees would call him "*huzoor*," and perhaps this is where he had taken a liking for it. But now, he insisted that his aunts, mother, so much so that his grandmothers also address him as "*huzoor*."

Often the working women would forget or maybe they just wanted to add some fun in their monotonous days and call him, "Adil" or "*Bhaiyya*" or "*Bachua*." And pandemonium would break over the shrine. All would together apologize, touch their ears, and swear by their gods that they would never repeat it, only then would he be appeased.

Adil was attending a public school during the day and went to a nearby madrasa in the evenings. Mazaar now had enough income to hire a regular cycle rikshaw for him to commute. One morning, he had not been gone for a half an hour when the rikshaw returned with him happily seated on it. The school had been shut down due to a Bharat Bandh called against price rise.

Fagged out after the back breaking work that had begun at five in the morning, the women had, at about 9 a.m., decided to take a break and were resting in the cool shade. It was middle of May and the sun was already beating down relentlessly. To control their breathlessness and provide some support to their exhausted limbs, they brought out two cigarettes at the same time. A bit of an argument, "No! Do keep some for the evening!" "I have more, come on light up!" was quickly overcome and both were lighted.

Adil was alighting from the rikshaw when the rikshaw-wala turning around saw the women smoking, grinned showing his yellow with nicotine teeth and exclaimed, "Dear Lord! What an eye-candy the smoking band is! These females are the pride of this shrine! All because there is no man around to put a check on them!"

No more instigation was needed. Adil jumped down from the rikshaw and charging towards the group of women, smacked the head of the first woman and yelled, "Witches! Didn't you find any other place to commit this filthy act! How dare you taint this pious place? Who granted you permission to sit here? And who said you can adulterate this place with your smoking?"

Then, he turned on the women from the Mazaar, "aren't you ashamed of yourselves? You belong to a respectable Syed household and mix with this scum? Get inside all of you! And you, get out at once! Never show your ill-omened faces at the Mazaar; you have turned the Mazaar into a den of drugs and narcotics! Get lost!"

Women, the Mazaar ones and the outsiders, all dazed and shaken were staring at each other and listening to the abuses falling from the lips of a ten year-old boy. Straightening each other's dresses and putting right their dupattas, all were alert and watchful; to teach women the criteria of shame and dishonor, indignity and disgrace, a person from the human settlement was preparing to become a man. Obviously, the humans who had become women had to be vigilant and cautious.

First published as "Cigarette wali Mazaar" in *Parikatha* (2016). Translated from Hindi by the author.

13

Billiee

Shajahana

Rehana's husband Raheem was a government employee. He often got transferred to nooks and corners of the district. The latest one brought them to this big city. Raheem had been counting days since his last transfer, anxious about finding a rented house. Thankfully, they found one on the third floor. He breathed a sigh of relief.

In smaller towns, people were generally cordial and always spoke nicely. Rehana wondered if they would find such people in this city. Anyway, they arrived at the new house with a truck load of stuff. The steps to the third floor reminded her of the steps to the top floor of Charminar that she had climbed in her childhood. She was annoyed at the number of steps that she had to climb. They had to pass the houses on the lower floors. She spotted a potted *tulasi* plant outside a house. A cat was taking a nap right next to the plant. It opened its eyes at the commotion but closed them immediately and turned to the other side as if it didn't care.

They got busy with unpacking and arranging the house on the weekend. Rehana arranged her plants in the verandah so that sunlight fell on them. She realized that it was an indifferent neighbourhood and that she had to spend the entire day by herself when Raheem went to work.

The first week went by lazily. It was Sunday again. Raheem brought half a kilo of good meat. It spread its aroma all around while getting cooked. She finished by sprinkling a bit of masala and coriander leaves.

After lunch, Raheem went out. She was alone in the house. The cat from the lower floor came up meowing. Rehana shooed it out. But it promptly returned. How much ever Rehana tried to shoo it away, it refused. It began to circle around her endearingly shaking the end of its tail, as if they were well known to each other.

Shajahana, *Billiee* In: *The Silence That Speaks*. Edited by: Haris Qadeer, Oxford University Press. © Oxford University Press India 2022. DOI: 10.1093/oso/9780190132613.003.0014

Unable to bear its haranguing, Rehana put together a few pieces of meat with all the left overs in a "rathendi" plate and put it out for the cat to eat. Cat went out, smelled the plate, and began to eat. Once it finished, it made a few rounds of the corridor and went down.

From then on, the cat visited her house whenever meat was cooked, and Rehana fed it. On one such Sunday, when the cat was eating its share of meat, the lower-floor woman came up to the terrace to hang out her thick blankets. While passing Rehana's house, during this climb, she spotted her cat and the meat in front of it. Swiftly, she went back.

Rehana thought she may have forgotten something. But soon, she heard loud screams from below. She climbed down four steps to see what was happening. The lower-floor woman turned her face away from Rehana and continued her haranguing, "I brought it up on milk and curd till now. This dirty food has polluted it now. Aren't you supposed to check who the cat belongs to. It is like a child in my house. It has never violated the rules or conventions of the house. Years of good upbringing has been destroyed in an hour … I have told the owner not rent it out to turakollu. He didn't listen to me … He is only after money. Now, I will see to his end."

Rehana felt that the cat was looking at her with a lot of sympathy.

She tried to explain "If I had known, I would not have … " Before she could complete a sentence, her husband called her inside, "Dakshayani, what happened? You asked me to come out but disappeared by the time I came out of the room. What is all this ruckus? Don't behave like low castes. Come inside."

She looked disgustingly at me and the cat, went inside, and angrily closed the door. The cat which tried to enter the house could not understand why it was left outside. It meowed pitifully.

Rehana was coming down the steps to buy vegetables. She saw that the cat was trying to enter her house, but Dakshayani came out like a stormy wind to scream at it, "You dirty bitch! How do you think you can enter this house? Not only did you get polluted but want to pollute the house also? Go away. Chi chi, go away. You will not get any food from today." She pushed the cat away with a stick and closed the door with a bang. Rehana wondered if Dakshayani's tirade was against the cat or herself.

That night, she dreamt only of the cats. Some cats wore sacred thread. They were battling with cats without sacred thread. It was not clear who won this battle. Every cat was injured and bleeding. Isn't it cruelty to animals, Rehana was talking in her sleep. In her dream, Rehana, after witnessing this battle, digs deep into ancient texts, writes valuable research essays on cats, and puts together a book on the subject. She goes to a meeting organized by an association and speaks, "All cats are meat eating, but some stopped through self-restricting rules. They thought they would distinguish themselves as superior by not eating meat. But as the meat-eating habit got inscribed into their genes, the secret desire manifests itself when meat-eating opportunity presents itself." But before she finished her speech, a lot of sacred thread-wearing cats jumped on her and attacked her from four corners of the hall. The stage collapsed and Rehana fell down.

She screamed in fear. She awoke and sat up in bed, scared by her own screams. Her husband was looking into her face like an angry cat and scolded her, "What are those screams for? Neighbours will think that I am beating you up after getting drunk. All through the night, you threw your hands and legs like a cat. As if it were not enough you scream like a character in a horror movie."

Raheem left for office at the stipulated time. Rehana got down two steps to check the state of the cat. She found an empty, dry plate in front of it. She realized that it would not have eaten anything in the night. Her heart was filled with pain.

She felt something was hanging around in front of her door in the afternoon. When she opened the door, she found the cat. It was so weak that it couldn't even say meow. Rehana went inside quickly, brought some dry prawns, and put them on its plate. The hungry cat cleaned it in no time.

Then, it started to follow Rehana wherever she went. It made a place for itself amidst the plants and went to sleep.

From then onwards, the cat was never found in front of Dakshayani's house.

First published in *Saranga* web magazine (2013) and later in *Randhi*, Telangana stories in 2013. Translated from Telugu by A Suneetha.

14

Chappals

Sara Aboobacker

Samira was agitated. She couldn't understand why. An inexplicable loathing for life seemed to have possessed her. The last several days had been a roller-coaster of emotions. On some days, she was cheerful, running about, laughing happily, but on other days, she was morose and dejected. She would isolate herself and sit in a corner. She would refuse to do tasks that she had gladly done before. Earlier if her mother told her to pick up her bawling baby sister and quieten her, Samira would do it immediately. But now she would refuse, saying she didn't feel like it. It had been so for most things of late.

Samira's behaviour was causing her mother Fatima great anxiety. But that particular day, something happened which just aggravated her mother's worries. Fatima had put her six-month-old daughter in the cradle and started her evening namaz, but before she could complete her prayers, the baby began to cry, thrashing her little arms and legs against the sides of the cradle. Samira, who would normally rush to pick up the baby and cuddle it to make it stop crying, was nowhere to be seen.

Fatima finished her namaz hurriedly and ran to the crying baby, picked her up, and gave her some milk. "Where has this Samira gone?" she wondered. "What is she so busy with that she can't even attend to the screaming child?" The baby finished feeding and fell asleep. Fatima put her back in the cradle and called out to Samira. There was no sign of the girl.

After looking for her in the inner rooms, Fatima came to the front of the house. From the window, she spotted Samira standing by the gate, minus her burkha. She was shocked. "What's happened to this girl? Why is she standing at the gate in broad daylight, that too without gosha? So many strange men pass by this road at this time. Has she gone mad or

Sara Aboobacker, *Chappals* In: *The Silence That Speaks.* Edited by: Haris Qadeer, Oxford University Press. © Oxford University Press India 2022. DOI: 10.1093/oso/9780190132613.003.0015 what? If her father sees her like this, he will break her bones," thought Fatima.

Fatima opened the window just a little, afraid that someone might see her, and called out to her daughter, "Samira, what are you doing there! Come inside."

Samira pretended as if she hadn't heard her mother's voice and remained where she was for some time. Then, she slowly dragged her feet back to the house. She didn't even look up at her mother as she entered the house and simply walked to her room. Fatima followed her daughter inside.

"What's wrong with you, Samira? Should a married Muslim girl stand outside, by the road without a burkha? The baby was crying, but you acted as if you hadn't heard it. What will happen if your mother-in-law hears about your behaviour?" Fatima went on and on ...

Suddenly, Samira snapped, "Enough, Umma! Be quiet. I'll live the way I want to, I'll do what I like." Her voice was filled with scorn, distaste, and disrespect.

Fatima was shocked. This girl, speaking so rudely to her, was not the daughter who had been obedient and respectful till recently. Actually, this behaviour was not recent, she told herself. Ever since her husband Shabbir went back to Dubai this time, something has come over her. She deliberately picks fights with her brothers with whom she shared a loving relationship earlier. Never a shirker for housework, she has stopped helping me with the chores, and if I ask her to do something, she mutters, Do it yourself, I can't. Fatima was confused; she didn't know what to do.

After Samira's odd behaviour continued over several days, a worried Fatima sent for one mantravadini, a female exorcist, to cure her daughter. The woman made some calculations in her mantra book and deduced that a spirit, a *shaitan*, had forced itself into Samira's body, causing her to behave in this strange manner. To get rid of the shaitaan, she wrote a few verses of the Quran on a piece of paper, rolled it up in a copper amulet and asked Fatima to tie it around her daughter's neck. She also wrote a few letters of the Quran on a tender coconut and told Fatima to keep it in the kitchen.

The next day, when Samira's brothers saw her wearing the amulet, they started teasing her. "Akka, why is a suitcase hanging by your neck? Going off to Dubai, aaah?" Samira shoved her brothers aside, ripped the amulet from her neck, and threw it away. Fatima quickly rushed in calmed the girl down and persuaded her to let the amulet remain around her neck. However, the charm didn't work, and the jinn didn't leave Samira's body. She continued to stand by the gate like a crazy woman.

Then one night, when Fatima's husband, Hassan Byari, came home, Fatima told him about their daughter's brazen behaviour. She told him what she thought. "See, we can't let her go on like this. Write a letter to her husband. He can come and do whatever he likes. Today, she's only standing at the gate, what if she steps outside tomorrow? What will be our plight?"

Even for Hasan Byari, Samira had become an enigma. The girl had absolutely nothing lacking in her home. Till she got married, she had led a happy, carefree life. Then, when his sister's son Shabbir went to a foreign land and started earning well, Hasan Byari got her married to him. Shabbir came home once a year loaded with everything they asked for. Mother and daughter had been wearing only imported saris since then. You could not find a single fault in Shabbir.

When he heard about his daughter's behaviour, Hasan Byari also felt it was best to inform his son-in-law. Fraught with worry, he wrote a letter to Shabbir asking him to come and do something about Samira, if possible.

A couple of weeks after receiving the letter, Shabbir came home and the first thing he did was to go meet his wife. Immediately he knew that Samira had changed. The Samira he saw was thin and gaunt. Her pretty face with its plump rosy cheeks was pale, and her well-rounded body seemed to have shrivelled up. She wore a dirty sari, her hair was unkempt, and her eyes had no life in them.

Seeing his wife in this state wrenched Shabbir's heart. He recollected how she had welcomed him the first time he came back home after their marriage—her palms and fingers decorated with henna, her hair adorned with jasmine flowers. She had sprayed herself and everything around her with the perfume he had brought her and she smelt beautiful. Is this the same girl? "Samira, what has happened to you?" he asked, drawing her into his arms, and kissing her lips. Samira looked up at her husband silently. While her eyes were still dull and lifeless, her lips livened up slightly to welcome her husband.

"Won't you talk to me?" asked Shabbir, putting his arm around her waist and seating her beside him.

At once, tears started to flow from Samira's eyes.

"Sshhh ... don't cry," said Shabbir, holding her close and wiping her tears. Suddenly, Samira pushed his hand away, rushed to open the door and ran out of the room. She went to her brothers and started harassing them. She, for whom her husband was her very life, behaved as if he meant nothing to her.

Shabbir did not sit around worrying about his wife's condition. He quickly realized that her behaviour was not because of any spirit or shaitaan. Although he was not sure whether she was suffering from a physical or mental ailment, he was convinced that it was not some spirit or shaitaan affecting her. He talked to his father-in-law and took Samira to a doctor the very next day.

The doctor asked Samira all kinds of questions, probing into her past. Shabbir also shared details about his relationship with her.

———-—

Samira's father, Hasan Byari, was a merchant. Even if he wasn't wealthy, he earned enough to keep his family comfortable. There was never a dearth of food or new clothes for the family. Samira was his eldest daughter.

When Samira had stepped into the eleventh year of her life, she was studying in Class 6. She used to walk back from school every day with her friends. That day too, they were on their way home, chatting and laughing. So engrossed in her conversation was Samira that she was oblivious to her surroundings. Which is why she didn't notice her father and his friend approaching them, or even when they walked right past her. She came back home and got busy with the housework.

When Hasan Byari came home that the night, he called out loudly, "Fatima!" Fatima dropped whatever she was doing and ran to him. "You called?" she asked. "How old is our Samira now?" he said to her, without any context.

Fatima counted on her fingers and replied, "In the next Moharram month, she will complete eleven years," she saidlooking at her husband's face, puzzled. She couldn't understand why he was asking this question.

"So, Samira has turned eleven, grown into a big tall girl. Should it not have occurred to you not to send her to school anymore? What kind of a mother are you? Does it seem right for a grown-up Muslim girl to wander around on the streets, that too without a burkha?" Shabbir's voice rose higher with every question.

"The thought hadn't occurred to me at all till now," Fatima stammered in a low voice.

"Yes, yes, this thought will occur to you only when someone steals her away from us. But shouldn't this girl know better? In the evening, while I was walking back with that Saidu, she and her friends were so busy in their own chatter that they were completely unaware of all the men around them. As we walked past, Saidu said to me, 'The girl in the middle, isn't she your daughter? She has not started wearing a burkha yet, has she? And you are letting her roam around the streets openly like this?' I had to hang my head in shame!" Hasan's words exploded like firecrackers.

And that was the end of Samira's education. Since unmarried Muslim girls were not allowed to go out, Samira was confined to the four walls of her home from then on. In fact, there was neither the opportunity nor the time to step out. Her mother was always either pregnant or had just given birth. Consequently, the burden of the housework fell on her. Samira, though, never complained. She performed all the chores with a smile and looked after her younger siblings with affection, protecting them from their mother's wrath. She was particularly protective of her baby sister.

At fifteen, Samira was married off to Shabbir. After the wedding, Shabbir was in town for only ten days. He spent a few days in his village and a couple of days in Samira's house. The ten days went by like ten minutes. The night before he was to leave, Samira laid her head on his chest and said tearfully, "If you go away, I will be very sad. Why don't you stay here only?"

Shabbir laughed at his wife's words. "I have no choice, Samira. I must go. But just for a few more years. After that, I will come back and set up some business here. Till then, you must be patient," he said to his wife, consoling her. "But tell me, when I come next time, what shall I bring for you?"

Samira sat up, wiped her tears and thought for a moment. "Will you bring one of those clocks that play music every hour? A car for my brother, for my sister, a beautiful doll . . . ," her list kept growing.

"That means you don't want anything for yourself?" Shabbir said, cutting into her words.

"Ummm, get me *Jannat ul Firdaus*!" she exclaimed.

"What?" Shabbir laughed. "Isn't that the highest paradise, the seventh heaven? How can I buy that for you? Haven't I been showing you that paradise every day?" he asked.

Samira's face turned red. "I didn't ask for the highest paradise, I asked for the attar by the same name," she mocked him.

With a mischievous smile Shabbir went to her, and Samira melted in his rough embrace, his smiling face, his thick curly hair!

Shabbir left for Dubai the next day. In accordance with her father's wishes, Samira returned to her maternal home. But she was no longer the innocent Samira who didn't know what the purpose of her life was, or which direction it would take. She was a young sixteen-year-old married woman, and even though it was only ten days that she had spent with her husband, he had shown her what jannat ul firdaus was. As the poets describe it, he had rained a shower of honey on her, made her float on a river of milk. But now that he had gone, the pangs of separation she suffered were unbearable. During the day, housework kept her busy, but in the night, when she lay in her room alone, memories of her husband kept gnawing into her. Whenever the thought that he was so far away from her came to her, she was engulfed in a deep sadness, no matter what she was doing or where she was. At night, her pillow would be soaked with her tears. Whenever she received a letter from him, instead of making her feel better, it only increased her sense of loneliness.

She went to stay at her mother-in-law's place a few times, but because she couldn't stop thinking of her husband even there, she returned home in just a couple of days.

The agony of separation and the endless housework gradually began to reduce her tolerance. Added to that, being cloistered within the four walls of the house, with no source of entertainment or other activities to distract her, Samira started to become mentally weak. Sadly, no one in her family could understand her plight.

Once, just before Shabbir was to return to Dubai, unable to bear her grief she told him how she felt. "Samira," he said to her, "don't waste your time doing only housework. Read your brothers' books and try to understand them. Ask someone to bring you story books to read. Your town has a cinema theatre, doesn't it? Take your brothers and go watch a film once in a while. You will go mad sitting at home like this all day."

"What did you just say?" Samira said indignantly. "I going to watch a film? Even when I was ten years old, I hardly watched one or two films. I haven't stepped out of the house since then. If I go out now, my father will skin me alive. He doesn't even like me reading novels. Never say such things again in this house," she admonished him.

One and a half years passed by. This time, Shabbir came back home on one-and-a-half month's leave. His suitcase was filled with all kinds of gifts: saris, soaps, perfumes, a tape recorder, and many more things. Samira's face brightened up when she saw all the gifts. She distributed them amongst her family members. But more than the gifts he had brought, the real reason for her happiness was the fact that her husband was finally with her. She blossomed in his presence. Her nubile young body, yearning for physical proximity, became alive. Yes, he was the biggest gift Samira could have got.

Shabbir took Samira to his village for a few days. Spending time with him in his village made Samira forget everything and didn't know how the days went by. She was constantly in and out of the house, she wandered around the hillocks, in the village with Shabbir, sat by the edge of the lake in the backyard when he went for a swim, playfully splashing water on him, gorged on mangoes and jackfruit... Like a shadow, she followed her husband, not leaving him alone even for a moment! The days grew wings and flew away.

In the fresh pure air of the village, the colour returned to Samira's face, her body filled out, and she felt as if a new life was infused into her. One day, after dinner, Shabbir said to Samira, "Staying here in the village for so long is boring. Let's go to Mangaluru for a couple of days. What do you say?"

Even though Mangaluru was very close to her own village, Samira hadn't ever been there. As a school girl, her friends would often talk about their trips to the city and describe its many wonders, and Samira's mouth would water! She would wish that she too would get a chance to see the big city. But who would take her? Even her own mother hadn't been to Mangaluru.

So now when her husband suggested a trip, she felt like jumping around with happiness. "Let's also watch a film there aanh!" she said.

"Sure, we will," said the husband agreeing readily.

The next day, besides his wife, Shabbir took his mother and brothers also to Mangaluru. After booking a room in a hotel, they all rested for a while. Shabbir indulged his family with food that they had never even heard of let alone tasted before. He hired a taxi, and they drove all around the city. His money flowed like water, and he immersed his family in an ocean of delight.

When Shabbir was setting out to see a film with Samira that night, he asked his mother to join them.

"Look, Shabbir," she said, "it is an act of *haram*. Till today, I have not done anything like it. Now with one foot in the grave, I do not wish to change that. I will live the rest of my life like this only. But you all go. Once you go away, Samira will be confined to the house again. Let her enjoy her time now at least."

"Umma is still living in the eighteenth century," said Shabbir with a laugh. As he didn't want to leave her alone in the hotel, he told his brothers to stay with her and after saying bye to them he and Samira went to the cinema. A dream that she had long dreamt of was finally coming true and Samira felt as if she was floating on air with happiness. In the dark theatre, she played with her husband's hands and rested her head on his shoulder. She saw herself and Shabbir as the romantic couple on the screen, and she was ecstatic. After a most enjoyable day in Mangaluru, they returned to the village the next day. As they approached the house, they noticed someone standing in the front yard, and automatically they quickened their pace.

Khatija greeted her brother the minute she opened the bamboo gate, "Anna, have you been waiting very long?" she asked with a warm smile.

Hasan Byari's face radiated displeasure. He was tired and annoyed. He must have been waiting for them for a long time. Shabbir quickly unlocked the house and invited his father-in-law inside. Everyone entered the house.

"Where had you all gone?" Hasan Byari asked sharply.

"Shabbir took us to Mangaluru," his sister replied.

"Oh, you went to Mangaluru? And what did you go there for?"

"Shabbir's leaving for Dubai in two weeks, and he wanted to take Samira to Mangaluru. He asked all of us, too," said Khatija.

"Did you all go to the cinema also?" asked Hasan Byari, his forehead creased in a disapproving frown. Shabbir didn't reply, but lowered his head as if he had done something wrong. Once again Khatija, who was close to tears by now, answered her brother's question. "Do you think

I would do something like that? They are young, let them enjoy themselves for a day, I thought and sent them. Once Shabbir goes back to work, Samira will have to stay at home. At least when he's here, let her not feel restricted."

Barely had she finished speaking when Hasan Byari became fury personified. His body shuddered with rage. He turned on his son-in-law. "What evil times we have fallen upon, aaanh? You took the women of the house to the big city and let them wander around? Don't you have any sense? You rented a room in a hotel, gave them a taste of outside food? Do you think your wife will continue to do as you tell her after all this? No one in our family has seen a movie until now. You have shamed us, ruined our reputation by doing this. You have all become the trash of hell!"

Then, he turned to his sister. "You have become so old and yet you have not got any sense? Dancing to the tunes of these youngsters. If I knew this is how you would treat girls, I would have never given my girl to your son," he declared and like a sinking ship, he slowly slumped to the ground, his head in his hands.

"It won't happen again, Anna. From now on, I won't send her anywhere ever again," said Khatija, to pacify him.

Shabbir stood on one side, listening to his father-in-law's rant with his head bowed. His brothers quickly ran out of the house. Samira had gone into her room and was sitting there weeping softly.

Finally, Hasan called Shabbir closer. Like a cool and gentle breeze that follows a raging storm, he began to advise his son-in-law calmly. "Shabbir, listen to me. You are a man. You can do anything you want and no one will stop you. But Samira is a woman. Don't spoil her by giving her a taste of such things. What if she decides to go to the cinema on her own tomorrow? Remember, women are like chappals. Use them when you want them and leave them in a corner when you have no use for them. The right place for chappals is on your feet. Is it right to place them on your head, tell me?" said Hasan, trying to soften his rough tone.

Upon hearing his father-in-law spout these words of wisdom, Shabbir was livid. "I wasn't born of a chappal. A woman gave birth to me!" The words came to the tip of Shabbir's tongue, but he somehow swallowed them back. He knew that if he argued with his father-in-law, his mother would get upset.

Samira heard everything her father had just said and was shocked. He had actually dismissed all women as chappals! She felt extreme anger towards her father. But there was no outlet for all that rage. It just kept seething and simmering inside her and eventually escaped as mere smoke. And because she was not used to arguing with her father or back-answering him, she swallowed all her rage and remained silent.

Finally, Hasan came out with the real reason for his visit. "Samira's mother has just delivered. A stillborn child. There's no one to take care of the little ones at home. So send Samira back with me."

Samira's heart sank when she heard her father's words. She wanted to stay with her husband till he left for Dubai, but once she heard about the stillbirth and her mother's plight, she forgot everything else. If she couldn't help her mother out at this time, who else would? She had to get home as soon as possible.

"Will you go back to your village, Samira?" asked a dejected Shabbir, walking into the room.

"I wanted you to stay here with me until I left. My father-in-law is using my mother-in-law like a chappal. Every year, he gives her a child. You are there, of course, to take care of her ... Once the chappal is completely worn out, a new one can be brought, isn't it?" said Shabbir bitterly. What could Samira say!

"You go now. I will come after one or two days," said Shabbir and sent her away.

Back at her mother's place, it was the same old drudgery. Samira slaved from morning till night. Even when Shabbir came home, she didn't have any time to sit and talk to him. She used to come to their bedroom only to sleep at night, and she would be completely exhausted by then. But she didn't want her husband to worry about her, so she pretended to smile and be cheerful when she was with him. However, as the date of his departure came nearer, she started to lose her self-control. She did not take any interest in housework; she was impatient and irritable with her siblings, lashing out at them unnecessarily. The night before Shabbir left, he held Samira close and stroking her head, asked, "Samira, what shall I get for you when I come next time?" Running her fingers through his curly hair, Samira was silent for a while. Then, she said sadly, "I don't want anything."

"Don't you want Jannat ul Firdaus?" asked Shabbir with a smile.

"If you are close to me, then that itself is Jannat ul Firdaus for me. Without you, even heaven seems like hell!" After a pause, Samira pleaded, "Please, take me with you this time; otherwise, my loneliness will drive me crazy!" The smile left Shabbir's face. Grimly he recalled the way he lived in Dubai. A long hall with ten beds, one of which was his. That's all the space he owned. How could he take Samira to such a place? He could neither afford to take her with him nor he could he get a better job. Since he worked in a hotel, he didn't have to cook for himself. What he didn't spend on food, he saved. That's all. But would Samira understand all this?

"Don't you think I too want you to be by my side always? If I get a good job, I will definitely take you there. But until then, please remain patient," said Shabbir assured her, comforted her. But that night, a deep uneasiness burned in both their hearts.

After Shabbir left, Samira remained at her mother's place.

One more year passed. Her mother became pregnant again. Since there was no childbirth the previous time, she became pregnant sooner. Whenever Samira looked at her mother, she remembered what Shabbir had said about her father using her mother like a chappal.

Her mother had once looked at her sadly and said, "What I am going through should be happening to you. I should be doing your work, looking after you, not the other way around. What kind of fate is this?"

Samira became more unhappy and restless by the day. She worked tirelessly all day but got no rest even at night. She missed her husband so much that she tossed and turned sleeplessly in bed. The loneliness, the drudgery of housework, the confinement within the house, with no entertainment whatsoever—did not permit her to be the Samira of old—innocent, gentle, soft spoken ... She started changing. She would complain if her work increased. She would quarrel with her siblings for no reason. She even started arguing with her mother.

Fatima couldn't understand her daughter's behaviour. She had everything—a perfect life. Her husband was working abroad in a good job; he came home once a year and brought gifts for them all—things that they had neither seen nor heard of before. As for the saris, they were too many to count. When he was there, he would spend money like water. As for Samira, she was his very life. What more could a girl want? She didn't face harassment from her mother-in-law or sisters-in-law. She was allowed to stay on at her mother's place. She was truly fortunate. So then how did one explain her behaviour?

section break

Hasan Byari decided to go to the airport to receive Shabbir the next day. Samira asked her mother, "Umma, shall I also go to the airport?"

Hearing his daughter, Hasan Byari thundered, "What? Your daughter wants to go to the airport? In the midst of so many strange men? Has she lost all sense of shame and dignity? I had told Shabbir that day itself, once you allow your woman to go around, as you had done in Mangaluru, she will demand to do it again and again. Women should be kept at home under tight control. Today, she's asking to go to the airport. Tomorrow, she will want to go to Dubai with him, the brazen hussy!"

The thunderbolts and lightning streaks her father threw at her destroyed Samira's desire. "Why did I ever open my mouth?" she thought. Despite her mother's coaxing, Samira didn't eat anything that night and went to bed. Would she ever escape from his hell, she wondered, and spent all night crying into her pillow. Early the following day, Fatima went into labour and gave birth to a healthy child. Mother and baby were doing well. But Samira dived into the depths of despair. All her hopes were shattered. She would not be able to spend the entire month with her husband who was arriving that day. She had to stay with her mother to take care of the child. Her dream of staying with Shabbir would not be fulfilled. So busy was she with taking care of her mother and the household that she didn't have the time to even talk to Shabbir.

"Samira, come, let's go to our village," said Shabbir. But she simply pointed to her mother and kept quiet.

Not wanting to seem insensitive, Shabbir didn't ask her to accompany him again and left for his village alone. For the next month, he kept shuttling between the two villages.

It occurred to Shabbir many times that Samira wasn't herself anymore. Her tinkling laughter was gone. Every time he had come home earlier, she had coloured her hands red with henna, had strings of fragrant jasmine flowers in her hair, applied the perfume he had given her and dressed in a new sari, and had come to him eagerly, uninhibitedly. She had tried to make each night like the first night, to retain the newness of the experience every time. But now that Samira had changed completely. Her tinkling laughter was gone. The henna had faded to an ugly brown, she didn't bother to smell of perfume, and her hair was generally dishevelled. She was dull and listless.

Shabbir noticed that physically too she had changed. She had lost weight, the colour of her cheeks, the sparkle in her eyes seemed to have flown away and hidden somewhere. A blank expression had taken their place. She didn't even try to look happy for Shabbir.

"Samira, why are you like this? Aren't you happy that I am back home?" asked Shabbir, caressing her cheeks with his lips. Her lips parted into the faintest smile, "Why won't I be happy when you are here?" she countered. "Then, why are you so sad? I have brought Jannat ul Firdaus. Won't you even look at it?" he asked again.

Samira's smile disappeared. "Why should I apply Jannat ul Firdaus? Where do I have to go? Just a waste of money, that's all," she said dryily. Then, burying her face in his chest, she sobbed, "Take me with you, don't leave me alone anymore." Her fingers raked his hair, twisted his curls, and for a moment, Shabbir felt as if the old Samira was back.

But Shabbir knew it was impossible to make her wish come true. His frustration turned to an uncontrollable rage towards his father-in-law. "What kind of a man is your father?" he said. "He's still giving children to this family, punishing not only your mother, but also you and me!"

What could Samira say to this? Somehow she managed to blurt out, "For you men, women are like chappals, aren't they? You use them until they are worn out, then throw them away and get new ones."

"Samira!" screamed a shocked Shabbir. "To me, you are not a chappal. If that's what you think about me, discard that thought right away. You are the queen of my home, of my heart, do you understand?"

"Next time I am here, the two of us will spend some time in Mangaluru, all right?" said Shabbir, trying to bring some cheer into his wife.

"You come down once a year and I get to spend only one or two days with you. What's the point of living if I can't even be with you? Instead of being born as a woman, I should have been born as a rock!" said Samira with a lot of pain in her voice.

Shabbir left for Dubai the next day.

Samira changed completely after that. She refused to do any housework. She would snap at her mother, answer her questions rudely, and ignore her instructions. Only if she wanted to do something, she would do it quite cheerfully. Otherwise, she would sulk and lie in bed all day. Both

Samira's parents were not able to understand what ailed their daughter. Exasperated and helpless, they finally sent for Shabbir.

The doctor once again asked Samira probing questions about her past, but she refused to reply. Shabbir answered for her as best as he could. The doctor was quick to diagnose the problem. He had been getting a number of similar cases recently: women whose husbands were away in a foreign country while they stayed back, lonely and isolated.

Turning to Shabbir, he said, "Shabbir, in the three years of your marriage, you can count the number of days you have spent with your wife on your fingers. The rest of the days, she has had no recreation in her life. She feels alone and isolated and spends her days desperately waiting for you to come back to her. You are a man, you have the freedom to do whatever you want, you can watch films, TV, and have other forms of entertainment. Nobody can find fault with you for that. You are not imprisoned within four walls like she is. Her situation is completely different. Besides being separated from her husband, she has to work like a slave in her house. Too many restrictions are imposed on her. She has had to face all these hardships at a very young age. So her mind has rebelled against them. She has lost her mental balance. I would strongly advise you to take her with you, or if that is not possible, spend a few months with her in your village. That is the only cure for her sickness." He then added, "One more thing, next time you come, please bring a tape recorder for me."

Shabbir was shocked to hear his last statement. He looked around the room. It was strewn with all sorts of imported objects. Shaking his head, Shabbir thought, "When our lives are in such a turmoil, how can this man even make such a request!" He bit back his words, because the doctor had to make Samira well again, didn't he.

"Very well, doctor," Shabbir said, "I will definitely get you the latest model of tape recorder next time I come. But for now, I am not going anywhere. I have decided that I will stay right here, in my village itself. My wife's health is more important than my job in a foreign country, isn't it?"

Translated from Kannada by Keerti Ramachandra and Varsha Rao

15
A Day in the Labour Room

Jeelani Bano

"Next . . ."

"So, what's wrong with you?"

She looked at her husband and I realized the situation. She always authorizes someone else to speak on her behalf.

The whole day I stand in the labour room, holding a knife, that cuts a woman's flesh, a pair of scissors, which tear her veins, and drugs which make her lose her consciousness.

Dr. Reddy is there to prepare the preliminary report of a patient but more often than not he is fed up of these weeping, whining women who come here. So he chooses to ogle at me. His eyes remind me of drones, hovering around, buzzing irritatingly. Ignoring them, I turn to this patient again.

"Doctor, she is pregnant, four month's down, but she doesn't want the child," says her male companion. She does not speak a word about what she wants herself.

"How long have you been married?" I ask her opening the register but again she looks at her companion, expecting him to answer for her.

Realizing the uneasiness that has descended upon both of them, I close the register.

"It is too late so let it be."

"Yes, that's right; let it be." The woman speaks for the first time, looking happily at the man.

"No doctor, no. She is very weak so I want . . . " he stammers . . . "er . . . she wants that . . . " he is visibly upset.

Yes, she is very weak. I give another look the women.

Somehow I think of all those terms and conditions which are put down on a "Nikah Nama" to be signed while purchasing land, car, and

Jeelani Bano, *A Day in the Labour Room* In: *The Silence That Speaks.* Edited by: Haris Qadeer, Oxford University Press. © Oxford University Press India 2022. DOI: 10.1093/oso/9780190132613.003.0016 women ... for this much of dower, in the presence of so and so as witness I say "Yes" without any compulsion or duress ...

And then comes a shower of blessing and advices. "May you be blessed with wisdom to understand your duties, to be obedient to your husband ... The decision of having or not having children (or their number) will entirely be that of your husband."

"Sister, take her to the operation theatre, and you sign here, please." Dr. Reddy pushes a form towards the man.

Dr. Reddy himself is a man, so he fully appreciates the agony of a man would be going through on such occasions.

The woman is, almost forcibly, showed into the operation theatre.

When I entered the room, she was lying unconscious, in complete surrender, which is so typical of women. I see this face of women quite a few times in a single day—compulsions of foregoing the rights over her own body. People may play with it the way they want, trample upon it, cut it up into pieces, and throw it away.

After the operation, she will come back to her sense but still look groggy. She will try to comprehend the world, which has always been beyond her comprehension, anew. She will feel a kind of dullness prevailing all around as if all the hues of her multicoloured dreams have been washed away by her tears. Now she will find everything empty—right from her womb to the never ending skies. From now on, she will die every minute. She will also go through the agony of dreaming of nurturing this unborn, incomplete child into an authoritative, commanding adult.

"The man who has come with her is not her husband." The nurse commented.

Perhaps the women could not explain to the nurse the relationship that existed between her and her companion, the relationship that made the woman offer her body as well as her soul to him and yet could not be given a name. In fact, now it became something to be ashamed of; something to be broken. And that is why the woman is lying on the operation table, unconscious.

I do not say anything in answer; just keep standing with a knife in hand which slits open every view of a woman's body. Now I have to deactivate that in-built scientific laboratory of her system, which after much moulding and processing turns out a complete human being.

Once my guide in the dissection hall chided me as I ripped open all the layers of a female body and reached her brain. "What will you do with her brain? There she does not have anything which could call her own." All my classmates had burst out laughing.

"Send it to the laboratory, it is an abnormal case." I said and put the incomplete blood-soaked foetus in a tray. Dr. Reddy came forward and took it in his custody. Now it will turn into a guinea pig, subject to a variety of experiments; people belonging to different branches of science will surround it . . . opening it up one side. Joining it up on the other.

Destroy a man's reproductive powers. Look into a woman's womb first lest she should give birth to a woman like herself.

I wash my hands, which are stained with blood and ask the routine question: Who is next?

A woman comes in. A lack-lustre face, a run-down body, and bulging belly. Seeing the agony on her face, it is not difficult to discern that she is going to deliver her seventh or eighth baby in a short while.

"Write your name here." Dr. Reddy shows the register towards her husband who is healthy, tall, well-built man. Dressed in a fine well-cut safari, he seems to be holding some high office. There is another woman who has come with the couple; middle aged, sharp, and smart, talking, incessantly. In all probability, she is the man's sister. "Bhabi," she addresses her sister-in-law. "Chanting the name of Almighty God, go in. This time, He will surely grant you a son. Your house will be filled with sunshine." Then, she turns to me and says sorrowfully, "By God's grace, we have everything except a male child. My brother is really unlucky in this respect. Doctor, we have come to you with great hopes." Hearing her babbling, the patient feels dizzy and slumps on the ground.

"Come on, quick, get a stretcher and get it fast." Bending over the woman, I examine the heartbeats of both mother and child. I realize she is not in good shape and feel worried about her.

"Oh, no doctor, please save my child." The man too is looking upset.

The child is almost dead. Its waning heartbeats are an indication that it prefers not to be than be and face the wrath in its father's eyes.

The overpowering desire of a delivering a male child before she breathes her last has made the woman highly worked up. She is trying to say something. There are lots of women whose lips move but voice is not their own.

"Next," I call out warding off the buzzing droves of Reddy's eyes with both hands.

Three girls enter together. They are young teenagers hardly thirteen or fourteen years of age. They are coming straight from school, wearing same uniform, nervousness … large on their face, trying to huddle behind each other. Seeing them, Reddy's eyes find a new target.

"Dr. Reddy, will you go out of this room for a while?"

Girls of this age usually come with complaints of backache. Unfamiliar faces frighten them and make them feel ill at ease. These girls too were nudging each other instead of coming forward. Then, the youngest and rather good-looking one of them all turned her face towards the wall and started crying.

"Listen girls, you are wasting our time. Come to the point, quick." The nurse started getting impatient with her.

Sensing their discomfort, I went up to the girl who was crying.

"Is there anything wrong? How much time are you overdue?"

She gave me a nervous look, covered her face with both hands and continued crying. Her friends came to her rescue.

"Doctor, Honey did not do anything. The teacher who takes special classes in the evening … he … he … "

"Didn't you confide in your mother or complain to your father?"

With lowered head, Honey kept standing, quiet.

"The teacher says you will get a bad name if you will tell anybody about it. You will also lose the chances of getting married."

"We have come here on the sly."

"We don't have any money either, doctor."

"Come to me … " I beckoned the girl.

She did not move forward, but her friend spoke.

"Honey says that she will now die."

I looked at Honey intently. A young teenager, barely twelve years old, who knows neither a man's love nor the joys of motherhood but has come to acquaint herself with the path that leads to death.

"Honey, why do you want to die?" Before giving anesthesia, I asked her at the operation table.

"I don't want to live in this male-dominated world." Her answer was simple.

"Stupid girl." I put my hands on her head with affection.

"All men are not savages. When you grow older, you will get a man's love as well as trust."

Honey vomited on the operation table.

She was trembling with fear and hatred. I slit her open and took out the baby which hadn't even acquired a shape—the baby of an unwed mother. Now she is going to face the divine wrath as well as social stigma, not to mention the legal hassles.

Is Honey a girl of depraved character? Loose morals? Religion and society both are going to ask her questions. Lawyers, judges, and spectators will gather in and around the court to have a glimpse of the girl who is at a tender age of thirteen went all the way . . .

"What's your name?"

"Where do you live?"

I wash my hands, which are stained with Honey's blood and call out . . . Next!

A blood-soaked woman is brought on a stretcher. A flustered-looking man, an ageing mother-in-law, and an old man follow trembling with fear.

"She fell from the staircase."

"A rock fell upon her."

"No, she slipped in the bathroom while bathing."

"Is the child still alive in her womb? What could it be, a boy or a girl?" The man is asking again and again. Holding her diary a lady police inspector barged in.

"Doctor, please help her to gain consciousness. I have to record her statement."

The woman's companions want to leave the room, but the door is locked.

I put my stethoscope on the woman's chest. "Take her away for the postmortem. Why do you bring dead bodies into the labour room?" My voice is laced with irritation.

"How am I to know as to which of these woman is dead and which one is alive?" The male nurse who brings in stretcher says angrily. "Bastards! They shove them on us when they are dead." He is swearing. Outside the ward people have gathered to have a glimpse of the injured woman.

"She is dead." They look at each other, satisfied.

Her husband moves towards her, sheet in hand. After all he is the one who has to draw the curtain after the final act is played out, but he flinches and takes a few steps backwards as he finds his dead wife's eyes staring right into his face. In fact, she stares at all those who come close to her—police inspector, doctor Reddy, relatives, spectators.

"How are we going to perform an autopsy on her? There is no part in her body which is not broken." The nurse says wearily.

"Her head is spared. Perhaps doctors will open it."

"No." Dr. Reddy smiles and looks at me. "Postmortem is not done on a woman's head."

"Next… Next… "

But now the bees are all out of my body, stinging. Scissors which I use to cut a woman open fall from my hands. I feel heavily sedated. Swatting the buzzing bees with my hands, I shout…

"Next… Next… "

Translated from Urdu by Zakia Mashhadi.

16

A TV of One's Own

Salma

A colour TV set brought home by Shaukat Ali from Dubai made the entire town sit up open-mouthed in amazement. As there was no space in his tiled-roof house to fix an antenna, setting up the TV turned out to be such a bother and a headache for Shaukat Ali. He thought of approaching Habib who lived two houses away, to find out if he could fix the antenna at their terrace. Shaukat's wife Mahmooda stopped him with her perfunctory comment, "*Aiyyo*, even if that fellow agrees, his wife Farida would not agree. As such, the entire town is on a heart-burn trip ever since the TV arrived."

True, indeed. Shaukat Ali had reached the town at midnight. Had it been daytime, the entire street would have lined up to count the number of suitcases that got off-loaded at his home. Mahmooda had warned him in her letter to be wary of evil eye. She had made a phone call to instruct him to board a late night flight to "avoid the town's evil eye and prying folks" She was not wrong. He reached home an hour past midnight. As soon as his car reached his door step, neighbouring windows were lit up and piercing pairs of eyes glared at him.

The Fajr, morning prayers culminated in neighbours paying him visits. Ajarat who stayed bang opposite his house asked him, "Why have you brought *shaitan* with you?" Shaukat was not surprised in the least. He expected Ajarat to refer to TV set as devil, indeed! He nodded at him and chuckled to himself. When Saiyadamma asked her neighbour Mahbooba "did you notice how many suitcases came out of the car" and chortled, Mahmooda sensed her envy pretty well.

"Since the past four years, he has worked day and night in the searing heat, was clueless whether his wife and children were alive or dead, had forgone food and nourishment … look at these people . how jealous they are … Be damned, I say," Mahmooda was furiously cursing and

Salma, *A TV of One's Own* In: *The Silence That Speaks*. Edited by: Haris Qadeer, Oxford University Press. © Oxford University Press India 2022. DOI: 10.1093/oso/9780190132613.003.0017 muttering. Shaukat, in the meanwhile, was seated at the *thinnai*, wondering how and where to fix the antenna.

He was not deaf to his mother muttering under her breath, "Far better to bring back cash, build a house. Look at him bringing home a TV, of all things!" He thought to himself, "Haven't I brought back cash reserves? Just an old TV set in my quarters that I lugged along. So much muttering and taunting over this?" He left his place at the *thinnai* to meet Habib at the marketplace. Shaukat was inwardly feeling very proud to have bought the first TV in his town. He wished to meet Habib at the market, not at his home. At home, his wife may object to his request for space to fix the antenna at their terrace.

"Hey! You look lost in thought, what's up?" Shaukat was taken aback and looked up. It was indeed Habib, standing before him. "Long life to you Habib, you shall live a hundred years! I was on my way to meet you." He warmly hugged Habib and greeted him.

"All good, my friend? Tell me, what brings you here?" Habib enquired.

"Good enough, I dare say. You see, I have brought back a TV set from Dubai. Only if the antenna is fixed at a height, TV reception would be good. Antenna looks like three small rods sticking out. Could I get it fixed at your terrace and draw up the wires to connect my TV to receive signal?" Shaukat asked.

"Oh, is that so," he pondered over it for a while. He then continued, "Alright, go ahead. I'm not going to carry the stuff on my head, right?" A moment later, Habib lowered his voice and enquired, "Boss, hope *thunder-wunder, lightening-shitening* would not hit those three iron rods, no?" Habib's lowered voice betrayed an uneasiness, a fear that perhaps he had agreed too quickly. Would there be a fall-out? Would I be taken to task by my wife? His inner agitation was palpable to Shaukat. He could sense it pretty well.

"What, macchan? Why such fears?", Shaukat began to panic that Habib might backtrack fearing his wife's objection. "You are a well-informed guy; I didn't expect such apprehensions in you. How many homes have TVs and antennas all over the world? What a worry, indeed!" Shaukat tried to win back Habib's trust.

Habib felt cornered. He is being seen as a well-informed guy;he can't possibly refuse his plea. "Oh, that's alright. You may fix it at my terrace," he conceded. But Habib's face had lost its earlier brightness. The fact that he had concurred with Shaukat without consulting Farida and his anxiety of winning her over could not be masked. Shaukat didn't wish to get embroiled in it but went ahead with his mission.

He managed to bring the dangling wires from the back alley of the adjacent street to reach his house. He pulled the wire out of a hole from his tiled roof, brought it down from a window sill near the ceiling and attached the same to the TV he had placed at the wide courtyard.

There was just a single Hindi channel getting beamed the entire day. Even that was getting disrupted whenever strong winds blew. The signal was lost, and one could see merely black dots! Programmes on TV could only be watched intermittently—human images for five minutes alternating with black dots, the following five minutes.

Shaukat Ali got really put off as he could not follow the language! So much effort to get such poor transmission in a language incomprehensible to all at home. He regretted bringing home the TV. And all the trouble and humiliation over fixing the antenna! He vowed not to go near this TV at all. But the pride of being the sole owner of a TV set in the town remained undimmed.

This was the state of mind of Shaukat Ali. Women and children, however, took to TV watching with great enthusiasm. At the stroke of half past six, in the evening, a sizeable brood of children and women from the entire street, lay siege over his home. Whether they understood the programmes or not, whether the transmission was good or not, there was no dearth of visitors. Initially, Mahmooda was happily serving them tea and invited relatives home with great pride and extended warm hospitality. Over a period of time, Mahmooda was fed up and thought of the TV as a troublesome Saturn. She almost regretted why it was purchased. Post eight o'clock in the evening, once *Chitrahar* concluded and the crowd of spectators left home, she had to sweep and mop the house to get rid of dust and sand left behind by the neighbours. She could hardly refrain from cribbing and cursing under her breath. As far as Mahmooda was concerned, TV had turned more of a burden than a matter of pride. Shaukat would feel sorry for his wife and regret her increased workload. Zakiramma from the next street would stay back and help Mahmooda in her chores.

Mahmooda would offer 10 or 20 rupees to Zakiramma, but she refused to accept any money for the help rendered by her. She would quip, "Don't I watch TV for free? Then, why offer me money? Let it be . . . "

In their town, the cinema theatres would put up a new movie once a week. On such days, Zakiramma would be the first one to queue up to watch it—first day, first show. She was around 58 years old. She was an ardent film buff.

Her husband Sultan would lose his cool over her obsession with the cinema. He would rant, "Listen Brother, does it become a family woman, that too, a Muslim woman to go mad over cinema, cinema like this? And if it's an MGR film, she would watch it every day of the week. All my earnings from lifting of luggage are reduced to ashes by this woman." To his clamour for justice on this score, Zakiramma would stoutly assert, "Yes, what of it? I love MGR. He is my heart-throb. I would not miss a single show."

"Hey, we survive on kanji but you want rosewater to rinse your mouth?" Sultan would scream at her. Often, Mahmooda and Shaukat had to watch this spat and arbitrate as if at a panchayat. One day, Mahmooda remarked to her husband, "Have you ever watched how lovingly Zakiramma cleans up our TV? The way she dusts it repeatedly, I am afraid she would break it or cause anything untoward."

At times, Mahmooda would collect the dust from Zakiramma's footfall from the streets as she went home at night fall. She would add salt, seven red chillies, and hay from the roof top to this sand dust, make Shaukat Ali sit down near the TV and at prayer time, whiz past this mixture over his head to ritually ward off the evil-eye. Shaukat Ali would mutter to himself, "Hmm, this as well, indeed!"

If Zakiramma had watched a movie the previous day, she would regale Mahmooda with its story, plot, and screenplay in vivid detail. As she went about washing the dishes, she would analyse the film and make Mahmooda watch the movie in her mind's eye. Hardly one or two women went to the theatre in this town. Zakiramma watched all the movies screened without any discrimination. Each movie was a source of joy. In her opinion, no movie is a bad choice for viewing. All movies are good and as delectable as a *laddu*.

Once, Shaukat Ali confronted her, "This one was such a terrible movie. I had watched it too, yesterday." Zakiramma replied, "Saar, how much money they must have pumped into this movie? How much hard work they must have put in to make it? We buy a ticket for thirty-five paise and criticize the film. Is this right? Is this just? I don't label any movie as a bad movie, saar." She went about dusting the TV carefully. Shaukat chuckled to himself at her comments.

Of late, Zakiramma's eyes had a dreamy look. Mahmooda often noticed her lost in thoughts in the midst of chores. She would call out, "Which profound thought has taken over you Zakiramma?" She would resume her task with a shrug, "Oh, Nothing."

Since the past two weeks programmes in Tamil, aired by Chennai Doordarshan, began to reach this town. Zakiramma's return to her home became erratic and infrequent. These days, Zakiramma hardly slept. She began wondering if it was possible to bring the movie screenings at her door step just as at Mahmooda's home.

The TV that sits at rich folks' homes, is it not possible to bring it to my home, she began to wonder. Her pre-occupation with this line of thought began to affect her routine work.

Zakiramma's work began to centre on putting her thoughts into realization. She began to hatch numerous plans. Her eyes had lost their sparkle by her monotonous washing of dishes. They now began to appreciate the smooth, shining glass screen of the TV set. She lost count of hours and enjoyed looking wistfully at the TV screen. This slowly led to her resentment of living without a TV at home. This particular lack weighed far more heavily upon her mind than the paucity of good clothes, jewellery, a self-owned house, or the absence of children in her life. Far from being considered a luxury, TV seemed to be a necessity and one that gave her happiness. Even such a thought made her happy. It seemed that she had completely forgotten about the aged Sultan's presence in her life.

One day, Zakiramma did not turn up for work until noon. A harried Mahmooda went to her house, looking for her. She could hear Sultan's raised voice reaching her even before she reached their doorstep. Being familiar with his rant, Mahmooda took this to be another routine spat. She pushed open the metal door and its screeching noise made Sultan turn around. He welcomed her.

"Welcome. Look at this audacity. Atrocious!" Mahmooda looked in the direction of his outstretched hand. A huge TV set with a cardboard box nearby was staring at her. Sultan thundered, "Is this needed at this home? This headless wretch has bought it for four thousand rupees!" Mahmooda stared blankly without grasping what was being told. A TV for 4,000 rupees? Where did the money come from? How did Zakiramma lay hands on such a huge amount? She turned to Zakiramma with a perplexed look. Zakiramma was seated on a wall divider near the kitchen with an air of majesty and composure. It seemed that she had not heard Sultan at all.

She was eyeing the TV set with exhilaration. Perhaps she was wondering at whose terrace she might get permission to fix the antenna. Mahmooda watched her in consternation. Sultan resumed his angry outburst, "Can you guess from where she got the money? She has sold off her golden karugamani—her thali made of gold and blackbeads! When I objected she insists plain karugamani will do. Plain blackbeads for a thali would do indeed! To whom do I turn to?"

Zakiramma was unfazed by Sultan's outburst or his anger. She calmly posed a question, "Hmm, so this man would hang around my neck only in gold, not in black beads? Karugamani is not good enough for him?" Mahmooda gazed at her in astonishment—Zakiramma sat unmoved by Sultan's screams in helpless rage. Her dream had turned true. This commotion would be swept away by the breeze for all she cared. Fascinated, Mahmooda watched this spectacle silently.

Translated from Tamil by B. Mangalam

17

Registered Post

Annie Zaidi

It was 7.30 in the morning, and my alarm hadn't gone off when Suhail showed up. I was still in my nightie when the bell rang and was just looking for a dupatta to throw over my chest, but Shahryar said he'd get the door, so I settled back into bed.

A whole minute passed. The silence outside was making me nervous. Nobody who comes to our door in this town leaves without saying a word or two, even if it is just *salaam*, *ram-ram*, or I'll show you bitch just watch. Milkman, postman, courier, goons sent by the other party after I've had a good day in court, everybody has something to say. Besides, Shahryar also always says something in response. I usually wait to hear the door clicking shut before I call out to ask who it was.

I called out to Shahryar, but there was no reply. So I rolled off the bed and ran barefoot out to the front door, and there he was—Suhail. He was dragging a backpack into the drawing room while Shahryar tried to wrest it from his hands so he could carry it indoors himself. Scruffier than I thought possible, though Achhi Khala did send us a photo after his last visit home. I had thought even then that this must be the scruffiest engineer on the planet. Bearded, greying, shabby in those stained jeans and a jacket that looked like he'd picked it up cheap at some Tibetan market. Even his smile was kind of shabby.

Shahryar made the morning coffee and took the joke manfully when Suhail clapped him on the back and said that I had trained him well. Then he stepped out, mumbling about 'Sunday Special' breakfast. As the sound of the scooter faded into the morning quiet, I turned to my cousin.

"Fifteen years, huh?"

Suhail was staring into his coffee mug. I poked a finger into his side playfully but regretted it at once. I could feel his ribs through the jacket.

Annie Zaidi, *Registered Post* In: *The Silence That Speaks*. Edited by: Haris Qadeer, Oxford University Press.
 DOI: 10.1093/oso/9780190132613.003.0018

I slurped up the dregs of my coffee noisily and wondered if I shouldn't just ask him outright and be done with it.

"So? Still gifting your millions to those wretched distillers in the hills?"

He smiled. "Is that the current masala item on the Rizvi clan's gossip menu?"

"That Suhail is a drunk? Yes. From Dubai to Australia, it is known. You're internationally famous."

He looked away, took a gulp of the coffee, grimaced, then drained the cup. "Your house is a bloody sugar factory!" Then, he reached out a finger and poked my belly. "And you're the same old lazy lump of corruption."

A second's pause, then he frowned down at my belly. "You're not growing things in there, are you?"

I pinched his arm hard, like I used to when we were kids. He settled back against the sofa, ran his fingers through his hair.

"You need a haircut," I said.

"I need a lawyer," he said. And then he told me that we were going to sue the Government of India.

What had happened was this. Cousin Suhail was busy destroying the lower Himalayas with his dam-building, and his liver with the local liquor, when there arrived a package. Inside it was another envelope, old and yellowed, addressed to Suhail Rizvi, c/o Sheeba Rizvi. The sender's name was Khushbu Rawat.

It didn't take long for him to figure out what had happened. The old letter had been sent via registered post fifteen years ago. Khushbu had written to say that her family was trying to force her into a wedding, but she would slip out of her house somehow. Suhail was to wait for her behind the Shia graveyard every night of the week. There were five trains leaving Ranipur between nine and midnight. They would board one and get married at the registrar's office in Delhi. The future would take care of itself, she wrote.

And it would have, but the letter had arrived 15 years too late. Khushbu Rawat was now married to one Umesh Tiwari and was mother to two school-going boys. Meanwhile, Suhail Rizvi had wasted his youth getting drunk and working on a series of infrastructure projects in remote parts of the country, as far away from home and his memories as he could get.

I had heard that Khushbu had tried to run away before her wedding, but her family had caught her and dragged her back. Half of Ranipur knew this. She was not allowed to use the phone or meet her friends, and when Suhail failed to show up, she had had no option but to go through with the wedding. It had cost the family twice as much, getting her married off, and they had to find an orphan from another caste, but it was a higher caste and things evened out that way.

I also knew that Khushbu had no desire to dredge up the past. Two years ago, I spotted her at the Saturday haat. I almost didn't recognize her—saree-worn *seedha palla* style, head covered, big red bindi, gold jewellery, haggling over the price of *tindas*. When I called out her name, she did not answer. I had run after her and tapped her on the shoulder. She finally turned, and I could see that she recognized me, but when she spoke, it was like she was crunching ice between her teeth.

"My name is Sunita Tiwari," she said. "You must have mistaken me for someone else."

I tried to dissuade Suhail. It was too late now; Khushbu had moved on. But he kept shaking his head, saying "That's not the point. That's not it at all."

"It" was that blasted letter. Now that it had arrived, it was driving him crazy. He had spent the last fifteen years thinking that Khushbu had betrayed him by marrying someone else, that she had quailed at the first sign of conflict, and that she did not fight for their love. Now he knew that she too thought the same—that Suhail had betrayed her and that he did not want to fight her family.

"The last time you were in Ranipur," I reminded him, "the Rawats thrashed you senseless and left you to die in the *nullah*."

Suhail shrugged.

"They'd do it again," I said. "Things aren't better around here."

Suhail shrugged again. By now Shahryar had returned with jalebis, masala milk, and kachoris from Chunnu Halwai's. I told him to drive some sense into our idiot cousin, but I should have known better.

"Lucky I had your forwarding address," Shahryar said. "When the letter was delivered, I didn't even see who it was from. I just sent it off to you. It reached you! Imagine! Isn't that a miracle? I mean, given your gypsy ways. Nobody knows how to reach you. But what is intended … " Shahryar was careful not to look at me as he said, "Perhaps this is what Maula intended."

I wanted to find the nearest door and bang my head against it. But I picked up a kachori instead and bit in.

"Just what I needed early in the morning on a Sunday. One drunk atheist and one impractical Sufi. Why don't you unroll the *janamaaz* and ask Maula what he wants, since you appear to have a direct line to him?"

Shahryar was unfazed. "Maula doesn't speak directly. He has angels to do His work."

I harrumphed. It's a standing joke between us—whenever I take on a case that I'm sure to lose and the client cannot afford to pay my fees, Shahryar touches my feet and calls me an angel.

"I won't do it," I said. "The court will throw it out in a minute. There is no case."

"Listen," he pressed on. "I took a *chakkar* of the post office. The new clerk, his name is Girish; he told me that he found this letter at the bottom of a drawer. It was inside the desk occupied by his predecessor."

"So?"

"Can you guess who this predecessor might be?"

I closed my eyes and thought of the Ranipur post office. Most of us had been going to the post office since we learnt to walk. We knew the names of most of the clerks and postmen. I remembered one particular desk, one particularly scowly face.

"No!"

"Yes. Banwarilal Rawat. Uncle of Khushbu Rawat. He retired last month. Forgot to clear out his desk properly."

So that was how I ended up arguing *Suhail Rizvi vs India Post*. Usually, the postal department is protected from litigation in the event of a delay or a loss of posted material, but if you can prove that a letter or parcel was held back on purpose, you can claim damages.

I did warn Suhail that we would most likely lose. Suing government departments is not for two-bit mofussil advocates like me. Land disputes and petty theft is what I do. Besides, he would never get a hundred crores. Indian courts do not award such sums even in cases of murder or industrial accidents, or medical negligence. It's unheard of. But Suhail would not be discouraged.

"Win or lose, I'm going to make you a rich woman," he said. "You won't need to stand outside the courthouse any more, pimping yourself."

I smacked him on the face then, and told him that if he tried to throw money at me, I'd throw him out of my house. As it is, he had quit his job. I would have to feed him until … Only Maula knew how long this would drag on. But I wasn't doing it for money. I was doing it for family. And pride. And even for my nation.

While I prepared my lawsuit, Suhail paced. My husband begged him to have mercy upon our carpet. It was the only expensive item from my dowry. Secretly though, we were both relieved. At least he wasn't drinking. When he didn't pace, he slept. Sometimes I caught him staring hard at the phone. But I had strictly warned him not to try anything funny. I wanted to petition on behalf of an upright, aggrieved citizen, not a stalker harassing a married mother-of-two.

On a foggy Friday morning, Suhail and I took a cycle-rickshaw to the court. We sat in my chamber, drinking cups of tea. The stench of urine hung heavy in the winter air. We hardly spoke and when we did, it was gossip about the extended Rizvi clan. The judge wouldn't arrive for another hour.

My neighbours Mishra-ji and Pande-ji were standing at their usual spot near the main gate. The chamber they shared was the one nearest to the toilet, and they couldn't bear to sit there for more than five minutes. Besides, they needed to accost hapless folk at the gates, those who had been summoned to the court and had no lawyer yet. "Foremost in the service of the poor" was their motto, they liked to say, and they hated my beef-eating guts because poor clients sometimes came asking for me by name.

Mishra-ji and Pande-ji had glanced at us that day, fake morning smiles smeared on their paan-stained mouths. They didn't come to my chamber to talk; they wouldn't have been curious about Suhail. He looked too scruffy to be worth much as a client. I wondered what they would say once they knew of our suit. "Cheap publicity stunt." That I was expecting. There was the religion angle to worry about. Ranipur is not the kind of place where you take it lightly. There are more takers for religion than for law and order, or human rights. We expected death threats. Witnesses could turn hostile.

I had managed to put the fear of the law into Manoj, the postman who had delivered the letter at my address, and Girish, the clerk who found the letter. They tried to say they didn't know anything about anything, but I said that we had secretly recorded the conversation, and they would be jailed for perjury if they lied in court. Besides, they only had to accuse Rawat, not India Post. They ought to be proud. The state would be proud of them, I said. I was lying through my teeth. The state would probably punish them. The Rawats certainly would.

That morning, my hands were shaking. Suhail clasped my hands between his own and smiled his old smile—the smile of understanding and humility and protection and a hundred other good things. When you saw that smile, you knew why a girl had been willing to fight family, caste, religion, Ranipur, all of India. That smile beckons to the truest part of you. It refuses to see how weak you are, how narrow your interests.

I pulled his beard and tossed back my head. "You have get presentable. Now just pray that the judge doesn't throw us out with a fine for wasting his time."

Then, I filed the case, and in the following weeks, all this happened:

- Judge Sharad Tripathi called me to ask: "What's this drama?"
- Mishra-ji and Pande-ji spread rumours that my brother was back in town to take revenge by sullying the Rawat clan's honour.
- Five local reporters called on my mobile phone, then on the landline at home. When I refused to talk to them, they parked themselves outside my house.
- The clerk leaked our petition to a reporter. The details of the case were on the front page of *Savera*, and every time we had a court hearing afterwards.
- Advocate Khan came down from Allahabad to represent India Post. He mentioned vexatious intent, frivolous waste of nation's time, etcetera. I smacked him down with Section 6, Indian Post Office Act 1898.
- I put Mohan and Girish on the stand.
- Banwarilal Rawat had been coached by Khan, but he was still a blubbering mess when he took the stand. I practically ate him for breakfast.
- Khushbu's father, Maninder Rawat, was in the courtroom, sitting right at the back. He looked like he wanted to murder me.
- Judge Tripathi admitted the petition.

- Shahryar bought *balushahi* from Chunnu's to celebrate. While we were eating it, somebody threw stones at our house and four windows shattered. Suhail and Shahryar kept vigil all night. At dawn, a rock came through my bedroom window. A piece of paper was crumpled around the stone. It said: "Muslim whore."
- Shahryar went to the police station. The inspector kept him there for three hours, asking questions like why did he marry a cousin, because didn't that make him a sisterfucker?
- A local TV crew took up residence outside our house. I refused an interview. I tripped over a tripod. They ran footage of me falling flat on my face.
- A women's group came into my chamber to "request" me rather "strongly" that I withdraw the case in solidarity with my "Indian sisters."

Then, there was a lull. Judge Tripathi had asked me to justify the lawsuit. I sought compensation for mental torture and loss of happiness. By preventing my client from marrying his beloved, Banwarilal Rawat had cheated him of hope, peace, and fulfilment. So the usual questions arose: Who can guarantee hope or happiness? How much happiness? Each minute of each day? Would every single night bring pleasure? Should the law care?

I argued that the law seems to care in cases of divorce. Wives are awarded alimony even if the husband did not prevent the wife from pursuing a career. Even if he did not want a child, he must pay for child support. The law assumes that people have a right to compensation when a marriage breaks down because we do invest in each other's lives and happiness. Marriage is a contract with serious human consequences. Therefore, a fraud that results in the absence of a good marriage is a serious crime.

I summoned some of Suhail and Khushbu's college friends to tell their story—hundreds of happy, fearless days; their trust that their families would come around; Khushbu's desperate letters, begging to be rescued from her family; the hurried wedding. Without any prompting on my part, a witness told the court: "If these two people could not find happiness with each other, then there is no hope for happiness and peace in the world." I was licking my lips with satisfaction.

Advocate Khan began to say that even if all this was true, the fault lay with social norms. "Our own cultural values have prompted clerk Rawat to act as, allegedly, he may—or may not—have acted. Why should the innocent taxpayers pay for this?"

"If society causes damage to the individual, then society must pay the price," I retorted.

Khan argued that this love–happiness argument was a tacky fantasy, a bad joke. I retorted that only those who experience marriage as a bad joke could make such an argument.

And so it went on until, finally, I put Suhail on the stand. He had shaved that day and was almost good looking again. I kept looking around the room, worried that somebody would throw a knife, or fire a gun. Ranipur is not the kind of place where a man can say he loves a woman, not if she's from another community. Definitely not if she's married.

The police had relented and given us protection but so far, the constable who was on duty at our house had done little except eat plentifully, doze, and read aloud the letters that had begun to pour in. Yellow postcards, blue inlands, gauze-wrapped parcels, registered letters—India Post was doing a fine job these days. It was from one of these letters that I got my next big argument.

One M. Kanji, a retired forest officer, had written about his own experience of love and parental control. While he was still in service, he had adopted an orphaned female baboon; he called her Meenakshi. He had held her in his lap when she was a baby, fed her with a tiny milk bottle. He let her sleep in a cradle next to his bed. He had trained her well. She wore frilly frocks, sat at the dining table, and used cutlery to eat like a little lady. She could hold a pencil to "write." She could even brush her own teeth. In short, she was the pride and joy of his old heart.

One day, a male langur got into the house, and though he bared his teeth and broke some glassware, young Meenakshi appeared to be more smitten than scared. Old Kanji did his best to beat off the animal, first using a stick and then firing an air gun. But, although he ran off that day, again and again, the langur returned. And each time, Meenakshi seemed pleased to see him.

How could Meenakshi bear this ugly stranger? Kanji simply didn't understand the attraction: he wasn't even a baboon but a langur! What was his little flower thinking? Besides, she'd never survive in the wild.

Where was the toilet? What about toothpaste? His baby did not even eat bananas without peeling them first like a lady. How could he hand her over to this feral animal?

Kanji swore that he would not let Meenakshi run wild. He would find her a suitable mate when the time was right. She was only a teenager (in baboon years) and didn't yet know what was best for her. He locked her up in the house.

Soon Meenakshi stopped eating. The lack of sunshine and trees to climb was making her ill. The vet advised that she needed to be out in the open air, so Kanji put her in a cage and suspended it from an old banyan in his backyard. At night, he would drag out a cot and a blanket for himself and he began to sleep outdoors, next to her cage.

The langur returned, of course. Kanji began to fire the air gun at him. But the animal was no longer frightened. Even if he was injured, this sturdy male hung around. He began to bring other langur friends to visit. They offered fruit, even sweets, which they must have stolen from the tiny hilltop temple inside the forest. Meenakshi accepted the gifts rather sweetly, and she sulked when Kanji took them away from her.

Then, Meenakshi went on hunger strike again. When her boyfriend came to visit her, she would just lie in a corner of the cage. The langur would go mad with anger. He'd rattle the cage with all his strength and then he'd make piteous crying noises.

Finally, Kanji opened the cage door and went inside the house. As he lay in his bedroom, he heard the langur arrive. He heard the swinging of the cage and a soft thud. He heard a scratching at his window, but he did not raise his head to look. The next morning, he went out. The cage was empty. Meenakshi had made her choice.

I immediately wrote to Kanji to come and tell the story in Ranipur. On the back of it, I could argue that even monkeys know one simple truth—no happiness is possible outside of love. This led to the following events:

- Kanji became a national celebrity for a week.
- Someone filed a counter-case in Allahabad, accusing me of insulting all Rawats by comparing them to baboons.
- An editor in Allahabad wrote an editorial in which he called *me* a baboon.

- There were cartoons in the papers about a monster chimp called Suhail who liked to abduct human girls.
- We got letters saying that my family was probably full of uncivilized animals, but what else could be expected from the descendants of Taimur and Ghazni?
- Shahryar went into a frenzy of writing letters to newspaper editors about the history of Islam in the subcontinent. Only one was published.
- Our constable got hurt on protection duty. The windshield of our car was shattered by a stone and he had to get three stitches.
- Judge Tripathi decided that the question could not be settled without hearing from the other side. Khushbu Rawat would have to testify.
- Khushbu Rawat's dough-faced mother came to my house and begged me to think about the reputation of my "sister." She said I was her "daughter."

The date for the hearing was three weeks later. It was supposed to give us time to summon the witness, but all the lawyers knew that this was actually because Tripathi-ji had already booked a family holiday to Nainital. Also, all the lawyers knew that Khushbu could simply "fail" to receive the summons. Since this was a civil case, it would be very hard to make her to appear in court against her will. Without her testimony, we could not prove that she had ever been in love with the petitioner.

For three weeks, Ranipur held its breath. Everybody had an opinion and expressed it at every opportunity. For instance,

- The cycle-rickshaw puller who often takes me to the courthouse gave me a long lecture on being content with one's lot in life.
- Chunnu Halwai delivered a soliloquy on misery within the institution of marriage while we waited for him to wrap up our *pyaaz ki kachoris*.
- My neighbour dropped off a pamphlet about the Radhasoami sect. She advised Suhail to immerse himself in devotional love in order to attain true bliss.
- A group of undergraduate students from Ranipur City College got into a heated debate about love and parental control. The owner of

the college canteen threatened to complain to their parents. They beat him up. He went to the police.

- The newspapers ran opinion polls about "happiness in marriage."
- A talk show on TV invited psychologists to explain the source of happiness and the difficulty of monetizing it.
- A twice-widowed woman called Naushi sent a marriage proposal to Suhail via an open letter in the newspaper.
- Sukhdev Baba came to town for a *satsang*. He delivered a sermon about love and marriage being two separate concepts. He said we must love everyone equally.
- Advocate Khan gave an interview saying that lawyers like me ought to be fined heavily for wasting the nation's time and resources.
- Suhail got ambushed when he was out for a walk. His face was rubbed with cow dung and he was garlanded with old shoes.
- Achhi Khala came to visit and begged us to withdraw the case. When Suhail refused, she bawled and beat her own head with a shoe.
- Umesh Tiwari, Khushbu's husband, was hospitalized after a minor stroke.

What were the chances that we could drag Khushbu to court now? I should not say "drag" though, because the truth is, she had already come to court once. She probably wanted to catch a glimpse of Suhail. She would have understood by now that there had been no betrayal, except the one by her own family. She must have heard that Suhail was still crazy about her.

It was in the early days, before Suhail's face was known to many people. The courthouse was littered with journalists, lawyers, and curious good-for-nothings, so it was easy for her to melt into the crowd. A burqa-clad figure entered after the hearing started and sat at the back of the room. Suhail says that his heart started hammering for no apparent reason and the back of his neck prickled. He looked over his shoulder and saw the veiled figure. Then, he went round to the back and sat down next to her. When she stood up and left the room, he followed.

On a deserted staircase, she drew back the veil and slapped him on the face. She said that he was destroying her peace of mind. She said that Khushbu Rawat didn't exist. She was now Sunita Tiwari, and he could never have her.

I had few hopes that she would take the stand. In two days, the family would disappear into some discreet corner of the country and wait for the noise to die down. Even if she did accept the summons and show up in court, she would say that she was happily married, that her family had been right to do as they did. But this did not happen.

On the day of the hearing, Advocate Khan informed the court that Ms. Rawat was not in Ranipur, but her father was present and he had a letter from her. But even while he was speaking, a woman wearing a burqa stood up. She walked to the front and quietly took her place in the witness stand.

I was giggling hysterically, partly out of sheer relief, and partly because of Khan's reaction. The crowd understood—it was "her." A susurration went down the rows. Khan went on babbling his lies. By the time he understood what was happening, the whole room was laughing. Someone tried to take a photograph on his phone. Judge Tripathi exploded. He banged his gavel and ordered the police to throw out everyone who was carrying a cell phone.

Then, I questioned Khushbu, and she told the truth. Khan cross-examined. He asked if she could have been happy in a marriage that her family strongly disapproved of. She said, yes.

He asked, "But are you not happy now?"

There was pin-drop silence in the room. Khan repeated the question. After a long pause, Khushbu answered. "In our society, we choose duty over happiness. In fact, we do not choose. It is taken for granted that everyone else's choice will be our choice. In other words, there is no choice. It is my duty to make others happy."

So, we won the day. But winning the day is not the same as winning a case. I still had to prove to the court that my client was justified in suing India Post for loss of happiness. And what price, happiness?

My client, meanwhile, seemed to have lost interest in his own case. Khushbu had vindicated him. Her family left Ranipur immediately after the hearing. Now Suhail went about looking like a deflated balloon. If I woke up in the middle of the night and peeped into the guest room, I'd find him sitting up, staring out of the window. He smoked endlessly. He no longer paced. My cook threatened to quit, saying that she could not bear to look at his sad face.

Shahryar suggested that we withdraw the case, or settle for nominal compensation, but I flew into a rage. To go through all this, only to withdraw when I was so close to winning? Oh no! I was going to fight this to the end. The fight, however, was going the other way now.

One day, Khan turned to face the crowd assembled in the courtroom. He asked for a show of hands: "Who can claim to be happily married? Who is hundred percent happy?"

No hands were raised. Not one. How could I prove that Suhail was not like other men? I did argue that some people kill themselves rather than live without love. Judge Tripathi was willing to accept my argument but, in a bizarre twist of logic, he decided to look at legal precedent for compensation paid to families for dead sons—young, educated sons who were expected to support the family.

I argued that you cannot reduce a person's life to the size of the pay cheque he might bring home. But Judge Tripathi pointed his gavel at me and said, "Enough! Your client has asked for money. So the court will naturally measure out his life in money."

What the court awarded us was rupees 6,12,500, plus legal expenses. An economist, a social scientist, and a psychiatrist from Delhi were consulted. They made calculations based on how much a male engineer's income was likely to be affected if he was not married or not particularly motivated over fifteen years. They referred to some foreign research paper about emotional security. They worked out a percentage increase in income as a result of emotional well-being and then they added medication costs in case of depression, and deducted from the whole amount a percentage loss that may have occurred due to marital discord. It amounted to a loss of rupees 6,12,500, apparently.

It was small change for the postal service. They could have sneezed it out without a sniffle of regret if they chose to pay rather than appeal. Even Rawat, the retired clerk, could pay off this sum, and he wouldn't even need to sell off one of his ancestral fields. Nobody was really put out, in short, except me. My shattered windows, my damaged car, so many nights spent worrying about our safety. What was the bloody point?

I sulked for days and threatened to go up to the High Court. My husband knows these black moods of mine. Whenever I lose a case, I'm like this. He makes sure there is a box of *barfi* from Chunnu's in the fridge, and he stays out of my way as much as he can.

As for Suhail, one freezing night, he went out for a walk and did not return for over two hours. Shahryar and I took the car out. The windshield was still missing. In the blinding fog, we drove around, stopping to peer into ditches and garbage dumps. When we found him, he was sitting outside the boundary wall of the Shia graveyard, holding a bottle wrapped in brown paper. He hadn't started drinking yet. He was just sitting there.

He saw us, put down the bottle, stood up, and quietly got into the car. The next morning, he told us he had found a job. In Africa.

"Don't be an idiot," I said. "Who goes to Africa? Go to Dubai. There's so much construction work there. What's wrong with Dubai?"

He shook his stubborn head. I knew from the look on his face that it was no use trying to dissuade him, but I persisted.

"Africa is so far. And it's such a poor country."

"It's a continent," he said.

I rolled my eyes, and we argued for the rest of the day, but it was only for the sake of having something to do. Shahryar and I decided to drive down to Delhi with him. We didn't want him to take the train alone. Besides, we too needed to get away.

We went to Suhail's mother's house, and she did her own share of weeping. She made her son promise that he would not marry a black woman in Africa. A week later, she softened. He could marry a black woman if she was a Muslim. The week after that, she bent further. She said he could marry any kind of woman if it made him happy.

Suhail refused to say a single word on the subject of women. Achhi Khala sighed and called upon Maula for help. She wanted to live long enough to see grandchildren. But once the subject turned to children, her attention was deflected towards me. I had been expecting that to happen, so I gritted my teeth and kept a polite smile on my face for the rest of our stay.

At the airport, we asked Suhail to call us, keep us posted, and to take care of himself. He nodded. But we knew he wouldn't. Afterwards, I asked my husband if we'd ever see Suhail again. I had only meant that he might not want to return to India, but Shahryar scolded me for having such thoughts, and then he burst into tears. What do you do with these Rizvi men?

Nearly a month passed before we returned to Ranipur. I unlocked the front door, and there it was—a letter on the floor. My husband picked it up. It was addressed to Suhail Rizvi, c/o Sheeba Rizvi, and at the back of the envelope, the initials 'K.R.' Shahryar waited just long enough to dump our bags inside the house, grab the letter from my hand, and then he was off again.

"What?" I called out. "Where are you going?"

He didn't answer, but I knew. He was going to the post office.

18

Rehmat's Red Calf Has Gone Missing

Eli Ahmed

"Rehmat's red calf has gone missing." It has been quite some days since the red calf last returned to the cowshed. Rehmat's wife Amina is feeling anxious at its absence. With every evening, her mind starts becoming restless. She stands near the bamboo post at the entrance of the house and casts a long look on both sides of the road. Then, she dejectedly returns to the house and sits silently by the feet of Rehmat who is lying on the bed, down with fever.

"What happened, haven't the cows and the goats returned to the shed?" Rehmat's question shakes Amina up, "Yes, they have returned."

"And the calf?" Rehmat asks her back!

"What does one say? It has become quite mischievous these days. It's too young, you know!" Unable to lie to her husband, Amina manages to somehow turn around the conversation.

Amina knows the fact that Rehmat's life is dependent upon the well-being of his cows and goats. He spends a lot of time in the evening affectionately caressing them as they return safely to their sheds. He makes sure to clear their habitation from insects and mosquitoes, yet he never ties them up with ropes. He has made small bamboo enclosures for the newborn calves besides the milch cows in such a way that the mothers can lick and tend to their babies whenever they want to. To ensure that the calves do not suck out all the milk from the cow's udders at night, Rehmat has strategically placed the mother and her calves at a distance of a small enclosure, separating them from one another.

It is Rehmat's job to mop and clean the cows' shed and the goats' stilt shed every morning, and disinfect them with phenyl, Dettol or any other disinfectant. During midday, children from the neighbourhood flock to the very shed and play games such as "bride-and-groom" and "marbles."

Eli Ahmed, *Rehmat's Red Calf Has Gone Missing* In: *The Silence That Speaks*. Edited by: Haris Qadeer, Oxford University Press. © Oxford University Press India 2022. DOI: 10.1093/oso/9780190132613.003.0019

Rearing cows is a passion that Rehmat has cultivated since childhood. Even though Rehmat's father, Azimuddin, had migrated to this village when the former was still a child, the father could not dissociate himself from the memories of his earlier habitation. Bakultol, the village across the river, was the birthplace of Rehmat's father. Close to their home in the village was the house of uncle Krishnahari Choudhury's, which was, for Rehmat's father Azimuddin, more like his own house. Separating the two houses by a few feet was a common vegetable garden, jointly cultivated by the members of the two families. During their childhood days, Rehmat and Krishnahari Choudhury's cousin, Bogitora, used to play hide-and-seek in the small vegetable garden, and it was through fun and frolic that both of them advanced towards adulthood. However, one day, snapping all ties of emotional bonding and togetherness, Azimuddin had to leave his ancestral village and settle down in a new locality across the river. This is a tale of woe and misfortune. Rahimuddin, Azimuddin's brother, was a notorious character. The two brothers were engaged in a long feud over the ownership of their parental property, and in the end, Rahimuddin, with some legal help, seized all the property to his name.

Following the court's verdict, grief-stricken Azimuddin left his place the very next day and settled down upon a new patch of land on the other side of the river. It was a pitiful sight: along with humans, cows and goats as well as ducks and roosters had to be carried across the dry riverbed. It was soon after that, Rehmat's father gradually began to break down in spirit as his physical stamina too began to degenerate. Even during such difficult circumstances, all the members of Krishnahari Choudhury's family continued their cordial relationship with Rehmat's family. A sisterly bond existed between Azimuddin's wife, i.e. Rehmat's mother, and Jetuki, Bogitora's mother. It was in the midst of such associations that a relationship of incorporeal love bloomed between Rehmat and Bogitora. It was as if passing a single day without meeting, seeing, or speaking to one another was unimaginable for them. During *Bihu*, an exuberant Bogitora would embroider her favourite floral designs on the first *bihuwaan* from her loom as a gift for Rehmat. On every such *Bihu* or *Sankranti* festival, wedding parties or rituals, a young Rehmat and a graceful Bogitora would invariably present themselves as a couple. Unbeknownst to them, they became a part of each other's minds and thoughts. Gradually, they also developed physical intimacy. These developments had not escaped the silent attention of Krishnahari Choudhury and Jetuki, and one day, they summoned Bogitora to a corner at the backyard-garden of the house, and attempted to explain the matter to her. Jetuki told Bogitora: "Can't you consider Rehmat as your brother? Why have you two gone so ahead in something that's frowned upon in society? This would invite trouble for Rehmat. You know how people react to such things; once they are incited to anger, it would be difficult for Rehmat to escape. Don't you wish for his well-being?" Bogitora wept bitterly upon hearing this. Despite Rehmat's repeated questionings, she declined to reveal the matter to him. Not that she didn't wish to tell, but simply couldn't bring herself to speak the truth. It was only her mother who revealed the matter to Rehmat:

"O Rehmat, a lot of people have been gossiping about it. Now it is up to you two to protect each other. I don't wish to see you go away. Our families are but two parts of a whole. However, it would not be possible to bring you close to us in this manner." That day itself, Rehmat moved away from Bogitora without a word of parting, and within a few days thereafter, his father passed away. Krishnahari Choudhury's family stood by Rehmat's family during these times of grief and loss. Bogitora too was grief-striken and heartbroken. Soon afterwards, Rehmat got weighed down by the pressures of maintaining his family in his father's absence. Following his father Azimuddin's demise, his mother suffered too was plagued by high blood pressure leading to paralysis on one side of her body. Rehmat, her only son, had a lot of things to look after now. Not only the livestock and the fields, but also his father's business. He also needed a lot of money of his mother's treatment. Jetuki from Krishnahari Choudhury's family visited them on various occasions, and, on each occasion, she used to put some money under Rehmat's mother's pillow. Bogitora too came and attended to Rehmat's mother. The society around them was appreciative of the bonhomie between the two families. However, there was an inkling of some doubt, some lingering premonition of a sacrilege or violation on the part of the already estranged couple—Rehmat and Bogitora.

Bogitora started having misgivings about even addressing Rehmat whenever she visited his place. Rehmat too began feeling too deep a pain in his heart to ask if she's going to come over the next day.

The village elders tried to reason with Rehmat—"In these times of your mother's illness, it is fitting that you get married and bring home a daughter-in-law. Your paralytic mother needs a female companion to tend to her health day and night; someone to attend to her daily necessities. It is inevitable that you would marry one day; it is better to do so a day or two earlier so that it would be a matter of a divine reward for you, son, to bid an appropriate farewell to your ailing mother on her journey to the other world while she receives the deserved service from her daughter-in-law. Mother's blessing is a great boon, son!"

Rehmat didn't say anything. The face of Bogitora flashed before his eyes. It was as if the social system had cruelly struck the lawgiver's hammer upon his head. He looked at his mother as if he woke up suddenly from a deep slumber. She started speaking in an indistinct voice: "Nazimuddin Sa'ab from the other side of our village wants to give his daughter, Amina's hand in marriage to you, son. Please do not refuse!"

It was after six months on that day his mother had spoken when she so painfully conveyed this to him. She took a lot of time to finish her sentence. Trying hard to understand what his mother was intending to convey, with so much trouble, through her facial expressions, he soon closed his eyes, and putting her hand upon his head, he eventually acceded to her request.

Next day, when Bogitora visited them, Rehmat took her to his mother. Putting her shaky hand upon her head, his mother told her—"Don't stop coming to our house, keep visiting us often. I just wanted to liberate myself from my social obligations with Rehmat's marriage. I am suffering terribly, my dear! I seek liberation. You too should help me to attain it." Bogitora swallowed a deep sigh inside her, and carrying a heavy burden in her heart, proceeded to her home. She felt the affliction weigh heavier with every passing day. Sighs after sighs remained unvented and were accumulated inside her heart—they soon threatened to burst out in agony. She stopped going out of her house. Her parents could understand the pain inside her heart. Both of them hastened to find a match for her wedding as soon as possible. However, amidst all, her father suddenly succumbed to high blood pressure and passed away. The house of Bogitora and her mother went silent. Unable to attend to the cattle at home, one by one, all of them were sold off. Time passed. Soon Rehmat's mother too went weak in her vision. The incoming days were full of woe and troubles. Bogitora was gradually moving past her youthful grace. One day, as her mother was stepping out of the frontyard of the house in twilight, she accidentally slipped and succumbed fatally to injuries sustained during the fall.

The river was gradually extending its breadth owing to constant erosion of land on either side. The heart of the river too gradually became shallow. However, within the expanding boundaries of the house, confined to one of the many rooms is Bogitora who has become a granny now. It is in that room that she cooks for herself and eats all alone. In the frontyard of the house, a few dogs lie about lazily scratching themselves. For Bogitora, whenever she remembers those days of the past, she feels as if she were living in a dream. However, just like dreams, she is fast losing memory of the bygone days. Forgotten those days of love spent with Rehmat, those ambrosial conversations of affection and intimacy and so much more! Now granny Bogitora cannot discern the boundaries of land across the ever-widening body of the river. Having married Amina under the obligation of his mother's last wishes, it seems as if Rehmat has forgotten to inquire about the well-being of Bogitora through all these years. His family, however, has expanded. With the arrival of goddess Lakshmi in the form of Amina to his house, there was prosperity everywhere, be it the fields or the cows and goats at home. Keeping a constant count of the number of cows and goats all these years while maintaining a happy and contented household, Amina herself has become an aged woman now. The cows have given birth to calves in the house; not one has strayed far from the house. The absence of the red calf for the past few days has therefore caused great grief to Amina. And while she is grieving the loss of the calf, Rehmat speaks to her in the midst of high fever:

"Cows and goats leaving the house is considered inauspicious. These are ominous signs! I may not recover from this illness. Where and why has the red calf gone away forsaking me in this manner? It must have taken some offence against me. How could I have looked after them with this ill health of mine?" Hearing this, Amina feels terribly bad. She asks her neighbour Bhadoram to stay beside Rehmat, and sets out on the road early morning in search of the red calf. Rehmat's words make her feel even more emotional. Lost in thought, she crosses the entrance of the house and steps on the road. She meets Jaymati, wife of Harekrishna, a friend of Rehmat, whom she informs about the loss of the calf. Jaymati admits to have seen the calf making its way across the village, and joins Amina as both of them follow the road ahead. Jaymati further tells her that once when she was crossing the river to visit her aunt's place on its other side, she saw the calf drinking water from this side of the river. On their way across the dry bed of the river, passing by small rivulets, Amina and Jaymati spot the red calf of Rehmat, sleeping peacefully in the frontyard of a dilapidated house. It does not take long for Amina to identify the home-born, familiar calf. She hurriedly wakes it up and tries to look for the white birthmark upon its abdomen in order to convince herself of its true identity when Bogitora, a time-worn old woman ravaged by woe and grief, appears at the door and says:

"It has been for a few days that it became my companion; I am otherwise very lonely, my dear! I too once had a herd of cows. I have none today. I don't know how it came here and started staying with me. I am very happy to feed and look after its well-being. Even animals are great companions to human beings. At least I am feeling a lot better these days. However, who are you?"

"We are inhabitants of the other village. This calf had gone missing for a number of days. It belongs to Rehmat, and this is Rehmat's wife Amina."

Bogitora stands still for a moment. The red calf yawns and stands on its feet and slowly makes its way towards the river. Bogitora sits down and gently runs her hand across the spot upon which the calf was sleeping; she closes her eyes feeling a warm sensation emanating from deep down the ground.

First published as *Rehmat'or Ronga Domorato Heral*. Translated from Assamese by Dhurjjati Sarma.

19
Azrael

BM Zuhara

I heard the hospital clock striking. I did not wish to count it. Two, three, or four ... I have spent many sleepless nights since the day I came here. The nurse hands me a small white medicine and some water to gulp it down with, after taking which I doze off to horrifying dreams. Most of the night then is spent foreseeing my own death wherein Azrael, the Angel of death, arrives to take my soul. I run to save my life. When he grips me tight, I slip away with excuses. I saw him even a moment ago. He left with a warning that I shall not be spared anymore. I heard the door creaking. It could be Him. I shut my eyes tightly.

The sound of footsteps forces me to partially open my eyes to the silhouette of the nurse "Rosamma." She's here for a routine examination of my vitals. I close my eyes, pretending to be asleep in order to avoid another pill being shoved down my throat. If I relent to it, I'll be back with the dizziness. My mind will be cramped with dreadful thoughts, even though sleep will evade me. The nurse flashes her torchlight at my face to make sure that I am asleep; satisfied, she leaves without a sound.

I constantly feel someone knocking me in my sleep. A gentle voice drifts into my ears. The ever-busy Azrael, angel of death, shall take away each soul from the world at the command of the Almighty. Sinners shall be severely punished. They shall bear a painful death. Their eyes would be, but a reflection of hell. They are the ones who shall be desperate for a drop of water under the scorching sun. They shall get burnt down to ashes. The good souls will leave the bodies without even a hint of pain. They shall be witness to the vision of heavenly garden, with meandering rivers. Enchantingly beautiful *hoories*, the dwellers of the paradise will welcome them, with platters of fruits and drinks. There will be lush greenery all around and mellow fragrance of flowers. The torment of the raging heat

BM Zuhara, *Azrael* In: *The Silence That Speaks*. Edited by: Haris Qadeer, Oxford University Press. © Oxford University Press India 2022. DOI: 10.1093/oso/9780190132613.003.0020 will be replaced by soothing, cool breeze. I learnt all of this while growing up. *Umma* (mother) always reminded me to pray hard in order to safeguard the soul from being led astray by *Iblees,* the Satan on the deathbed. But, I often forget. Usually, my prayers sound like this: please help my son score well in exams, please safeguard my husband, please help us overcome the financial distress, and so on. Thoughts of death haunt me only when I am sick. Therefore, I was certain that the version of Azrael I encounter will be the furious one. But His gentle voice pacified my soul, and astonished me too. He nudged me lightly to wake me up, and like a prophecy His voice echoed.

"Aysha, it's time. You forced me to resign several times with petty reasoning. What excuse do you have today?"

"I don't want to die here in this hospital. I want to go home. My son is in the tenth standard now. His exams are in the offing. He is bad at Maths. Usually, I teach it to him. He will fail, if I don't. If I die, my son and my husband will suffer a lot. Give me some more time ..."

"I do not expect to take you with your consent. I am not using force because of your good nature. Do you think that your son and husband will be grieved if you die?"

"If I am not there, I am sure the whole household will be in a mess. Who will cook food for them? Who will wash their clothes and iron them neatly?"

"Your worries are unfounded. Even if you are not there, they will live happily. Your husband will remarry. Your son will not even get time to think about you. How can you be such a fool?"

"Please spare me one last time ... Let me reach home ..."

Suddenly, I heard someone slamming the door or the window.

"Ok! I am retreating this time. Do not drive me away empty-handed next time!"

The noise came from somewhere close. Isn't it aggressive this time instead of a soothing one? My heart started throbbing heavily, sweating along. But I was relieved to have successfully bargained my life back, one more time.

Relieved, I opened my eyes to a room full of light. The nurse stood there with a thermometer.

"Gone, right?"

"Who was it, *Umma*?"

"Azrael?"

"*Ayyo* ... That is a country, right? Where would it go? You might have had a dream at this early hour of the day, *Umma*"

The nurse inserted the thermometer inside my mouth and started examining my pulse. Taking it out from my mouth, I asked: "What is the time right now?"

"It's already five. Today is Sunday. Your husband and son will arrive early morning itself. Aren't you getting ready, Umma?" She asked while marking my temperature on her chart.

"hmm ... " I replied, grimly.

"What happened, *Umma*, you seem to be dull today. Usually on Sundays you wake up early. How about the pain, is it severe?"

When there was no response, she closed the door and went to another room. It is true that I usually wait for Sundays. My husband comes in the morning itself along with my son who narrates to me every single incident taking place in his school. After that, I teach him Math while my husband lies on a bed nearby, reading a newspaper. At times, he too joins our conversations cracking jokes in between. Then, we have our lunch together. And I don't feel the passage of time. Today, however, I feel very detached. I am filled with a sense dread. It's only his words resonating in my ears. He is the one who knows everything. He speaks the truth. Even if I am not there, they will live happily. They will forget me, even before I turn to dust.

My mind refused to be at ease even while brushing and performing ablution for the morning prayer. I didn't feel like taking a shower. I quickly changed into a saree from the nightdress I was still wearing and sat in a chair near the window. By then, the convent servant "Gracie" had come with a flask of tea. She poured me some tea with a small serving of local news and went back.

Run by a Christian missionary, the hospital is located at a hilltop twenty miles away from the city. It is well maintained. Mother superior visits and assures the welfares of patients herself. The chief doctor is my husband's friend. So, I don't have anything to worry about, here. The doctor stays in the hospital quarters nearby. If something special is being cooked at his home, my share of it is sure to reach here. Most evenings, the doctor's wife nourishes me with her wit. Initially, my husband used to pay me a visit daily. But, because of my insistence at staying alone until the operation, so as to not trouble him, he doesn't now. The doctor had also agreed with my suggestion. But the date for this operation hasn't been fixed yet.

Will it be Azrael's next scheduled arrival then? If He comes, I certainly have to go. It would be unfair to send Him back again. There are no excuses left anymore. The cold breeze forced its way through the window making me shiver. I took a shawl and covered myself. Sipping on hot tea brought a bit of ease. I checked my watch. It is only six.

Here, in the hospital, time seems to crawl. Back home, even though I wake up at five in the morning, the clock strikes eight at the mere blink of an eye. When I enter the kitchen after the morning prayers, my busy day starts. My son wakes up at five to revise his lessons. By then, his tea and boiled eggs should be ready at his desk. My husband wakes up at seven and heads straight to the balcony to pick up the newspaper. His tea should reach him there. Before leaving for office, he needs at the least four cups of tea. After that, I get caught up with breakfast and lunch preparations. And by then, my son would have already whined several times for extremely trivial things.

"*Umma*, you did not polish my shoes? *Umma*, I cannot find my socks. Where is my school diary?"
My husband also needs me for everything.

"Aysha, heat this *khuzamb* (medicated oil). This shirt lost its button. Where is my kerchief? Who misplaced my spectacles off the table? I never find anything in its designated place."

I loved this busyness! But the past few days have drained me of all my strength. Nights have become sleepless. I get startled by nightmares each time I close my eyes. It's only at the dawn I get some sleep. Thus, the first routine to get disrupted was that of waking up at five in the morning. And when the household chores started to get affected, my son and husband burst into complaints.

"If *Umma* is sick, why don't you consult a doctor? Or employ a house help. Even yesterday, I reached school after the final bell."

"Why didn't you keep the lunchbox in my bag? I almost starved."

There is no salt in the *sambar*. *Iddli* is not soft. Fish fry is not crispy enough … All these complaints began to take a toll on me. That's how Aamina *di* was employed for our help, which turned out to be a good decision. Even if am not there, she ensures a smooth running of the household. She is a good cook as well. She worked at my sister's place for many years as a domestic help. Seeing me struggle, my sister decided to send Aamina *di* here to aid me. I never tolerated anyone else in my kitchen, before her. Everything was very organized. Each container was labelled properly. I was always adamant that whoever takes it should keep it back in its designated place. Everything might have been in a disorder now. But my husband and son seem to be happy. The last time they paid me a visit, my son spent the entire time praising Aamina *di*'s culinary skills.

"Aamina *di*'s chicken biriyani is delicious! Even if you stand upside-down, *Umma* you cannot make such tasty biryani!"

"True! Though expensive, we are getting tasty food."

Every Sunday, Aamina *di* cooks something special and sends it for me. But I do not feel like eating it. Without any particular reason, I find myself getting furious. I just take some rice, sambar, and sour yogurt from the convent and try to gulp it down. As for Aamina *di* dishes, I give it to Gracie who really enjoyed chicken and fish.

"I'll be writing my exams soon. Couldn't you have come here after I was done with it?"

My son's words were a clear indication of his aversion to the hospital visits. I insisted that he come here only after he was done with the exams. My husband too must be tired of all this. Bereft of a choice, he conceals his displeasure. I never asked them to take me to the hospital. I was silently bearing the excruciating pain. But one day, I fainted and could not get up despite my best effort. My body was writhing in extreme pain. He was the one who called the doctor, ignoring my protestations. My life has become limited to sheets of X-rays now. They have scanned my brain from all possible angles. Many different blood tests and several other experiments followed. Several days rolled under the fancy name called "observation" and finally they decided on an operation! I had asked them to keep it after my son's exam. But to no avail, Doctor disagreed. It's been almost a month since I came here.

"Hello! Good morning. Are you daydreaming?"

Oh! It is the doctor. Without uttering a word, I went and sat on the bed. The doctor's stethoscope began to examine my chest. He glanced at the chart prepared by nurse, and asked:

"Slept well at night?"

"Can that tube also read thoughts?"

When I retorted with such a question, the doctor tried to smile and asked:

"What happened? Your plan is to baffle me with philosophy today?"

"Please be kind to me. I do not have a disease right now. Even if I have something, it will get cured once I reach home. If I stay here like this, many people will suffer. My son has exams next week, Doctor, please!"

"Ok. Don't worry. Let Muhammed come. You have a slight temperature. Nurse, please give her a paracetamol. I will send you home soon."

The doctor tried to calm me down with a gentle hand on my back. By then, my husband had entered with a carry bag. He kept the bag on the table and shook hands with the doctor. When they left, I walked towards the window. I wanted to see the sky ... trees, flowers, and leaves ... What if I cannot see them tomorrow? The sky was heavy with thick clouds. I so wished for a heavy rain that could give me some peace. I could see the high mountains and the green valley from the window. Was this valley so enchanting yesterday? In the garden beneath the window, a statue of Mother Mary stands tall surrounded by a host of differently colored Bougainville. Yellow, green, pink ... Roses in the pot. Oleander in full blossom. These flowers carpet the whole land. The gardener was watering the plants. And mother Sister was standing nearby giving him instructions. When she saw me near the window, she raised her hand to greet me. I waved back.

Hearing footsteps, I turned around. My husband stood behind me with wearing a worried expression on his face which was pale as a paper.

"Hmm? What is it?"

"Day after tomorrow is the operation?"

"Where is it?"

"Head ... You need to shave your head today ... "

He swallowed the unfinished words. The hair I had nurtured with the best natural oil and shampoo ... I ran my fingers through the rich black strands of hair, soft as silk. I was frightened at the mere prospect of imagining my face with a bald head ...

"You did not eat anything from the morning, right? I bought *pathiri* and fried meat, Shall I give you some?"

"I will eat later."

But without minding my words, he served me a plate of *pathiri* smeared in coconut milk, along with some fried meat. I was not hungry and ate merely for the sake of it. The rest of it went into the trash. He was blankly staring at my face even as I poured milk from the flask and gave it to him.

"If I ask for something now, please do not dismiss it. For the time being, let us postpone the operation. I want to go home. I want to relax on my bed. I gave Him my consent. I made him leave, even today. I cannot postpone it anymore."

"Aysha, what are you talking about? How can we go home now? Let the operation be done!"

"I cannot! I want to reach home today. If necessary, we can come back after two days"

"Why are you being so stubborn, like a child?"

"I won't trouble you for anything else. Please fulfil my wish this time. Do not deny it."

My words fumbled and eyes filled with tears. Without putting up a strong defense, he walked towards the doctor's room.

As I started packing my things, I could only hear Azrael's gentle voice echoing in my mind. No, I will not break my promise this time. I will come. Without uttering a single word, I will come. I won't let you use force on me.

"Lying on my bed at home, with kindness and eternal peace … " I mumbled continuously.

Translated from Malayalam by Ayshath Shamah Rahmath.

20

Bidda Lives On

Zakia Mashadi

Imili ke patta, nava nava patta,
khada raho beta,dalle chhu,
dalle chhu,dalle chhu
(New shoots on the tamarind tree; come on son, stand and see,
I am coming to touch you, touch you, touch you)

Chanting the ditty, the *kabaddi* players could be counted in dozens and the ruckus they created made one feel the day of judgement had arrived. A player from the opposite team was out; the din gathered more volume . . . ho ho ho.

November chill was in the air. The cold breeze swept in the house carrying high-pitched voices on its wings. On the hot iron girdle, Amma's thinly rolled chapati puffed up like a balloon. Taking it off with a pair of tongs, she babbled. "These urchins seem to have been fed with lion's fat or else why wouldn't they feel the cold? It is already time for dinner and they are playing *kabaddi* on the street. Even their parents do not seem to bother . . . "

Safia chuckled. Worrying her head over the matters that belonged to others, Amma used to drive herself crazy. She not only kept her own children cooped up like poultry but wanted the whole neighborhood also to follow suit.

"What is there to laugh about?" Amma really got angry. "A mound of leafy greens is waiting to be cleaned. The dinner will get late again!" Safia pulled the wicker basket close to her and started separating tender leaves from mature stalks. Heat emanating from the earthen stove felt soothing. Another sign, heralding the arrival of winter.

Zakia Mashadi, *Bidda Lives On* In: *The Silence That Speaks.* Edited by: Haris Qadeer, Oxford University Press.
 DOI: 10.1093/oso/9780190132613.003.0021

Suddenly, an earthquake seemed to rock the house, kitchen, and all. It was Bidda pounding up the stairs, taking two at a time, calling out to Safia at the top of her voice ... Sappho, hey Sappho Rani ho ...

Now this gross distortion of her name irked Safia no end. She had tried to correct Bidda so many times but "f" in Safia remained the same "ph." Actually, Bidda's own name was a distortion of Vidya, and there were hardly four to five people who knew it. These included the Panditji who had presided over the name-giving ceremony sixth day after her birth. Rest of the world did not know what Bidda stood for and did not bother to know either.

Calling out her own version of Safia's name, making Safia's blood boil, Bidda darted straight into the kitchen. Plump and fair, wearing a wristful of glass bangles, vermillion in the parting, Bidda was all of fourteen and already given into marriage. This year, her "*gauna*" ceremony was due. She would formally be sent to her husband's house to start living with him, but first Panditji had to decide the auspicious time for it.

"Hey you, won't you decorate the dollhouse this time?" She addressed Safia, panting. Her anklet bells tinkled as she continued. "Tomorrow is *dhanteras* and day after, Diwali."

"Yes, why not? We will do it tomorrow itself," suppressing the excitement in her voice, Safia rejoined.

Bidda was extremely conscious of her marital status and also of being a little older. Both gave her an edge over Safia, also the authority to find faults in her house work and give a word of advice or two. Right now too, she plonked herself on the kitchen floor and started taking out some stalks from the already-cleaned spinach leaves. Safia pulled a long face. "Oh come on, they will all soften and how do a few matter anyway?"

"Oh yes, even the 'hands and feet' of a goat soften once they are cooked and gobbled up by you so fondly." Bidda, who was a vegetarian, always teased Safia for gobbling up "hands and feet" of poor goats. She knew Safia loved trotter curry.

Amma started laughing. "This friend of yours is really clumsy, Bidda. If asked to peel potatoes, she peels them so thickly that only half of them go to the cooking pot; the rest land in the dust bin. Why don't you teach her some tricks of the trade? Like you, she too, will get married one day."

Bidda rolled her kohl-lined eyes mischievously, picked the rest of the greens in no time, pushed the basket towards Amma and got up to leave.

Safia gnashed her teeth and decided not to go to decorate Bidda's dollhouse, but the next day, no sooner did she hear Bidda calling "Sappho," than she bolted down the stairs like an arrow.

Taking great care, Safia mixed colours in small bowls. Bidda pulled out a terracotta plate from the heap of toys of clay and filled it with *pedas*. Safia loved this special Diwali sweet but did she need any bribe for splashing colours on the traditional dollhouse, an integral part of Diwali celebrations? In no time images of gods and goddesses, lotus flowers, ducks in a pond, rising sun, flying birds, and clumps of trees, all came alive on Bidda's *gharonda*; this year too hers was the best in the entire neighborhood.

"Long live my Saphho." Bidda hugged Safia, winked at her and said, "Diwali over I will come to you to have the letter written." Now what irked Safia next to being called "Sappho," was being winked at, that too by Bidda. Irritated, she retorted, "Why don't you ask Kalu to write it for you? Now he is in class six; can do the job well."

"You shameless creature! Can a girl ask her brother to write a letter to her husband on her behalf?"

Now this letter writing business was something rather weird.

Bidda was a primary school dropout. Once she left school, she forgot even what little she had learnt. On the other hand, the boy she was married to had not only done his matriculation; he was quite romantically inclined, too. He wrote regularly to his bride, who had not joined him yet, and expected just as regular, love-lorn letters in reply. Bidda not only took time in writing one, she also made many mistakes. Dictating the letter to Safia was the easy way out. As a good friend, she was ever so ready to oblige.

Safia really felt sheepish. How could she be so daft as to expect a brother to write his sister's letters addressed to her husband? But teasing? Yes, he was the most appropriate target for that, especially when he happened to be younger. "Kaloo! Bhaloo!! Khaloo!!!" Wiping her colour-stained hands on a rag, she shouted out loud.

Kalu's half yearly exams were scheduled just after Diwali holidays. He was learning tables; at the same time wishing death to all his teachers, especially the Maths teacher. Exercising great control, he tried to ignore the insult of being called Kalu the bear and Kalu the uncle.

Seeing no reaction, Safia tried a more effective measure:

Two billy goats, reared our dear Kaloo,
One died of coughing,
Of sneezing, the other, too.

Kalu could never imagine anyone rearing goats in his family, not in generations that had passed neither the ones that had yet to come. Besides the ludicrous doggerel could be tolerated if chanted by street urchins, not when this chit of a girl recited it. The table had also gotten stuck at eighteen sevens. So the big fat math's exercise book was thrown at Safia, which landed right on her head. Just then, dabbing her face with the end of her sari, Kalu's mother emerged from the adjoining room. "You wretch! Don't you know that you are insulting the Goddess of knowledge by throwing the book like this?" she shouted. "Instead of helping decorate your sister's dollhouse, you are harassing poor Saphho who is doing it. Go to live in a pig sty." Muttering her favourite swear words of sending people to a pig sty, Kaki disappeared just as she had appeared a moment ago. Kalu tugged at Safia's long plait so hard she barely escaped a fall. Bidda gave Kalu two tight whacks. Mayhem ensued.

Mayhem and Kalu were almost synonymous. The very sight of the prankster made Safia itch to say something which irked him. But on the day of Bidda's "*gauna*" ceremony, her heart went out to him. The boy, who always behaved like a bull in china shop, was sobbing like a little child who had lost his way in a jungle with no exit in sight. She went close to him and put her reassuring hand over his head. The feel of Kalu's thick silky hair lingered on her palm for a long time. A few years later, a similar feel was retained by Kalu's hand when he put it on Safia's head at the time of her departure to her husband's house. His eyes had brimmed over thinking of Bidda who was so wrapped up in the affairs of a life of her own that her visits to her parental home had become few and far between. Decorating dollhouses of Diwali had become a thing of the past; there was no one to fight with, no one to receive the sweet scoldings from. Forgetting he was a man who is not supposed to shed tears, he burst out crying.

As Air India jumbo jet touched the ground at New Delhi airport, the chanting of those small town children playing *kabaddi* on the street got superimposed on the impeccable English of the air hostess announcing landing. "*Imali ke patta; Nava nava patta*," voices, that dated back to almost quarter of a century. Perhaps with children creating ruckus as usual, they still reverberated in the lanes and by-lanes. Early in the morning, the wizened *halwa* vendor would still be calling, "Halwa, fresh halwa, dripping with ghee!" His shrill voice, just as cutting as the chilly winter morning, would be making children sit up in their beds, demanding money from their parents and just then, some elderly person would comment, laughing, "The crook! He makes halwa with vegetable oil, only smears some ghee on top," and Kaki would still be giving a nudge to this stubborn brat Kalu shouting, "Go to the pig sty," and during Diwali Bidda must be erecting her dollhouse—without Safia.

Imali ke patta … imali ke patta … even during train journey from Delhi to her home town children played kabaddi along the railway tracks, peered through the widow, hovered around her, passing years notwithstanding.

When the train pulled up at her destination, Safia, without waiting to get down, craned her neck to see whether the old Gulmohar tree was still there. Yes, it was. Taller and greener, it had become immense. The years that had gone by had done it good. The air smelt of Diwali. Mounds of milky white puffed rice, and delicate as air *batashas* were selling on the road. Small little earthen lamps, toys of clay, specially elephants and dolls washed in a mixture of lime and mica, to give them that glitter, icons of goddess Lakshmi and Ganesha. All so familiar. Any minute Bidda will appear carrying a large platter of puffed rice and an assortment of sweets with an extra packet of *pedes*, especially meant for Safia and their faces will brighten up in the light of *phuljhadis*.

Safia's ten-year-old son who had not visited his grand parents' house after the age of one and a half years was watching everything in wonderment. All this was quite amusing for him but the tears rolling down Safia's cheeks while climbing the stairs of her parental home were beyond his comprehension. "Why is mummy crying incessantly for no apparent reason? She had never been so daft!" He mused.

"Aapa would always be welcome here but she has chosen the wrong time." Safia's younger brother's wife was saying. "Thanks to God, she hasn't brought her daughter along." Her tone made Safia uneasy. Why wrong? She deliberately wanted to come during the festive season. There in Dubai she missed Holi and Diwali so badly. Their lights, their colour, the rustic, colourful toys. They figured in her dreams. And that semi-literate childhood friend, who could not write her letters herself and tormented Safia to write them on her behalf, that too to her husband. Why should she not have come now? Diwali is such a beautiful festival. Bright and sweet and loving!

Safia came to the terrace. Pushing the reed curtain aside a little, she peeped outside, her eyes scanning the neighbourhood. All those children were there. Real—of flesh and blood. Under the thatched roof, Tahir Miyan's sewing machine was running as ever. Sitting by its side his billy goat was merrily chewing the cud. Chhote Lal, after having a hearty breakfast of fried vegetables and kachories, was belching noisily in satisfaction. Shopkeepers were decorating their shops to lure the *Dhanteras* customers who will come thronging in the evening.

Suddenly, the street came alive with raucous noises. Sharp and threatening and laced with abusive words, Safia's sister-in-law came out, exasperated.

"What is happening, Aapa? Whatever has happened?"

"Can't say. Perhaps some people have started a quarrel. All at once." Safia said nonchalantly.

"May God help us. Your brother is not back yet. Had gone to buy some sweets for you."

"Altaf must be coming. Why are you so worked up? Squabbles of this kind are so very common."

"You don't know what the atmosphere is like these days," she said suppressing irritation in her voice. Just then, some child burst a loud cracker; she jumped, fright writ large on her face. Her young teenage son, Amir, too, joined them. His mother pulled him behind but he protested, "Let me assess the situation," said he. In that instant, Safia found Amir growing up beyond his years. Grown up and serious. But just the next minute, the whole neighbourhood heaved a sigh of relief. Residing in the adjoining by lane, from a family of goldsmiths, someone had been drinking the whole night. Inebriated, he had returned in the morning, now creating a racket. Some women had also jumped into the arena, making their contribution to the commotion that had ensued.

Safia started laughing. On such occasions, Noor Mohammad Chacha, with his long, quivering beard, used to come out to give his free services as trouble shooter; some time by making people see the light, sometime by giving them a good dressing-down. Every one listened to him. "Now he has no say even in the matters that pertain to his own family. Old and rendered powerless, now he skulks in a corner of his house. And, why only Noor Mohammad Chacha? All those old fogies who talked of peace and goodwill are obsolete, a thing of the past."

"And Kaki?" Safia was perturbed by the bitterness in her sister-in-law's voice.

"She died some three years ago."

Safia drew her breath in. Staggering under the yolk of life, producing and raising children, stretching their limited resources like rubber, arranging marriages, extending a helping hand to whoever needed it, neglecting their own requirements, kaki and Amma both were gone. Last time when Safia had come home, they were there. Safia's son, at that time, was about a year old. She sent a message to Bidda's village who arrived the very next day. In an embroidered shawl her plump, fair, youthful face shone like the full moon. She, like a magician, produced a thick silver band from under her shawl, slipped it on the boy's wrist and, rolling her khol-lined eyes as usual, said, "Have a look at me, son, and don't you dare forget, I am your *mausi, your mother's sister.*" Then, showering him with blessings, she scooped the child up in her arms. After sometime came Kaki, whose eyes were dim with cataract and knees were bent with arthritis. From the end of her old, crumpled sari she took out a five-rupee note and quietly slipped it into the child's palm.

After Kaki had left, Amma said, "consider this small amount a treasure. After her husband's departure, poor woman does not have any cash at hand. Kalu is earning enough, but he thinks that after two square meals, an old woman does not require any money. You give it to her, she will splurge unneceesarily." Taking a deep sigh, she added, "my sons do not think any differently either."

When Safia tried to give some money to Amma, she got very angry. "Can I take money from a daughter? And a married one at that! Your friend Bidda too, had insulted her mother in the same manner. She was so furious that she hit Bidda with a chappal. You deserve the same, but I am a milder person. Don't worry, I am not all that broke."

Bearing the cross of same Indian middle-class values, Kaki and Amma both had disappeared from the earth they had walked together, once.

"Any news of Bidda? Does she come visiting?" Safia asked her sister-in-law who gave her a blank look.

"Bidda who? Raja Ram's sister?"

"Who else?" Safia's voice betrayed irritation.

"She is also no more; she died when her mother was still alive." She informed nonchalantly.

Safia was dumbfounded; a giant blow knocked off all the Diwali lights, entire town went dark.

After a long silence, Safia gathered courage. "Is Raja Ram's family still residing here?"

"They are very much here."

"Can you send someone to inform them I am here? I am sure Kalu will come running. If he doesn't, I will go." Altaf's wife did not say anything. Quietly, she got busy in the kitchen.

Evening had started getting darker. Safia's desolate heart ached. Was it the age to die? She would have hardly entered her fifties. Sorrow swirled around like mist. In a weak effort to ward it off, she turned to her niece, Reshma. "Haven't you bought some fire crackers. I love *phuljharis*."

"I am very scared of them," said Reshma, quietly.

"Why? Did you ever get burnt?"

"That Diwali the whole town burnt, Phoophi." Reshma's voice was bitter, the face a mask of fright.

Somebody put a knife through Safia's heart; disconcerted, she came out on the terrace again. Carrying a large brass plate, covered with crocheted doily, taking long strides, a little girl was coming from the opposite direction. She looked uncannily familiar. Reshma who had followed Safia, said, "She is your Kalu … er, Raja Ram's daughter."

"Call her, Reshma, call out to her. What's her name?"

"Ok, I will call her, but I don't think she will come." Then, she shouted her name, "Manju..u..u, hey, come here. Someone wants to see you."

Manju stopped short near the raised platform and looked up. By then, Safia had bounded down the stairs. Pushing the reed curtain aside, she beckoned to the girl. "Come on in child, come on in."

Very reluctantly, the girl obeyed. Safia put her arm around her and pressed her close. She started staring at this strange, expensively dressed, middle-aged woman in wonderment. "Tell your babuji … " "we call him papa … ." The girl interrupted. Safia laughed. "Ok, tell your papa that

Altaf Chacha's elder sister has come. She wants to see you. And ask him since when he has become Raja Ram. His name was Kalu." Holding the girl still close to her, Safia whispered into her ear, "Not only Kalu, it was Kaloo … Bhaloo … Khaloo!." Surprise got replaced by a beautiful smile, and next moment, she burst out laughing. "May I know who you are?" The little girl could not curtail her curiosity anymore. Safia suddenly turned serious again. Putting her hand on Manju's head she said, "I am your *phua*, child, your papa's sister." Saying so, Safia felt that she had paid a little of Bidda's debt back. She wiped her eyes.

Manju was again taken by surprise. How can her phua be in this house? She had some faint memories of Bidda phua. But affection is not beyond her comprehension. Going back, she turns to cast a glance at Safia, smiling.

Kalu did not turn up. Safia insisted on going to his place in spite of Altaf advising her not to. Raja Ram does not visit us anymore. We just exchange perfunctory greetings if we happen to run into each other. Sometimes I feel that both of us try to evade even this much of courtesy"

"Reason?"

"Aapa, you are not all that naive; you only love nitpicking. He has joined a political party. Some two years ago, the town went through severe communal tension It was proved that his party had a great role in it. Raja Ram himself was involved in writing provocative slogans on the walls of the town."

"Altaf, you and Kālu went together to the same school" Safia said plaintively.

"Yes, and together, we stole guavas from Noor chacha's garden."

"And when your school started a cleanliness drive, shovels in hand, you cleaned the overflowing drains together." Safia's heart was feeling heavy as lead, yet a faint smile crossed her face. She had teased Kalu no end calling him a sweeper. The little boy, who fought Safia, flailing his arms and legs all at once, is now running a successful business, is married, and has sired many children. From Kalu, he has transformed into Raja Ram but where has his innocence gone during the process? Who has polluted his mind, heart, and soul? Who has made him xenophobic?

Next morning, she went to see him.

Sitting on the raised platform, which made the frontage of most of the houses, he was scrubbing his feet with a pumice stone. The platform was the same; the whole ambience was the same. In one corner of it, holding its head high stood the dollhouse of his daughters. Come evening and the earthen lamps adorning its edges will shimmer like hope in human hearts.

Their eyes locked. He was startled, kept looking in disbelief. Many years rolled by ... "Hey, you, know who I am or have lost your wits completely?" She addressed him in the dulcet local dialect which only people here, in her home town, could understand, no one in Dubai.

"Yes, I do. Safia *didi*, When did you come?" His voice was bereft of any enthusiasm or cheer. Safia's spirits dampened still she managed to say, "I am sure you knew I was here, why didn't you come?"

He started scratching his head. "Business is expanding, life, too, has become demanding with so many family affairs to look into." Then, he called his wife, "Manju's ma, look who has come?" Safia continued, "Altaf says you hardly visit them. What is the matter? Have you two fallen out with each other? He looked sullen when I enquired after you." Kalu did not respond to this, scrubbing his feet he called his wife again, this time asking her to bring two glasses of tea.

"Kalu, how did Bidda die?" Her voice was laced with tears. "Where are her people, children?"

Just then, tea in hand, his wife appeared in the doorway. Putting the tea tray on a nearby stool, she greeted Safia. "Now direct all your queries to her. She will tell you everything." In the same breath, he told his wife, "She is Bidda didi's childhood friend. Sit and talk to her." He got up without even his tea. "I have to leave now. Have already become late for the shop."

"Kalu, I don't want any tea. It is to see you and your family that I had come." She said angrily, but the sadness too could not be put under disguise. With a sense of defeat, she also got up.

Suddenly, Safia saw Manju, eyes sparkling with mischief, come running. There was a boy behind her, giving her the chase. A little older, he looked like her brother. Seeing Safia, Manju stopped short. For a brief moment, her eyes reflected surprise, but the next minute, a shy smile, like rays of the sun peeping from behind the rain clouds, brightened up her face. Two little dimples appeared in her plump, fair cheeks; black beady eyes looked directly into Safia's. Spitting image of Bidda!

"Papa, papa, She is my *phua*, I told you about her, didn't I?" Coming very close to Safia, touching her with her little hand, she said. And, in her angel-like countenance, Bidda came back to life.

First published as "*Bidda Mari Nahi*." Translated from Urdu by the author.

21
To Be Myself

Huma Kidwai

Knock, knock. Knock.

The sound was soft, like a hesitant tap really, as though the visitor was not sure that it was the right door. Ratnamma groaned in exasperation, finished scrubbing her arms and face with the rough lye soap, washed up leisurely and tied up her hair into a knot, before walking unhurriedly to the door of her one room, asbestos-roofed tenement. Whoever it was, was unwelcome. She had had a hard day sweeping the streets under the hot summer sun. The sun had burnt dark patches on her exposed skin and no amount of water seemed to quench her thirst. She had only just returned to her tiny hovel by the railway track, a few hundred yards from the Khairtabad railway station.

She reluctantly opened the door to two women standing to one side in the shade of a scrawny, twisted, thinly leaved shrub by the door. One of them was old, wrinkled and completely grey, decked out in her few pieces of artificial jewellery and her saree worn in a very unfamiliar fashion.

"Does not seem to be from here," thought Ratnamma with surprise. "What could she want from me?"

The other woman standing behind the first one seemed to be hiding, cowering close to the gnarled tree trunk. She was unbelievably emaciated and the posture—slightly bent—was one of pain and disease and suffering. The saree she wore was threadbare and dirty; the hair in a short plait was matted and tied with a very bright pink, now almost brown, ribbon. This woman now turned to face Ratnamma. At first, it was an unbearable sight. But the eyes were very familiar. She heard her own muffled scream. She felt she was sliding down in a spiral, but pulled herself together with a desperate effort. She grabbed the two women and pushed them into the house, shutting and bolting the door in a single unbroken

Huma Kidwai, *To Be Myself* In: *The Silence That Speaks*. Edited by: Haris Qadeer, Oxford University Press. © Oxford University Press India 2022. DOI: 10.1093/oso/9780190132613.003.0022 movement. Then she collapsed on the floor in a heap, at the feet of the two women.

"Whatever has happened to you, Narsing? Who has done this to you, son? You … you are a … ?" She couldn't say the word. She ran to the corner of the room where a small drain represented the washing area, and was sick. She held her head in her hands and sat there for a long while, gathering the courage to return and face her long lost son.

The skeleton was shuddering. Was it sobbing or was it shivering from fever? Ratnamma came back to the centre of the room and turned to the elderly woman silently, a hundred questions in her eyes, but no words on her lips. The stranger put a sympathetic hand on Ratnamma's shoulder and started to speak in a hoarse whisper in Hindi. She was not from Telangana, obviously.

"These people are very kind and take care of their community very well, though they live in a slum. Nargis was very sick. She kept asking in the delirium, whether you will let her into your home. The Guru asked me if I would accompany her. I did it for the blessings." The kind, pragmatic, old woman said it all in a few words. That she had rendered Ratnamma and her son invaluable service, did not occur to her. A mother should see her dying son, which was the only objective of the immense effort and expense that this poor woman had borne quite unselfconsciously. This was the sensitive face of the apparently indifferent India.

"I must take the evening train back. I have to go back to work tomorrow. At the supari factory. Peeling the areca nut. My work."

Ratnamma nodded in a daze. She was staring at the raw and calloused hands of the old woman. She nodded yet again. Yes she knew. She did not dare to speak. The trembling in her limbs was threatening to turn uncontrollable. "Am I coming down with a fever? No I can't afford to now," she thought stupidly.

She mechanically lit the stove and put the rice to boil. She would get the details when she could think. Right now, she felt she had turned into a wooden doll, stiff like the Kondapally toys from childhood. The brightly coloured, handmade wooden toys lay in an untidy line on the second-hand black and white television set in the corner by the tiny window. She had bought the TV with great difficulty, paying in monthly instalments for two years. But it was not for entertainment. She switched it on whenever she was at home, just for the flickering light and the sound of many voices from it, which brought a crowd of virtual people into her loneliness.

Staring into the flame of the kerosene stove, hearing the laboured breathing of her son through the loud hiss of the stove, she suddenly felt like throwing back her head and letting out a long drawn howl, just like the stray dogs did in the dead of the night. Perhaps they were tortured souls, reincarnated as dogs in this lifecycle. Placing the hot vessel of rice and an earthen jar of pickle in front of her guest, she finally raised her eyes to look at the benign face of the stranger.

The weather beaten wrinked face looked kindly.

The old woman finished her meal, curled up on the reed mat and fell asleep. Ratnamma took a spoon and tried feeding her son (she still could not accept that he was a 'she' now) warm rice starch. He gulped with difficulty, but seemed better for it after a while. Too weak to speak, he lay quietly, watching her from deep, dark sockets. Ratnamma shuddered inwardly. "What shall I do now? What?" The question kept going round and round in the tiny room, buzzing like the plastic bee on a string toy that you whirled in a circle to hear the buzz. A sensation of ants running down from her hairline, to her neck and her back, made her continually rub her forehead and neck in a nervous gesture. Ratnamma did not notice the dusk falling and the darkness entering her hovel. The ground tremors of the many trains that ran on the tracks nearby were so much a part of her days and nights, that they did not disturb the tranquillity of the tiny room. The skeleton was motionless.

When the old woman rose from her nap, Ratnamma gave her some tea and tried in vain to press some money into her gnarled hands, which she refused. Then she stood up to go, turning to give an affectionate glance to her ward of two days. Ratnamma came out on the street with her, locked the door and tucked the key-on-a-string, into the dirty little satchel that hung at her waist, partly tucked into the folds of the saree. She walked the two hundred yards to the railway station, beside the old woman, in silent gratitude that defied expression. Between them, they sensed the whole range of emotions; from empathy to gratefulness to the heart-wrenching agony of a mother who faces the trauma of sexual transformation of her child. The massive presence of death, in the form of the skeleton, lay between them. The old woman asked Ratnamma to go back to her son and not to wait for her train. In an expression of her gratitude, Ratnamma embraced the stranger and burst into silent sobs on her shoulder.

They both wept; for wasted life, for the cruel hand of fate, for being women in a hostile world, for the strength, they always had to summon to face poverty, pestilence, male brutality, back-breaking labour to keep body and soul together and for Death that was never far from their door, in the filthy slums of posh high-tech cities. They wept for the city lights that stopped short of their streets, the water lines that ended at the train tracks, the garbage and filth that was never cleared from their lanes, the stink filled air, the constant fights at common taps and ration shops, the grip of vice and crime on their children, the longing to sleep in a clean soft bed—just once. They had a thousand years of crying to do, but that too was a luxury they could ill afford. Ratnamma started on her path home, turning to look back several times, through misty eyes at her benevolent sister from a faraway land. They both reached out to each other in that feminine understanding of their souls.

Ratnamma walked slowly, reluctant to get back to the bad dream that had gripped her in its talons. She paused before her door, straining to hear in the dark for footfalls of her neighbours. Except for children playing cricket with a plank as bat and a rubber ball, under the streetlight by the railway yard, most one-room shacks showed a pale light from a square hole, which was the standard window by the door. The doors were slightly ajar with jute sacking for curtain to satisfy a long held desire for some privacy. There would be thick rice and tamarind juice with much red chilli powder for dinner in almost all homes as usual.

She quickly entered her house and shut the door. The pile of bones stirred slightly. Ratnamma sank down on the reed mat and forced herself to look at her the stranger, who had been her mischievous, wayward son five years ago. He had large beautiful eyes and had been teased by other boys for being 'pretty.' He had always been negligent in studies. The government school a kilometre way was not capable of inspiring academic excellence. The frequent teacher absenteeism, the caning at the smallest provocation, the mindless learning by rote, was not for a spirited young boy like Narsing. He liked to play marbles or fly kites in the kite-season, or steal fruit from the gardens of the middle-class and the rich. He also secretly dressed in his mother's saris and danced alone inside the house when she was at work. She often cuffed him and said, 'Be a man!' He wanted to grow up into a beautiful woman like the voluptuous Telugu movie heroines and own a pair of dark glasses like them. He failed in almost all the classes and was 15 when he sat for the seventh standard board exam. He studied very hard and his illiterate mother worked harder at keeping him from venturing out in the evenings to hang out with the street children at the railway station.

Living by the tracks, Narsing knew a great deal about the trains, the life of runaways, the opportunities of the railway network and the names of cities his mother had never heard of. On the day the results were to be put up at his school, he told his mother she had nothing to worry. She said, "If you do not pass this time, don't come back. I am exhausted and there is no money to feed an idler".

It was true that Ratnamma had struggled a great deal, as do most women of her caste and class. She was a Kamati—the caste that sweeps and cleans. Curse though her caste was, it also proved an advantage in securing the job of a sweeper in the Municipal Corporation of Hyderabad. It was comparatively a well-paying job with benefits like pension and healthcare. Most importantly, it provided secure livelihood with no fear of being fired as in private employment. In fact, she had dreamt of getting her son the job of a sewage pipe cleaner on her retirement, if he failed to study further. She had been as harsh on him as any other single mother who desperately wants her child to escape her fate and the marshlands of her caste, which sucks you under, no matter how hard you try to get out of it.

That fateful day when Narsing did not return until nine o'clock in the night, she became uneasy. He had surely failed the seventh class exams and was scared to face her wrath and the green cane that would certainly be applied to the back of his legs without mercy. "He better know that life is not merciful to those who fail. The sooner the better," she thought. "But, where could he be?" "Perhaps at his maternal uncle's place, or at the railway tracks, watching the crowd surge and scatter at the coming and going of trains. He should return now." She picked up the green cane and locked the door of her home and stepped out in the alley, leaping over stagnant puddles of dirty water covering her nose with the edge of her saree when passing by public toilets. That night she searched for Narsing for three hours. She called his friends in the basti to come search with her. Her neighbours, men and women and children, all ran helter-skelter in and around the lanes and by lanes. For the children, it was a thrilling hide-and-seek in the middle of the night. No one seemed to have seen him after he left in tears, not having found his roll number on the list on display at the school.

It was two weeks later that his number was released from the 'withheld' (no one ever knew why there is a 'withheld' category of results) list and his teacher told Ratnamma that her son had just cleared the exams. By then it was too late; Narsing had disappeared. By now, there was a general consensus that he had left on a train to some unknown destination. Ratnamma had visited the police station every evening for weeks, but the officers were too busy on bandobast duties or breaking up protests or running errands for some political leader's wife or attending to rich people's petty domestic quarrels to pay attention to a trivial matter; that of the disappearance of a boy from the basti. These women could not control their wayward children, nor did they have the money to put into search by the police.

Now, Ratnamma squatted beside the recumbent body of her son, wondering what to do. He had no energy to get up, and no control over his bodily functions. Ratnamma turned her head away, every time she was called upon to clean him. How can she save her son now? "I will take you to Osmania hospital?" She asked tentatively. Narsing's hollow eyes darkened with fear. With great difficulty he haltingly whispered, "No! Doctors don't attend … Hijras. I have … AIDS. You will … be thrown … out … this house. Don't … don't … let them know. I … die soon. Wanted to … to … see you." Inside her, Ratnamma broke up into tiny bits of searing pain. Tears ran down her withering, sun burnt cheeks, as she went about attending to him.

Over the next three days, she tried not to hear his story of pain about those hapless five years. She wanted to go back and undo it all, to give up her own life to erase from her son's mind and heart all that torment. He could not give details and thank Deva for that! His story was very sketchy and her ignorance did not allow for filling it out. Deva be thanked for it again!

How had he, who made so much fuss over food and comfort, who made demands of TV, fridge and bicycle, how could he bear it all and survive? Survive? He had not survived it!

Narsing was grateful, ironically, for his sickness, which made it impossible to recount the details of his terrible life away from home — the home that until the fateful day when he left it, had seemed to him to be unliveable, lacking in the amenities he wanted and where his tyrant mother never failed to make him the butt of her wrath. He had not had the occasion to appreciate the love and security that his mother provided. He lay waiting to die. The unease of being desperately sick was relieved only intermittently when he dozed off into naps lasting a few minutes at a time. Several times he relived or dreamt—he did not know the difference — of the past he had not shared with anyone.

The day he left, he just blindly got into the most crowded compartment, hoping to lose himself into the dense mass so that the Travelling Ticket Inspector would not ask him for a ticket. His friends who lived on the railway station had told him how to dodge the authorities. But an hour into the journey, the smell of sweat from a hundred odd bodies and the rising temperature from them in the summer heat, locked into an iron shell became unbearable. He tried to get his face out of the door, which is what almost everyone wanted to do but like frogs in a bucket, were pulled back by others. In a way this was a very democratic space. Lowest fare, no frills, no mobility; everyone here was desperately poor and trying to go where they desperately needed to go. This was no holidaying class, only need and desperation supported by dollops of forbearance. The TTI did catch Narsing. His body language, trying to shrink and disappear, his terrified eyes, all gave him away to the experienced eyes of the TTI. What ensued was the usual: the shouting and threatening by the official and the cringing and pleading of the defaulter. The crowd just giggled and laughed and some even shoved Narsing. The crowd always sided with the stronger.

The conductor pushed him out on the platform at Wadi junction into a seething evening crowd. He tried to get into another door of the same train. This time, the passengers of the reserved seats took umbrage. They hit and punched and kicked him, until two fat, kindly men came to his rescue. They said they would accommodate him on their berth. They gave him water and asked him where he was from and why was he alone. They even ordered a plate-meal for him from the railway canteen, as they did for themselves. He came to know that they were brothers, Babu Rao and

Manik Rao. When the TTI came in, they greased his palms to let Narsing ride with them. The fatter and older one, Babu Rao offered him a job with board. He nodded, not because he wanted the job, but he needed to get off the train. They disembarked at Sholapur and took a rather dated and rattling car out into the dark. They came to a wide road called the 'highway' with thinning density of shops and then only fields on both sides. Finally, after what seemed like interminable driving, they reached a 'Petrol Pump' with a shack some distance behind it and what looked like a single storied house attached to it.

"This is your home from now on!" both men chorused.

The door was opened by a thin, tired looking woman, in a green sari with red border. She looked at Narsing and at the brothers with coldly indifferent eyes. "Another?" she asked. "Hm."

She took Narsing to a tiny, windowless room lit with a zero watt bulb and spread a mat on the floor. She handed him a thick cotton sheet, with dull blue and white woven pattern of leaves and left without a word. Narsing promptly fell asleep, deeply.

The next day, Narsing learnt that he would be working in the shack, which was a garage, from 10 in the morning to 10 in the night and the food would be sent to him there. He would sleep there as well, with another thin, dirty looking boy, a year or two older to him. Over the next two years, Narsing was taught how to repair cars and two wheelers. He was beaten with whatever tool happened to be near any of the two brothers, and by Chandu, the other boy. When he tried to run away, he was caught and chained. He now spent all day and night, chained to a ring in the floor but working all day as usual. Chandu even tried to molest him on and off.

At the end of one year and some months, though it seemed a lifetime, he fell ill with diarrhoea and vomiting. They had to unchain him. He was too sick and weak to run away, in any case. Narsing remembered the thundering of his heart in his ears, as he stepped out in the dark and just sailed through the tall millet and maize fields all along the highway. Only a few hours ago, it looked like he was dying, but the lightness of freedom, its elixir, took over his body and mind. He was thinking with great clarity. He knew they would look for him in the direction of the city or along the road. He took off at an angle, going deeper into the fields. He broke a maize stalk to clear his footprints. He kept moving in the direction of the setting moon, just to be sure he would not walk in a circle. Past the maize fields, the millet fields, almost crawling through the corner of the groundnut patch because they were low plants and half bent through the cotton fields. He avoided the villages and the wells. As dawn broke behind him, he took two maize cobs and found a ditch in a grove of Keekar and slid in and fell asleep.

He was not sure how many nights he walked, crawled, or dragged himself. He found himself in a small town. His memory now was patchy and chronologically mixed up. Why did he remember vividly, only this part of his five-year self-imposed exile? Why the rest was only flashes; many happy ones and a few painful? He could only recall with difficulty, the truly terrible episodes of a very eventful life. After the fateful escape, the next year or less, he had wandered from place to place, sometimes working in a roadside dhaba, cleaning dishes, some days in the railway coaches, singing and selling peanuts and getting into fights with other runaway children. He was raped several times by older homeless boys on threat of being cut up by a razor. The first time, he wanted to commit suicide. But some survival instinct kicked in.

Some days he collected plastic and metal from garbage bins in a town. A boy he had befriended on the street had introduced him to the business. It was then that he had first started to smell glue for light intoxication. It led to trying other things like rags dipped in gasoline and snuff and grass. In the evenings, young boys like him, even younger, sat on the parapet wall of the basti's drain and smoked, what was euphemistically called the huqqa or sheesha, in long pipes. Sometimes the local constable shared it with them. What was amazing to Narsing, was that the same man used his baton indiscriminately on his huqqa-sharing friends, when out on the main road. During one fight over the quantity of the intoxicant sold to him, three older boys, who materialized around the peddler and brutally attacked him and his young friend, surrounded him. He almost gave up hope of surviving the attack. He could hear his shinbone break and his arm twisted behind his back almost dislocate. Then suddenly the hitting, twisting and spitting stopped. He had blacked out and fearing the consequences, the trio fled the scene.

A group of Hijras found him very early next morning, behind a pile of debris, close to a garbage dump near the local train tracks, yards away from Thane Railway Station. He was unconscious. The hungry dogs would have torn him to shreds. The Hijras did not shy away from picking him up. The other 'normal' people did pause to look at him curiously, but moved on surreptitiously. The Hijras took him to a nearby government hospital. The doctors were not sure if he could survive at all and then, it was a medico-legal case. But the Hijras kept by his side. It took him a week to regain consciousness and a month to leave the hospital. Where would he go? They asked him. He went with them.

He could relive the happiness he felt at being in the midst of caring family members in the 'House of Shyamala,' the Hijra Guru. She had five disciples, who were now his 'sisters.' Nilima, Dia, Surveen, Meena, and Laxmi. Shyamala was the matriarch. There was much laughter and dance and music and going out to the bazar. They all shared the housework and even massaged the swollen feet of their 'Guru.' They were keen to send Narsing back to his mother, once he recovered. It took two months. Narsing had by then learnt to love their happy camaraderie and a kind of egalitarianism, he had not seen in the larger society outside. They were not as poor as Narsing had been at Hyderabad. There was a general atmosphere of celebration, as though by being beyond the pale of the mainstream society, absolute freedom was a natural state of being and hence the joy. It did bother them much that they are treated with scant respect beyond their community's four walls. But several men came visiting and they went out singing and dancing to houses where there was childbirth or other life-cycle rituals. He was slowly drawn into their routine and livelihood issues and was loath to leave. He started to dress and dance like them and he was surprised that he actually liked it all. He now thought of himself as Nargis—she, not he.

Then, in October that year, Nargis went with her 'family' on a pilgrimage to Yellamma Devi temple in Belgaum. There, she met hundreds of members of the Hijra community. She was surprised that they were Muslim Hijras there, as well. She also learnt of the many problems that besieged the Hijras and how some of them had acquired education and worked for the community's welfare and the rights of the 'third gender.' She resolved to go to the night school run by an NGO near their locality. After returning from that pilgrimage, Nargis approached the Guru and asked if she could give up her male identity. There were several meetings; of the five Gurus, of her sisters, of herself, and the Guru. She was asked many times if she was willing and prepared mentally. There could be no going back. Nargis was resolute.

There was much ceremony, and she was dressed in whatever finery they could afford. There was singing and dancing and drinking for three days and three nights. Finally, Nargis stood in the centre of a circle of all the Hijras of her locality and they whirled around her and she was given copious amounts of drink and as the chanting rose to a crescendo, she felt the blinding sharp pain between her legs and then it rose and rose in intensity until she blacked out. The next several days, long days at that, were only a muddled memory of searing, burning, deep unbearable pain and unconsciousness. Since surgeons do not accept to perform castration in hospitals, the benefit of anaesthesia and sterile conditions to avoid septicaemia is not an option. Recovering from the crude procedure is a chance with one in two probability. She wondered why law did not allow medical intervention when there was consent. She was taken to a sympathetic doctor who had his clinic just outside Hijra Galli. He, as usual, struggled to save one of them but it was too far gone. Her immune system had already weakened by HIV. It was then that she wanted to go to her estranged mother.

Ratnama sat cross-legged beside Nargis, her pupils wide in half-light, a small slight dot showing the beginning of cataract in her left eye. "Why did you do it, Narsing? Why?" She sobbed silently.

"To be like them, Amma. To be myself too."

22
Lost Paradise

Rubina Shabnam

I have known her from childhood. Today, when I saw her talking to passers-by in the bazaar after a long time, I came to a stop. Surprised, I went closer and I saw that she was asking everyone just this question, "Do you know where the paradise under my feet has disappeared?" Her repetition of the same question dragged me back several years into my past. . . .

For about twenty odd years, the bounties of Nature and her mother adorned her youth with a great deal of hard work and dedication because a very important duty was to be assigned to her . . . the creation of a human being . . . After fulfilling this responsibility, she would be a part of the legion of the world's well-known and respected personalities of the world. Paradise would be at her feet. She was herself overwhelmed with joy that Nature had chosen her for such an important task and considered it to be her life's ambition to accomplish it; even her own personality would be complete only after fulfilling this duty.

One day, she came to a forest as she was walking. She stumbled upon a stone idol lying by the wayside on the desolate path. She picked up the statue, and thinking that it was a statue of creation, she clasped it to her bosom and brought it home. At home, everyone looked at the form and face of the statue and tried to convince her that it could in no way be a statue of creation, but she ignored them and began to worship this statue of creation day and night. Who knows why she was convinced that it was sure to help her in achieving her mission in life. Every day she tried different wiles to make it happy so that it agreed to help her. She made new offerings daily, but all to no avail. Since she had a positive attitude to life, it was not in her character to be easily disappointed. So, several years went by in this cycle of hope and despair.

Rubina Shabnam, *Lost Paradise* In: *The Silence That Speaks*. Edited by: Haris Qadeer, Oxford University Press.
 DOI: 10.1093/oso/9780190132613.003.0023

Gradually, reality began to dawn upon her … reality that she did not want to accept even after coming face to face with it … a reality which had made her soul shiver as soon as their eyes had met. Had reality hit her or had some divine catastrophe struck her? This tender-hearted girl was bemused … no, she was dismayed … or perhaps not … She herself could not understand how to react. There were thousands of questions … what happened … ? How did it happen … ? Whose fault was it … ? Yes! Undoubtedly it was one hundred percent her fault that she had mistaken the god of tyranny and misery to be the god of creation. She had worshipped it for years … The rigours of her adoration had turned her golden body to ashes. She, who had erased her footprints, who had burnt her boats and travelled along the path … for her all roads to return had been closed. And what was the remedy now? To fulfil her life's mission and to fulfil that important duty, she returned to worshipping that god of tyranny and misery and her god began to extract a new tax every day. Her sense of modesty, decency, pride, dignity, and all ornaments of femininity were offered to her god one by one … what remained now was only a skeleton. Yet her god's heart did not melt. Every night she dreamt of flowers and buds blossoming in her courtyard; and every day when she opened her eyes, the sorrow of her deprivation gripped her heart. One day, an old crone told her that if her god bestowed just one atom from the stream of life during the fourteen nights of the burgeoning moon, she should plant it in the soil of her being. "Just see, one day it will blossom as a flower in your courtyard; and if you are able to do this during the nights of the waning moon, then a bud will emanate fragrance in your courtyard." Now there was she … fourteen moonlit nights, fourteen moonless ones, and her cruel god. She often wondered how and from where the stream of life would flow if her god was made of stone, but the very next moment she would shake off her thoughts and begin to worship her god with renewed energy and enthusiasm. She was convinced that her prayers would one day melt the stone to wax and she would be able to find the element she desired in the wax. She had to achieve her life's ambition at any cost, and then there was the question of finding paradise at her feet. But days turned into months; and months into years. Neither did any bud emit fragrance in the garden of her body nor did a flower blossom. Nature planted seeds, but her god kept her deprived of the stream of life. Finally, Nature stopped strewing seeds in the garden of her body … the realization stunned her … The aim of her life trickled from her fingers like grains of sand and she could do nothing about it.

Now the situation was such that whenever she saw flowers and buds in any courtyard, a hammer seemed to strike her heart. These blessings were so dear to her that she kept humming these lines from Wordsworth's poem, "Lucy Gray":

"The sweetest Thing that ever grew Beside a human door!"

She began to seek refuge in an imaginative world. Slowly, gradually she began to feel that Nature had blessed her with these gifts, but her cruel god had stolen these gifts from her and hidden them far away from her. Her god had estranged her from divine blessings … The poison of hatred for her god filled her being. An arrow of deprivation and failure pierced her heart. She offered all the poison in her heart to an arrow; and that very arrow … that very poison-tipped arrow she plunged into the heart of her god. In a state of frenzy, she screamed one question again and again … "Tell me, where has the paradise under my feet disappeared?" But the god was made of stone … it was lifeless. She banged her head repeatedly against the stone statue and bled profusely, but no spark of life stirred in it. Since then, she has been accosting all passers-by in a half-crazed state and asking, "Do you know where the paradise under my feet has disappeared?" Passers-by are not familiar with the background of her question. They pause for a moment; and the very next, murmuring, "She's mad," they move on.

First published as "Gwachi Jannat." Translated from Punjabi by Hina Nandrajog.

23

The Men and The Woman

Tarannum Riyaz

Aasima Begum woke up with a sudden premonition; such a horrible dream it was! She looked around her and then through the window of her room. The sound of Salman sniffing his nose and of a stream of running tap water coming from the bathroom brought a sigh of relief to her. She sat up and slipped her large toe into the arch of her velvety black slippers and walked into another room. Usually, she would step into the lawn after getting up and look at the sky. Today, she only returned after repeatedly touching the door handles of her sons' rooms. The handles were ice cold, which meant that they had been peacefully sleeping in their air-conditioned rooms and that her dream was not true. There were no paparazzi armed with cameras at her husband's car. Her sons' friends did not stand outside the house gates with motorcycles and cars, having good-natured, naughty questions in their eyes. Aasima Begum swept the sweat over her forehead with the silken sleeve of her nightgown.

She dragged a chair from the dining table next to the kitchen and sat down to make tea for herself, planning to take the cup to the patio. But then, she decided that she would bring out the tea trolley when Salman came out. But her mind was occupied somewhere else, she had very little time.

"*Maydum* ... " (Madam).

Sundari had come out of the kitchen at the sound of a chair being dragged.

"I found fresh jaggery, *Maydum* ... " Saying so, she picked up a crystal bowl off a spotlessly white tray with crushed jaggery in it, and put the granules in Aasima's cup with a shiny engraved spoon.

"Please stop taking this fake sugar, *Maydum*. Sir had told you too. It causes bone diseases." She put away the sugar pot and looked into Aasima's eyes.

Tarannum Riyaz, *The Men and The Woman* In: *The Silence That Speaks*. Edited by: Haris Qadeer, Oxford University Press. © Oxford University Press India 2022. DOI: 10.1093/oso/9780190132613.003.0024

Aasima Begum stood up saying, "Alright, listen ... I've decided ... we have very little time." Sundari, who was bent stirring tea, straightened up with the cup in her hands. Aasima walked out into the patio and Sundari followed.

"The road that goes that way ... see, from there ... " Aasima pointed outside. "Turn around the corner there ... in front of Balaji tent house, the one with a picture of a bridegroom on it ... which says ... oh ... you cannot even read ... Well, in front of that is a poster of a child being given polio drops ... "

"I know Ponio (polio), *Maydum* ... had suffered from it when little."

Sundari placed the cup and saucer on a white marble table. Aasima overcame the temptation of her Earl grey tea, which had been a family favourite since her grandfather's time and said, "Really? ... yes, yes ... now listen to me first ... there will be a red cross next to it ... I mean a symbol like this." She crossed the index fingers of both her hands to show Sundari a cross.

"Do you understand? Or are you just ... there; on the ground floor itself is the place ... "

"Yes, *Maydum* ... I understand ... "

"You understand nothing, even after being told twenty-times!"

Aasima settled herself on a wicker chair.

It was about a year back when they had sent for a maid at the placement centre; and this girl was sent with a representative. It was difficult to guess the girl's age, but she seemed pretty young. She had a small, tiny body, complexion slightly lighter than dark, a long face with prominent bones and small eyes with pupils that appeared to go in different directions. There were streaks of white in her black hair and her teeth were rather large and long.

"Where does she live?" Aasima asked the man who had brought her. She glanced at the girl and then at her cook, Kamal, who had been employed with them for two years. Within a second, he shrugged his shoulders, screwed his face, and turned it away. He was showing disapproval of the girl.

This made Aasima turn to the girl again. Aasima's old mother sat on the sofa beside her. She looked at everyone from behind her glasses and softly asked the girl, "What is your name, child?" Reactions like those of the cook and Aasima were probably not new for the girl. She mumbled something that nobody understood.

The mother nodded as if in appreciation of the name and said, "Alright, alright; and your parents?"

This time, to everyone's surprise, the girl replied loudly, "My mother dead . . . have stepmother."

"Oh, I see . . . go, freshen yourself up," said mother, pointing towards the rear lawn.

The man who had brought her said, "*She in town first time. No know language.*"

"You seem to know the language very well," said Kamal with a naughty glint in his eyes. Aasima looked at him with disapproval.

" . . . *but she learn*," he quickly added. Then with a smile said, "*I too learn language here*, had come from Jharkhand last year." He did not comprehend the sarcasm of Kamal, who had picked up speech better over the passage of time.

Aasima's mother looked at Kamal in dismay and said, "You are being harsh to the poor, motherless girl . . . "

"No . . . I was only . . . " he shamefacedly went into the backyard saying something.

"And you, my dear, are all alone in a way . . . God has given you no daughters . . . take her as your own . . . she'll give you company . . . "

"Yes, mother . . . but she does not know the language, let alone work!"

"She'll learn, it is her first time in the city . . . poor, motherless girl," said the mother with sorrow in her voice. She was going to say more when Kamal barged into the room, saying, "Ma'am! I had gone out to get clothes off the line . . . she was combing her hair . . . near the other gate . . . "

"So? Can she not comb her hair?"

"It is dark outside . . . I got scared . . . she looked . . . just like a witch!"

Mother kept gazing at him and said with displeasure: "Quiet! God has created her. She has a stepmother, wonder if she gave her enough to eat . . . the poor girl is weak . . . you should not say such haughty things!"

She then looked at the clock on the wall and rose holding the armrest of the sofa, her fair, wrinkled fingers moving on her rosary. She did not know how to read the time on the clock with Roman numerals and would usually look at the clock and then ask someone the time. This time she did not do so, and just walked into her room quietly.

The girl was hired.

Her name was Sundari, and she knew neither language nor work. However, she tried to do all of Mother's work as long as she stayed. Mother's schedule consisted of staying up late for prayers, and Sundari used to stay up with her, lest Mother be troubled by some work. The servants' quarters were in the backyard. A door of Mother's room opened into the backyard, which Sundari used to knock upon in order to enter. Mother would be reciting her prayers most of the time, so her conversations with Sundari consisted of a few sounds and signs. She used to drink warm water and often had tea. These were the only things she would require Sundari for. The signal for tea was raising an invisible cup to her lips. For water, it was a cupped palm being brought close to her chin. On cold days, she would ask for a hot water bag by shuddering and clattering her teeth.

Mother would say, "Did I not tell you that she'll learn?" in praise of Sundari. Kamal would complain to Aasima, "Even a deaf and dumb person could do this," in the absence of Mother.

Aasima would conceal her smile and ask, "Is it necessary for you to comment on all matters?"

"No Ma'am, I was only saying ..."

Sundari was trustworthy and used to keep herself tidy. The undersides of her dark feet were radiant and her slippers were neat and clean. She would tell interesting tales of her homeland.

One day, she said to Kamal, "I cook good rat, you know?"

Kamal dropped the spoon he was using and asked, "What! What do you cook?" This caused hot oil to splash over his hands. But this did not make him any less curious. "What did you just say ... ?" he asked while holding his burnt wrist under a stream of water from the tap.

"I said rat ... I cook good ... there is fat rat in my village ... " Sundari said without looking up from the spinach she was cleaning.

Aasima heard water run for long and entered the kitchen asking, "Why are you wasting water ... what's wrong ... oh, you've burnt yourself!" She quickly walked over to the wash basin and asked "Did you get a boil?"

"No Madam, just saved myself ... would have died."

"Why what happened?"

"Ask her, Madam," he replied seriously.

"Why are you always pointing fingers at her? What had happened Sundari?"

"Nothing *Maydum*, I did nothing," she innocently answered and looked at Kamal in surprise.

"Tell *Madam* about what you can cook," said Kamal.

"Oh, that! I cook good rat. My grandmother used to eat, she taught me. She cooked excellent; there are no animals or birds to eat."

Aasima looked at her with surprise and laughed when Kamal asked, "Did you eat it too?"

"I did not eat ... " Sundari finally lifted her head, smiled at both of them and got back to work.

"Must have tasted some, while cooking it ... " Kamal inquired while wiping his hands off a towel.

Aasima left the kitchen with a laughter. A smile had remained on her face long after she was in her room.

Salman had told her a lot of interesting facts about that region. The north-eastern part of India had always been a hub of astonishment. Due to migration of various tribes from all over the Indian subcontinent, the region represented a mélange of different cultures, languages, and human physiques. However, political experiments had left their deep impact on their original culture.

The British had introduced the locals to Christian faith in order to clicit their loyalties. The introduction was not a new one and had been previously done by German priests around a hundred and fifty years ago. Gradually, other Christian sects including the Roman Catholics and Anglicans followed the suit. The local worship houses called *Sarana* were turned into churches; priests only changed local names into Christian ones during baptism and did not insist upon a change in lifestyles. Therefore, changes did not seem very apparent or drastic. Land, the only source of income, got annexed by the British. Accepting the faith of the rulers appeared to be the only medium of gaining a livelihood.

There was no dearth of people who understood this and rose against it. Birsa Munda, known as Birsa Bhagwan among the local tribes, stood up against imposing Christianity. This grew into a local freedom movement and echoed Birsa's slogans along with the issues he raised. Later, education too was taken up as one of the causes.

Aasima woke up when she heard something clank in the kitchen.

Sundari was a careful worker, but the frequency of mistakes ranged from rare to very regular. Knowing this, Aasima would often call Kamal for a chore and Sundari would appear with soap bubble covered hands saying, "Kamal bhaiya go to market ... I washing dishes."

"Do that and come here when you are done," Aasima would say.

The clatter of glass would make Aasima move into the kitchen and ask, "What did you break now, Sundari?"

"The one glass left out of six," said Sundari in a matter of fact tone as she moved towards the bin with broken glass bits.

"Why, Sundari? What is wrong with your hands ... always breaking one thing or another?"

"Oh *Maydum*, I had *ponio* (polio) when I small ... could not walk at all ... took medicines and get well ... "

"Yes, you had polio ... but you are fine now," said Aasima with a sigh.

"I am fine, but sometimes ... "

"And what is this?" asked Aasima, with distress, moving towards the kitchen cabinet. She noticed a chipped end of her favourite gold outlined, fine china saucer with painted blue and pink flowers.

"O ... I don't know ... that Kamal bhaiya must have done ... not me," Sundari replied with innocence while looking up from the glass she was washing, and accidentally striking it against the tap.

Aasima could only stretch her hands and say, "Oh! Be careful ... "

"Sorry, *Maydum* ... I forget tell you one thing," Sundari said, sliding her finger around the chipped rim of the glass in her hand.

"No, no ... you'll cut yourself," said Aasima, putting forward her hand to take the glass away from Sundari. She smiled at her use of the word "sorry" and left for her room. Sundari followed her.

"How many times have I taught you to spread the sheets right, Sundari?"

"Is it not spread right ... see ... if you could just pull a little from there ... " Sundari would say with confidence and tug at the sheets. Aasima prized Sundari's self-confidence.

After Independence, priests from various local tribes were selected for churches. People demanding a separate state of Jharkhand, in 1949, were almost all Christians.

The state was separated from Bihar in the year 2000.

Except for self-governance, there was not much change in the living conditions of people. Governments were made by calling people to be loyal to their religious faiths, or by emphasizing the de-communalization of politics. The issue of livelihood remained untouched.

People like Sundari were affected by this issue, Salman had said so.

Sundari had left the room but her face remained in Aasima's sight. A proper diet had turned her hollow cheeks fleshy as a result of which Sundari's dark complexion seemed lighter. Her teeth no longer looked too large on her full face when she laughed. Her crossed eyes escalated her innocence to the level of naiveté. Aasima Begum moved into the kitchen.

"I'll teach you an exercise for your eyes," she told Sundari.

"What will it do?"

"Make your eyes beautiful. Whenever you are sitting idle, look at the nail of your index finger and move it close and away from your eyes in line with your nose."

"*Maydum*, I had to tell you something ... "

"Sure, tell me."

Sundari spoke as if delivering a joyous report. "When I was small, I went blind ... my uncle asked me to get the radio for him and I fell over, so he scolded me saying that I am blind."

Her expression became serious and she went on "*Maydum*, he should have told me that I was walking wrong. I did not know because I had gone blind. It was not my fault, he told me to come so I did. I did not even know that I had gone blind ... "

Sundari looked at Aasima to get a response for her story and saw Aasima bending in laughter. So she too joined in her laughter.

"So you did not know that you went blind ... " Aasima said in between guffaws " ... fine, then how did you recover?" She finally held back her laughter and asked.

"Then I got *tamin* (vitamin) capsules from the medicine shop and ate them for a month ... then I got well."

Kamal received a call from his village that his wife had delivered their baby. They had to let him go, even when he had already been on a holiday this year. His return was not assured, for his last child had not survived. The hunt for a new servant began.

Sundari tried to manage the chores all by herself. Aasima noticed the pulled down looks on her face and while checking her wrist softly asked "Have you got a fever? Why do you look pale? The work is too much for you, right?"

"The work is fine, *Maydum*, but ... ever since Kamal *bhaiya* has left ... I don't feel like eating," replied Sundari in a sad voice and got back to work.

A few days later, another tribal servant was hired. He had a broad jaw, flat nose, hoarse voice, and lot of scars on his face. His name was Faltoosh, and it was his first time in the city. Sundari confidently ordered him around. He learnt to work and speak in broken words. In Sundari's absence, he would rush at calls for her and say "I'll do that" while quickly batting his eyelids. He too was sent by the placement centre on an eleven-month contract and was quick to learn chores around the house.

Sundari went to fetch him from the quarters one day, when he did not turn up for work till afternoon. She quickly returned, saying, "*Maydum*, he'll cut me into pieces ... he told me."

"What ... who?"

"Faltoosh told that to me."

"Why?" asked Aasima with surprise.

"I did not do anything ... he had taken the rope cutting knife today ... it was in his hand ... brought it near my face and told ... shut up or I'll kill you ... he has a short temper!"

"Do you think he can do that?" Aasima had read several incidents of assaults in newspapers.

"I don't know *Maydum*, but he sure has a short temper ... I learnt that today."

Faltoosh had been employed for six months. Aasima narrated the incident to her husband. He was a law abiding, political man. He used to solve such matters instantly.

"Did I not say that he is good for nothing? Fire him immediately, could be a dangerous criminal. Call the placement centre, they send in just anyone ... humph!" he said, and kept looking at Aasima with diabetes medicine in one hand and a glass of water in the other. This was just the answer Aasima had expected from him. Salman removed his eyes from Aasima and swallowed the pills. Instead of going out, he sat on the sofa and asked Aasima to call the driver inside. "Ask him to go and drop the servant at the placement centre first, I'll go later," he told Aasima.

For the next few days, Sundari had to manage the work alone. The chores were done but in a disorderly manner. A new servant was hired very soon and order was restored. He was an innocent-faced boy of eighteen or nineteen. Sundari had informed Aasima that he was a good singer and imitated film actors very well.

"He is nice … but younger than me … calls me *Didi*," she told Aasima with seriousness.

"So? He is younger than you, what else should he call you?" Aasima looked at her with surprise.

"Yes, my age is more … and medicines have made my hair white, but I colour it so that my hair looks good. I don't like him calling me *Didi*, I will ask him to call me by my name."

Aasima tried to grasp the meaning of her words and said, "Sure, do as you please," while lowering her head and moving into the next room.

The chores around home were done better now. Sundari had trained her new assistant, Chaman, well. Chaman worked willingly and well. He did not seem to be looking forward to a vacation. Aasima was about to take pleasure in this fact when Sundari came up to her with a deeply troubled expression.

"*Maydum*, *Maydum*! I did not get my monthly period," she told Aasima and quickly lowered her head and collapsed on the floor beside the bed.

"There is nothing to worry about. You'll get it in a few days, it gets delayed sometimes."

"No, *Maydum*, yesterday was the fourth day … today will be the fifth," she said while showing the number with her fingers. The expression on her face was extremely disturbed.

"What … what do you mean … did you … " Aasima quickly asked. "Making a mistake does not give you period; it gives you a baby … are you … ?"

"*Maydum*, Chaman caught me … " she looked at her and lowered her head.

"What are you saying! When?"

"Last week."

"So why did you not tell me all these days? I'll send the rogue to the police … I'll … " Aasima stopped in mid-sentence and asked, "How many times did he catch you?"

"Three. It was not my will."

"Oh, so it was not your will?" Aasima sighed deeply and asked with astonishing disbelief, "Did Faltoosh catch you too?"

"Yes, many times ... I used to worry a lot, but he said that he knew nothing would happen ... and I used to get my period."

"And Kamal?" Aasima asked with further amazement.

"Yes. But he was smart; he knew where to find what in the market ... used to bring it ... I was never worried."

"Shameless girl!" Aasima raised her hand to slap Sundari but held back with clenched teeth. "Did you not call him your brother? And the rogue used to say that with open hair you look like ... like ... " Aasima was running short of breath. "You were with my pious mother too ... " she said in a trembling voice.

"No, *Maydum*, I used to bathe," Sundari quickly said.

Aasima felt dizzy and held her temples with her fingertips. Moments passed by in silence.

"Fine. Why did Faltoosh say that he'd kill you?"

"I did not get my period ... and I told that I'll tell *Maydum* about it and that you touched me. Then he got angry."

Aasima felt numb and just gaped at her. "When was the last time?" she asked.

"The day you and sir went out for dinner with the children. I was wearing a churidar ... I went to the Tuesday market with the money you gave on the *animasry* (anniversary) ... "

"Shut up!" Aasima said raising her voice. "When did you last get your period? The date ... " She asked lowering her voice.

"Oh, the period ... on the day I asked you to let me buy groceries because I wanted napkins ... I got it on the day after that."

"There must have been a date!"

"I don't remember, it has been a long while ... "

Aasima tried to remember the date. She had taken her elder son's girlfriend for lunch at the Sheraton that day. Sundari had asked for napkins that day, upon her return. But she had taken the girl for lunch twice—once at her son's request and once out of her own fondness for the girl and out of the desire to fill the void of a daughter figure in her life. That day she had also selected a dainty chain with matching earrings to gift Deeba. Aasima remembered how drops of sweat had glistened on Deeba's fragile neck even in the hotel restaurant's sixteen degree celsius temperature. That was strange in a sweet way, because she did not know that Aasima was quite fond of her.

A slight smile appeared on Aasima's face, but she quickly and intensely realized the seriousness of the present situation. She pushed away her thoughts and looked at Sundari.

"What do I do now? There is no option other than sending you back to your village." They had a long moment of heavy silence.

"Are you really pregnant or … "

"What pra … *Maydum*?"

"Nothing, just get out of my sight!"

Aasima just sat thinking and stared at the floor for a long time. Her elder son was a young man, and the second one could be thought of as a young man. Salman looked youthful too. If Sundari were really pregnant, people would cook all kinds of stories. Chaman had asked for a holiday, yesterday; and for an advance salary of two months. The placement employee had taken away a month's salary as his commission.

Aasima moved her eyes away from the crown of a nightingale seated among delicate red hued lavender flowers on a thick green vine against a blue sky, on the silken Kashmiri carpet of her room. She looked outside her window; a torn kite stuck among trimmed tree leaves looked shabby.

What if the crook runs away after taking the money? What was Aasima to do of the girl? She would send the shameless creature away. Sundari could go to hell. Aasima had been fooled all this time while this girl was indulging in mischief. Sundari can go back to her village and exhibit herself. Aasima was going to report the entire matter to Salman.

She removed her gaze from the window with contentment. She lifted a crystal deer from a table that was placed between two sofas. It had legs like lion's paws.

But Sundari's stepmother would make life even more difficult for her, might make her pregnancy known all over. Without a mother Sundari was probably never told about these things. The stepmother who would thrash her with a spatula for seeking another serving of food would find a reason to hit her. She would humiliate Sundari in front of her father. The abortion would be done by some inexperienced mid-wife in the village. There would be a lot of blood; carelessness could lead to …

Aasima had been through a horrible experience after two months of her marriage. The doctor had suggested complete bed rest in the hope of saving her unborn child. Aasima silently lay in bed out of needless coyness at her young age. She was losing blood, along with the hope of saving the child. Only after the blood had streamed down her twenty inch rubber mattress and dampened the bed boards, did she realize that her hands had gone extremely cold. Her feet had remained cold during the entire pregnancy, but she had an ominous feeling now. She had almost died, they said at the hospital.

Losing an unborn child also meant losing the hope to live. If Aasima could undergo such an atrocity under the care of the city's best doctor, then what would poor Sundari have to bear. She was only concerned with riddance, but how much blood would Sundari have to lose for that . . . and what if the fetus remained attached even after losing a lot of blood. Unless she was treated by a skillful professional . . . but how could the poor girl afford proper treatment?

Aasima walked towards the kitchen as she heard the loud sound of dishwashing.

"Sundari . . . I have decided that . . . "

"Yes, *Maydum*?" Sundari said without looking up in a sniveling voice.

"Oh, look at me . . . have you been crying?"

"What do I do? People in my village will . . . " she sobbed.

"Silly girl, I won't send you away in such a condition. We'll see what happens next, there is nothing to worry about. I'll see for myself, you are confused about the father now." Aasima wanted to stroke her head but did not.

"Wait for four more days, and then I'll take you to the hospital for a urine test. I don't think it is time for your period yet . . . Do you feel hungry at proper times?"

"Yes, *Maydum*."

"Ever felt like throwing up or dizziness?"

"No."

"Fine, leave the rest upon God and trust me. Whatever has been done is done. Now to bring you out of this problem . . . "

Aasima spoke as if to herself while looking at Sundari. "I won't leave you alone." Sundari lowered her head in agreement.

Aasima returned to her room, thinking. How would she take Sundari to the hospital? It might become a scandal. Sending her alone was not an option for she did not know the way. Sending with the driver could be one. It was no longer a crime. These days, they don't ask girls about marriage or about the name of the fetus' father. Abortion was legal now.

Salman returned very tired from work. It was inappropriate to trouble him with the matter now. Aasima wondered if discussing the matter with him was appropriate at all. He might add to Sundari's trouble with his strictly professional attitude. She just looked at him unknowingly.

Aasima lay in a nightmare-haunted slumber. Her last dream plunged her into deeper thoughtfulness.

She walked into the lawn and spoke to Sundari without looking at her.

"Look there, across that lane ... where you see the road. You already know the way up to Mother dairy. Turn left after the first right from there. You'll see a large board saying 'Balaji Tent House'. In front of that is a poster of a doctor dropping medicine into a baby's mouth. It is right there, go straight inside. That is the government hospital, just 10 minutes away. Don't worry, I'll ... "

Aasima turned towards Sundari who looked eager to say something.

"I got it, *Maydum*," she said with a smile.

"Meaning ... you mean ... you aren't ... " Aasima said with an excited smile.

"Yes, I got my period."

"When ... ?" She held Sundari's shoulders.

"Last night."

"Really ... ? Thank God!" said Aasima while looking up at the sky. She then looked back at Sundari and pushed her away while holding her shoulders and said, "Don't ever make such a mistake again. Or I'll really send you back to your village."

"I swear never to do it again, *Maydum*," she said with a smile.

"Chaman has left, *Maydum* ... "

"Really ... when?"

"I don't know, he was not at his room this morning ... "

"What did you go to his room for?"

"I did not go, the door was open ... I just saw ... all things gone." She continued with an expressionless face, "Now I'll have to do all the work on my own."

"Well, the insolent can go to hell! Why will you have to do it all ... we'll get another servant, it's just a matter of a few days. The work is too much for you alone. Plus, a male is required for most of the boys' work. Anyway, I'll ask the centre to send a decent fellow this time ... and you must be careful too."

The decent fellow arrived the next day after that.

"*Maydum*, he is here ... " said Sundari when she saw him at the main door with someone from the placement centre. "Shall I open the gate?"

"Sure, do it."

The boy was better looking than all previous servants. His hair was styled according to the latest fashion. Aasima looked away from him and at Sundari, who was looking at him intently. The boy went into the backyard to put away his things and Sundari walked towards the kitchen with a smile. Aasima followed behind.

"He doesn't look like a servant, right *Maydum*? Looks like one of your children's friends ... " Sundari said while taking a bottle of water from the fridge.

"Whatever he looks like, Sundari ... spare him, for God's sake! Or I'll really send you ... " Aasima said in a counseling tone.

Sundari started giggling and held her ears.

"I promise, *Maydum* ... " her expression turned serious, as she tightly pulled her ears. A smile spread on Aasima's face. Sundari started laughing while still holding her ears. Aasima just looked at her childlike laughter; it was an innocent, carefree, and peaceful laughter.

"Don't you understand? Look at me, Sundari ... now please don't create a mess ... " Aasima's expression was desperate. "You want me to beg with folded hands?" She asked as she folded her hands.

"No, no, *Maydum* ... I'll swear on whatever you want me to," she said while holding her ears and kept laughing. The sight of Aasima's folded hands did not stop her laughter but had widened her eyes. One eye was directed towards the right and the other to the left.

"No, please don't do that, Maydum, I really swear ... " she said looking at Aasima's hands. "I swear on God, *Maydum* ... I swear on my dead mother ... I won't repeat it," she said in between giggles and took a step towards Aasima with her head lowered.

"I ... I ... I swear on you, Maydum ... please forgive me ... " she said in a soft voice and kept smiling.

Aasima noticed tears floating in her eyes.

Translated from Urdu by Miraan Punjabi.

24

A Letter to the Sky

Asrafi Khatun

Dear Sky,
It has been a long time! I could not come to you earlier. The situation is a miserable one. Everyday, it gets crushed under the complex wheel of life. I want to tell you a certain things — a few things that you may not have seen the same way as I have. I have seen them very closely. The little girl you loved dearly, lives in a hostel now.

Actually, we never wanted to send the little girl to the hostel, but we had to take the decision. We also had to think of the future of our son. After his matriculation, he was adamant about not continuing his studies at the missionary school. He would study in Kolkata but in a different school. His refusal to study in a good school pained us. We were forced to admit him to a different school. But the problem was: who would stay with him? After a long discussion, we decided to rent a house. The father would stay with him. Then, what would happen to the younger daughter? She is in standard III, and soon, she would in standard IV. After a lot of discussions, we decided not to prioritize the daughter's education for the time being. The son's future was more important for us. He was everything at that moment — the centre of all worries, all care, and all attention.

The father was not in a good mood. What would happen to his business? He was unsure of the money that he would earn. But, still, that amount would be enough for paying the rent and electricity bills of the shop that he runs. At times, he could also buy a few items for his shop. At least, everyday he could get a sense of peace when he sat in his shop. His friends visited his shop. They drank tea, gossiped, and and did other things to kill their time. It was not his responsibility to run the family. '*Laage taka debe Gauri Sen*' is a Bangla proverb which means, 'if you ever need money, Gouri Sen will arrange it for you'.

Asrafi Khatun, *A Letter to the Sky* In: *The Silence That Speaks*. Edited by: Haris Qadeer, Oxford University Press.
 DOI: 10.1093/oso/9780190132613.003.0025

It was about twenty years ago, he saved a helpless girl, who had a BA honours and a JBT degrees, by marrying her. He rescued her. So why worry? The golden egg would be laid by the hen in due course. What else to seek for! After the marriage, the couple had to wait for almost three years for their baby.

The girl got her due for all nights long studying, for her hardwork, and for her great struggle with poverty. God bestowed His mercy on her! Asna got a job at the high school after offering a donation of a lakh rupees. What else to wish for now! Now, it was the time for her to enjoy and relax. But, after working hard for the entire day, Asna would go to the station bazaar to buy vegetables, fish, and other groceries, and only then, she could enter her house. God again showed His mercy! The bicycle that her younger brother-in-law gave her when she was studying in B.Ed in Kolkata, proved to be quite useful. Her husband, Masiul could not afford to pay for her daily fare of twenty rupees, and almost everyday, the matter became a bone of contention. One day, her younger brother-in-law saw them quarreling; he felt bad for his sister-in-law. He said: "It's fine. I shall buy a ladies' bicycle for my sister-in-law. After all, I have a job now; I am still unmarried, so I don't have many responsibilities."

Initially, Asna felt bad about it. She also felt a little humiliated. If a married woman continues her education after marriage, it is her husband's responsibility to bear all the expenses. But she was not so lucky; her husband was unemployed. Her only fault was that she wanted to continue her education and be self-dependent. Was it a serious crime?

Her parents were in hurry to get married as if she was going to dishonour her family by eloping with someone. Asna remembered her elder sisters, Boro Bubu and Mejo Bubu—as she used to call them. Both of them were very happy when they reached their class X. They would be appearing in their matriculation examinations. But, then one day, out of a sudden, a Maulvi Sahib came to their house. He liked Boro Bubu; he told that he had a nephew; they were from a Syed family, and had a *peerzada* lineage. Syed Abubakar Shah, his great-great-grandfather, was a *peer*—a saint. That was enough! My mother did not feel the need to enquire about anything else. What did the groom do for a living? Where was his ancestral place? If he owned any property? Whether the Syed sahibs had enough food in their house? All these questions became unimportant for my family. My family did not even bother to enquire about the education of the prospective groom. It was all like the famous idiom: "*Uth chhuri tor biye/dhuchni mathay diye*" (Get up, girl! You have to wear the wedding dress, it's your wedding now.) It just happened in the same manner. The grandmothers, aunties, uncles—they all warned my mother, but she had seven more daughters to worry about. She had to marry all of them — one after the other. If she doesn't take the decision for one, how would she think about her other daughters? As my parents could not follow their plan in daylight, thus, they used the darkness of night. One day, around midnight, my parents took my sister to the Maulvi Sahib's house. Following his sacred advice, they got her married off to the chosen groom; they also bid her farewell then and there.

Asna was surprised to learn about the matter when she woke up the next morning. She was in class V. Even at that tender age, she was wondering why her mother had to do it in the dead of night! Boro Bubu was good-looking enough. She was good at her studies; she was also very good in household chores. Was was the need? Why? It was like immersing a golden idol secretly, hiding it away from the public eye. She could not think of any other example. She felt like crying loudly. Just two days ago, she went to the school with Boro Bubu, Mejo Bubu, Sabur bhai, Achintyo daa, Samad Bhai, and Jayanta—all the way to the school, they were laughed and chatted happily. The past came alive before her like a living figure.

Samad Bhai whispered to her, "You know, I like your Boro Bubu so much."

"Why don't you tell her ?" Asna asked.

" I am scared." Samad Bhai replied.

Asna still remembers the day. Her thoughts and memories were circling in her head. She had a good laugh that day. "Is Boro Bubu a tiger or a bear who would eat you up!"

Samad Bhai was from a rich family. The family owned a grand house in the Paschim Para—the western part of the village. His mother was a very simple lady. She was also our distant aunt. They had a big coconut garden and orchards of other fruits such as mango and jackfruit. My sister and I visited his house for the sake of fruits on the pretext of studing there. His mother used to give us dry coconuts. Our frequency of visiting the house would increase during the summers. We could never control our greed for ripe mangoes and jackfruits.

Boro Bubu would ask me every now and then, "Asu! Shall we go to Samad Bhai's house?"

I used to say, "Why?"

"Don't you remember what the aunt told us the other day? She said, 'Come after two days . . . the jackfruit will be ripe; I shall give it to you. The mangoes are also becoming reddish in colour, I will get them plucked by someone. You must come.'" Boro Bubu replied.

Boro Bubu was a little greedy about eating. Since my childhood days, I have been seeing her eating leftover food. She used to ask everyone for their leftover food, "Give me, I will eat that." My mother often scolded her for her behaviour.

My mother would say, "Greed for food is not good for a girl. After your marriage, you will have to go to someone's house. What will people say then? They would say that the parents have given birth to a she-demon; they have never fed her enough."

Boro Bubu would make a silly face and say, "What did I do? Munna only told me that he would not eat and would give his leftover food to a dog. It is better that a human being eats the food instead of a dog."

My mother would say, "Stop your arguments. Don't pretend to be extra smart. Now help me in the household chores."

When we talk of greed, I think it is better to reveal that I am also greedy for fruits, especially for mangoes and jackfruits. We went to Samad Bhai's house secretly in the afternoon. His mother gave us a big jackfruit and *Golapkhas* mangoes weighing almost one kilogram. She said, "It is quite heavy. How are you going to carry it? Wait. I will give a bag."

When we were coming out of the house with the big bag of fruits, we found Samad Bhai standing near the backyard entrance. When he saw Boro Bubu carrying the big bag with difficulty, he volunteered, "Give me the bag. I will carry it for you to your house." Samad Bhai was elder to Boro Bubu, so he used to address her as "*tui*" (informal Bangla word for you).

Boro Bubu appeared to be quite adamant, "No, no, leave it. I will can carry it." But, Samad Bhai snatched the bag from her, "Enough of your pretenses now! You will not be able to carry it, still, you don't want to give it to me. Hand over the bag."

My mother was happy to see Samad Bhai at our house. She was very fond of him because of his gentle nature. After seeing the bag, she asked, "What is in it? Did your mother send something?"

"Yes." Samad Bhai replied.

"You sit down, son! I will offer my evening prayer." My mother said.

" Azera, give him a cup of tea." My mother commanded Boro Bubu.

"No, no tea for me. Am I a guest in your house?" Samad Bhai replied. He sat quietly on the string bed in the courtyard. His face looked dark in the dim light of the evening. If someone noticed him closely, he would know that his mind was turbulent with thoughts. He must have been thinking about why he was unable to express his feelings to Azera. He was determined to confess his love that very day. He thought of telling her just before leaving the house, "Azera! I love you so much."

But while leaving, he stopped at the gate and called Azera, "Azu! Listen, I want to tell you something." When she went to him, he held her hands and started shivering. She asked, "What happened? Tell me what you have to."

Samad Bhai's words got stuck in his throat. He ended up saying, "Come to our house tomorrow. My mother has asked you to come. I shall tell you then, do you understand?" He ran away after saying that.

Azera could not understand anything. What was he trying to convey? The plan to express love was never materialized. The next day, Azera went alone to the aunt's house. She innocently asked , "Did you ask me to come over?"

"When? No. Who told you so?" Aunt asked.

"Samad Bhai told me that you wanted me to come today." Boro Bubu replied immediately.

Samad blushed as he listened to the conversation from the adjoining room. He got angry at the stupidity of Boro Bubu, "Stupid girl! She insulted me before my mother. She could have come secretly and asked me … but no. She is revealing the secret before everyone. Dumb girl! She doesn't understand anything. Go. I will never speak to you ever again." He left the house in haste, ignoring Azera, telling his mother, "Mother, I am going out. I will be late."

Azera foolishly looked at him as he left. She suddenly said, "Aunt, I am also leaving." She too ran away. My aunt understood that something was going between them. She smiled and went back to her household chores.

It went like this for a while. Both of them did not speak to each other. Then, one evening, Samad held Azera's hand, and asked: "Why did you tell everything to my mother that day?"

"When? What did I say? You were the one who told me that your mother wanted me to come." Azera made a foolish face.

"One does not need money to become insane. If money was needed then nobody would become one." Samad got angry and said.

"It's ok. I will never say anything, anymore..."Azera replied with a stony face.

"You are such a stupid girl! Will you be able to keep secrets?" Samad was annoyed.

After being scolded by Samad, Azera entered the house with a pale face. She could not focus on her household chores.

Before their drama of love and anger was over, Boro Bubu was married off to another man in a dark night. Samad Bhai could not get up from his bed for three days. He suffered from high fever. He is still unmarried. He often tells me, "Your Boro Bubu did not marry me. Who else shall I marry now?"

Mejo Bubu also did not lead a happy life. She too was married off to a spoilt son of one of our relatives. After marriage, her husband harassed and humiliated her. As long as his father was alive, he lived a comfortable life. The family could afford to have their daily bread and butter. They faced difficult times as soon as the father suffered a stroke. Although he was a school teacher, his son did not study much as he fell into bad company. After his father's death, he did not get any job except for a peon's. He was not eligible for any better job. He did not accept the job offer despite his mother's requests. He harassed his wife and mother to give him money to start his own business. Their financial condition deteriorated by the time the couple had a son and a daughter. There was no one left to look after them.

My mother was also in a miserable condition. She got her youngest daughter married off to an unemployed man by giving a part of her ancestral land as dowry. The man sold the land to start a betel-leaves shop. He also married another woman. The youngest and most loving daughter of my mother returned to her parents' home. Her in-laws took away her three-year-old son. Her son is under the custody of his stepmother. My mother felt so sorry for her daughter that she forgot about her other daughters.

One day, my mother came to know that she was suffering from a fatal disease. She wasn't keeping well for a while, but she could never imagine that she would suffer from a deadly disease. To whom she would ask to look after her youngest daughter? What about her treatment? All her daughters were busy in their own lives. As a mother, she never thought that it was her responsibility; she had married all her daughters, and was not required to look after them. She was only concerned with the youngest one who was abandoned by her husband. My mother was helpless now. So, she called her daughters:

"I have no one to call my own except you all. I need money for my treatment. If I don't survive, who will look after my youngest daughter? I want to sell the small plot of land near my house. Does anyone want to buy it?"

"I am almost a beggar. How can I buy?" Boro Bubu said.

"No, no. I do not have the money to buy a land. You did not give any dowry when I was married." Mejo Bubu said.

"What nonsense! Mother is ill, and now you talk of dowry! Leave it. Money is needed for our mother's treatment. If we are unable to save our mother, what will happen to the little girl? Who will look after her? I shall buy. Mother, I will get the money even if I have to borrow. How much will it cost?" I said.

"Forty thousand rupees." Mother told in a sad voice.

Our relatives started criticising her. The adjacent house was sold for only twenty thousand and she is asking for forty thousand from her own daughter. What kind of mother she is!

I had arguments with my husband. I sold my jewellary and took loans to collect the amount. But, one day, I came to know that my mother called Mejo Bubu and her husband for giving them the land. I went to my mother's house to know the truth.

"You heard it right. I am giving it as a dowry to Zarina. We could not give her much at the time of her wedding." She told me.

"What about your treatment? How are you going to afford a doctor? How are you going to manage the money for your surgery?" I was agitated.

"Whatever happens, let it happen! One has to die anyway. I may will die a few days before. None of you should be worried for me." My mother replied.

I was deeply hurt! Ah! my mother would not get her treatment because of paucity of money. If I had enough money, I would have given it to her without any return. But Mejo Bubu was her daughter too! How could she not feel anything for our mother? Was getting dowry so important for her? That too, when mother was on her death bed? Did she understand that land and property are not everything in life? Did she understand that we would never get another mother if she leaves us?

"How much is the fees for the doctor and the treatment? I will bear all the expenses for your surgery." I said to my mother.

"How are you going to manage it? Your husband is unemployed. You have two children. You can't even run your own house properly." My mother said.

"I shall take more tuitions. I will stitch saree-falls; I will stitch border of sarees; I will stitch *lungis*." I told her.

"What about your children and your family? Who will look after them? Won't you have to appear for job-examinations? Why did you study so hard?" My mother replied.

My heart ached. She was right. I bled as I walked on the path of progress. I gave tuitions. My mother would oppose me during those days. I tolerated everything in my life. Often, I only had puffed rice to eat. Sometimes I slept with half-filled stomach, and sometimes, even without any food ... how I earned my graduation degree with honours, I cannot even describe! I also completed a Junior Basic Training course with a lot of hardwork. I only had one aim in life—to get a job. If my parents hadn't hurried for my marriage, I would have got a job.

The days passed quicky. Months passed by. I roamed around with with strange thoughts. The taunts of relatives affected me. Whenever I visited my mother, I gave her whatever I could afford. My mind was not at peace. Through out the whole time, I lived with some sort of pain and uneasiness.

While crossing the vast ocean of sorrow, I see an island! My life has brightened with a hope to live! I feel that my husband and children are very close to my heart. I also remember my mother, but she has passed away, and is sleeping peacefully in her grave. I often visit her grave, and tell her: "Mother, you could have waited just for a few more days. I have a job now. You did not get enough time in this world! You went back to your Creator. You were so worried about your youngest daughter. Do you know that she went to meet Boro Bubu to her village? May be she was also getting ready to meet you! That's why she left us one day with a smile on her face. It is only I who is still holding on. I don't know how long will I be able to? When shall I be free! Whether I will be free or not . . . I don't know. You pray for me. Bless me!"

Dear sky, It has been days since I looked at you! Although I see you everyday but where is the time to talk to you? It has been long since I felt your cool touch. It has been long since the last I dived into your cottony and cloudy mind. Do you remember the advice that you gave? You said, "If you want peace, write letters. It doesn't matter if you send them or not. That is not a big deal! Your mind would lighten up if you write your thoughts on pages. A day would come, when you would have a big collection of letters. Then, you can send all those letters to me. I will make a garland of your pains and wear it. I shall be be happy to do so. You are a poet too. You can also write a few poems for me. It will lighten up your mind." So, after a long time, I missing you so much today when I started my life's journey with a heavy heart, I remember making you a witness. I sailed for uncertainty. I faced uncountable storms. You always supported me wholeheartedly. Today, I remember all those terrible days again. Memory of the past brings more tears. I feel at peace to tell you about those bygone days. I feel reassured thinking that you would never laugh at my pains, no matter what others may think. So I am here to tell you about my my past. You know the truth . . . people may say that they do not want to remember their pasts. We often want to forget our past and move on, but it is impossible to do so. Our past teaches us ways of surviving the present.

What else! May be some day again, I shall come to you at a sluggish moment on a stormy day. I will write wholeheartedly to you. I know that you will never throw away my letters without reading them. Because nobody other than you, knows that life oscillates between pain and pleasure.

Stay well. Take care. Be happy. That is only my wish!

Sincerely Yours,

Yours own.

First published as *Akash ke Chithi*. Translated from Bengali by Arzuman Ara.

25
Green Tree Stumps

Sami Rafiq

"Don't paint with numbers, lines and circles, paint with your heart" was an utterance that was her.

Pegah was finishing the morning frying of parathas, eggs, toast, and tea. She had forgotten to switch off the old toaster in time, and it was the third toast that she had burnt that morning. Then, she was helping her mother make the beds, and her mother grumbled that she could not do anything right, she couldn't even pull a sheet straight, " 'butter fingers' (as she referred to her in third person) had already burnt three toasts and even the milk had boiled over."

She had an aching desire to run away outside and sit and dream on the wooden swing under the lush mango trees.

There was something about those mango trees in the back yard and the invigorating scent of mango blossoms that always brought her solace and comfort.

But the image in her mind, of the swing moving dreamily back and forth in the company of the mango trees, dissipated as other perils awaited her.

Amidst the rantings of her mother, she thought of the high school result that was due to arrive by post that morning. She knew the result would not indicate the emotional intelligence that she had gained in the company of her friends at the boarding, though it would sum up her mathematical intelligence as low. Yet from her parents' side, she feared the worst because she had performed poorly in the Mathematics examination.

Her father had expected her to get an A+ in Mathematics and then they would go to the hills for the vacation.

But she knew there would be no such trip as she was sure to fail and even worse she would be loaded with extra tuition and in addition the

Sami Rafiq, *Green Tree Stumps* In: *The Silence That Speaks*. Edited by: Haris Qadeer, Oxford University Press.
 DOI: 10.1093/oso/9780190132613.003.0026

grave prospect of the loss of family honour as family honour was the golden cage in which a Muslim girl lived.

"Who knew whether she would even pass the Mathematics test a second time if she had to give a re-test!" she had thought wiping the cold sweat and swallowing her cold tea.

"You are not looking well!" her mother said which was a rare utterance from her, and Pegah knew it was more of an assertion than an inquiry of concern.

Her mother could interpret Islam on her own terms and so she felt every good Muslim girl should be obedient and tidy even if she knew nothing about the Quran. Her purpose in keeping Pegah in the boarding was that she would learn to be a good homemaker as according to her that was the ideal life for a Muslim woman.

Of course, her staunch religious father had his misgivings about the boarding school where the girls wore skirts and sometimes their sweaty shirts revealed their body outlines. But he was in competition with his brother who could not send his kids to an expensive boarding school so he had bitten the bullet with a grimace.

Pegah was rather tall for her age with a pale pimply skin and thin body; with lank dark hair that seemed to interfere with everything she did. Nobody ever thought her pretty except perhaps Sajid.

At home, she never tied it, but in the boarding school, she had to plait it and tie it with ribbons.

She hated the ribbons and the exacting discipline of the boarding school but loved the friends and the freedom found in that cloister.

There was no mother and no father to pester her to study or to do the mundane household chores. She was particularly weak in Mathematics but she made up for it in the art class.

Fast forwarding into the future, they were the same old tasks day in day out as she waited for her husband to come home.

He would sometimes call and say that he was not coming home for lunch then she would eat alone.

She was standing near the window of their four-storey apartment and watching the cars go in and out in a posh society in a foreign country. There were many picturesque oak trees that stood all around.

A globe shaped hanging light gave off reflections of her in its glass.

But it also reflected the universe outside of giant, kindly, gnarled oak trees. This was where they lived after their marriage.

It had been just two years since they had married and left India. He was an engineer by profession, and she a housewife though she was loaded with degrees in fine arts.

When the phone rang, he was on the line—"I will be home in exactly five minutes. Put the food to warm—I'll eat two rotis, two spoons of sweet curds, one bowl of rice, two helpings of lamb curry, and a three fourth cup of salad," he said hanging up.

She was standing, intently watching her image touch the image of a massive oak tree which stood right outside their window.

She attempted to recall the amounts as they had been uttered … because she couldn't see how Mathematics could fit in with one's appetite.

"Even the oak tree is kinder to me and will forgive me if I count or colour its branches in a violent manner," she uttered as she laid the plates all the time fearing that he would count the spots on them.

He was a genius with Mathematics and had a passion for learning up all the numbers around which their lives revolved, the monthly electricity bill, the grocery bill, the insurance, the savings etc.

She would withdraw into herself when he would rattle off the exact amounts without even having to calculate them on paper.

It was only much later that she realised that even she was only a number in his life and that sex too was measured out in numbers … in perfect timing and of course the oak appeared more gentle, more kind when she thought of its biological side.

With the passage of months, the apparent attractiveness of her face had worn off for him, and he began to distrust her as far as numbers were concerned.

Her fear of Mathematics had started when she scrawled number five in an inverted way in her class I and the teacher had slapped her hard.

It was then that she decided that Mathematics was not for her and not her cup of tea.

By the time she reached high school, she thought she could get rid of the measly numbers and opt for something more pleasant and peaceful like fine arts.

She had always excelled in the subject for there was no compulsion for numbers in the pictures that she painted.

The neem and banyan trees figured prominently in her school paintings. She knew that their numbers were dwindling but no one was counting them.

Nobody was counting the clouds, or houses or streets either and neither was she forced to come up with a solution.

But her father had never been easy about her escape from the Math demon, for he believed that numbers had in them a romantic beauty.

She thought she may have fallen in love with a grey-eyed boy in her art class, but she was painfully aware that he would not find acceptance in her house. Sajid was an artist like herself; while she found her peace in water colours, he found his haven in oils and tapestry.

He had startling grey eyes and golden hair which, according to her, reflected his artistic and angelic soul.

They would put their painting projects side by side and try to evaluate them. Nobody appreciated her work like he did, and no one could gage the nuances in his work like she did.

Once Sajid had said, "Look at that mango tree in your painting and the crooked village road in mine ... you and me are like the colours of a rainbow ... "

"But you don't get to see rainbows every day," she had replied not looking up from her painting.

She knew silently that Sajid thought that they were always meant to be together even if her father did not like him.

When one morning she had seen the mango trees being axed and logged away in their yard, she knew Human Math and Nature Math were severely at odds.

It was as she had suspected all along that her father had other plans for her and sure enough he found a suitor for her, who had mesmerized him with his genius for Mathematics.

"And I hope he will teach her something about Mathematics ... the poor dumb thing ... I can't see her going anywhere without it," he said to his wife.

Pegah's mother had replied, "But she hates Mathematics" to which he did not reply as he was calculating the wedding expenses.

"Now I suppose I've some money for her wedding after logging those ugly old mango trees!" he went on.

After an appropriately calculated courtship, Pegah and Nasir were married.

At that moment standing near the globe of light, she remembered how she had been unable to screw the bulb that morning.

Her husband had given her a look of derision and pulled the bulb out of her hand and had hastily screwed it matching symbol with symbol and mumbling.

She had seen the image of the oak tree vanish in the bulb in his hand.

"That's the third bulb this week . . . you should be watching the electricity bill . . . it has almost doubled!"

"I didn't know that the bill had doubled . . . all I did was fix a more powerful bulb in my room to paint better," she had replied.

"Do you know how much it costs, the rupees, the paise, the income tax . . . it all comes to fewer savings . . . ugh! . . . " he said disposing the old bulb with a crash.

For a few minutes, she felt that the images of the oak tree and her had changed into the picture of a goat in the glass globe.

To her troubled mind came the memory of a glass lampshade that she and Sajid had painted together.

For both of them, it was a masterpiece and love had enhanced its beauty.

It was the picture of a wild and obstinate *peepal* tree that had begun to break through a wall of their school.

There was no fight between the colours that both of them put into it and the tree appeared a sheer living force of nature.

"One day, the poor tree will be discovered as a non-mathematical addition to this universe and will be wrenched and pulled out and no one will even hear it cry . . . and yet . . . ," she faltered.

"And yet . . . " there was questioning in his grey eyes.

"Its roots will continue to hold on . . . "

"At least we are preserving its beauty," he had answered putting his arm around her neck.

When they had put a bulb in the lampshade, the sheer majesty and ecstasy of the colours was illumined in a sacred way.

A stranger in one of their art exhibitions stood a long time before that lighted lamp shade and said, "never have I seen such an effulgent light of cosmic love in all my sojourns in the universe of art."

Her father, however, flung it at the wall and its shards flew about like stars from a crashing galaxy—when she mentioned that the guy who gave it to her wanted to marry her.

She never saw Sajid again after that ... and she knew that the galaxy could never be put together again.

Even the poor peepal tree had met its fate.

Presently, she desired to smash the bulb that her husband had just fixed.

She couldn't help but feel remorse that her husband was only a more diabolical development of her father's Math mania.

The day the high school result card would be opened would be the day all her hopes would be shattered.

She had trembled on the creaking swing under the mango tree and shivered at the dining table though it was a hot summer's day. Her father had promised that they would go for a vacation in the cool hills and that he would buy her a new camera and a new watch.

She knew that postman was at the door, and there would be no vacation or camera or watch.

Her mother slipped the large stamped envelope on the table before her.

"Your high school result, probably and your father will see it when he gets back."

Mathematics had not spared her in the present moment either. That morning after her husband had left, she had decided to go to the bank to withdraw some money. The money was in a joint account between the two of them.

After the episode of the bulb in the morning, she had realized that she was tired of painting in a closed room.

She hoped that she would be able to ask a neighbour for a lift to the nearest market where she would buy all the art material and sit outside under the trees and paint portraits of people and get paid.

She knew she had to have her own money.

She stepped out of the neighbour's car at the door of the bank.

"Do you want me to wait for you?" the lady asked.

"No, thanks," Pegah said and went into the suffocating, air-conditioned bank.

She was nervous in her white T-shirt and black trousers and her hair in a thin pony tail. This was the first time she had come to the bank on her own. She wondered whether it looked odd.

She finally wrote out a cheque of 50,000 rupees and with shaky hands took the money and slipped it into her purse.

The gatekeeper eyed her with surprise as she slipped out like a thief.

She settled in a busy place of the market under a giant shady tree and pulled out her aisle and her brushes.

Very soon, she was painting her first portrait of a teenage girl and her boyfriend. They loved it, and they paid her even though she refused as it was her first painting.

They were followed by an old lady with her grandchild. The tolling of a bell reminded her that she had to get home as her husband would be home for lunch.

Although she wanted to tell him about the bank and the portraits over lunch she was unable to. He seemed to be in a cheerful mood and didn't seem to mind that the rice was a little under cooked and she had not served his favourite dessert of sweet curds.

When he was gone, she realized the enormity of her crime.

She knew he hated painting, and he never encouraged her to go to the bank on her own. She was also aware that he would know by evening that she had withdrawn cash from the bank.

It was so like the day when the high school result arrived and her father would see her failure at the end of the day and then all her dreams would be shattered.

It was the same when her husband would arrive at the end of the day and would see her crime and then all her dreams would be shattered.

He commented some days later, as he stood by the glass windows "look at that stump of an oak tree destroyed by the lightening last night … "

Fast forwarding into the future, she was painting the portrait of a middle-aged man and the grey eyes and golden hair seemed familiar.

"Don't paint with numbers, lines, and circles, paint with your heart," he said slowly and effortlessly.

He seemed to hate Mathematics like her and then she was reminded of how her Mathematics copy would be assaulted with angry red marks from the teacher, and the biased teacher would cancel out even an equation that she had done correctly.

In contrast to this non-mathematical gentleman's words, her husband's cold cash like tone reverberated so many years into the future, " … you said you drew fifty-thousand rupees, but the account update says five lakh . . . "

Even though it was the silly mistake of adding an extra zero, she had accepted the damning verdict that she was a failure. Failure however had no place in her portraits and her last visit to the oak trees and mango trees showed a smidgen of green.

26

Sending the Lord Away

Nasira Sharma

Returning from the university, as soon as Farzana entered her house, the basket of sweets lying in the halls informed her that news of her wedding date getting fixed had been floating in the air. She wanted to quickly secure a *laddu* in her mouth, although, she hesitated. As soon as Chanda saw Farzana, she rushed from where she was picking the trash in the courtyard and announced elatedly, "the bride is here!"

Farzana felt jittered by this attack. Each woman of the house came towards the hall, leaving whatever they were up to. Badi Phuppi greeted her with an *Aadaab*. She sent Farzana's misfortunes away by crunching her knuckles and embraced her. Her Khala-Ammi kissed her forehead, and at this moment Chanda began singing: "*Banno teri akhiyaan, surmedaani*" (Bride, your eyes are kohl-pods!).

"Quiet, *wretched one*! Your throat makes the sound of a cracked bamboo!" Ammi rebuffed her.

"*Begum* sahib, are we going to get any *neg*, any cash or presents or not?" she spread her *aanchal* before everyone.

"This one is quite all-rounder! She could be *mirasin, nayan, maniharin*[1]—all at once!" Badi Phuppi took a note out of her purse and put it in Chanda's *aanchal.*

"I don't stop any work, now, do I?" exclaiming which, Chanda went on to pick up the trash from the hall.

"She's come tired from a long day. Your face is all so small with fatigue, dear bride! Will someone please ask Shabbo for some sherbet and food?," Badi Phuppi patted Farzana's face. Phuppi's remarks made Farzana hungry. She gaped at the basket. Had it been any other day, she

---

[1] Mirasin—women performers; Nayan—women from community of barbers; Maniharin—women from community of bangle makers.

Nasira Sharma, *Sending the Lord Away* In: *The Silence That Speaks.* Edited by: Haris Qadeer, Oxford University Press. © Oxford University Press India 2022. DOI: 10.1093/oso/9780190132613.003.0027

would have swooped and picked up a *laddu* and eaten it without any care, swaying her legs; but this was her . . .

"Painters will turn up tomorrow morning and this Queen Elizabeth of ours has not been able to sort the odds and the ends!" Shabbo grumbled and went across the courtyard with the breakfast tray.

"I am not giving you anything, do you understand that?" Chanda was irritated.

"There are plenty who will provide me. After all, we are not trash-pickers, now are we, who else will take care of the garbage!" Shabbo swaggered her way as she placed the breakfast tray and then returned.

"As if I don't know, that there are several pals of yours, you innocent one!" exclaimed Chanda, and laughed. Shabbo frowned. Palpitating, she cried out, "Your brain is full of worms, which is why you indulge in such ill thoughts. *Arré*, I meant . . . "

"Ah, leave it, you. I am well aware of what you meant," saying this, Chanda went on with her trash-picking. Shabbo giggled and stared at her, and then swiftly moved towards the kitchen, banging the batten on the floor.

"Are you people ever going to shut up?" Ammi scolded them both.

"Farzana went to her room and was all fazed. Parading in her solicitude, she held her bed and contemplated upon how at all she agreed to get married so easily! She wanted to do an M.A. She wanted to sit for the I.A.S. entrance exam. Ammi and Abbu liked this one guy and turned a blind eye to her aspirations. They do not remember anything now, neither their promise nor her dream. "It is my marriage, and no one even bothered to ask me. Simply . . . "

After the lamps were lit in the evening, all the men of the house too gathered in the courtyard, all washed up and tidy. Phuppijaan and Khāla-Ammi were snoozing after having sent half of the baskets of sweets in the neighbourhood. Farzana too lied on the bed in the courtyard and appeared to be busy reading a magazine, but her ears were attentive to the talks surrounding her.

"Has the amount for *meher*[2] been decided, Irshad?" Badi Phuppijaan asked her brother.

---

[2] A payment, in the form of money or possessions paid by the groom, to the bride at the time of marriage (payment also has circumstances on when and how to pay). While the *meher* is often money, it can also be anything agreed upon by the bride such as jewellery, home goods, furniture, a dwelling, or some land. Meher is typically specified in the marriage contract signed during an Islamic marriage.

"We were waiting for you. So far all the weddings were arranged within the family. Conventionally, it has been somewhere around fourteen thousand rupees."

"The count of fourteen is auspicious, fourteen being the number of the immaculate ones. But this marriage has been arranged among outsiders," Phuppi expressed her worry.

"Considering this, Phuppijaan, *meher* should be settled at one lakh twenty-four thousand rupees; it's quite a lucky number too!" speaking with a sombre voice, Firoz then stared at Phuppi.

"How so?" Phuppi rolled her big eyes.

"*Arré*, so far there have been one lakh and twenty-four thousand Imams," Firoz exclaimed with gravity.

"You are right, indeed," Phuppijaan was lost in thoughts.

"Their business is running well, they will agree Phuppijaan," Firoz tweeted.

"Since when have you been keeping your nose in other people's p's and q's?" *Arré*, talk about what has been going on in our family," said Khala, disgruntled.

"One lakh is not too much now. Isn't it, *Baji*? It's not that time and age where like in Bibi's *nikah* we settle the *meher* in three rupees. There are thousands of risks, don't we hear a new story every day. The girl should have some firm ground, after all, she is our only daughter," Ma expressed, feebly.

"Maulvi Imam visited yesterday. Said it is futile, however much you settle the *meher* for! The groom's side will agree to it in their opulence since anyway they do not even give a do it at the end. It's all a matter of pleasing, settle for whatever amount; nevertheless, the Islamic ritual is to pay the *meher* immediately after the *nikah* ceremony. But who is to listen! Everyone is making new rules as is convenient to them. They do it in the name of Islam—but I think those who are meaning to settle the amount will do it anyhow, be it before or after the marriage. Look at my case, your brother-in-law gave the house in lieu of *meher*. I now sit respectfully in my own corner. The same is the case with Fiza, she got orchards of guavas and mangos in lieu of meher. She eats her share in peace now," said Badi Phuppi.

"They will agree to whatever amount, fifty or seventy! They are after us, saying, Asghar master is highly respected, and the girl is educated too.

This is exactly the kind of home we were looking for, one which would help in growing our prestige even more! Money comes and goes like dirt in one's hands. That's why we won't accept even a single penny for dowry," said Irshad.

"Ah, what does it matter what they say! Would we send our daughter away empty-handed? *Arré-waah*!" Badi Phuppi was infuriated.

"I think, Shammo, fifty thousand is an appropriate amount. And then, it is also about mutual credence. Rest we should leave in the hands of God," said Khala.

"Alright. Fifty is a fine number ... they might not agree to one lakh anyway. Things could be left to air, or it could cause some sort of distress as well," Irshad added, pensively.

"What distress are you talking about? Fifty thousand rupees have no standing today; it will amount to nothing tomorrow," said Ammi.

"Phuppijaan, one lakh twenty-four thousand—it is nothing but a plain loss of seventy-four thousand rupees," Firoz said softly.

"Quiet, you spite! Joking all the time," Badi Phuppi said in a manner of anger, but smiling slowly, and placing her nephew's head in her lap she started stroking it.

"Other than love, there are thousands of other issues that now exist in a relationship between a man and a woman, otherwise, why would this mayhem bother us?" said Irshad.

Listening to all these conversations provoked Farzana. Everyone is concerned about the money. How much will the *meher* be settled for, how many pairs of clothes, jewellery, sugar, and sweets will go in *bari*,[3] instead, no one is asking if she will be allowed to study further? Will they let me go to the university? Will they let me compete for I.A.S.? Her anger came out in the form of tears. She used to make claims in front of her friends with such pride, that I will not get married already, I will study, but ...

"Don't cry, child. Every girl has to leave her father's home one day. Both paupers and the kings have to send their daughters away," Khala began to weep as she exclaimed and with her everyone's eyes were moist. Saving herself from everyone, Farzana ran towards her room, stomping her foot as she threw the trail of cups and shields that she had received as rewards,

[3] Gift of dry fruits and bags of sugars, etc. that is given to bride's family by groom's family.

all off the cornice, and taking the framed certificates off the wall. Had Chanda not held her hand, the certificates would have been shattered into pieces as well.

There were about six to seven days to the wedding. Farzana had stopped attending the university. In any case, her exams were over too. She had no enthusiasm towards the measurements of the clothes that were being stitched in and outside the house, or in looking at jewellery, kitchenware, or towards buying things of her choice. A fear consumed her—how will she sleep in her new house. Up and asleep a face would appear in front of her eyes and she would sit upright, in shock. However, much she jittered; she would always find that face dancing in front of her eyes. She had met Zubair at Khala's elder brother's wedding. A tall, well-built man, dark in complexion, who was different from all in his manner of talking and moving—everyone's eyes were fixed upon him. She too did not find him bad, but that did not mean that her family should have been on her back to marry him!

"My dear child, what are you thinking?"

"Nothing, Chanda."

"Can I say one thing, my child, *nayan*, *mirasin* will be here from your village in a day or two. That's why you should give your old clothes to me. You could give a couple of old ones with holes in them to Shabbo too, I will not mind," said Chanda, stroking Farzana's feet.

"I can hear everything . . . aren't you satisfied with all the clutter that you have collected, that you are here asking for clothes from our daughter?" Shabbo stood all alert as she swept the room with a broom.

"You are going to be here, innocent one, I am only advocating for you. And instead, you are fighting with me?" Chanda exclaimed in wonder, with her finger on her nose, jerking her waist.

"I know all your manoeuvres—you plan to swipe this house clean with your smooth talk!"

"Chanda—where are you! Come here and fold-out this bedspread," hearing Khala's voice, Chanda sprinted away.

"Such a spite, this one," exclaimed Shabbo, and full with gusto began to sweep even faster.

Relatives started gathering even before it was evening. It was Farzana's pre-wedding *majha* ceremony today. Phuppi prepared the mix. Everyone began to apply *ubtan* (paste of turmeric and gram flour) on the bride.

Wedding songs were being played and amidst all the friskiness; Phuppijaan was making small talks with other women and the elder women were applying *ubtan* on their hands, throwing it here and there as they did so.

"*Ae* sister, everyone had their eyes on that guy. Achhan Miya's wife was green with envy when she heard it! Same was the case with Batool Bibi."

"The marriage procession will land at your doorstep tomorrow. Let the jealous ones be."

"I heard, the groom has plentiful wealth and property!"

"Right, he runs a business of his own ... They run a shop for embroidery and one small factory where they make plastic bottles ... he has two sisters, both of them have been married off to their new homes. That's about it, it's these three brothers now, eldest of whom is Zubair Miya."

"Allah bless them, it's a lovely name ... May it be prosperous for Ishrat, everything should go well."

The rest of the conversations died under *mirasin's* taps on the *dholak*. *Nayan* lifted Farzana in her lap towards her room. Draped in yellow attire, Farzana could sense a change in her. Her irritation and anger were now turned into melancholy. She became aware that her home would be left behind. She was struck by a quiet. Her sisters and sisters-in-law were teasing her, making jokes and having fun. Her heart had also begun to tickle, just a little.

The activities and arrangements involved on a wedding day were all over the place in the house since morning. *Ubtan*, massage, *mehndi* and then by the time it was evening, the *nikah* happened involving the nose ring and *missi* decorations, and the red *dupattu*, along with the amount of fifty thousand, promised as *meher*. Now, her name was not the same. Her home and relations were not the same either. There were only a few hours left for the new life to begin. Romantic ridiculing, fun-filled anecdotes, a decorated *sehra*, swirling clothes, and whirling smells made her unconscious. Several scenarios were taking rounds in her head. Her childhood, youth, home, school, university, scenes of the wedding night from films, and the instances about the "first time" as she had read in books—all knitting a dream of romance. And then with everyone's crying as they held each other, she didn't realize when it was that she was made to sit next to Zubair in the car. With the assurance that her brother will pick her up on *chauthi*, the fourth day from the wedding.

"Your daughter-in-law is but a slice of the moon ... I am sure they had donated wheat to the poor."

"Has got quite an amount as dowry as well ... I have heard she is a *degreewali*—she is a degree-holder."

Around midnight, after finishing the ritual of meeting people at her in-laws', she was made to move towards the room. Her whole day was spent sitting, and she was sent-off from her parents' early in the morning at four. Now her eyes were heavy with sleep. Young-little girls, daughters of her sisters-in-law, would sit in her lap sometimes, or stroke her face lightly. It was only after the dinner tables were set, that everyone had left her alone in the room.

She took a deep sigh. But by that time, amidst the calls for *neg*, customary presents and cash for closing the door, jokes, and laughter, clanking bangles, and impish anecdotes, Zubair entered the room. Farzana's heart began to throb. Anxious, she coiled around herself and resigned her head down. She thought Zubair will lift her veil now and ...

"You are educated and sensible. That's why I want to say something to you ... I hope you are listening?"

"Yes," Farzana was startled by this sudden attack. Opening her eyes, she spoke in a feeble voice and changed the position of her arms and legs.

"I am a businessman. And that's why I see the reality of life beyond the world of books ... are you getting what I am trying to say? If you will respond in 'yes' or 'no'. Should I continue."

"Yes," the same feeble voice and the bundle moved. "I have read all the books of our religious law and have heard several *maulvis* as well. That's why I want the matter to be clear and there should be no apprehensions from your end too. Lawfully, I should handover the amount of fifty thousand for *meher* at this moment, and it is only then that I will have the right to lift your veil, and touch your body ... that's why."

"Yes," Farzana exclaimed, agitated. She was not able to understand anything. While she was walking with her, Bhabhi had mentioned completely different things. And here, instead of romantic conversations, the groom is giving a premeditated speech. What kind of first night of marriage is this?

"See, if you want the amount due for *meher*, I do not have an issue, we belong to the business class. I can write a cheque at this very moment. But the issue here is something else. The woman who exempts the *meher* from her husband on the first night of the wedding is considered to be auspicious. She is deemed as pure and chaste."

"Ok," Farzana was panicking a little. No one had mentioned this. What should she say now? Nervous, she lifted her gaze and looked at Zubair from behind her veil.

"Trust me, I am not going to touch you until you take a resolution on this. I am not one of those uncouth men. You are mine now. That is why, I have faith, and patience, I can wait, but whatever step I am going to take is going to be in principle with law and religion, I will never cross the line. You must be thinking that I am one of those people, behaving as if I am a *Maulvi* myself. That I have conservative beliefs. It is not so, but before we begin a new life together I wish to complete every custom as it should be."

Farzana felt unconscious. Her father's tearful face began to float in front of her eyes. Tonight she had to decide between marital bliss and *meher*. This was a trying time for her.

"You haven't said anything ... " said Zubair.

"If I forgo the *meher*, I lose everything on the first night itself. No claim, no power, nothing whatsoever ... if I don't do so, then I let go on love—bearing the charge for my whole life that I preferred money over love," Farzana introspected.

"I am not sure why are you so scared ... I should leave. You should sleep without any worry and call me whenever you are ready to answer." Speaking thus, Zubair took a step further.

"Wait," Farzana was unsure how she was able to utter. Her face was hot with humiliation.

"Yes," Zubair turned.

"*Meher* is indeed not dearer to me than you are," Farzana spoke, exhausted, and her eyes were now brimming with tears.

"That is what I was expecting from you. Are you going to waive the *meher*, then?"

"Yes," a failed voice stemmed out of Farzana's throat, and she soaked in her tears with all her might. She had to prove her innocence without any experience. Even in the absence of any contest, she had to announce the other side as the winning side.

"Now I have the right to see you and touch you," saying which, Zubair lifted Farzana's veil and put a beautiful necklace around her neck.

Farzana appeared quite tired and upset to everyone when she visited her home on *chauthi*. She cried her heart out, holding her father around her arms. Her mother became doubtful, her girl is not happy. Khala, Phuppi, Bhabhi, Nayan, Shabbo, Chanda, every single person enquired her persistently, but in vain. With Zubair smiling, it seemed everything was alright, but Farzana's dismal countenance, pensive eyes . . . ?

Several days were past. Farzana came back to her parents' house from her in-laws' once again. One day, she found a chance to speak with her brother, that she is quite worried, and that she wanted to say something to him.

"Why, what happened?" said Firoz.

"Brother, if Abbu comes to know, I don't know what it will lead to. First, you have to promise not to tell anyone."

"Will you at least say something . . . what is the matter anyway?" Firoz was stressful.

"Zubair . . . " Farzana's face was flushed.

"What? Was there a fight? Did he say something inappropriate?" Firoz wiggled his sister's nose in affection.

"No, brother. That amount for *meher* . . . he got me to waive my *meher*," speaking so, Farzana took a deep breath.

"What are you saying? I didn't understand . . . he *got you* to waive the *meher*? Tell me the whole thing, so that I am able to get exactly what you are trying to tell me and . . . " Firoz stood there in surprise, unable to absorb the shock that her words evoked.

"Zubair explained how by letting go of the *meher* a woman is deemed auspicious for her husband," Farzana spoke in a shattered voice.

"And you appreciated this flattery by . . . and how is it that each woman of this house is so wretched, that . . . your immaturity . . . all of you young women do not understand anything at all!" Firoz was red with anger.

"No, brother, it's not my fault . . . he had put a condition that he won't lift my veil until either he pays the amount for *meher* in cash or if I let it be . . . "

"My lord! I have never heard this one before. I cannot believe this is happening in our society. Did you talk to Ammi about this?" Firoz tied his fist in anger and despair.

"I have been too afraid to bring it up with anybody . . . I was thinking about Abbu. He was already so concerned regarding the whole *meher* issue. I don't about Ammi, how is she going to deal with this?" All of a sudden, Farzana's eyes were teary. The grief on her face was showing deeper.

"Anyway, you should not get too worried. I will get in touch with Maulvi Imam. I will bring you along; I can smell something suspicious here. I will not let that man be! That treacherous one." Firoz was clenching his teeth as he spoke.

"I used to say that I want to study further, but ... " Farzana said, sadly. For a little while, Firoz kept staring at his sister. And then spoke as he felt stable, "Look, Farzana, use your head, you have the *nikahnama*[4] with you, right? All the conditions have been duly recorded. What's there to be scared now? You have only waived it verbally, you haven't given anything in written, now have you?" Firoz said as he was spelling it out to himself.

"No," Farzana spoke as she wiped the tears falling across her cheeks.

"We will fight this as and when we will need to. God forbids! But you should be patient. Law seeks evidence. It responds to legal, official documents. Verbal agreements don't bear a stand anywhere. That is why you should keep your cool and stay happy, we make these oral obligations to each other, good or bad. You should forget this," Firoz reassured his sister and took a sigh of relief himself, for the disaster had been deferred for the moment.

The gloom on Farzana's face faded after the conversation she had with her brother. The heaviness of her eyes had turned into a twinkle. Firoz, on the other hand, was worried after listening to what Farzana had to tell him. He had never heard of such a thing ever before. He had seen the amount for *meher* getting settled sooner or later, but he could not believe that well-educated, prosperous men would do or think as such. The only thing that was in favour was that his sister did not settle anything with signatures and had agreed only verbally. On the other side, Farzana was experiencing ephemeral contentment, but there was something that was troubling her like a lump inside her heart, that why was she stripped of her right? What will happen to her in the time to come? Why was her

[4] A binding contract and a fundamental element of an Islamic marriage. It describes the rights and obligations agreed upon by both parties (the bride and the groom) which confirms the consent of both the husband and the wife.

security taken away from her by putting her between the devil and the deep sea?

It was quite difficult for Farzana to spend her day at her in-laws' home without there being anything for her to do. She would miss her university, teachers, and her friends. One day, she tidied up her father-in-law's cluttered desk, out of sheer habit. She arranged the documents into files. She was fond of organizing her father's books since she was a child. When he returned in the evening, her father-in-law was upset seeing his desk, thinking all the documents have been lost to cleaning. Gauging his anger, Begum smiled. His *pandan* (betel nut box) seemed all too decorated, and noticeable! This small gesture by Farzana filled her parents-in-law with so much love, such that she wasn't even able to know it. Instead, she was cleaning dry leaves off the plants with a trowel.

It had been two months since the wedding, and today a custom known as *Handiyan doi chulwana*[5] was to be observed. Both the sisters-in-law had prepared something sweet and savoury in the morning, discreetly, so that Farzana doesn't have to bear any insult on account of being an educated one who is otherwise good for nothing. That is why mother-in-law could sit in pride amidst the guests, without anything to worry about since everything had been taken care of. Unaffected by any of this, Farzana was immersed in preparing a dessert called "Onion-Kheer." Her brothers-in-law teased her quite a few times—"Bhabhi, don't end up putting salt in the *kheer* instead of sugar!" looking at her manner and execution, Mama ended up gloating all over her. She spoke softly, "When did you learn all of this amidst your studies, dear daughter-in-law?"

"We had to study home science during my school days, Bua. I used to see Ammi cook at home as well," said Farzana, wiping her sweat. She was anxious, wishing for everything to go well. Phuppijaan used to have her make this *kheer* quite a few times before her marriage so that when the time comes, this custom could be accomplished appropriately. This was a new thing. Everyone applauded Farzana. Most of them were surprised by the fact that a *kheer* so sweet and aromatic could be made using something as foul-smelling as an onion! Only educated girls could perform such a wonder!

---

[5] A ceremony in which a new bride cooks for the first time.

It was Zubair's Khala's wedding next week. The whole family was to go to Jaunpur. It was as if one whole compartment in the train was reserved by these people. Sisters-in-law and their husbands, kids, father and mother-in law, and brother-in-law were engaging each other with jokes and laughter, and in food—so much so that they didn't realize when Jaunpur had arrived! Farzana's heart was blooming with happiness.

The new bride was the centre of attention at Khala's place, but Farzana was no old bride either. Hence, she was receiving her *muh-dikhayi*, a token for meeting her for the first time, from the women who could not make it to her wedding. During the night, all the women and young girls lied beside each other on the mattresses spread on the floor and chatted. Jokes and anecdotes were being shared. Afsana remarked out of the blue, "Bhabhi, let me show you some drama," saying which she got up and sat with a woman who was sitting by herself, and stared at her as the woman ate tobacco from her pouch. And then she spoke, "Nani Amma, when did you get married?"

"My *nikah*? Silly girl, what are you asking, it's been some fifty ... oh, no, sixty years! What should I even recall, nothing remains now, neither my beauty, my age, nor my youth," she sighed as she spoke, and pulled her purse's string, licking the remaining lime off her fingers.

"Say something," the women and the young girls requested altogether. Everyone had mischief beaming off their faces.

"She is our old Dai, Anna Bua ... Every elder one in this house has been raised by her," slowly, someone slipped this information into Farzana's ears.

"Tell us, won't you, how did Nana see you?"

"You must be looking splendid!"

"Of course, Bibi, in that age and time, wherever I stepped, I used to swipe the land off from under people's feet. I was quite popular. Your Nanu had gone bonkers over me. He said that he would only marry me and no one else. That's it; we were married to each other in a jiffy! But, good heavens, how he had scared me. On the night of our wedding, amidst pleasing chit-chat, he spoke out of the blue that he would jump into the well if I don't waive the *meher*! I too was quite mischievous. I said impishly, "do whatever you wish to, I am not excusing it." Little did I know that there really was a well in their courtyard! As soon as he heard me, he jumped onto the wellhead. He said, "So, are you going to let it go or not?" I couldn't believe that what I thought was a joke would lead to this. Wailing, I ran towards him and convinced him to come back. He was laughing as I was crying. God forbid, he had quite a funny bone. Whenever he wanted something out of me, he would rush in the direction of the same well ... It was only after a long time when I saw that that well was brimming with waste, I had finally felt a sense of relief."

"And then?" someone asked.

"And then, what, I had already let go *meher* anyway ... Alright now run away I have to get some sleep." Laughing, the girls got up from where Anna Bua was resting, but Farzana was quite upset.

Her in-laws' place had everything that she needed; there was nothing more that she could have asked for. She had even sought her father-in-law's permission to pursue her studies further. She had won her mother-in-law's heart by serving her left and right to her pleasure. But she was not able to hoist the flag of her triumphant femininity against manhood. In her heart, she wanted to know the truth behind the whole *meher* issue. After a lot of thinking, she could think of one thing that she could do. When she started to read certain religious texts, the happiness that her mother-in-law and father-in-law felt knew absolutely no bounds! However, they were not aware of the sift that was going behind these godly texts.

When Farzana was visiting her parents' home on the occasion of Eid, on her request, her brother had called Maulvi Ali Imam, who was a friend of their Phuppi's brother-in-law. Firoz mentioned the issue at hand when everyone gathered after supper at midnight for some tea and dry fruits. Hearing which, a master in Political Science and a degree from Najaf, the Maulvi could be seen red as he said, "Lord Almighty ... what craft is this! This is but a man's gambit in a man's world so that he can steal every weapon from a woman's hand, either with love, law, or sometimes with despotism. I don't know why, in their greed for wealth accompanied by their fear for any woman's independence, men have resorted to illiterate maulvis. I have been arguing over all of these issues with them. And when I show them *Sharia*, *Hadith*, and the Quran, I realize that these fools know absolutely nothing! Neither do they study nor do they wish to learn."

"And what about the learned ones who engage in such things?" Firoz wanted to augment the discussion.

"They're selfish, egotistical, nitwitted, educated men who are hardly learned at all. They want to snatch away all that they can fetch out of a woman but do not have a giving heart themselves. They are afraid of well-educated women. I am telling you, the law and the women won't benefit anything from these bastard *maulvis* and lawmakers. Women will have to educate themselves in *Hadith* and the law, and fight for their own selves … that's what I think. That is why be it the government or the common man, they hesitate in front of me … in matters of advice and counsel, you will always find an army of illiterates in every newspaper along with their photographs. People gain pleasure in making an issue out of non-issues.

The hand in which Maulvi was carrying the *Tasbih*-beads was now shaking. Firoz thought it appropriate to end the conversation there. Hence, he extended a fresh cup of tea towards him and signalled towards his sister to not ask any more questions. For a while, there was utter silence.

"Chachajaan, what is the connection between *meher* and marriage such that there are so many issues regarding *meher*? It is often said that *meher* is the monetary worth of a woman, which a man pays … " Farzana enquired after some time.

"Wrong! Absolutely wrong! The meaning of *meher* is—love and affection, and not … Lord Almighty! … none of this is worth discussing. It's far removed from the truth." Ali Imam expectorated and continued, "*chair cheezin*[6] things are necessary so that the marriage is lawfully valid—one, the girl must be asked if she agrees to be married; two, there should be two witnesses, who should be men. In the absence of a man, testimonies of two women shall be considered equal to that of one man. It is important that the *nikah* is performed in front of an audience; *meher* is of the utmost importance because that is considered as a "token money" or *shagun* for that agreement wherein he has promised to take care of the woman the groom is marrying. If there is even one thing that is absent, the *nikah* or the marriage will be deemed invalid. In fact, in the case where someone promises an amount of *meher* which is beyond their financial capacity even that is considered void since in this situation, the foundation of the marriage lies in fallacy. That is why, the amount of "*meher*" should be the

[6] Four things (here, essential to a lawfully valid wedding).

least—according to the rules it should either be gold in the size of the seed of a date or an amount of gold that holds the possibility to be paid pronto. This amount is the guarantee that the man is not going to sit on what the woman owns, and instead, he will earn the bread and feed her and will take care of her comfort. Among us, marriage is a contract. In case of a breach of even a single clause results in the breach of the agreement or the marriage could be considered null. The girl can make potential use of her right. She can say no if she has been wedded against her wishes. That is precisely why it is advised to conduct the wedding in front of a number of people, and not in secret. I will send you the books, you may read them and try to understand . . . speaking of which, why are you asking me these questions? Is there a problem, or . . . ?"

Farzana's face began to change colours. Her earlobes were turning red with humiliation. A rebellion rose in her head—what is the point in going back to the house of a husband who is but a liar, an ignorant! She should stay here at her parents' place instead and teach her parents a lesson that she should have been allowed to pursue her education further instead of marrying her off. If it was so important for her to get married, then why was she not taught about what marriage, divorces, the relationship between a man and a woman is all about, why was she pushed into darkness!

"This means that *meher* is in a way a security amount for the integrity that the husband has to prove later with his conduct and character. Or should it be explained in this way that *meher* is not a woman's price but a man's bail-money." Firoz spoke as he began to contemplate.

"You are getting it absolutely right. If only everyone could understand this. Many a time, people make the mistake of understanding *meher* as the amount paid for a woman's sustenance, or dowry. In reality, it is a promise of a life that will be led in prosperity and equality, which a man presents in the form of *meher*. Although, right, that when the relationships break off, leading to a divorce, there is no role of *meher* there; instead, there is this whole issue of alimony. That is an entirely different matter of concern.

"If *meher* is supposed to be paid off right away, then why do people pay it off in old age or at the hour of death, in the form of houses, shops, property, gardens, and so on?"

"So that after their death their wife should not be left at others' mercy. That is why instead of a cash amount, they offer the amount in the form of immovable property. This is a romantic expression of those noblemen, who have a soft corner for their wives in their hearts and feel a sense of responsibility towards them.

"But then, this task can be accomplished earlier too?" asked Firoz.

"Yes, indeed, but they would have just started to earn. They would have not inherited any property as yet. Even then, there can be several rightful owners of that property. They have some money deposited in the bank. If the amount for *meher* is settled in accordance with their social and financial status, then they can pay it off as soon as it is possible for them to. I have conducted several *nikah* in this country, of wealthy families who believed in *Hadith* and not in this transaction of money. They settled *meher* for a rupee and a half or three or a guinea worth of gold, which was paid off by the groom to the bride right at that moment. On the other hand, grooms from families with an average financial background had to settle for an amount as big as one and a half lakh rupees. Dowry is prohibited in Islam, despite that it was paid only in order to show it off to the world. The fundamental was compromised for the worldly. More than often it so resulted that the woman never returned to her in-laws' place from her parents' and the man was married to another woman. His home was now prosperous with the dowry gained from his first and his second wife. Misdeeds of such devious nature are now commonplace because people are adopting what is convenient and criminal, in place of leading themselves onto the righteous path. What does Islam have to do with such instances, that the blame is imposed on the religion," saying which, Ali Imam took a long, deep sigh and was now preparing to leave.

"Do you believe that in following all that is there in *Hadith* one can attain peace and justice" Firoz enquired in a rather sombre tone.

"It isn't just about *Hadith*, but about choosing the path of honesty. One should have some insight about their life. When you walk on that path, the chances of falling off it are lesser, and you will benefit from the peace and justice that has been promised by the religious law. Else, you will have to abide by the law of the disorderly, and there will be no end to your worldly grieves." Ali Imam tied his shoelace and set his countenance and placed the black turban on his head.

"All the religious writings are in Arabic, and I do not know the language in the first place," said Firoz.

"It is not so. There have been several translations in English and Urdu. It is about showing interest and knowing oneself. You will not be able to comprehend the expanse until you understand the roots, and in believing in the wrong kind of knowledge you will end up assuming yourself as weak," Ali Imam spoke, placing his hand on Firoz's shoulder.

"I enjoy conversing with you," Firoz exclaimed smilingly.

"You can enjoy alright, but my dear young prince, be cautious of these things in your wedding," Maulana chuckled.

"Yes, that shall be the testing hour," Firoz responded to him with a grin.

"Whatever you do, do not do it in a fit. Anger is the most innocent declaration of losing a war. A woman has every weapon that a man doesn't in order to attain what is rightful," spoke Ali Imam, responding to Farzana's greetings, placing his hand over her hand fondly.

"Yes," Farzana was caught surprised. She understood that Maulvi Imam has gauged everything.

"Character is a much sharper and shinier weapon than wealth, power, prosperity, because it holds a person's being," saying which Ali Imam exited the room, obliging Farzana with newer grounds to contemplate upon.

Even there were volcanoes erupting inside Farzana's head, but from the outside, she was trying to present herself as calm as it was possible for her, but by all means, her anger wouldn't lessen concerning the fact that her marriage was partially valid and partially unlawful. Whenever Zubair used to bring his hands close to her, she would feel as if she was being raped. She would grow so violent inside that she would fear doing something horribly wrong. By his craft and guile, he first enfeebled the woman, and then showed affection, but I am determined to destroy the hold of this noose, using the same wit and diplomacy that Zubair had employed in manoeuvring me on our first night together. This cold war will have last until she comes out victorious.

Whenever she was alone in her room, she used to stare at the ceiling the whole time, making several plans, clenching her fists, and sailing along her long, heavy breaths. She was living two lives now—one where in her head she was Zubair's enemy. And another, in reality, as his wife, listening to and abiding by all that he had to say to her. Her whole attention was focused on how can the purpose be served without having to facing any consequences herself, what will happen to Zubair? If she stays sulking at her parents' house, then it won't take him long to bring another bride home and reap all the convenience that he can in the name of Islam and in lieu of saving her pride she would end up losing her self-respect instead—this did not seem appropriate. It would only make sense for her when the water in this river of convenience is made to turn the other way around, only if she could teach Zubair a lesson if she could cut the beard off that illiterate maulvi, but how? How at all?

It was summertime. Farzana had come back to her in-laws' place. When Zubair used to return after a long day out in the sun, a glass of sherbet from Farzana's hands would relax him immensely. During the night, whenever Zubair would try to touch Farzana, she would turn around and tell him, "please Zubair, it is too hot tonight."

Listening to this Zubair would find the desert cooler's cold breeze hotter than the summer's loo, and the night would turn into a journey in the sun. On the other hand, for Farzana, every intimate touch of Zubair was nothing but a trap, and Zubair a fowler. The raging storm inside her hadn't rested yet. She would stare at Zubair's discolouring face and would swallow down the bitterness that was ready to spurt out her mouth thinking that it was enough for today since there is no wisdom in giving a patient all his medicine all at once.

One day, Farzana was embarrassed by seeing that two men had come along with the guy from the factory in order to install an air conditioner. The whole house was brimming with joy. Both her brother-in-laws gathered in the room to look at the A.C. being installed. Somewhere in her heart, she was comforted to know that Zubair cared for her. She cooked some fine delicacies and changed the room's upholstery, spreading an aura of festivity in the whole house. Seeing this, when he returned in the evening, Zubair was elated and took the whole family out on a long drive in the car.

During the night, in the room soaked in blue light and snowy breeze, there was the fragrance of Rajnigandha diffused all over. Farzana felt a pull by a newfound attraction in Zubair's countenance. She was responsible for creating this mellow ambience. Then why was she hesitating? Everything feels so strange, why? On one hand, their relationship was gaining a solid foundation of love; on the other, the scuffle between self-respect and logic was attacking her sense of sympathy, leading her into a sea of agony. She could follow her heart and persist the short-lived beauty, and drink a handful of love, not disappointing Zubair, and to not getting immersed in grief herself, but her conscience is stopping her—do not follow the flow of emotions, there will be several such beautiful nights, have some patience. Compromising the future for today's pleasure will knock back, where she will have to stroll in the streets of sorrow.

"Who should I listen to?" Giving up, Farzana began to roll her fingers into her hair. She was breaking down. She was feeling weaker.

"What happened?" Zubair looked at Farzana in some astonishment as he entered the room in his nightgown after having brushed his teeth.

"Nothing," replied Farzana, smiling as she puffed away the clouds that were blocking her vision.

"Is it a headache?" Zubair looked at her pallid countenance and as she nodded, he began to rub her forehead slightly.

A beautiful night was slipping away, gingerly. Zubair slept as he was rubbing her head. She took Zubair's hand and pressed it against her lips first and then lightly against her breasts.

"How long will this go on for? Expressing my anger in this manner should not lead to any unpleasant consequences. I will have to gather the courage to speak my mind, or else this martyrdom will go waste in silence"—Farzana was contemplating. She wasn't feeling sleepy either. She would look at her husband's body with eyes full of love, and then at other times, she would cover the tears shining in her eyes by stuffing her face into the pillow.

Zubair was inclined to deliberate upon Farzana's regular excuses. Despite several trials, he was not able to look beyond the love and attraction that he felt towards Farzana. Each passing day, the closer he was to Farzana romantically, physically they got further away. Somewhere he felt that Farzana did not feel attracted to him anymore. Was this his loss or…

"What are you looking for in these books all the time?" Zubair asked as he moved the pile of books lying on the bed.

"You," Farzana looked at her husband smilingly.

"Me?" Reaching for the bed, Zubair found himself rather surprised. Books lied between him and Farzana.

"Yes, you said in our first meeting that you have read quite a lot, you know sufficiently about religion as well, since then I felt inclined that I should carry forward your interest, but so far, even after reading so much, none of the *Hadith* or the *Sunnah* have mentioned that a woman has to exempt the amount for *meher* on the first night." Farzana said rather innocently, collecting the books.

"Oh, that … that was just," Zubair stuttered. He did not expect this conversation especially since it had been a while.

"I am doing just fine. But what if my daughter faces any difficulty? Meaning, what if she waives her *meher* and later she is not able to stay with her husband … and she also doesn't have *meher* in her right too … meanwhile, due to any unforeseen circumstances, if your business also … or what if we have so many kids that we are not able to feed them … I am always surrounded by several such concerns. That is why I wish to go to the bottom of certain things, so that my daughters do not have to face any difficulty," Farzana's tone was full of concern and her face full of despair.

"All that is fine, but we do not have kids as yet. You are counting the chickens before the eggs are hatched." Zubair giggled.

"I will not have a child born out of rape. Even if that makes people call me barren … " Farzana spoke, gritting her teeth.

"Did you say something?" Zubair was startled.

"No, nothing," Farzana flipped smilingly.

"I see. My ears must be ringing then," Zubair spoke, baffled.

"I want you to make me meet that *maulvi* who told you this law so that I am able to understand the law that is not available in these principal texts and are now getting popular as conventions," Farzana said in a playful manner and laughed as she looked deep into Zubair's eyes.

"I don't know any *maulvi*. I don't believe in these kinds of things anyway," Zubair spoke, rather confused.

"Does it mean that you lied to me on that night," Farzana's smooth fingers got lost in her husband's hair.

"Not entirely, although, partly," Zubair smiled feebly. He was caught in a trap, unaware.

"Why?" Farzana was shocked and batted her eyes dramatically.

"Because my friends had advised me that I should deal with the issue of *meher* on the first night itself, or else … " Zubair beamed at his victory.

" … or else, what?" all of a sudden the look over Farzana's face had changed.

"Forget it, why are you concerned about those fifty thousand? You are wearing a jewellery set worth one lakh as we speak, my love." Zubair extended his hand to embrace Farzana.

"No, Zubair. First, you'll have to give me an answer—or else what?" she bounced off to the other end of the bed.

"Ah, just like that, to make you agree to my terms on the first night would have entailed that I could lead by the nose for the rest of our lives, else you would have bullied me into listening to you, these kinds" Zubair spoke, comfortably, straightening his legs and sliding further into the bed.

"But you could not imagine what would happen if and when I come to know about this? If you will lose your worth?" Farzana's tone had changed.

"Women are not aware of these kinds of things. For them, whatever the husband and the *maulvi* say is the truth." Zubair laughed.

"Women are not aware of these kind of things," Farzana's tone was harsher now. Zubair had never seen her in a temper. That is why, despite not having gauged the root of the issue here, and without conjecturing much, he spoke in an assertive tone—"Yes, because they do not hunt for the truth like you do, instead, they believe in what their husband has to say, and hence, live contently. You are keen to turn your heaven into hell. Will you be able to get any love by insulting me?"

"Now, is this another precondition?" Farzana asked sarcastically.

"No, or maybe yes, I don't know ..." Zubair said bewilderingly.

"Look, Zubair, I die a little every day along with you. I am scared that I am going mad. I am always prodded by the terms that you had put on the first night, everything that you had said. The more I try to forget, the less I am able to. Maybe it is because it was wrong from the religious point of view, it was false—the foundation of our love is false and deceitful. I pine in its clenches. Try to understand my pain, will you? This pain will not die by wearing jewellery worth lakhs and crores ... " Farzana's eyes were brimming with tears.

"You're crazy. It is nothing like you think it is. My love for you knows no bounds. Let it go." Suddenly, the anger cast on Zubair's face began to settle like dust.

"But I fail to love you even if I try. Whatever you had said on that night hits me hard all the time; it tells me that you took advantage of my helplessness and my innocence. After our lord, it is only appropriate to bow against your husband; but, pray tell me, will I be able to revere you wholeheartedly? Would you bow your head against the lord who is not truthful to you?"

"Stop it, Farzana ... I didn't do any of it deliberately, or even understanding much of it. It was all done in a whim—of my masculinity, of my power, my pride, of thinking of myself as superior to you. I committed this mistake in that spell. You can punish me in any way that you want, but please, do not leave me!" Zubair exclaimed as he saw Farzana opening her suitcase.

"Yet another ruse, a new trap that you are setting in the name of love? If you are regretting it, you would also know how to atone yourself from it. I am but punishing myself here for my nerve. I will let this womb be barren, I will not bear a child of the man who would whirl the flag of his authority in the name of love, who would snatch a woman's right by deceit and declare his victory when discovering her unarmed. That land will not sprout, ever." An angry obstinacy rested on Farzana's face.

"I am mortified," the gravity on Zubair's face was biting the dust.

"If you had to break customs, unleash a mutiny, you could have built the foundation of a new life, which would have had its own rules. If you had to rebel against the rules of this religion, you could have subverted it as an atheist, but you did not want to risk any such dangers. By accepting a life of rules and religion you conveniently chose those rules in your favour which profited you and slammed the ones that you thought would favour the others, is this not a crime?"

"You are bent on destroying everything! Keep your cool, what is the point of all this? We are happy, as we were and will be."

"I was never happy—I was living a sham of a life, gathering courage, searching for the truth and today I want to make a decision if I want to live with you or live my life alone." Farzana declared as she was packing her suitcase.

"Have you lost it? Zubair was angry.

"I have come to my senses, I am awake now. I do not wish to continue to live this life full of compromises, where I am made to feel helpless and where I am denied the rights God and the Prophet have granted me. The future is unpredictable—what foundation can possibly be laid on this swamp land?" As emotions took over, Farzana's voice was bolder than ever.

"Speak softly, there is someone in the hall ... unnecessarily ... " Zubair placed his hand over her mouth in panic. It was still for a while.

"Do not touch me ... I have been stressed to the extent that I can shatter into pieces right at this moment. I had the power to endure until I was quiet. Now that I have opened my mouth, my patience has reached its capacity. I will need some rest for a few days, the silence before the storm. Please drop me back at my home. Do not come to take me back, until I say so," Farzana's gave her final judgement as she locked the suitcase.

Farzana had left. The in-laws' house felt empty. Farzana's strategy was successful to an extent. Since she had won their hearts from her service and dedication earlier, they were now pining for her. By spoiling everyone, her name would be on their lips all the time, and Zubair was perturbed by the way their house looked like now, with his parents insisting and his brothers full of questions. Until now, there was this one demand—so many months have passed and our daughter-in-law still had not been expecting a child. Farzana had laid that truth bare. The question that he has been asked now is why was he not going to his in-laws' place? Why is he not bringing Farzana back? Only Farzana could undo this knot. At times, he would beat his head over how law, education, and medical facilities have only made lives miserable.

In the meantime, her parents-in-law along with their two younger sons came to visit their daughter in law. They tried to dig deeper into the matter, but they could learn nothing about the situation, except this that Farzana's mother had not been keeping well, and the doctor had advised complete rest. A month passed by in this way. Zubair did not receive any message from Farzana.

Zubair would feel angry at Farzana at times; at other times, he felt affection towards her, but he was never able to fathom where his fault lied. If Farzana had access to the safe full with ornaments, the bank which had every penny that belonged to the family, the keys to the house which his mother had handed over to Farzana, Zubair couldn't seem to realize why an amount of fifty thousand rupees was so important to Farzana. She alone is the owner of at least four times of that sum. After all, what was lacking? Despite all this, why has she left all her jewellery here? On the other end, his friends convinced him, "Let it be, mate. Women throw such tantrums, one has to whack them once or twice for their mind to be in the right place. Our wives not only exempted us from the *meher* but they also forgive us for our mistakes every day. All I know is that without tightening the *dholak*, and without suppressing a woman, they will make nonsensical noises. My sister-in-law isn't married yet, I can ask for her if you wish?"

Learning and listening to everything they had to say, Zubair got distanced from his friends. Everything was scattered in their home, there was clumsiness and a feeling of helplessness in the relationships. Had Farzana not taken care of everything like she did, he wouldn't have realized how she was so much better as a wife than the wives of men that surrounded him. She is a better daughter-in-law, a better human being. But? I had put my heart and my whole being at her foot. I listened to everything she said, fulfilled every wish of hers ... despite that she pulled a tempest in a teapot ... maybe she had gone crazy. If she continues with such behaviour, then I will keep loving her lesser and lesser. I could teach her a lesson by remaining indifferent. I could go to the mountains for a few days, making an excuse that it is for the business. At least I will get an escape from Abba-Amma's questions. She too would realize that instead of making efforts in her praise and persuasion, I have left for a tour myself.

On the other side, awaiting Zubair every day, Farzana would wonder if Zubair was so unwise that despite having told him everything he could not free her of the knot that was entrenched in her head and her heart. Where did his love disappear? Has he forgotten me? Or is he under the spell of his masculinity all over again? If men and women do not respect each other, don't take care of each other's bliss when in love, it does nothing but kills the very drive and desire of being. I think I was not able to make this known to him, nor did he want to understand. If not the whole male community, at least a part of it is quite self-obsessed.

When the second month was about to get over too, Farzana assumed that she would have to spend the rest of her life at her parents' house, and if she makes her peace with all of this and tries to call Zubair, what would he do when he comes? What would she do if she leaves with him? Would she have to live with this agony day and night? Would she live a lie in the name of love, ashamed, like someone out on bail?

Even her parents began to be suspicious of her account. Her mother would explain to her that second to their God, one is only allowed to bow in front of their husband, and hence, the figure of a husband is that of a *majazi khuda* - "God on Earth." What's the point of being upset with that worldly God? By engaging her in such conversations she too advised her to return to her husband's house, where, quite cleverly so, Farzana used ill-health and her need for rest as an excuse to attract her mother's attention towards herself, but how could she have escaped Firoz? One afternoon, he engaged in a conversation with his sister.

"What is the matter?" Firoz stared at her.

"Nothing is the matter, brother," Farzana replied in a weary voice.

"Is Zubair undergoing a training period?" Firoz's eyes sparkled with mischief.

"Probably," Farzana giggled.

"Do not change the topic by laughing it off, dear sister. Abbu and Ammi are worried, and there your parents-in-law are concerned as well."

"Bhaiya, I am not able to live with what happened, it is emptying me as it destroys me from within. It is as if my future is hanging like a sword right above my head. All that I have, it is as if..."

"Does Zubair know about your anxiety?"

"Yes, he does. We discussed it openly one day. He is humiliated and terrified, but..."

"But, what?"

"He does not know how to reach me."

"Then, who is going to tell him that?"

"Let him search for his way himself, Bhaiya. When I left him, I asked him not to come until I ask him to."

"And that fool agreed?" Firoz ended up laughing.

"I will not lend that fool a piece of my mind and end up living a life of compromise. He should understand what the issue is as days are passing." Farzana spoke in a manner of humour.

"If there were a few more women like you they would teach men a lesson and liberate them from the hold of *maulvis*, helping their husbands in becoming normal human beings. But Farzana, what is going to happen is exactly the opposite of what I just said. All of the liability would descent on you. You will be blamed, and he on the other hand will marry someone else. That is why, I think you should take it slow, and act wisely after having a sense of the situation at hand. If you were to listen to me, then I could jump in and handle the situation."

"Not at all, Bhaiya! I do not need any help, Zubair has to handle this himself, and I have come a little too far to go back on my decision now."

"Then, what can I do for you?"

"To be patient with me for a few days, and to grant me the permission to stay in this house."

Firoz was tearful hearing Farzana's last statement. He placed his hand over his sister's head and then left the room quietly. His heart was full of questions of many kinds—in any and every relationship a woman plays one definite role, and that is of love and affection; however, the roles that a man plays in a relationship always revolves around fabricating, manipulating, and his own ego. He does not think anything of anyone under the whims that he bears of his power—be it his sister, his mother, or his wife. It is only when he becomes a father to his daughter, his whole disposition changes into something so meek, wretched, and depressed. He thinks of the whole world as evil. By the time he understands the relationships of his lifetime from the point of view of a woman, he is closer to the dusk of his lifetime and he finds himself unable to share his experience with anyone. Introspectively, he might as well be regretting his deeds over the span of his life, but from the outside he blames the system and the society. Kudos to the men of the world!

Returning from his vacation, Zubair's fatigue turned into sorrow when he found out that no letter or message from Farzana was waiting for him. He was shattered. His parents were somewhat annoyed with him as well. His brothers were involved in their whims and fancies. They would come back home rather late at night, they would be careless with their work, and looking at the bad state of affairs of the factory, he felt as if the ship that he has been sailing on was now sinking. Everything was coming to an end. For several days, he was trying to cope up with his devastated condition. And then when found himself completely broken and shattered into pieces, a thought crossed his mind—Farzana had said that she would call me, she did not say anything regarding me visiting her on my own, but why did I agree to everything that she had to say? I will go there, I will definitely go there. I will not listen to her. After all, I too have some lien of my own! I need her. I cannot live without her anymore."

Farzana's distressed face and her awaiting eyes vexed her brother. As the days were passing by, Farzana could feel the ground beneath her slipping away bit by bit. Firoz would bring brand new magazines and novels every now and then and she would merely flip through their pages and put them away on the table. That was about it—all her attention was focused on that one spot, and it was mining all her energy. Sick of this, Firoz invited Maulvi Ali Imam—their Phuppi's brother in law—and his friend Maulana Wahiuddin who was visiting him. Phuppi and Khala also came by. After some talks about this and that, Maulvi Imam asked out of the blue, "Beti, since when have you not been at your in-laws' place?"

Farzana stuttered, "Yes ... yes, I did go," as if her theft has been caught. Maulvi Wahiuddin noted her anxiety and her distressed countenance.

"It is your time to make merry and feast. And, after all, if you are engaged in the kind of things that interest you, your face should reflect some humour. Knowledge is wealth; indeed, it can end the darkness that engulfs one's heart and mind. He is my friend, and in several of his books he discusses women in the Islamic times. You should talk to him," Maulvi Imam suggested.

"He is my friend, what do I say now ... yes, I am somewhat keen on learning and writing. Tell me, have you ever heard of 'Hajra'?"

"Yes ...," it was all Farzana could utter.

"Never mind, it doesn't matter. Right, there is a saying in English which goes like 'Behind everything good, there is a woman's hand'. Now, listen to this ... Hajra and Sara were the two wives of Hazrat Ibrahim. Hajra left Egypt and started living in a desert taking the child that she bore along with her. Ibrahim dropped them there. The assumption was—the city space destroys the human essence. That is why, by living in a desert, one learns to survive hunger and sacrificing the worldly desires. That is why, the child should be brought up there. That little child, Ismael, was now growing up and later because of Ismael, the desert began to populate—which would later come to be known as '*Saheba Giroh*.' That is from where our Prophet belonged. Hajra and Prophet are two and half thousand years apart. Now you can imagine the determination of the woman-being who not only reared a child by surviving the sufferings that a desert has to offer, but also founded the whole population on her son's pedigree and her own principles."

"Yes," Farzana nodded. Rest of the women present there, among who there were women of his own family too, were listening to him from a distance, all ears.

"Inside that desert there were two rocks by the names of Safa and Marwa. In order to find water for her son, Hajra had to anxiously pass through those two rocks seven times. Remembering her sacrifice which led to a better human race, anyone going on Haj in today's time is supposed to walk the distance between the two rocks seven times. My only purpose of telling this to you is to let you know that the woman who led us to the Prophet, and whose footsteps are measured till date—that woman's lineage doesn't have to be hopeless. I am not interested in knowing what distresses you, but in the fact that you should realize your potential, your power, and your worth."

Farzana looked at Waheed Saheb's face in shock, which made him smile and say, "People call me liberal-minded. I am not a liberal at all. My truth is what is written in *Hadith*. I do not believe in building up narratives in order to present what is false as truthful. I am a sincere believer, a loyal *maulana*, who believes in *Hadith*."

"Such great things to know, making the heart and the head feel stronger," said Farzana's mother.

"If only women knew anything," exclaimed Phuppi.

"You will not know unless you read about yourself," *Maulvi* Saheb replied.

"Not every *Maulvi* is Wahidudin," Ali Imam interrupted and erupted into a laughter, which everyone was a part of.

Since after that night, Firoz could sense a new confidence in Farzana. She was enthusiastic all over again. Someone has rightly said—diamonds cut diamonds. I was trying to occupy her with all the wrong things. I did not realize that the weapon that attacked her could cure her as well.

Firoz was worried for his sister on several grounds. He couldn't eat or sleep properly. He realized that Zubair's family might as well have acquired all the wealth that they could, but they lacked the etiquette and wisdom that a good education can bring about. And Farzana, on the other hand, had a little too much wisdom and knowledge. She has been brought up extraordinarily. What if this difference turns their lives into hellholes! It would have been so much better if Farzana would have pursued a Masters in Arts and prepared for competitive exams. Now she is stuck between the devil and the deep blue sea. She might have to spend her entire life alone. Everything has turned into a mess. Would Zubair be able to deal with this? How long will Farzana be able to hinge onto this self-assurance?

Farzana was sitting on the roof with an open book. Marking it with a pencil. The manner in which Prophet Moses had pleaded for water given the severity of his thirst, the daughter had praised that discipline in front of her father as she returned to her home. Looking at that traveller, the father had decided to get one of his daughters married to him, but unfortunately, Moses did not have the money for *meher*. Hence, it was decided that for the next two years, he was going to pasture the goats which belonged to that house. Farzana would stop in the middle of a sentence and stare at the road, thinking Zubair would drop there flying with the help of the wings on his back, like an angel.

"Do you know, *meher* are of two kinds—one that is paid off immediately, and another that can be paid off later. I was going to give it to you later, but you turned out to be overhasty. Here, have what is rightfully yours ..."

Farzana would grow tearful, her daydream would drop off her eyes like a night star, and she would find herself looking at the colourful paper-kites in combat with the falcons soaring in the bright blue sky.

Whenever Zubair found himself moving towards Farzana's house, he would recall what Farzana had told him. His enthusiasm would fade off like that of an exhausted horse. What if he goes there and Farzana chides him away? He would lose his reputation if their mutual disputes were to get exposed. What would people think about him? As a matter of fact, during his engagement, his relatives had mocked him over the predicaments of marrying an educated woman and questioned him if he would be able to pursue it. They would say—we have never had a girl child go to the university, and this one not only has been to one but also presents programs on radios and televisions! She speaks English like it is no one's business! And then her nails are so sharp and pointed too. Who is to say if she is going to cover her head or not?

Zubair was now trying to find any means to escape the situation, instead of resolving it. He was experiencing an unknown fear concerning Farzana. It was also terrifying for him to realize that if Farzana does not return, his relatives would be mocking him to no ends claiming that he had got what he did not deserve, and it did not work out for him. What should he do? Should he run away somewhere far, where no one would bother him, or ask him any questions that he doesn't have the answers to ... he came to know about the lack of money in their house when he was a child, and since then he had been determined to earn as much as he could. He left his education in the middle and bought and lodged everything that his house could ever fit in. What did he get in the end? He found himself challenged by books.

On the other end, with every morning star setting, Farzana's hope would rise with the rising sun that finally, today was the day when Zubair was going to come to her. Looking into the mirror as she batted her eyelids and applied a sleek surma, she seemed to be talking to herself—"Why am I waiting for you, Zubair? Why does my heart insist that you will come here despite me telling you otherwise, breaking all the barriers that you may confront, and standing before me with a newfound reason?—there are thousands of excuses for you to return and thousands of reasons for us to settle what has been unsettled. But for that, you have to enter the palace of my desires and my feelings ..."

As the afternoon went by, she would confine herself inside her room and ponder, "Why doesn't she surrender herself by letting go the crown of her pride and withdrawing the sword of her rights? Why doesn't she accept who she is, annihilating the centuries-old laws? For how long is she going to wait for her other half? What will she achieve by doing this? For now, no one is aware of this tug of war between them. If she returns, everything will be alright. One has to sacrifice a lot in order to achieve something. There is no reason in leaving heaven behind and embracing the fire of the hell. Every woman around her seems to be doing fine. She is no different than others; this is nothing but a delusion that her relationship is standing on fragile ground, bearing no roots or foundations. What would she do if she returns to that ground?"

Zubair wanted an escape. He found it. He signed a five-year contract. But he did not find it important to declare it to the members of his family. All that he mentioned was that he was going to the Saudi Arabia for a week's duration. If he deems the place appropriate and if things work out, he could think of staying there. As he stepped on the plane, he felt that he was able to steer clear of a number of problems all at once—at the same time, he was apprehensive about leaving the matters as they were and just run away from there. What would Farzana think if and when she will come to know? Not a thing, probably. She was unaffected even while he had been travelling quite regularly lately. But this time ... I am leaving for five whole years ... Farzana's face danced in front of his eyes. There was still time. He could get down. This fear from Farzana could be a mere misconception. He felt a jolt. He looked outside the window. The airplane began to rush through the runway and took off into the blue sky, spreading its wings across. Closer to the clouds, he felt a sense of relief—everything had been left behind. Whatever happens in the future can be looked after as it does. He shut his burning eyes.

Every night Farzana would dream that Zubair has returned.

"Did I hurt you with how I treated you?"

"No, I deserved this treatment. You were helpful in bringing me back to my senses," Zubair spoke in a feeble tone.

"And what about your male pride?" Farzana batted her eyes in astonishment.

"It is there, still, but only to fight with the world, and not to inflict any pain on my wife or my family. I learnt a lot while I was living alone. I have now understood that misusing one's power, and that too in the wrong context, is a way for one's weakness."

"Zubair! I cannot believe that those snares of ignorance in your mind have been cast away and how! Have you changed for real?"

"Yes, Farzana, believe me, I truly have changed for good. Think for yourself! If our Lord is merciful, then how can the worldly lord be so cruel? Better late, but at least I have finally understood that a human being is supposed to care for every other human being's rights and happiness, and not merely his own. That is why I have come back to you."

"Then this beloved's prostration to you shall be reckoned fair?"

"I have not returned to you as your lord, but as a mere human being and that is what I mean to be from now on," Zubair laughed.

"Oh, Zubair! Half of the world has changed for me when you have!" Farzana chuckled in her sleep.

Farzana was caught in shock on hearing her voice. She stared into the pitch darkness of her room. It took her a while to have a sense of where she was. Several exhausted birds settled onto her heart as if they were asking her, why wish for the nest that you have left behind? Who was waiting for you there, to understand you?

First published as "Khuda ki Wapsi." Translated from Hindi by Kanupriya Dhingra.

27

Loving, Dying

Ather Zia

The young girl in this story is looking out from the window, of what at one point must have been a large house, now divided into slim columns, probably amongst its heirs. Built with tiny scorched bricks that are held together by mud, the partitions are discernible by windows of different colours. Most of the homes in this town of Maisuma, which is called the heart of Kashmir, are conjoined like this, and at some visceral level are waiting to be separated from each other. The rundown buildings are worn with history and often lean dangerously exhausted against each other. Shops, industrial buildings, bus-yards, and garages stand entwined in this maze of a place which sits on the bank of river Jehlum that now has become an embittered swamp full of raw sewage and grease-oil. Broken parts of buses and trucks line the waters' edge where shanties erected by professional beggars, who pour into Kashmir during summers from India, overflow with soggy bundles of clothes, cardboard, and pieces of random trash—found and pilfered for recycling. Sturdy pieces of metal have been turned into seats in the makeshift courtyards. Young garage hands come here to smoke and flirt with panhandling girls, who are single-mindedly focused on lightening their pockets.

Tangles of electric wires can be seen hanging over the narrowest alleyways, so low that the static buzzes in your ear and sparks (not the enlivening kind) fly. The girl in the window looking down on one such alley is reminiscent of a native scene from a postcard, someone sent from an inexpensive holiday. It is around lunchtime. The air around the neighbourhood is thick with the smell of green tea brewing in old copper pans, sweet frying onions, and traffic smoke. Grandmothers are done with sunning themselves and cleaning collards on the slightly raised pavements, which doubles as their porch. Snatches from old Bollywood songs and

Ather Zia, *Loving, Dying* In: *The Silence That Speaks*. Edited by: Haris Qadeer, Oxford University Press. © Oxford University Press India 2022. DOI: 10.1093/oso/9780190132613.003.0028 pleading beggars mixes with the shouts of hawkers selling pain balm and cigarettes. Men are heading home for lunch; some bargain with the pickle seller on the alley corner, who swears by his mothers' grave to prove no cheap food colour has been used, and that the mixture has been fermented for more than a month. Army bunkers sprawling at every nook and cranny are abuzz with gustatory activity too. Dogs congregate as they hear the dining trucks rolling in to feed the soldiers. They follow the tall stacks of aluminium boxes packed with sizzling hot lentils, meat, pickles, rice, and bread. The soldiers kick and hit their rumps with sturdy boots. The dogs yelp, keep distance, and wait till the soldiers are ready to throw leftovers generously towards them.

Our young lady is about twenty years of age. She has a waif-like face. A wisp of a scarf is stylishly perched on her hair. A soft wave of brown hair falls over the side of her face reminiscent of the Bollywood actresses. The white tunic that she wears, with small red tulips on the neckline and hem, which she has embroidered herself, remain hidden beneath the windowsill. Her eyes are fixed on the wooden lamppost near the Masjid next-door. An old cough can be heard behind her and someone shouts. She seems to pay no mind.

An all-too-close call for prayers booming through the public address system jars the air. A young man, also around twenty years of age, appears at the mouth of the alley. The girl's face opens like a sunflower; it looks as if her prayer has been answered in advance. The boy wears a white T-shirt that says, "Coke" in red—the brown bottle placed on the right side, just below his heart. A white skullcap covers his well-groomed hair. He leans against the lamppost that is leaning dangerously. It tilts some more and the greasy bulb on top begin swaying only to still some seconds later. The girl always worries that the lamppost might fall on him. The gutter gurgles around the boy's feet. He continues looking towards her, arms crossed against his chest, eyes intent and unsmiling.

The girl always wants to see him a bit closer. Feel those hands that she has touched so many times in her dreams. She has seen him up close only once—the first time. She was buying dried chili powder from his father's grocery store. Everything smelled like turmeric, and some vague spice that never seemed to leave the shelves. His gaze was unbroken as he passed the packet of chili to her. She saw it had a hole but could not summon the courage to ask for a different one.

She felt rooted to the spot. After paying and forgetting to take the change, she broke into a run. She felt his eyes stuck to her back. Her hand was burning and stained red by the chili that escaped in tiny puffs with each hurried step. She sneezed the entire day. Her chest felt light and heavy. The world seemed awash in a golden haze. It had been four months since then, when she saw him for the first time.

The boy began to come every day and linger around the lamppost awhile. His eyes would keep darting towards her window. As the time for prayer drew close, he would mingle with other congregants, and then vanish into the Masjid. On the way out, jostling for exit, he would steal looks at her, while she peeped out of what now would be a half-closed window ready to be shut till the next afternoon. Then, in a flash, he would be gone. She would spend the rest of her day reliving the thick slice of time that had stood between them. The silent minutes of their distanced tryst would unfold like a video in slow replay. Each moment was a lifetime of glances, yearning, and inexpressible joy. Every moment spoke, as no word ever could. The next day would take forever to come.

The pain in her heart would continue growing, only to abate a little when he appeared. After he was gone, her body would be filled with more and more agony. At night, she would peer out of the window. She imagined a silhouette walking towards her. Her reverie would be broken by the barking of dogs that were roused by army patrol and the firm kicks and slurring shouts they delivered on everything that moved or not. Her mother's exasperated, muffled shout reminded her to close the window or face a bullet or worse. She saw that today, the boy did not stop at the lamppost but walked hurriedly towards her window. He raised his arm and threw something at her. She ducked. It fell into the corner without a sound. Moving swiftly, she picked the soft sweaty ball of paper, crushed around a piece of clay. She opened it, trembling. It said—"Be laghey tche balai." "I will die for you." One could argue that the phrase is a placeholder for *I love you* in Kashmiri. It was written on the letterhead of the "Paradice Garage," where the boy probably worked. There was a picture of a black tire and a shining hand holding a wrench in the corner. The night was unending. The redness that appeared in her cheeks when she first read the note became deeper. She tried to write back. Nothing seemed adequate. In the end, she repeated his dear words—"Be tih lagai tche balai" (I will also die for you). She tucked the well-kissed note under the pillow. The clock seemed to be stuck at midnight. She filled the emptiness in her room with a litany of soft sighs, whispering sweet nothings. Her eyelids drifted shut. She saw herself hanging from the long hand of a giant clock, pulling it to move. She felt her feet dangling in air and there was nothing to catch her underneath. In a distance, she heard slogans, shouting, and cries of all kinds. Shots rang in the air. She hung between her dream, and an eerie wakefulness, undecided where the dream ended and reality began.

The morning arrived without the call to fajr (dawn) prayers. Usually, she would have welcomed the silence, without an entreating congregation at the Masjid rousing God's pre-dawn beneficence and her sleep-deprived ire (and probably the rest of the neighbourhood's as well), but not today. The only sound she heard was the army jeep announcing the curfew. There was an order for "shoot at sight." Protests had started all around the valley after the police beat a young boy to death. People were staging anti-India demonstrations and there were incidents of stone pelting. The soldiers fired on unarmed crowds, and many were killed. Usually, the girl would make hasty prayers much to her mother's consternation. "This does not seem to be a mark of patient bowing before the Lord, it seems more like an impatient bird pecking at the grain," her mother would complain. Today, the girl fell into frequent and prolonged prostrations. She shifted uneasily; thousands of needles seemed to prick her body. Her eyes kept darting towards the clock. The note, which had her answer, was balled tightly around a piece of clay and felt like hot metal in her hand. She longed to throw it to him. She wanted to see his face once when he read it.

At noon, she opened the window just a crack. Only a cow stood at the far end, chewing on a wet cardboard box. She heard noises from afar. Smoke rose in the slim crack of sky between the windowpanes. Suddenly, a running figure appeared. It was him. Blood rushed into her face. Her hand fell and the window came ajar with a swift noise. There were shouts, curses, jangling, and running footsteps. A contingent of army-men in riot gear, their visor-hidden faces and bodies, preceded by guns, were behind him like an unending camouflaged flurry. She threw the sweaty ball of paper towards him when he was near the window. Shots burst in the air and sparks flew. For a moment, it felt like fireworks at a wedding. A strange and a very sharp heat bolted through her breast. The boy lunged at the paper-ball and smiled at her—for the first time ever. More shots, and then he fell. Her face sank into her chest as she saw the blood seeping into her tunic and the tulips, which she had wanted him to see some day disappeared. She fell into one limp heap. Later, in the evening news bulletin, the boy and the girl were included in the list of people killed by stone-pelting that day. No one found the girl's note. It was probably mangled in the dirt, under the feet of running and falling crowds, which would not cease for days to come and still has not stopped. No one would ever know how well the young pair of Kashmiri lovers delivered on the one and only promise they made to each other in the alley of Maisuma where the gutter still gurgles below the tilted lamppost. The window in which the girl stood looking at the only boy she ever loved, now remains open all day and all night.

28

I Am Reminded of You

Kasema Khatun

"I am starving for the last two days. Master, please give me two rupees."

I was returning from the poet's meet on linguistic harmony on the occasion of National Integration Day. Being the only poet in the district, I was fortunate to be given the opportunity to say a few words in the meeting. Till the time human beings continue to sow the seeds of violence in their hearts, the day of harmony would not arrive. What will come out of organizing communal harmony programmes (*Qaumi Ekta Diwas*) for seven days every year? If one cannot purge one's heart of religious bigotry and prejudice, what's the use of organizing events celebrating communal harmony? "You are a Hindu, I am a Muslim, he is a Bodo, he is a Santali"—as long as such narrow-mindedness exists, these occasions would serve no purpose. I was lost in these thoughts as I was walking back home from the programme. I was taken by surprise when I heard someone's voice calling me. When I turned back, I saw an emaciated and skeletal boy of seven or eight years extending his hands in supplication. His eyes though looked sharp and intelligent. Because of hunger and thirst, his belly was curving inwards; his eyes recessed into their sockets, and his skin appeared utterly shrivelled. I looked intently at the boy for a few moments. I repeated to myself a few lines spoken at the meeting: "All children of this earth are of the same nature; only the surrounding environment helps in moulding the habits in an appropriate manner." My mind was bogged down by an inexplicable ache; I somehow felt compassionate towards the boy. I asked him, "What is your name?"

"Gajanan Basfor," he replied.

I asked him again, "Where are your parents?"

The boy replied in a mixture of Hindi and Goalparia Assamese dialects: "No master, my mother is not alive. My father has run away, leaving

Kasema Khatun, *I Am Reminded of You* In: *The Silence That Speaks.* Edited by: Haris Qadeer, Oxford University Press. © Oxford University Press India 2022. DOI: 10.1093/oso/9780190132613.003.0029 me all alone. I have been sleeping in the verandah of Pushpa Hotel for the past seven days. I have no place to go in case I am driven away from there." I immediately arrived at a decision—I shall take the boy home with me.

"All right," I said to him, "Take these two rupees. Go and eat something from that tea stall. You shall accompany me to my house. At home, I live with my wife and a little boy who is of your age. You two shall play and study together. You are coming, right?" The boy nodded in affirmation.

I brought the child home and told my wife, "You know what Alyssa, this boy is a *harijan*. His parents have abandoned him. We shall educate him. He shall grow up alongside our son Iqbal." Before I could finish my sentence, Alyssa lost her temper upon seeing the boy. She yelled, "Don't you have anything else to do? It is so difficult to take care of one child at home and you have randomly picked up another one from the street, that too with no knowledge of his caste. You will realize it later—when our society will ostracize us for this misdeed. You shall then understand the consequences of poking your nose into unnecessary issues."

A writer-friend of mine visited our place about two days after this incident. He was highly appreciative of my conduct with the boy. But, to my surprise, the very moment I told him that the boy was a *harijan*, he scrunched his nose in disgust, Whereas, two days before, he was the one who had spoken at the communal harmony programme—"We shall remove all traces of caste differences; we shall get rid of all kinds of communal prejudices and religious bigotries." All littérateurs who had assembled at the meeting that day had profusely praised the liberal attitude of this friend of mine. Nevertheless, in accordance with the wishes of my wife, the boy was rechristened Ghazibar; he was admitted to the same school where Iqbal was studying. In the meantime, Gajanan became known to everyone as Ghazibar. Through word of mouth, the news reached the local journalists.

One fine day, a group of journalists came to interview me. They also took photos of Ghazibar. The story was published as a long article on the front page of the newspaper with the title in large bold fonts—"The Role of Littérateur in Integration." And about two days later, I noticed that Ghazibar was not attending his school. Upon enquiring the reason, my wife told me that his schoolmates make fun of him and call him "an untouchable whose body stinks of faeces." I was quite worried about the incident. In the evening, I saw Ghazibar sitting dejectedly at one side of the carpet in the drawing room. I asked him if he was feeling unwell and checked his temperature. I was unable to sleep properly that night. I kept thinking of the ways to resolve the present complex situation.

About a week later, the writer-friend of mine revisited, but this time, he came with a newspaper to congratulate me on the news story. I was hailed as a true liberal—amongst all the attendees who had adopted resolutions on the communal harmony day, I was the one who showed the way by translating words into action. He spoke highly effusive sentences, replete with appreciatory adjectives and nouns, in praise of my actions. I was however not attentive to what was being said; for my friend possibly had no inkling of the fact that about three days, following the appearance of the story in the newspaper, Ghazibar had gone missing. I was secretly carrying out investigations seeking his possible whereabouts. Bereft of his friend, Iqbal was sitting dejectedly beside his study table. Alyssa too was restless and was unable to sleep at night. And what about my own condition? I was trying to divert my mind by reading something or scribbling nothings on paper. Sometimes I lifted the curtains from the window to cast a glance at the road with the hope of seeing Ghazibar coming back and waiting at the gate to come inside. I was terribly anxious remembering that fervent look on the boy's face. Who knows, somewhere on the roads, braving all kinds of weather, with his gaunt and unaccustomed hands extended in supplication, Ghazibar might once again be crying out to stout faces in the crowd—"Master, I am starving for the last three days. Please give me two . . . "

First published as "Tomaloi Monat Pore". Translated from Assamese by Dhurjjati Sarma.

29
Origin

Semeen Ali

Nukta-chīñ hai ġham-e-dil . . . *

I remember the June afternoons. How electricity tested the patience of numerous households on such days. A sadist. The days when the wood pigeon would choose the perfect time to sing its sad song. It was in these hours that she and I used to sit outside in our veranda every day at 2 p.m.—when the rest of the house had fallen asleep. She used to sit on the cane sofa—at times softly singing an old ghazal—staring at the plants that were wilting. The hoarse voice of an ice seller (I always believed that he used to have ice creams for lunch and dinner and therefore, always had a bad throat) used to snap her out of her reverie. Her only escape. "*Do ice cream dena*" (Give me two ice creams)—Looking at the tiny figure running up to her excitedly—" *Ruko! Teen ice cream dena*" (Wait! Give me three ice creams).

The orange ones were my favourite. She loved the coffee flavoured and the chocolate ones. The ice creams that were forbidden; the horror if anyone found out we were having them! Her cupboard was my treasure island. A wooden box contained *atrs*—tiny glass bottles of perfumes with flowers painted on them that were fading away—empty, smelled of a past that had been shut down permanently. A few books—frayed but well preserved, with names that had long grown up and left. A silver filigree box that contained coins for our secret food sessions were amongst the few things that held my fascination.

Nukta-chīñ hai ġham-e-dil usko sunā.e na bane
kyā bane baat jahāñ baat batā.e na bane

* Ghalib's ghazal: *Nukta-chīñ hai ġham-e-dil* (She is a critic, the sorrows of the heart). This ghazal was close to my grandmother's heart.

Semeen Ali, *Origin* In: *The Silence That Speaks*. Edited by: Haris Qadeer, Oxford University Press. © Oxford University Press India 2022. DOI: 10.1093/oso/9780190132613.003.0030

My Nani was used to visitors. Not that they provided her relief from the silence that she had deliberately surrounded herself with, but sometimes she required a jolt—a necessary one to save her from herself. We lived in the older part of the city—Nawab Aga Ali Khan and his family had lived here. My Nani's father. Maybe the family lineage created a wall, maybe it made her free. She kept her inner thoughts to herself—maybe singing was her escape, maybe the silence she wrapped herself with. Young women research students covering their heads with chadors used to come to our house and at times drew her ire and much to the horror of those poor young women, she would proceed to remove the chadors from their head—"*Duniya se khud ko kyu chupati ho*? *Koi bure kaam toh nahi kiye hain jo chupi rehti ho parde ke peeche*?" (Why do you hide yourself from the world? You haven't done anything wrong that you hide behind purdah?)

Memories turn into stories if left untouched, and there were millions of them in her heart that she wanted to talk about. She lacked listeners. She had tested a few in the past including me, but we all fell short of that ability to hold on to the thread that she wanted to use to create her fabric of memories. She carried a box of them every afternoon—the only time she and I connected, the only time she was herself. Old Persian and Urdu couplets were at her beck and call—at times stumping my grandfather in front of his students. Suraiya was her favourite singer. It is 4 p.m. and time for the rest of the house to wake up—for us, it was time to say goodbye till the next afternoon. Bua—a permanent fixture in our house made tea and would brace herself for another lecture from Nani. *Bua*—a name she was called by in our neighbourhood. No one knew her real name. She had once posed for my camera-throwing her *jhadoo* down; she had removed her *dupatta* covering her head, patted her *mehndi* coloured hair and smiled at the camera. Bua and Nanima were always at loggerheads. Never a day went by when Bua had not complained to my nana about Nani interfering in Bua's work.

Bud had cried the most when Nani passed away.

Ghair phirtā hai liye yuuñ tere ḳhat ko ki agar
koī pūchhe ki ye kyā hai to chhupā.e na bane

It is difficult to tie down a life into a few paragraphs or pages. Life like *camera obscura* lies open to interpretations and at times misses the point it is trying to make through an individual. Our family was a collection of camera obscuras. I still have those two photographs of my Nani—bearing a toothy smile, standing against a grape vine like a glow worm surrounded by dark leaves. My aunt had bought a black and white reel, and I was her photographer. We had decided on a photography session one early winter morning. We already had our photo bomber all armed. Nani. Exasperated, my aunt had given up posing for the camera and the only subject left—an excited one—was Nani. Wearing a half sleeve sweater-knitted by her years ago, she had stood with her hands by her side. Attention! Smiling as if she was in love with the camera. She had chosen the grape vine as her background. "*Aasmaan bhi aana chahiye*" (The sky should feature as well). She had instructed. I still have those two photographs. I never got them framed. They have started to turn yellow. Even black and white colours stand to lose themselves with time. Disintegrate.

Moharram—the first 10 days when time stopped at our home. Nani's strict instructions were followed regarding the dress code and of course, no form of entertainment was allowed. I remember singing softly a Hindi song and being immediately reprimanded by Nani. Nani was in command—the only time Bua was in awe of her. Those 10 days were Nani's, and we dared not cross her path. The *Zuljana* procession was the highlight of the 10th day of Moharram. *Duldul* or *Zuljana* was taken around to every house where people fed this symbolic horse with sweets and milk. Nani always used to feed *Zuljana* these sweet orange-coloured *boondis* sweets. I remember waiting with her for *Zuljana* to reach our home—an open plastic packet between us filled with boondi. Her eyes on the front gate and mine on the boondi. Silently, she would scoop out a handful of it and put it in my lap. By the time I would finish eating, *Zulajana* would arrive to have its share.

Both vo sar se girā hai ki uthā.e na uthe
kaam vo aan padā hai ki banā.e na bane

I want to remember her in snapshots. I came to know a woman who was never a prisoner of time but now I want to imprison her memory. A paradox of sorts—maybe she left before I could start unravelling her. Maybe she never wanted a listener.

Seems like yesterday
It was a yesterday
when we decided to open our eyes
You - to a crumbling world
And I - to one that refused to move
For hours we would sit
In the veranda, looking outside
You - a remnant of the world forgotten
You - who had mistakenly ended up in the present
Those grey eyes
Beginnings of glaucoma
You had begun a conversation with yourself
Surrounding you my collections-
Chandamama, *Champak*.
Skimming through the pages to ask you-
"*Bhujo toh jaane*?"
The cries of an ice cream seller
would interrupt your questions
and mine.
Pulling us out of our worlds

It was 5 a.m.
when you decided to leave.
The house became saturated with cries
I remained silent.
I had sat alone in the courtyard
staring at the ground
where they had washed you
before your burial.
It is growing dark.
I sit in the veranda looking outside.
I have just begun a conversation with you.

30

Maina

Return of the Bowls

Asma Anjum Khan

"*Ari laga abi zor se, Munni badnaam hui...*" (Put on the volume!) A roaring laughter erupted, all feminine but not a bit beaten down.

Dry neem leaves were lying all around, unswept. The courtyard smelled of goat-shit. Walk cautiously, take care not to crush those tiny grey pop-ups, in abundant supply here. Multiple rooms squat around this open shitty verandah named Bakshu ki kothi, and this is Soorti moholla, right next to Laxmi market. As you roam around, you hear in the next hole of a home, a noise typical to the place; a woman shouting hoarse. She has refused her man; fresh funds for, "his two pegs only."

God alone knows why these sons of their fathers, remember their mothers at such somber occasions. Why can't there be a ruling that says:

O, You men, those drunkards among you; can't marry.

Why not nip the devil in the bud?

Talking about evil men would be my favourite digression but I am not doing it now...

Today, I want to tell you the story of a woman called Maina and a man called Yaseen Moulana.

Mehrun or Mahjabeen, only God or the clerk, issuing birth certificates at the municipal corporation, know what she was named by her parents but the whole moholla knew her as Maina. The younger lot added the common generic suffix of *aapa* (elder sister) to it. She was the apple of her parent's eyes. Being a clever scrap dealer dealing with old junk, her father was adept at disposing off things at a swifter pace.

Subhan Ali was fifteen years older to Maina but had a steady government job, in the railways. What more can one want? "My girl would roam

Asma Anjum Khan, *Maina* In: *The Silence That Speaks*. Edited by: Haris Qadeer, Oxford University Press. © Oxford University Press India 2022. DOI: 10.1093/oso/9780190132613.003.0031 all around all over Hindustan (on a railway pass)," the father in him, had smiled contentedly.

Subhan Ali had three sons from his first wife. The eldest was only four years younger to Maina. The first wife, as is the general habit of the first wives, didn't take kindly to the new arrangement by her husband. Two children and countless quarrels later between the two war maidens, a day came soon when the younger one left. How could she not? The younger one had been second to none at her mother's place, so why should it have been different over here? The daily soap operas of quarrels (and battles among womenfolks now) stopped at the Tank street and landed, in the muddy lanes of Soorti moholla.

Situation had already deteriorated there. Her late father had married off the three remaining sisters, causing a financial meltdown. Her lazy brothers were finding it hard to deal with the dwindling scrap business. The financial take over followed soon. The crumbling business was revived with the capital of Maina's wedding jewellery. When the little birdie Maina started dealing in scraps; she left no scrap unturned for bringing shine to the crumbs of her venture. She would cut corners, save the commissions, walk the talk with the brokers; quickly peace them out with pieces thrown here or there, if need be, etc. Now there was weekly *rice pilaf* with occasional *kebabs* on the plates and cakes or pastry in children's tiffins; a little respite from daily veggies. Her 'good for gambling' brothers, now had more time at their hands and myriad recreations kept them busier. The progress was rapid and astonished many except Maina.

Now it was time for branching out. A business expansion, this sort of undertaking is often just round the corner in places like Soorti moholla. She thought of starting a business of money lending.

People in this community are thought to be in perpetual need of the loans, that banks are never ready to offer them. There were no visible sign boards for, Maina: The Money Lender; the new proprietor was prudent enough. It started well. The interest was robust, but the new venture was full of rash exploits. The misadventures kind of got reported to the police, by the loan taking salmons; consequently giving birth to the contingency of the new loan shark and the *Khaki* (police) becoming close pals.

Bakhshu ki kothi had got buzzing. Their Eid-parties were now attended by people from the Khakhi moholla, adding to its stature by leaps and bounds. They would come in hordes if belonged to the lower ranks, and discreetly; if from the "Sahib" category. One such sahib, Inspector Rajesh soon became pally with Maina. The phone calls started stretching long.

Maina had one weakness, common to the felines of the human species... Looks.

Before each such feast-meeting, her elaborate preparations would begin, and maids would be summoned and presented with the ritual query.

"How do I look?"

All this while, the freshly arrived loan-shark would be inspecting herself in the tall new mirror bought for the purpose. The maids would be all aglow, set to put some shine to the ageing vessel.

"*Aapa*, you don't look even thirty!" Zaibun squealed.

The expert comment would be brushed off, quite in style; with pretended nonchalance. But the maid, the other maids, and Maina herself knew how soothing it was for her small, a bit overwrought ears. While she would be busy, kneading the pleats of her sari; which she tied just, I mean just above the navel, the maids giggled. The elder Rafia sniggered at them, while weaving words of praise around her mistress.

Poor Maina!

She was no exception to the maxim. You can never fool a woman, except with these sought after, three words:

"You are beautiful!"

Maina was short to a fault. In fact, if she tied her fuzzy hair into two tight and oily ponytails, you would take her for a chubby school girl, lazy and sluggish. She was fair with a slight parrot twist, at the nose tip. The full blown cheeks cascaded down towards her chin, giving her an appearance of plumpness. Heavy bosomed with a thin waist and wide bottom, she made a colourful human spectacle of a woman. Her maids laughed behind her with the pseudonym given to her after a popular vote: *Rangit Buddhi* (colourful old woman).

The women of the locality shunned her and ran a well-oiled whispering campaign against. Perhaps these hapless women hated her guts. She had done the thing most despised by the community. Maina had the daring to leave her abusive husband which many of these whisperers would gladly do but for their own cowardice and compulsions. She understood the whisper campaign and would fill the air with her huhs, "they didn't have the courage *himmat* and I had it, still have it." By *himmat* she meant the courage to leave "her husband" that is such a big deal in the subcontinent and the ignominy of returning to her mother's home.

Business bloomed and parties raged. Eid Party in particular, with *seekh kebabs* on the hot irons. Inspectors would come and leave after a little chat and a piece of *kebab*, followed by the constabulary, who hung around for a longer while, devouring the savories. Inspector Rajesh would visit with family in toe as special chief guest. Every "local" VIP in the vicinity from Shabbir chacha, Sai-Raj Baniya of the moholla to Hamid barber and all the sundry vendors and neighbours, would attend. Some people were *persono non grata*, or even family non grata, like her only uncle Husain chacha; who despite calling her his daughter had not yet got the entry ticket. Old property disputes die hard.

In short, every VIP of the moholla came to attend the Eid party, but one person avoided it, despite several oral and written invites by the staff of our little birdie Diva.

He was Yaseen Moulana.

Younger to Maina by five or six years, he was the newly appointed *Imam* of the Moti masjid of Soorti Moholla. With Yaseen, everything ran on *haram* or *halal* lines, the forbidden and the permissible according to Islam. With him, there were specific ways of sneezing, yawning, eating, and drinking. A spree of soft abuses, mixed with a generous sprinkling of *Lahol wilas* and *Astaghfirullahs*[1] came to him with a spontaneity, peculiar to the profession. Strange amalgam of graduating in English literature, along with an *Aalim Masters* degree from a madarsa and he would sheepishly call these "Arabic refrains," a professional hazard. This he would utter in a deep throated voice, used as he was to teaching children, the recitation of the holy book. This kind of recitation reserved for the more pious and was called *Tajweed*. To make it sound emphatic, you need to squeeze in and out your larynx your voice box etc. or else this particular way of reading the Quran would fail. This *Tajweed* was basically to take the recitation closer to its Arabic roots. Being used to such frequent squeezes (of his voice box and his larynx), he developed the habit of speaking in longish tones, that would linger on for a while on the

[1] *Lahol wilas* and *Astaghfirullahs*: There is neither power no ability save Allah and I seek forgiveness in Allah. Generally these sentences are uttered to express feeling of annoyance and displeasure at something that is not permissible in Islam.

air waves, particularly if he were angry, excited or both. Day or night, he would be seen, rushing in and out of the mosque, at the appointed hours, heaving profusely with droplets of water in a spontaneous spurt; dripping from his beard, face, and hands. In this rush of running back and forth from the house of Allah, the new enthusiastic Imam would often forget the house of Saeeda.

Life was a grind. Saeeda, his better-half would shout and fidget, like all normal wives do, and Yaseen would try convincing her how he being busy in God's work is more rewarding, than him, bringing pulses, and salt for her gravy at home. Like all poor wives she had learnt to pretend to "understand" and life would grind on. Grind, grind, grind, and grind some more.

The life of Yaseen as an Imam was steeped in orthodoxy; he brushed his teeth with a *miswak* stick, all the daily rituals began only with his right hand, as is preferred in Islamic theology. He would never spit to the direction of Makkah; calling it *Ehteraam* (respect), touching his ear lobes with tongue sandwiched between his teeth. When the pre-evening, call for prayer would ring; he could be seen, rushing after the teenage boys, extending official invites for the prayer. Things reached to such a pass that the urchins began to scoot, whenever the new reformer was seen stomping near the playground. The reformer himself would not be satisfied unless he ran after a few. What's more, once he had even invited Seth Basharat for the pre-evening prayer!

Seth Basharat, the *Matka* (Gambling) King was the chief patron and sponsor of the Masjid Committee. He was into the natural habit of nouveau riche, of being waited upon. Several pet and paid cronies; hovered around him at his, once a week, Friday appearance. They would clear the walk way for him and take him to the space designated for him in the mosque, unofficially of course. Seth Basharat wished to keep the account of his deeds, clean and clear. Yes, yes, even those into betting and gambling, have conscience, and who doesn't want to earn some extra brownie points that come by just being in the first row behind the Imam? Basharat Seth and former Moulvi Ashraf were childhood chums; one played on chance, and became 'the Matka King'; another earned healthy commission, with his chance pleading to Allah for special clemency, of his financier. *Khutbah* (pre-prayer address by the Imam) on Fridays would have to depend for its length on the first glimpse of Basharat Seth by Moulvi

Ashraf. Seth performing his ablution, near the mosque entrance, could be seen from the pulpit where the Imam stands to preach, to the worshippers. It was an open secret which the duo took as a covert understanding strictly between them.

For those faithful lazies, who can't say their prayers daily; Friday is seen as a special divine arrangement by the divine Himself, when mercy of Allah runs like an unlimited corporation and where everyone can take a share of the profit or at least, a few stock options. Seth Basharat had become the Santa Claus for all the former and serving moulvis, a harbinger of unexpected gifts, which they preferred to call, the divine mercy. And anything even remotely divine must be accepted without question… or that was the idea.

Former Moulvi Ashraf was a far-sighted man who knew how to keep his *deen* and *duniya* (religious obligations and worldly temptations) in balance and separate from each other. Post paralytic attack, he had to relinquish his Moulvi post. From then onwards, his junior carried on the show with the enthusiasm of a new bride, eager to cook every sundry dish in the kitchen to please her people. The difference here was that the junior was trying to please his Creator, whom he affectionately addressed as, Allah sahib.

The first Friday show, by Yaseen received mixed reviews. It was termed a disaster by some and an adventure by the others. Yaseen strangely seemed to care only about Allah! The financier Seth didn't seem to bother him. The retiree moulvi Ashraf literally tried every trick in the book; winks, light whispers protracted fingers on the temples and Shshs from his awkwardly curved paralytic mouth. Moulvi Ashraf tried fingering his ears first and then moved his slightly rightist head (tilted to the right, okay?) like when one does, refusing to gulp down a bitter pill, but all he got in return was this. Refrain by the new Moulvi:

"Allah listens to your whispers (and watches your winks!)"

The sane advice in the form of winks and *sh … shs*, fell on Yaseen's frozen ears; because when they met, after Friday noon-prayers; he quickly started reminding the seventy-year-old former scion of the mosque of the wrath of Allah. There was also something about the mismatch and vanishing of the masjid-fund account books. The words Yaseen spoke were so intense that the old moulvi Ashraf started feeling the heat of the far distant hell fire in which; the new moulvi declared, the old one, would have to burn. He didn't forget to add, the burning would be for thousand plus years, by the super-computing calculations of the hereafter.

That year, the Santa Claus of Moti Masjid had to bear the insult of arriving earlier than usual for the jumma. The things didn't end on this.

It so happened that the traditional first bowl of *sheerini* (sweets), on *Shab-e-Meraj*, the Night of the Dead, was chomped on by the false yellowish dentures of Zully. Zulfiqar was the ill-paid sweeper of the masjid and he was retiring, that very night, after thirty-five years of service. Earlier this honor of "the first bowl" of *sheerini* was reserved for the Santa Claus. This minor yet significant incident sparked off different reactions; some people clucked their tongues in despair, some looked away, others were shocked awed, and some just shrugged it off as some new spiritual formulae, by the new excited Imam that runs a successful show; for the first few days. But when the show started getting an extension, people spruced up their antennae and paid attention to the freshly arriving episodes, in and around Moti Masjid.

The extension episode proved to be more thrilling as it involved the new doyen of Soorti moholla, our dear Maina. Bowls of *sheerini* had arrived at the masjid on *Shab-e-Baraat*, like the year before. It was believed if you give away food to the poor, it reaches your dead relations, in the heavens, via the mouths and tummies of your earthly relations. Hence that night, all the dead members of the family would be watching from far above *helplessly*, as their dear and near ones, wolfed down, chicken biryani, mutton qorma, naan along with sweets, and "hoped" to receive it via the invitees at the night feast, also called dead people's feast. This time too, *Khaki* had been invited for the *fatiha* prayers.

In getting armored, for the night of the dead, Maina was draping herself green, in front of the large mirror, she stood in her high heels, adjusting *pallu,* the wayward end of her parrot green sari. On the opposite wall was a large portrait of a film actress, Madhuri Dixit smiling with pursed lips. On the settee, was lying her ensemble of the day recklessly and on the door were hung some colourful dupattas. As she folded the pleats neatly and was trying to tuck, them into her parrot petticoat, she heard her mother shouting at someone.

"Who could it be at this time?"

She came out, holding one end of her parrot green sari in her left hand and the other end; tucked away somewhere, roughly in the long matching skirt. Behind her, was Kaliman whimpering, asking her to not trip in the sari:

"Madam, be careful! You might fall."

Touching her mother's shoulder, she asked, "Why are you shouting?" Maina's thick accent pierced the ears.

"Moulvi sahib has sent back the bowls of sweet," Asghari Begum, the old maid of the house, waved the tray full of six bowls of hot *sheerini*, in her face.

"Who is he?" Maina's face could be seen flushed in a reddish hue, off-setting the green of her ensemble.

"He is Yaseen," her mother's voice crackled in the din.

"And who is this damn Yaseen?" The green feathers ruffled.

"He is the new moulvi sahib," her teenager nephew's tongue was sour with Americanisms. Maina had sent him to an English medium school, set up in the old stable of Haji Shaukat Ali. The accent had nothing to do with the poor buffaloes that were shifted to the next yard, once it was cramped with youngunns of the moholla, desperate to learn English.

"The Return of the Bowls" became quite phenomenal in the history of Soorti Moholla. According to "da" new moulvi, the sweets from Maina were "*Haram*" not "permissible."

Usury is forbidden in Islam.

From this time onwards, the loan shark began noticing the harrumphs and *Lahol wilas*.

Maina and Yaseen were neighbours and like all good neighbours they began having a history. When the Bollywood song "*Munni badnam hui*" began playing from Maina's new audio system, Yaseen's harrumphs and *Laholwilas* would get shriller. Sometimes, you could not differentiate who was louder, Munni or Yaseen! At such fierce contests, Maina would ask the volume to be heaved up, further. After some more angry *Lahol wilas*, Yaseen would migrate to the mosque; and Munni would stop singing.

But this was new for Maina. In the not-so-distant past, Moulvi Ashraf would himself come to take the offerings of the sweets, from the home of Bakshus now Mainas. Like buy one, get one free, monetary rewards came free, with the bowls of sweets. Ashraf instinctively loved freebies, might be considered generic to his tribe.

"Moulana sahib seems to have lost his mind." Maina was now trying to tuck away, all the loose ends of the sari, into her, not so slender a midriff. The long skirt now looked like a large green ball.

"Oh, really now!" Maina raised her hands gesticulating, in mock anger. Her hands had left the company of the sari and the pallu ends now went haywire. Rahiman quickly gathered these, in a small heap, behind her mistress.

"Leave it," Maina came out of the irritating green puffed up ball. Completely. To her big relief and to the alarm of her mother. In that small ill-fitting cloth, that figment of a blouse and the long parrot skirt, tied below navel, she looked like a large green apple. The apple sat at the settee and began blabbering both on and off the phone. It was Rahiman who saved the developing crisis, by quickly grabbing a dupatta hung, on the door and planted it on her mistress' heavy boxer-toned bossom. Maina remained oblivious to the wrapper cloth or her mother's piercing eyes of disapproval.

Usury is haram; Maina heard the detailed report patiently. Allah himself comes to fight with those who do it, the new Moulvi had said. The wounded tigress fumed.

He says, "It's illegal money." Her mother reaffirmed in a placid tone. She had often, mildly disapproved of her daughter's new business venture of interest laden loans.

The servants, the maids, all appeared calm, that promised a storm.

Maina kept staring at those seven bowls filled with soft creamy kheer. She had herself supervised the preparation. The seven bowls, seemed to her like those seven dwarfs, she had once seen in her school drama. After the play was over, she wanted to go backstage and bring one home. It required some persuasion on the part of her teachers, to convince her of the impossibility of the situation. The next day she had chased the boy nonstop, who had uncanny semblance to one of her favourite dwarfs, all over the school basketball ground. After this incident, whenever that tiny dwarf boy saw her, anywhere in the school campus, he would begin to run for his life; as the little birdie Maina could never resist chasing him. But soon Ashish became a friend with whom she was more than happy to share her tiffin and toffees.

Maina was unusually quiet. Refusing her offering was a daredevilry on the part of the new spiritual guru of Soorati moholla. But the prodigal diva didn't want to do anything in haste. She was amused with this new moulvi, who thought not of his bread but his beard while returning the bowls. No one in her five long years of stupendous career of lending money, had dared criticize her business and here this man was calling it *haram*!

Inwardly, she respected the man for his honesty. Yet, Maina the lender, had to hate him.

Some people are honest to the extent of foolishness. Plain and stupid. Yaseen fell on the borderline. Maina ran down memory lane, but came back soon; there was not enough light there. Few moments forward and backward, sparks flew and she could see Yaseen counselling, Sameena. Lo and behold the moulana was expounding on the virtues of obeying husbands, to a visibly bruised wife!

Maina was now strolling down the overcrowded, memory lane, where she saw herself going over and almost punching Samina's husband. To say the good moulana was stunned would be an understatement. Yaseen was clearing his throat, looking at the man-husband, adjusting his glasses but avoided to look at Maina. Most people from his profession, didn't. No direct eye contact with women, to avoid the sin original or otherwise. The first look, that is cast accidentally is okayish, the second becomes sinful. The man-husband again uttered an abuse for his wife and down came Maina's hand, a jaw bone crackled somewhere near the Moulana.

Yaseen was too stunned to speak. Obeying husbands had just become a dangerous business.

Return of the bowls was the beginning of a strange relationship between Yaseen, the moulana and the money lender, Maina. Now the obedience of the wives and haram-ness of usury started getting special mentions during Friday *khutbahs*. And there Munni started singing at a louder pitch. Consequently, *lahol wilas* suffered an intensity that touched near frenzy. Maina began shooting a mischievous Salams towards Yaseen if the duo happened to cross the lane at a matching time. All she got in response was a *Lahol wila*; and a hootish laughter chased the new Moulvi sahib, long after, he had left the lane. The next Friday *khutbah* naturally talked about how Allah himself along with his army of angels, wants to fight those, who commit usury. Maina saw Yaseen moulana wage the war and decided to send peaceful salvos, from her new surround sound system.

If the story of Maina and Moulana were made into a film, you would have to get a tall lean man to play Yaseen and you already know what description fits the female protagonist here. Sketching a Muslim moholla would be not that challenging. You must although make sure, it should reek of bakery and gutter smells mixed in naturally occurring proportions (with the added goat shit pop-ups for decorative purposes), the houses must be struggling for space and constantly rubbing each other on their shoulders with open drains, welcoming the visitors with open arms and heaps of children playing in close proximity to the trash spread around. Make sure, tiny shops with tinned roofs are selling sundry daily items of use and loud speakers blare *azaans* and DJ songs at suitable times. Some tents for marriage, etc. must be blocking the already loaded constrained roads. For a real Muslim ghetto, you need to have something more, but that, later.

The air was brisk that day, and all rituals went normal, including the songs and the Lahol wilas, with added *Astaghfirullahs* for effect. The night arrived quietly, and then the phone rang. The sharp shrill voice of the woman was tearing up the chill of the long night. For the people of Soorti mohollas, it seemed the longest.

When someone throws a pig in your mosque, you take it out, wash the floor with Rin Supreme detergent, forget about it, and go for your next prayer . . . this is the standard procedure.

If you are a bit adventurous, you report it to the police. But what do you do when a Mohsin is *caught* talking to a Shilpa? Oh, then, the religious brigade, has to jump into action. And people have to come out, on the street. In this kind of riot, the girl's side is more furious generally. Women are fruits of war. Fruits from other gardens always appear alluring.

Things were heating up in the city, with the Muslim lover Mohsin was being taken to the court. A small crowd had gathered to show solidarity with the seventeen-year-old Romeo accused of exchanging messages with his sweet sixteen neighbour. Shilpa's people had filed a complaint of attempt to abduction, against their, "*might be*" son in law. They had been brought home, after a week of escapade to a nearby town. Shilpa was shedding tears, begging everyone not to harass Mohsin. This was irony at its worst. The court was now, a debate hall, where the two religions got the best of the best moments to berate each other. By the evening, the crying women, the runaway bride, her mother, *might be* groom's mother, all had created a perfect ruckus. Amid this beautiful chaos, the two parties, a little reluctantly, a little helplessly agreed on some reconciliation. You can now spout those preserved like pickles, clichés: Love wins, hate loses, etc. As the things reached happy endings in the court, the matter had become quite sour, outside. The court of the fanatics was not ready to forgive and forgo such a chance that came walking in through the door, uninvited. You don't get such opportunities every day. They were right. The business was slack since some bilateral relations were getting better, through some sundry moholla committees.

The group of young men was tired of sitting idle. Their leader, a little fellow, ordered some *Som-ras* (alcohol) before embarking on the assignment. All they had to do, was roam in "their" gully and deliver shouts of *Har Mahadev*. The aim was to shock and awe, touch and go. Thus, thunderstruck the enemy, and taking care not to try to bring any democracy to the moholla, for they already, lived in one.

The gang was now on the prowl. The night was not dark as it usually should have been for such nocturnal activity, but the boys were naturally excited. When their first shouts of "*Har Har Mahadev*" boomed in the not so dark a night; the *azaan,* the call for prayers, was soon to begin wafting in the breeze. There was a stunned silence, as if asking, "Whatta this?" in pure American accent, perhaps because, Sakeena English medium school was near. Undeterred the gang continued.

"*Har Har Mahadev. Har Har Mahadev.*"

"*Allahu Akbar*," a solitary voice rose sharp, suddenly, in response to their "*Har Har*", to use a cliché, out of the blue, right behind from where they stood.

An uncomfortable pause followed and then someone spoke falteringly as if unsure:

"Who is Akbar?"

Madhav, a boy who had failed his twelfth class thrice in a row, was awestruck.

Some giggles and chuckles, quickly filled the night air and muffled laughter, crept in slowly. A low voice rose that spoke sharp:

"Stop! Fools, you have come to riot or laugh like idiots.

Look straight, be quiet."

"Quiet? But don't we have to shout '*Har har Mahadev*'?" This was Bantu, the compounder at Joshi Clinic.

"Thanks, for not asking who is Mahadev." The sharp yet low voice was full of scorn.

"He was Mahadev, the king of Gods." The voice came from someone, the leader could not recognize, but was startled bad, he began shouting, at the top of his voice:

"Har har . . ."

And before he could complete, someone shouted loud and clear, from afar:

"Allahu Akbar"

There it was again! He could not complete his slogan, and the enemy interrupted him, quick enough.

That solitary voice seemed to be coming from the front of where they stood. Now there was an awkward silence. And it all began again:

"Har har..."

"Allahu Akbar."

A creative and dynamic scene of unique communal harmony was being enacted, right in the midst of about to begin a riot.

It didn't even feel absurd.

"Don't mind. Keep moving, and don't talk, don't laugh. Clear?" The leader was trying hard to appear, undeterred.

The man turned around to look at his boys. They stood all attention; their silhouettes could be seen moving to the left now, as per orders, from above. This "above" was exactly five feet above the sea level.

The topography of the minority region had been studied well in advance.

To the left lies, Soorati moholla and if you take the right turn and walk straight, you landed in Sherkhan Basti. It was a large open tract of land, while the former was a mosaic of crisscross lanes which had been enveloped from every side. Its narrow lanes cut into each other, at several intersections. One narrow lane opened towards the main road; a small temple sat there pensively. Beside it, under a tin shade, a tea stall. This was an important spot for making a swift escape after a rapid fire assault.

The whispers were gathering strength and Maina woke up. There was an uneasy quiet in her room. She came out, wrapping a shawl around her little shoulders:

"Munna, where are you?"

"They have surrounded the moholla."

"Who? Where?"

And then, the world had to see that lone wolf of a woman Maina, coming out of the big iron gates of her home.

"Who is there?" Her voice looked calm, as if she spoke to inspector Rajesh on the phone.

Soon her eyes could see in the dark; a bunch of boys was trying to thrust their way forward, into the moholla. Old Rauf; who slept in the tin shade of the tea house, was standing there, like a barrier. The boys were, "being playful" with him. The muffler noose was tightening around his old fragile neck.

"Leave!" She plucked out the knot with her hands with a sudden jerk. Rauf fell in a heap, on and around his own feet; his breaths were doing fast runs.

"Why have you come here? Get lost." The boys had seen a short plump woman coming towards them.

"*Bai*, you go inside, this is not your job. Are your men all impotent, that you have come to see us?" They laughed.

This brought an unexpected blow for the speaker. Maina's hand rose up and the next moment the guy, who had foolishly tried to inch closer to the indefatigable feline, was rubbing his cheeks, with bewildered eyes.

"Dust laden you, get lost from here." The feline roared.

Maina, the woman with a little birdie name was fuming like a tigress. She was not huffing or puffing, true to her nature, she was unruffled. The gang was totally taken aback by this twist in their tails and of course the tale of the riot.

"Get lost, in five minutes or you will face the consequences." The thick voice came from the corner. It soon appeared at the front rows of the battleground. A man shorter than five feet was speaking through his hooded mouth. The gate near where Maina stood was creaking perhaps from the fear of what was going to come.

Maina looked stunned for a moment, then the little crowd saw her, surging forward, and in a blow she had ripped open the hooded mask.

"You?"

"You?"

There was a sort of staring match between them that lasted for a few seconds.

Then.

The shorty with a thick voice, started running.

Maina sprinted after him. The world saw a Muslim woman running after a Hindu man, under a riot situation. It was sheer bad luck that brought the Hindu thick voice shorty down to the ground. An old cycle tyre had clean bowled his left foot. He cursed his mother while sitting up. Herself puffing and cornering her shawl into a heap, her voice rose:

"You forgot?" He was asked.

"No, Maina, I haven't. It was just that I didn't know you lived here. In any case we just came for a round up."

"*Ae*, bring some ice for him. He has got a bad swell." She called out to someone, turning back. Four legs rushed towards the fallen Hindu. The little birdie was chirping. She sat near him on a big boulder lying near the cycle repair shop.

"Would you like to have some tea?"

"It just felt like school," the thick voice shorty said smiling.

Maina smiled too, under the moonlight.

The public was gathering to watch the spectacle. Hot tea came with *Parle* biscuits. The inhabitants of Soorati moholla had almost stopped breathing inside their homes, amid the crying shouts of "*Har Har Mahadev*." Yaseen had sat on his mat that whole early morning, like a cat that doesn't leave its cozy space, for some reason. All this while, he had used the loo, at a greater frequency than the usual and his wife could not resist commenting. He preferred and pretended not to listen, like a normal well-conditioned husband.

The next morning was calmer. People spoke in clichéd hushed tones, gathered in small groups.

So it was a woman who sent the rioters packing? They wondered, clucked their tongues in awe, and generally seemed impressed.

After the breakfast, Maina spread herself on the sofa, when she heard the familiar harrumphing:

"Rahiman, where were the soldiers of Allah, last night?" She spoke loud enough.

A muffled *Laholwila* was heard, as expected, followed by a long-strained harrumphing.

In the background you could hear, *Lahol wilas* and some long squeezes of a particular voice box. But these were in muffled tones. The little birdie had got its social index; re-fixed. Now women invited her over to their homes, as she walked to the market passing through the narrow alley. There were little to none, harrumphs and laholwilas, one day Yaseen Moulana even salaamed Maina.

On that cold winter morning, old Rauf with a leg still bandaged, had come to pay his respects to the little birdie doyen of Soorati moholla. Slurping tea like a pro, he was bombarded with tiny stuffed *samosas* and questions.

"I don't understand one thing," Maina rued, "who was the person, who was sloganeering *Allahu Akbar*? That night?"

"Har Har; Allahu Akbar."

Old Rauf went roly-poly with laughter, with his peculiar *khi-khi*, he spoke:

"Aapa, Lahol wila . . ."

"No *Laholwila*, who was it? Tell me," the birdie persisted.

"Har har ... " it was Zully, her driver, also roaring in his big dentured smile.

"Allahu Akbar!"

Pat came the reply.

From the other side, which had until now, only reverberated with *Lahol-Wilas* and harrumps.

A visibly stunned Maina turned around to see the maker of that anthem.

Where had she heard that familiar strain before?

Mouth wide opened, the shark gaped.

Yaseen Moulana was standing there, clearing his voicebox for the next round of harrumphs.

31
Penguin Life

Sheeba EK

Ignoring the elegant Ford Fiesta with tinted windows, Dr. Junaina Hyder picked the spring-green Scooty Pep from the car porch. Gearing it on full swing towards the gate, she did not pay attention to her slipping hijab. The security guard, Ibrahim Sulaiman, who came running to open the gate stared at her in disbelief. Silky strands of hair perfectly cut to her shoulder were blowing in the mild breeze. A crimson red chiffon shawl swirled around her fair slender neck. Feeling a prick of conscience, he quickly turned his gaze away.

"*Assalamu alaikum* Doctor!"

She did not reply. Ibrahim stood there dumbstruck while the scooty rushed through the gate towards the busy city lanes. It has been eleven years since he joined as a security guard. Doctor Junaina's family has been staying there since the last eight years. When they arrived, she was doing her PG after an MBBS. Her husband, Ali Hyder, is a paediatrician at Al-Ameen Hospital. They had two sons, and the youngest daughter was born after they settled there.

Theirs is a rather conservative family on the religious front. Most of the families in this flat are like that. Mostly home to professionals, all of them are well educated and socially sophisticated. Here, socially upgraded women always observe purdah. Doctor Junaina was also one of them. Covering her tightly pulled hair in a hijab, looking straight ahead, she walks exuding confidence. This sight is familiar to everyone around. The public attire of all the women here is almost similar. They lead a life strictly rooted in religiosity. They don't prefer movies or any other entertainment program. Quran classes, religious speeches, iftar parties, and gatherings on Eid days are more important to them. Quran classes are often conducted by women who are stay-at-home moms. When they

Sheeba EK, *Penguin Life* In: *The Silence That Speaks*. Edited by: Haris Qadeer, Oxford University Press. © Oxford University Press India 2022. DOI: 10.1093/oso/9780190132613.003.0032 walk together across the white-tiled floors of the vast courtyard, they look very much like a group of penguins waddling around—with both their attires as well as attitudes being extremely similar.

Years back, when he was working as driver in Saudi Arabia, such visuals of penguins amused him. He has worked as a security guard and a driver for many reputed families there. He observed how the young beautiful ladies of princely families drape themselves in purdah while stepping out from their homes, only to strip themselves of it in shopping malls.

When he came back to his hometown after years, he witnessed the arrival of these penguin drapes along with the gush of gulf money. Around this flat sometimes, he still feels like he is in Saudi Arabia. Even some of the young girls, who should be flying high on their colourful wings, seem more attached to the purdah.

But what happened to Doctor Junaina Hyder? Ibrahim Sulaiman's thoughts were stuck on her. He had always seen her in a *naqab*, covering her whole face except the eyes.

Doctor Junaina Hyder was racing with a white *i10* on the highway. When the wind tossed her hair, she felt like laughing merrily. She could feel the lightness of her body swinging itself in the sky, sprouting wings …

It was the same insane happiness she had felt while snuggling in her mother's arms after performing the final step of Bharatanatyam in St. Thomas convent school. Like the deep sigh of relief that one gets after standing on the peak of the conquered land.

It was twenty-three years back. She was Junaina A Rahman then, the only daughter of Abdul Rahman, a PWD Engineer. Along with the wind, she felt the gust of all the lost colours of the past. It was a time when she owned the stages of classical dance, music, speech, poetry, clay modelling, and painting. Her friends always teased her, that even if she doesn't score well in exams, Junaina can easily get admission in any college. Piles of certificates … they were right! But she never performed poorly anywhere, not even in academics. The legacy continued until she got admission in a medical college. Her roommates there were stringent followers of the religion. Initially, she found it difficult to adjust with their lifestyle and dressing sense, since it was totally different from hers. They led a life devoid of all forms of entertainment. She would stick posters of Anil Kapoor on her bedroom wall; keep humming the whole day long, go on weekend family trips to watch movies, keenly wait for family holiday trips, etc. Whenever she compared her life with theirs, a dry and fady image appears in her mind.

But for them, it was delightful!

They would argue that a life entirely devoted to the Almighty God is bestowed with eternal peace. Those five years of companionship drastically changed my life as well as those of my parents and relatives, though we could have never expected such a radical shift. My father's colleagues were surprised to witness these transformations. The anxiety stemming from the consciousness that we humans live at the mercy of an omnipotent God led us towards a religiously conservative life. Some of our relatives and friends followed us on this new spiritual journey. Attending the classes and speeches spiritually rejuvenated many of them. The women, who fancied sleeveless dresses and lipsticks, began to cover their bodies in the black shade of purdah. The girls who loved to wear jeans intentionally started to cover their hair in *maftha* (hijab). Most of the books I read during those days were of a religious nature. My thoughts were limited to accumulation of good deeds. The life I had lived till now seemed unreal. Nothing was right. Dancing is a grave sin; only God has the ultimate power to create rendering the creative arts like painting and even the very thought of sculpturing, a sin. Classical music became the devotional chanting of other religions. Those were the taboos.

I have to get rid of the fancy outfits I had used till then. I was relieved only after I gave all those half sleeved tops to the servants around. When I found solace in a dress that covered my whole body except arms and face, my heart whispered that this life is a mere journey towards the eternal life in the hereafter. When I saw the colourful lives around, I only felt pity for them. Poor things, they are living in great ignorance!

I earned contempt from friends by scolding them for not wearing the hijab or for not extending the length of their sleeves. Those were the days when I had a firm belief in my convictions being the ultimate truth. For marriage queries, my only demand was that the groom should make me devout. As per my wish, Doctor Ali Hyder became my life partner. He came from a renowned family from Kodungalloor, religiously firm and socially well bred. We went to the medical practice together, Quran classes, pilgrimages, iftar parties, gatherings on Eidgah … For the past fifteen years, life went on smoothly. The greatest blessings from the

Almighty God were my kids, for whom I chose divine names. Life moved on along with their joys and bustles.

When and where did I begin to feel flawed…

Was it with one of those dreams where I passionately dance on the brightly decorated stages of St. Thomas school?

Or was it the parched life with a heavy heart and a face masked all desires, shattered all of a sudden… I'm not sure…

Where did Junaina A Rahman, the charming modern girl fade away… Or did she perish altogether from this mortal world…?

Where did that girl vanish, the one who tossed thick silky hair on her face, which her friends always relished with a tinge of jealousy; the one who caught everyone's attention by trying the latest fashion trends…?

Since the past few days, whenever I wear purdah while going to the hospital, a strange reluctance creeps from within. I feel like I am recoiling from this world only to seek refuge in a distant, lonely cave. The distress at wrapping the hijab over tightly tied wet hair during summer was deeply felt. Will the Almighty God, the epitome of kindness punish me for a few stray hair strands? Even if I cover my head, He who can sense anything and everything in this world, might know what is concealed in our hearts… The Almighty God, who is praised for His boundless mercy by every religion… Stretching between the fears of hell and the bounties of heaven… aren't we forgetting His endless kindness?

It has been weeks since I stopped observing purdah while going to workplace. I received a lot of amused stares, but people respected my privacy and kept to themselves. I had readied several answers for their queries… internal struggles… Will they agree with my arguments… But no one asked, possibly because of the fear of sharp retorts from the brave Doctor Junaina Hyder. During work hours at hospital, Doctor Hyder was embarrassed to notice the sliding headscarf of his wife. He liked her better when she observed purdah. Even when she suddenly started wearing churidars while going out, he did not intervene. But now she had even stopped covering her head, what was her intention?

Nowadays, Junaina prefers slippery chiffon shawls over cotton shawls. She could feel a strange pleasure in the slipping away of her shawl.

But today, it was for the very first time that she was travelling through the city in an open vehicle without covering her head… what would people think ... Perhaps, they will poke their noses wondering what happened to the religious determination of the woman who lead a "deeni" life until then ... She wanted to scatter words into the wind ... "Hey, do you know yesterday I prayed without covering my head!"

No one knew about it. That was a secret between me and my Lord. I have seen women wearing skintight purdah, revealing curvatures of their bodies. Only the hair is covered decently. I do not feel that my hair is more desirable than their curvy bodies. Keeping something hidden in your heart and pretending something else for the sake of others is the greatest sin which the Almighty God—the one who sees and hears everything—will definitely sense. I am doing what I feel is right. If I find any other revitalizing truth in the future, I may act accordingly. Heaven or hell, mortal life, everything is within me ... whispering to herself, she increased the speed of her bike ...

Is Doctor Hyder chasing me along with the family psychiatrist?

Ali Hyder may say that his wife who was firmly religious has started to behave oddly. The anxiety visible on his face since the past few days was evidently signalling his worries.

She raced the bike to its maximum speed. I don't need the walls of a psychiatric clinic now. What I want is some fresh air, sunshine, breeze, music, dance, colours, and spectacular visuals—all that I dismissed for the past fifteen years ... I have to retrieve everything ...

Along the sea shore, like another long wave, Doctor Junaina Hyder tossed her lengthy hair into the wind and galloped through the blazing sunrays ...

The wind blew away her red chiffon shawl ...

"Ya Allah!"

A group of black penguins, returning from morning walk, knitted their eyebrows and groaned collectively ...

First published as "Penguin Jeevitham" (2013). Translated from Malayalam by Ayshath Shamah Rahmath.

32
A Lady and Her Husband

Seemin Hasan

Our story commences in the boarding house of a prestigious convent school in India run by Irish missionaries. The century is late twentieth, and the time is dead of a winter night. A group of five teenage girls is huddled under a blanket in torchlight focusing on a coin with their fingers on it. They gasp as it moves on the chalk alphabets, and they read with horror its deadly prediction. "Rukhsar," whispers Anjali, "The spirit says you are destined to kill your husband." The coin moves again, and the girls fearfully read the second prediction. "Wailing in a well will break the curse." The coin stops and a tense hush falls over them. A few seconds later, giggles ensue and they scamper off to bed before Matron can lay her hands on them and instill in them a fear of hell and damnation.

Rukhsar Zehra had been in the boarding for five years now. Her father, a bank manager, in a neighbouring town, had taken her from the clutches of her over-protective mother and a home environment which was making her progressively lazy, and put her in a boarding school so that the nuns could shape her into an independent and refined lady. Highly miserable at first, with a schedule beginning at 5.30 a.m. with a run around the hockey field, followed by a breakfast of boiled eggs, bread and butter (she missed her crisp parathas and omlette for sure), concluding with the washing of her own socks and handkerchief (she missed Riyazi Bua more than her mother at this moment) before bedtime, she gradually adapted to the rigorous routine and spent within the fortress-like colonial structure, as she later claimed, "some of the happiest years of my life."

Rukhsar cleared her ISC exams with a decent enough percentage and before she could fall into the loving arms of her pampering mother, her father swept her off to Aligarh Muslim University for the final grooming. Abdullah Hall, though a totally different experience from the convent,

Seemin Hasan, *A Lady and Her Husband* In: *The Silence That Speaks*. Edited by: Haris Qadeer, Oxford University Press. © Oxford University Press India 2022. DOI: 10.1093/oso/9780190132613.003.0033 had its own merits. Before her departure to Aligarh, she enjoyed shopping with her mother for *shalwar-kameez*, pretty dupattas, and matching earrings. Kaneez Phuphu, her father's youngest sister, a proud AMU graduate, lecturer in Chemistry at a local college, plied her with advice like, "Keep your eyes down and don't smile if a boy passes a comment" and "If your roommate's brother comes to visit her, don't go with her to the gate."

The undergraduate years in Women's College passed in a whirl, with the realms of English Literature unfolding high thoughts, values, and romance before her eager eyes, her performing roles in the annual play, winning a medal on Sports Day, putting up a palmistry stall in the fete and finally the tearful farewell party. While a number of girls left to pursue courses in their native places and others to be married, Rukhsar opted for admission to a master's course on the same campus. Now, well settled as an Aligarian, she impressed her professors and classmates with her grace, confidence, and good manners. She won accolades in academics as well as extra-curricular activities. She was appointed president of the literary society and received the certificate from the vice chancellor himself. Her father was so proud of her, and he had absolutely no objections when she returned to savour the indulgences of her waiting mother, Kaneez Phuphu and Riyazi Bua. They discussed, sadly, how thin she had become and fed her all her favourite food and let her sleep as long as she liked and showed off her medals to visiting neighbours. The days passed engulfed in a haze of happiness.

Rukhsar was waiting for an opportune moment to broach her mother about her plans to return to Aligarh for a PhD, when her father, in his typical blunt manner, announced that "some people" were coming to meet them on the weekend. And so that was it. The visitors were pleasant and lived on and maintained an ancestral estate, not too far away from the city. And he, Shad Ali, was a charmer. He had graduated from All India Institute of Medical Sciences, New Delhi and now worked in London, the city of her dreams. Without much ado, her fate was decided, her finger ringed and a big, fat Indian wedding arranged. Finally, Dr. & Mrs. Shad Ali arrived at Dilkusha Estate.

In her heavy *farshi gharara*, adorned with the full range of exquisite ancestral bridal jewellery … *tika, jhumar, jhumka, naulada haar,* … *shauqband,angoothi, kangan, pazeb* … Rukhsar sat in a high-ceilinged room lit by an ancient *fanoos* that spilled stars onto the carpet. The *masehri* was high and large and stood firm on heavy, silver paye. She saw her reflection in the large dressing table mirror and felt herself being sucked into it like *Alice Through the Looking Glass*, and she whirled back in time to the cold winter night long ago and heard Anjali whisper, "You are destined to kill your husband" and passed out. She faintly heard her mother-in-law's voice saying, "It must be the stress. She has had a long day." She awoke in the wee hours of the night and saw Shad's concerned face near her own and asked, "Is there a well on the estate?"

A few days later, Shad offered to take her on a guided tour of the estate. "Wear your sports shoes as there will be a lot of walking in the orchards and fields," he said. When she told her mother-in-law about the proposed outing, the kindly lady advised, "Dulhan wear a gharara and some jewellery as the estate people are eager to see you." And Mrs. Shad Ali, being a law-abiding citizen, did as she was told and boarded the olive-green Scorpio in a gharara with sports shoes concealed underneath.

The estate was large and well maintained. Shad's father was in his office and welcomed them affectionately. As they went through the orchards and the fields, the workers saluted them. She admired the lush, green environment and looked with a keen eye for the well. The last stop was a small school for underprivileged girls run by Shad's family. Dilkusha Training Centre prepared girls for independent careers in computers, tailoring, dress designing, cookery and catering, etc. while simultaneously educating them to high school level. Rukhsar was highly impressed by the high enthusiasm of the learners and their eagerness to elicit praise from her. She spent a happy hour going through their colourful handicrafts and tasting the fresh and healthy snacks they had made. They finally bid goodbye midst much cheering.

"You must be tired" Shad said, reversing the Scorpio. "Let's go back."

"Oh no! I must see the well," said Rukhsar.

"The well?" he said in surprise, "Haven't you seen one ever?"

Shad stopped at an old half-wrecked hutment. He called out to an old man who walked with a branch he used as a stick. "Chuttan Baba," he said, "Lead us to the well."

Chuttan Baba walked laboriously towards the Scorpio and lifted a menacing finger and hissed, "Nooo! Dulhan Begum cannot go near the well. It is cursed. Shad Mian, take her home. Go back to the haveli."

Rukhsar shrank in her seat and trembled as she thought, "Chuttan Baba is so old, and so in sync with nature that he knows my deadly, dark secret." But something had to be done, mused she. Time was running out. In another week's time, she would board the flight to London.

Tareequn Bua was old and frail, but she dominated the zenana. She muttered to herself all the time but kept all the younger maidservants under her thumb. She hounded them all day about their inefficiency and lack of concentration. Rukhsar could hear her telling Shehnaz, one of the girls who lived on the estate and came for a few hours each day to help, "You call this turpai? Do you have fingers or thorns?"

When she saw Rukhsar, her face lit up, "Come Dulhan, raunak of the haveli. Girl, get up. Bring a chair. Do you have eyes or stones? Can't you see Dulhan is standing." Embarrassed, Rukhsar pulled a cane chair and sat down. Bua looked at her lovingly. Rukhsar mustered up all the courage she had and said, "Bua, I went around the estate yesterday, but Chuttan Baba did not let us near the well." Tareequn Bua's face changed colour. She hit Shehnaz on her back and said, "Get away, girl. Always listening to people's conversations." Then, she turned to Rukhsar with a conspiratorial look, "Chuttan is a fool but sometimes he is right. The well is cursed. Never go near it."

She waited in ominous silence and chewed on her paan. Then, she spoke in a hushed tone, "Shad Mian's grandfather, Fahad Mian went to vilayat to study vakalat. He returned after two years with a gori mem. His mother was devastated. The mem wore frocks and would sing when she was happy. After a few months, she stopped singing and hid in her room and wept all the time. The villagers could hear her wailing. One night, she secretly left the house and jumped into the well, right behind the big barn. The villagers heard her wailing for a long time, particularly on the night of Fahad Mian's wedding. She takes the bali of one young girl every year. The first was Hari's daughter, then Bansi's, then Rauf Mian's, and so many more. Many maulvis, nujumis, and pundits have come, but none could break the curse. The last nujumi came just before your wedding. He, too, failed to do anything. However, he said that the curse would be broken if a daughter or daughter-in-law of the haveli would wail beside the well on a moonlit night.

My child, never tell anyone about this curse. It is evil, very, very evil." Tareequn Bua hauled herself from the peedhi and said, "It is getting warm. I will send for a nice glass of shikanji for you. Shehnaz, you good for nothing brat, where are you?"

Rukhsar shivered despite the heat and thought, "What mysteries, secrets, skeletons in the cupboard are stored by the human race!"

That night, Rukhsar lay still beside Shad, watching him sink into a deep sleep. She waited for the moon to climb high into the sky and then she slipped out of bed and into her sports shoes. Fear gripped her as she silently moved out of the side door and began the kilometer long walk to the barn. She imagined she heard footsteps behind her and started to run. The footsteps changed to a run. But they stopped when she stopped. So, it was just her imagination, wasn't it? She was sweating profusely when she reached the barn. She went around it and there it was … the well! She drew a deep breath and bent over the parapet and wailed long and loud. Lo and behold, the gori mem wailed back at her. Rukhsar screamed and stepped back into the arms of Shad who had followed her. She felt relief flooding into her and closed her eyes. Wordlessly, Shad escorted her back to the haveli.

When she was settled in bed, Shad demanded an explanation. Reluctantly, she told him all about her conversation with Tareequn Bua and how she wanted to break the curse forever. Shad could not help smiling at the innocence of his lovely wife. After extricating a promise of secrecy from her about the whole incident, he turned on his side and slept.

Rukhsar lay awake for a long time. The curse was finally broken. Two curses were broken, even if Shad did not believe Tareequn Bua's tall tales, as he called them. She had told Shad the truth. "Only half the truth," she thought as she fell asleep, "but then, there is no way in eternity that a lady can tell her husband that she is destined to kill him, is there?"

33

My Share of Happiness

Tasneem Khan

Jasmine, the flowers of the night were in full bloom. The entire household was deeply suffused in its sweet fragrance that wafted in with the gentle breeze through the windows and engulfed everyone—young and old, in sweet slumber. It was a full moon night, and the courtyard was bathed in silver rays. There was silence everywhere. Everyone had gone off to sleep. But there was one person who was wide awake. She was sitting all alone on one of the steps leading to the terrace. Her back was against the wall and her feet entwined in the balustrade of the staircase. She was gazing intently towards the moon lost in deep thoughts as if seeking an answer to all her woes. The silvery glow on her face was unable to hide her grieving heart as one solitary tear slowly trickled down her glowing cheeks. She was weeping inwardly.

This mystic moonlit night and the sweet fragrance of jasmine flowers were not for her tonight. "Can the fragrance of this sweet scented moonlit night ever be divided into two? How can anyone agree to it? No, it is not acceptable to me … " She hid her face between her knees muttering to herself. But did it make any difference to anyone whether she agreed to it or not?

It was past midnight, and she was not the only one who was still awake. There was another pair of eyes which understood her anguish. They too were lying awake with her. They too were filled with tears. Wiping the tears with wrinkled hands and mustering her feeble strength, *Amma* called out, "Nighat! Nighat! Come on dear, come and sleep now. It's very late."

Nighat was completely lost in her own world. She did not hear anything. Her gaze was still fixed blankly on the moon. Her mother in-law knew that she would continue to sit there the entire night but despite that

Tasneem Khan, *My Share of Happiness* In: *The Silence That Speaks*. Edited by: Haris Qadeer, Oxford University Press. © Oxford University Press India 2022. DOI: 10.1093/oso/9780190132613.003.0034 she never failed to call out to her. She would plead with her to come down and go off to sleep. The only difference was that the names she called out were different depending on which day of the week it was. On some evenings, she'd call out Nighat's name, and on some evenings, it was Meena's name that she called out. It wasn't as if she was unaffected by the tremor in *Amma*'s voice. The tears that she'd been trying to control all this while automatically found an outlet and started rolling down her cheeks. She felt all alone in this beautiful moonlit night yearning for her husband's love. She'll have to go through the agony of seeing her own husband in the arms of someone else for the next two nights as well.

Nighat tried to console herself that it was a matter of only two more days. Then, everything would be fine. The weight of her unshed tears made her eyelids heavy. They now refused to stay awake. With a heavy heart, she slowly climbed down the stairs and moved towards her room. It was three o'clock by the kitchen clock. As she reached the threshold, she again burst into tears. Wiping her tears, she went in and lay down next to her children. Her ears were completely attuned to the muffled sounds that she led herself to believe were coming from the adjacent room, although there were none. It was around 5 o'clock in the morning that Nighat woke up again. When she came out to wash her face, she saw Meena humming softly to herself, drying her hair with a towel. The sight made her extremely envious of Saifuddin's second wife. The day was nothing short of doomsday for her. But she controlled herself and ignoring everything she quietly slipped into the kitchen and began preparing breakfast. She knew very well that the first thing that her husband liked after his bath was a cup of hot steaming tea in his hands. She wanted to be there with his tea when he came out of his bath. And that's how it happened. As soon as Saifuddin came out, Nighat was there in front of him.

"*Arrey wah*!" said Saifuddin handing her his towel and taking the cup from her hands. That small utterance was enough to make her happy. She forgot about her miseries and she felt as if Saifuddin's "*wah*" was for her and not for tea. She retraced her steps back into the kitchen but not before noticing that this had upset Meena.

Nighat was completely charged up for the rest of the day and in a jiffy she finished off all the household chores from making breakfast to lunch. Today, she had made potato curry, Saifuddin's favourite dish. She wanted to do everything and anything that pleased her husband.

So what if the night wasn't hers, she could mold the day as per her own desires. She then turned the attention to herself. She freshened up and touched-up her makeup. She wanted to look pretty for her husband. Nighat didn't want to appear any less attractive than her rival, Meena. She knew quite well that whatever she'd do, she would never be able to bridge the wide age gap that lay between them. Meena was ten to twelve years younger than her and was pretty as well. Whereas the signs of age were clearly visible on Nighat's face. But when she saw her *sautan's* ruffled demeanor, who was trying her best to find solace in her emroidery, she felt vindicated.

This was invariably the daily routine. There were times when Meena used to feel elated and times when Nighat used to feel elated. There were times when Meena used to feel dejected and times when Nighat used to feel dejected. They would both run around Saifuddin like butterflies, ever eager to do his every bidding. And this wholesome attention that Saifuddin got from both his wives made him feel rather special.

That day was Meena's turn to do the kitchen work, but she got some respite as everyone was invited to attend a marriage function. At the venue, they met many old acquaintances and relatives. Among them were Saidan *bi* and her daughter in-law. Saidan *Bi* and *Amma* were old friends and were delighted to meet each other. She also blessed Nighat whom she had met earlier but was meeting Meena for the first time. "Who is she?" she asked.

Nighat and *Amma* looked at each other while Meena smiled coyly. "She is the second wife of Saifuddin," *Amma* whispered softly.

Saidan *bi* was taken aback but she blessed her a little hesitatingly nevertheless. Her daughter in-law, on the other hand, made her shock and displeasure amply clear. She immediately confronted Nighat, 'Do you stay together in the same house?

Nighat threw a glance towards Meena and replied smilingly, "Yes, we all stay together."

Meena also promptly chipped in, "We live like sisters."

Kishwar was completely aghast, "You don't face any problems?"

"What problems? She works in the mornings and I in the evenings. Even 'he' doesn't give us any reason to fight as he sleeps three nights with her and three nights with me and one night with his mother and his children. This way there is no scope for any kind of conflict between us."

These words left Kishwar totally baffled; she pitied Meena's naivety and artlessness.

Nighat face grew red with embarrassment and she quickly changed the topic, "And how are your children? What are they doing?"

Ás the night deepend, Nighat felt more and more restless. She felt a constriction rising in her throat. The moon was still the same and so was the fragrance of jasmine flowers. Earlier they never failed to please her, but tonight they both were driving her insane.

"Of what use is this fragrance? Life itself starts stinking when you are forced to share your husband with another woman."

All those evenings when Saifuddin was with his second wife, life became unendurable for Nighat. She would never be able to get rid of the presence of the other woman from her life. Meena's voice kept echoing in her ears, "We are like sisters ..."

"If sisters become co-wives, do they still remain sisters? And moreover she's not my ... " Nighat mumbled to herself.

Everything was going on fine. She had an affectionate husband and a doting mother-in-law. They had two sons and two daughters. Nighat was the mistress of the house, well loved by all. She was the only daughter in-law and *Amma* used to shower all her love on her. She too was very fond of her and used to take good care of everyone. Saifuddin also loved his wife dearly. He wanted Nighat to spend more time with him and he used to get upset when he found her always engrossed in household work. In the evenings when he used to come back from office, he wanted Nighat to attend to him. He wanted her to sit with him. He wanted her time, her company. But Nighat had thrown herself so deeply into her household chores that she started neglecting her husband's needs unkowingly.

He always used to complain, "you have time for everyone in the house except me."

And she would smilingly add a rejoinder, "But my entire time is for you only, dear."

"No, you've changed! You are not what you used to be. These days, you don't even come to me. Even at night you don't sleep with me. The entire day you are only bothered about the house and the kitchen and the children. You don't have time for me at all. And what is this strange habit that you've taken up of sleeping with children?"

"What can I do? The children have got used to me sleeping with them. And after a full day's work, I get extremely tired... that is why..."

As the days slipped by, distance began to creep in between the two. They drifted apart gradually. Saifuddin also become indifferent. He started spending more and more time outside the house. There were days when he did not come back even at night. Gradually he stopped complaining. He stopped loving her. He stopped seeking her company. This aloofness and indifference used to bother Nighat, but she found a way out of it all by throwing herself deeper into work. It was a Sunday, when Saifuddin dropped a bombshell. He came and announced his decision, "*Amma*, I'm marrying Meena, Kausar *khala's* widowed daughter."

Amma, who could never get up on her own without complaining of pain, was so shocked that she stood up instantly. Nighat, who was massaging her mother in-law's feet, also rushed to his side completely flabbergasted, "Why are you doing this to me? Where did I go wrong? Why are you bringing in another woman as my *sautan*?"

"Because what I need is a wife; that is why..."

"You already have a loving and caring wife, why do you need to marry a widow?" *Amma* rebuked him.

"*Amma*, what's wrong in that? I'm not doing anything unusual. Everyone keeps a second wife. Why *Amma*, you should be happy and proud of your son because I'm doing a big favour and a good deed by marrying a widow and helping her settle in life," said Saifuddin unashamedly and unrepentantly.

"No, you can't do this to me. What about our children? What would happen to us?" Nighat burst out in tears.

"But I'm not deserting you or divorcing you. Your own sister in-law lives with your brother's second wife amicably; they are like two sisters under the same roof."

"No, I would never be able to accept another woman's presence before my eyes."

"If you can't, then you are free to leave. I wouldn't stop you," retorted Saifuddin callously and went out of the room.

After this, Saifuddin did not speak to anyone, neither to his mother nor his wife nor his children. It was a stalemate. When things did not work out the way that Nighat wanted to, she left her husband's house and came to her parent's house along with her children. Saifuddin also did not budge from his decision. He neither went to Nighat to bring her back nor gave up the idea of a second marriage.

And then came a day when Nighat got the news of her husband's second marriage. She was devastated.

"Look Nighat, these menfolk are all the same. They don't understand what we have to go through. What Saifuddin is doing is nothing new. Men do it all the time. Look at yourself, you also have two mothers. I too had to go through all this and live with my *sautan*, your father's second wife. You also would have to adjust yourself to the given circumstances. What else can a woman do? Where would you go with your children? I think you should relent and make peace with your husband,' her mother advised.

Nighat was heartbroken once again. She felt helpless. Without uttering a single word, she gathered her belongings and left her mother's house.

The sun had already gone down by the time she reached her *sasural.* Saifuddin was very pleased to find her back. He happily took the luggage from her hands and brought her into his room. She then went to *Amma's* room to pay her regards and came back to her room without uttering a single word. Neither she nor the children spoke a word with Saifuddin. The sons, Amman and Ayan, too were very upset with their father because while they were away, he had given their room to Meena.

There had been a wedding in the house a few days back and a new bride had come. But instead of the usual festivities, there was an eerie silence everywhere as if someone had passed away in the family. Nighat too had withdrawn into herself. She had stopped talking to anyone. She would finish her work and retire behind closed doors. She had stopped sitting with her mother in-law too. She believed that *Amma* was equally to be blamed for Saifuddin's second marriage to her widowed niece. She should have stalled it. The daughters too tried in vain to comfort her, to console her but were unable to break her silence.

"*Amma* is calling you, mother," Almaas's words broke her reverie. Adjusting her *dupatta*, she went to *Amma's* room. Meena was already standing there.

"Listen Nighat, whatever has happened, has happened. We can't undo that. Both of you have equal right on Saifuddin and that is why Saifuddin and I have decided that he should give equal time to you both. So, he'll sleep with you for the first three nights and the next three nights, he'll sleep with Meena and one night he'll sleep with his children and mother. In this way, rights and interests of both of you would be taken care of. I want both of you to be happy," saying this *Amma* heaved a long sigh. But there was still something that weighed heavily on her heart.

After the evening meal, Saifuddin came into Nighat's room, which meant that the next three nights of the week he'd be sleeping with her. Initially, for a very long time, she just kept quiet, but when Saifuddin pulled her into his arms, she burst out in tears. All her pent-up feelings found a release. No words were exchanged. She kept sobbing in his arms, and he kept caressing her till she calmed down. Saifuddin knew womenfolk were extremely soft and delicate and would simply wither away without support. As such, the question of letting her go did not arise.

The next day, the situation had improved considerably. Nighat began to take good care of herself. She put on a new dress, used some makeup, and wore a nice fragrance. She cooked Saifuddin's favourite dishes and when he came back home in the evening, she devoted all her time to him.

Saifuddin too was extremely happy. He was on the seventh heaven. Earlier he used to yearn for the attention of one wife; now he had two wives, and both overeager to do his every bidding to please him. They would both make sweet delicacies for him. One would cut watermelon for him, the other mango. One would make *murg-musallam* for him and the other *chicken biryani.* Both would run around him trying to please him. They'd put new clothes and makeup and behave as newly married brides. They both were completely devoted to their husband and left no stone unturned to please him.

"Nighat… Nighat, come on dear, come and sleep now. It's very late in the night," *Amma's* voice broke her reverie. A single solitary tear escaped from the eye and rolled down her cheek. "You always wanted it this way Saifuddin … yearned for physical intimacy … " She recalled that after her children were born, she had lost the desire to sleep with Saifuddin. Gradually, she had drifted further and further away from her husband and started sleeping with her children. But ever since her rival in love came, she started vying for his love and attention. Her needs have changed, now her body doesn't want Saifuddin, but how could she tolerate the presence of some other woman in his life. How could she allow herself to considered any less superior and that too in her own husband's eyes?

"Just one more night has to be endured . . . ," she thought as she came into her room. The light of the moon had begun to wane as did her grief. "Just one more night," she consoled herself and closed her eyes.

Today, Nighat seemed to be a different person altogether. She was in a very jubilant mood. She took a lot of care in grooming herself, put on new clothes, and applied makeup. She made a liberal use of perfume too. Seeing her so happy and at ease with herself and her surroundings, *Amma* also felt very relieved. The ordeal of three nights was over, and Saifuddin was back with his first wife. Tonight the moon-lit night had brought a cool and embalming breeze with it.

But the cries were far from over. The steps leading to the terrace were still crying out in betrayal. It was Meena's turn now. She was sitting on the staircase gazing unblinkingly at the moon. Tonight the moon wasn't full. She too felt incomplete. She felt a kind of affinity with it, "Oh moon, who'd be better equipped to understand the deep ache and agony of incompleteness than you . . . tonight's night is not my night! Wasn't I better off being a widow and sitting in the dark than . . . "

"Meena, Meena! Come on dear, Come and sleep now. How long will you sit there? Come down, it's quite late in the night . . . " called out *Amma* entreatingly as she wiped the tears off her face.

First published as "*Meri Hisse ki Chandni*." Translated from Hindi by Jyotika Elhance.

34

Riding Rakhsh

Mariam Karim

I will soon be a hundred years old. So it's time I told my story. I was the youngest of three sisters and I didn't want to be anything - very unlike my sisters, who wanted to be professors or intellectuals or freedom fighters, or married well. In our family there were no doctors, although we were considered some of the best before my father died. My sisters also wanted to be good daughters, good mothers, and good wives. They wanted to be well considered in society, and among the Muslims. I had no such ambitions. Perhaps because I was the youngest and my mother loved me well just as I was. We were homeschooled, as girls still weren't sent to school or college in the early nineteen-twenties. My sisters Sajida and Zakia, (I called them Apabi and Bajia), were married off to a doctor and a lawyer respectively soon after they turned twenty-two which was late in those days, but they had degrees from private exams.

Just about that time, Abbu died, and I was only seventeen and we had no brothers to take care of us. Ammi didn't seem very interested in either my education or my marriage after Abbu left us. She became fatalistic and reclusive. We rented out the larger part of our immense haveli to an English family and began to live in the outhouse which was enough for Ammi and me. Our servants continued to serve us, and became employed with the English family as well. But we weren't so well off any more. We had kept two of our horses and the small car. I wasn't allowed to drive, but I did go riding some mornings towards the mango orchards. I can't say our changed circumstances had any ill effect on me.

We didn't interact much with our tenants and Shabbir Chacha did all the financial transactions for us. I could understand English and I read all the classics, but I couldn't converse in English. The four sons of the English gent thought I didn't know the language at all. So we just smiled at

Mariam Karim, *Riding Rakhsh* In: *The Silence That Speaks.* Edited by: Haris Qadeer, Oxford University Press.
 DOI: 10.1093/oso/9780190132613.003.0035

each other when we crossed, coming and going out of the estate and they made a respectful bow to my mother. She spoke only Urdu.

My story is of interest as my not wanting to *become* served me well. I cared not to be beautiful or popular or noticed. I was self-contained and content, whatever the circumstances. I knew after Abbu's passing no good match would come my way. Apabi and Bajia weren't clever enough to help me, although Ammi thought they ought to have. I didn't hold it against them. They were ensconced in upper-class society in a way I would never have enjoyed. Joint-families, weddings, and ceremonies such as *aqiqas, qurankhwanis*, elaborate *iftaars*, women's *majlis*. They really didn't have a voice in the freedom movement as many others did. Ammi, on the other hand, emerged from her apathy, and interacted, along with Shabbir Chacha, with gentlemen from the Congress Party and the Communist party. She had an opinion on political matters. Our very small home now became a meeting point for freedom fighters and intellectuals.

Rasheed was an assistant to a forest officer, and he was considered suitable for me. He was twelve years my senior and of an unprepossessing appearance: if my mother was unhappy with the match, she didn't show it. She was too involved with trying to browbeat the Muslim League. I went for an early morning ride on the grey flea-bitten horse, "Rakhsh." I had never been a romantic and Rasheed seemed acceptable to me. I was Ammi's favourite and her *dua* would always be with me, I said to myself. The morning air was bracing and fresh. I met the English boys on the way, and they bowed and smiled. I nodded briefly.

I started wearing saris after I got married as many women did in those days, and I really loved them. My sisters preferred *ghararas* for occasions, but I couldn't afford them. I kept the two made for my wedding safely in a trunk. I had some cotton *ghararas*, but it was hard to iron them. I felt far more free and more unobtrusive in my saris.

Rasheed was already forty, and I cannot say we were passionately in love. I moved with him to a small town by the Gomti. They were simple people, and I was from an illustrious family. They expected nothing from me, nor I from them. I wasn't looking to be the best daughter in-law in the world. Nor the best wife. Our first child died within the first week of life. I never conceived after that. Rasheed never complained. He continued to be as considerate and respectful as before. Rasheed took me along on all his outstation duties which were numerous. I wasn't expected to stay at home and look after his parents. I was also free to visit my mother's home or stay a few weeks with my sisters. They were alarmed at my freedom but also envious, I suspected. Their oppressive joint families left little space for freedom. I didn't envy them, their full lives, with children and grandchildren. I was filled with contentment just to see them. They were careful not to let anyone treat me like a poor relation. They bought gifts and gave them to their relatives on my behalf so I shouldn't look small. If they pitied me, it wasn't apparent.

Soon my in-laws, already old, were gone, and there were just the two of us. We had to be very frugal, and I grew some vegetables in the garden. The land was very fertile. I think our lives were so idyllic, those days. We went for long walks along the banks of the Gomti river. There were crocodiles and wild boar. Deer in the distant forests across, on the other side of the river. Nilgai had to be literally chased away (they loved eating our vegetables). The undergrowth was fragrant. Sometimes we spotted a tiger. Hyenas and leopards were a common sight. We had to be careful. Rasheed carried a shotgun. I dreamt of riding Rakhsh at times. Ammi had sold the horses to the English gent after I left. Often we stayed in tents in the lush forests. We had to keep a fire burning in case of wild animals. Hyenas were bolder than the big cats. They came after our guard dogs. The birds in the early mornings made such a clamour no one could remain asleep.

I think I've lived so long because I just was, and never wanted to become anything, or anyone. Rasheed was the ideal match for me as he never expected anything more than I was prepared to offer. Our unusual understanding had a beneficial effect on him as well ... his earlier apologetic expressions of social and financial inadequacy in regard to me slowly waned. He too began to appreciate the beauty of not being anyone, of existing day to day in a natural world full of unexpected wonders. The freedom which comes from not *having to be someone*. The less I expected from him, the more he appreciated me. The small joys of our lives were like the joys of children, finding a wild mulberry tree in the woods with sweet purple fruit, discovering the hiding place of the honey badger, witnessing the birthing of a fawn, were riches far, far beyond the gracious evenings of silks and jewels of my sisters' lives, their associations with nawabs, talluqdars, writers, and poets.

We seemed to be in a perpetual state of calm happiness where one day was like another in its basic essence. When I went to visit Ammi, it was a different world. There were large gatherings of politically active gentlemen and ladies in our little outhouse. The Muslims who didn't want a Pakistan. Those who didn't want to live in a country based on religion. Those who wanted to live alongside the Hindus the Christians and the Sikhs. Who hated the idea of a religious state. Who were vociferous and emotional. Then the Partition came. I fled to my own home by the Gomti in the Terai. We were nearer Gomut Taal, not close enough to Pilibhit town to experience much upheaval. The excursions had been suspended. The forest officer had had to leave for Britain. I told everyone we knew that we were not going to Pakistan and they should not either. Soon the Sikhs started trickling into Pilibhit. Refugees. And Bengalis, from East Pakistan, now your Bangladesh.

Rasheed and I, and our servants, stayed close to the land and to each other, grew vegetables and sent cooked food to the refugee camps nearby our homestead as and when we could. It was a hard time for all of us. But I was glad we weren't going. Many of my parent's relatives had gone. They thought they would get a better deal. Or help build a better nation.

It's been more than forty years Rasheed is no longer by my side. He gave me a good life, though we were poor. He was a good man. I came away, selling our land and the house. I came to my grandparent's ancestral home in the village surrounded by mango groves. I've lived here since. I'm glad I'm not going to be around much longer. All our reasons for not going to Pakistan, for opposing the Partition, are now taking shape around us in our Hindustan. People divided on the basis of religion, community. A huge machinery working towards, clamouring for, a religious state, like Pakistan. The end of the *Ganga-Jamuni* culture. The end of Hindustan as I have known it. For the first time in the nearly hundred years I have lived, I am not contented.

I still dream of riding Rakhsh.

I am waiting.

Ya Khuda, teri raza kya hai?

(Oh, Almighty, What is your decree?)

The story is dedicated to my father's sister, Begum Razia Fatima Zaman, who lived to be a hundred.

35

The Sunset

Sulema Khatun Kajol

1971. It was the month of March. A joint meeting was taking place between the Indian border forces and the East Pakistan border forces—a white-flag meeting for peace and harmony. People from both countries have joined the meeting. The Kamalpur camp of the border-guards, on the other side of the border, is not very far from the camp at Mahendraganj on this side of the border. The venue of the meeting was the no man's land, a buffer zone in the middle of the two camps. Depending on their understanding, people were talking and gossiping about the meeting. They all were very curious about the meeting. People were excited and hopeful of getting a chance to see their relatives from the other side of the border, the relatives whom they had not seen after 1947. Their relatives who had migrated from one side of the border to the other side, facing thousands of problems. These uprooted people … some went willingly, some were forced to migrate. One country was divided into two. But the love and affection of people were not divided. No one could draw a border on the hearts of the people; no one could take away their unity.

I have seen various colours of different emotions on multiple occasions. I, myself, have felt happy on various occasions. But how do I describe the emotions that I witnessed today! All the colours fail to appropriately paint a picture of the emotions. Some were excited with happiness. Some were heartbroken with pain. Some were breathing long sighs! Some were depressed; some were doubtful; some were disappointed; some were disheartened; some had high hopes. Colourful games of different emotions were being played on their faces.

Women are trying their best to finish their household chores. They may also get a chance to see a relative from the other side. A long and eager wait after finishing the chores.… Some of them were unable to

Sulema Khatun Kajol, *The Sunset* In: *The Silence That Speaks*. Edited by: Haris Qadeer, Oxford University Press.
 DOI: 10.1093/oso/9780190132613.003.0036

focus on their work as they were depressed. Their pain, which they have been hiding in the core of their hearts, suddenly, erupted. Some of the women came to this side of the border as newlywed brides, they have not the faces of their parents, brothers, sisters, and other relatives for years. After being uprooted from their native places, their hearts were severely wounded and pierced.

Time passed like this. A large number of people are walking towards the border like the rows of ants—old, young, children—all of them except the women of the village. They were peep from their houses . . . they try to get a glimpse from afar. The women, especially the newly wed ones, could not understand what was happening there. In my village, as a tradition, women cannot participate in men's discussions. They have to be satisfied with whatever bits and pieces they can gather from here and there.

Many elderly women spice up the stories that they hear:

"Do you know, the men in my house are telling that there might be a fight."

"Yes, I heard that. It is something like a food distribution ceremony. India is giving things to Pakistan."

"Not at all, Sheikh Mujib will come to deliver a lecture."

"The Government will build a road—my brother heard that."

"You don't know anything. I heard my husband telling his friend that Indra (Indira) Gandhi is opening a trade centre. We all will be able to buy and sell things."

"Do you see there are a lot of people disguised as insane people? My husband says that they are CIDs, the government spies. Be careful! Don't just say whatever comes to your mind."

I heard men were discussing about the meeting. I also heard women discussing the same. I was not a child then, I did understand some of their concerns.

Everyone finished their daily rituals earlier than the other days. Many had fears in their hearts; they had their own doubts: "God knows, what will happen at the meeting!" "It is a meeting of two parties of the border security guards; common people will also be there . . . Surely, there is every possibility for both good and bad to happen," "Are you sure, there will be no fight among the border security guards?"

East Pakistan is going through a time of turmoil. Under the leadership of Sheikh Mujib, they are fighting against the rule of the government of

Pakistan. They are fervently fighting for the freedom of Bangladesh. In Pakistan, the prime minister, Yahiya Khan, is in deep trouble. The *Pathan* soldiers are torturing the Bengali people brutally. A meeting in such a troubled time is beyond the comprehension of the village folks. The Armed Forces, on both sides, are ready with their arms and ammunition to meet any eventuality of a war. That itself is sufficient to arouse fear and speculations.

"But it is a White Flag Meeting, we should not worry."

Still, the limitless worries and uncertainties persist.

Still, the limitless enthusiasm persists.

Still, the people are walking towards the venue of the meeting at the border, much ahead of the stipulated time. All the hurdles of fear, uncertainties, and doubts have fallen before the flood of emotions – all the repressed pains and emotions are going to merge to form an ocean of love and humanity. How long could the fear and doubts hold them back! All fear and doubts vanish as the people are engulfed with strong emotions. The crowd ignored everything and rushed towards the spot.

One hour.

Two hours.

Time is passing.

Suddenly, I hear an uproar in one house in the neighbourhood.

"What happened? What happened?" I yelled.

"Their relatives from the other side of the border have come to see them."

"The border is only open for two hours to allow people to visit their relatives on both the sides of the border."

Like many others in the village, I ran to that house to see what was happening.

As the duration of two hours was a very short time, people are rushing in large numbers.

Many of them are meeting each other after a long period of time; nobody is able to control their tears. God knows when they may get another chance to meet!

While watching the people crying in one house, I hear the sounds of wailing from another house. After I reach there, I hear cries from another house. Within a few minutes, all the houses in the village have visitors, and the entire village is echoing with the sounds of sobbing and wailing.

Perhaps, after seeing those tears of joy and pain, I realized the importance of the day. I expected people to be happy and joyful with laughter. But now I see the opposite. I don't see anyone without tears. All those were joyful tears of happiness!

Who can look at the eyes of the others! All are busy wiping their tears. Unable to bear the stress of a long wait, some faint at the sight of their near and dear ones. Some are writhing on the ground; their traumatic cries that can tear the sky apart. Some are embracing their dear ones and mumbling as they are unable to utter any words. The throats are choked! Only the lips are trembling! And tears are flowing incessantly. What a devastatingly painful sight it is!

I became speechless.

I go from one house to another and see a similar sight. Suddenly, I hear the same is happening in my house too. I run to our house. Our forefather's relatives have come. They brought countless tears with them, and those tears were flowing from their eyes towards their hearts. I watch them with a gaping mouth. My siblings and I have never seen them before. I do not know who is what to whom in relation. While we are busy watching them, my grandmother comes running and wailing, "Oh brother! Oh my brother!" Her dearest brother has come. They had lost their mother and grew up together being very close to each other in their childhood. They were separated at a tender age and did not meet each other from their then to now. She could not recognize him till he was introduced by someone.

Suddenly, I hear my mother's choked sighs! Her maternal uncle has come to meet us. Our mother's maternal uncle was in front of us! We have never seen him before. What a surprise! Mother embraced her uncle. She started crying more remembering her dead mother. "Mother wanted to see you before dying. Her wish remained unfulfilled." My mother muttered with her choking voice.

We did not have a maternal uncle. My mother was a single child. Seeing our mother crying, all my seven siblings wept. After some time, we wiped our tears.

Mother's uncle exclaimed, "Oh Allah! Why did you write this in our destiny ?" He tried to console by blaming the Supreme one.

"Oh brother! Oh sister-in-law," crying this, someone hurriedly entered into our house. He is Ebol Sangma, a local tribal man. He stayed in this house for four years, for his studies. He is a very good football player. My father is also very fond of football; he is very affectionate towards him. Mother also treats him like a younger brother. In the last thirty years, Sangma did not forget our love and affection. Everything is fresh in his memory like a freshly-bloomed flower.

"Ebol! Ebol! Didn't you go to see your relatives?"

"My relatives are in Dalu and Porakhasia. Those places are far from Mahendraganj border. So within two hours, it won't be possible to visit them."

All are staring at Ebol now with sad eyes, feeling pity for him.

"It is unfortunate that I have to go back from here," Ebol said in a painful and apologetic voice. He has to be happy with meeting his brother and sister-in-law only.

Two hours. Only two hours. That too passed quickly.

How could people leave their pieces of hearts behind, after meeting them just for two hours! There was not enough time even to wipe the tears. Their feet refuse to move. The love that made them run to this side of the border, is holding them back.

With heavy hearts and heavy steps, people are returning back.

Out of a sudden, an announcement is made that after seeing the love and eagerness of the villagers to meet their relatives, the visiting time was extended till the sunset. The border guards are unable to control the emotions. Today, after seeing the flood of people moving across the border, they have become sympathetic and kind. So, they have extended the time till the sunset.

Till the sunset. Till the sunset. TILL THE SUNSET... that unbelievable phrase is echoing everywhere.

Now everybody's eyes are set on the sun. They have to return to their country before the sunset. Probably, except the poets and artists, no one has ever given such attention to a setting sun. Today, everybody is looking at the sun, again and again.

The sun rises every day with its smiling face and sets in the same manner. But today, the sun is not smiling while setting down. Today, it seems to be busier than the other days. Perhaps, it is unbearable for the sun to witness such painful tears. It might be thinking that it is better to get rid of this painful scene as soon as possible. It set too early towards the western horizon. And a black cloud appeared out of nowhere, perhaps to save the face of the sun.

Today, at the border, there was little laughter and few tears; there was little happiness and little pain — it all lasted only for a day.

The way the sun disappeared on the horizon today, it never did before. It never again will!

First published as "Suryasth." Translated from Bengali by Arzuman Ara.

36

Blue-Winged Girls

Husn Tabassum Nihan

The girls are growing up. While growing up, they are giggling; they are laughing; they are humming. They are running freely; they are sprinting ahead. It is as if they want to reach ahead before time and touch the finishing line. They are writing love letters. While sitting for on their study tables, they read something very secretively, and smile slowly like blooming buds of red flowers.

On their roofs, kites passionately kiss them and fly away. They wave their *chunris* in the wind.

Ude Jab Jab Zulfein Teri . . .

(Whenever the breeze wafts through your hair)

They are riding the clouds as they desire to touch the sky. They are running recklessly . . . They are running away from their homes . . . running away, and they shall never be caught.

Never . . . ever . . . never . . . never.

Aaj main azad hun duniya ke chaman mein . . . (I am free today in the garden of the world).

They know that they will have to be on the run for ever. But they are running just for the sake of running . . . fearlessly, confidently, and silently!

Razia's feet got stuck into a muddy pothole. "Yuck . . . yuck," she made faces, jerked her feet out of the pothole, and rubbed it on the dry ground. After rubbing her feet from every side, she felt a bit satisfied and wore her slippers back. She walked to a *sheesham* tree, sat underneath it, and looked in all the four directions.

"Where has he gone? It is time for the train's arrival." She looked at her watch, and dialed a number on her cellphone. A shrill voice emerged out of her cellphone: "Your call to the number is not possible at the moment. Please . . . " She got frustrated. "Such a big liar!"

Husn Tabassum Nihan, *Blue-Winged Girls* In: *The Silence That Speaks.* Edited by: Haris Qadeer, Oxford University Press. © Oxford University Press India 2022. DOI: 10.1093/oso/9780190132613.003.0037

She redialed the number, and heard the same answer in the same feminine voice. She held her head in her hands.

"What will happen now . . . ?"

"Well, I should go and look around at the station; he might be sitting there. Cellphones, often, betray you at such crucial moments. These days, round the clock, there are innumerable issues with cellphone network."

The evening was gradually sliding into a deeper darkness.

With hurried steps, she proceeded in the direction of the station. But where? Even after reaching the station she, like a lost kid, was looking cluelessly into the crowd.

"Where did he go . . . Where?"

"Meanwhile, I shall buy the tickets." Her eyes were still looking all around:

"Where did he go . . . Where did he go? What if train departs before he comes?

"Yes, Madam . . . where do you want to go?"

"I . . . I . . . ?"

She had not even thought about this question. Baffled, she took the money back from the clerk's hand, and came out of the queue. The abominable gazes of the clerk and others followed her. She went back to the far side of the platform and sat on a seat near the toilet, and closed her eyes. She held her bag tightly against her chest.

Her family must have started looking for her by now. What a long and lengthy letter of twenty-one pages she left for them! She gave a long lecture to her family. She also told them not to search for her. Today, she might be going away physically, she had already abandoned them a long time back.

"I have disappeared from everyone's sight. Nobody needs me. I roam around as a stranger in my own house. I feel alienated in my own father's courtyard . . . I am a stranger . . . the birth of a girl child is a curse!"

And whenever I applied for a job . . .

"No . . . no . . . what will people think? . . . " Abbu outrightly declined.

"Marriage . . . ?"

Marriage was fixed with the eldest son of eldest aunt. He is an acclaimed businessman! He has a car and a bungalow. He is also famous . . .

Why don't people understand? She was in a dilemma. I am the one who has to fall in love; I am the one who has to get married. Who are these people to dictate? Marriage can be forced upon us, but not love. They will decide whom shall I fall in love, and they will chose a husband for me... What sort of dictatorship is this? Can these things be forced upon? It is supposed to happen on its own!

Rani had accepted her defeat. What eventually happened to her? How Ashraf loved her! He used to send expensive gifts to her. Ashraf went mad when Rani fell ill. How bitterly he wept while praying for her health! How envious I was with Rani's fate! "Well, If one has a lover, he should be like him ... " But that envy ... no longer remains an envy! "Abracadabra ... " Poof!

Rani's father turned down the proposal, "You won't be married off to a man of lower caste. If you want to go with him, you will have to walk over my corpse." After a week or so, she was forcefully married to a boy from her distant family. Her marriage ceremony was performed at an *Ijtemah* (a religious gathering). She went away with a heavy heart, and was welcomed with Abid's punches, kicks, and blows. She turned into a living corpse – only her funeral procession and her burial ceremony were left to take place. One day, Ashraf self-immolated at her doorsteps. Abid was furious. He thrashed her badly, worse than before. She felt immense internal happiness. It is said that on the very same day, she committed suicide by poisoning herself and her husband. Although it was at the very last moment, atleast she had done something useful. If she died alone, other women would have to undergo the same humiliation and torture. It was a good idea to kill "the devil" along with herself. But why do we have such prisons ... such limitations ... such traditions. Which religion tells you to marry only within your own community and caste? Which book states that an Ansari has to marry another Ansari? Or Muslims will only marry within their community, and Hindus will marry within their community? Although Rani had a terrible death, her father was finally happy! But, was that of any use?

Thankfully, Sheeba was much smarter; she mustered up a little courage. Currently, she is on the cloud nine. She is the queen of the sky, and the princess of the entire world. Tauseef was from Naddaf community and Sheeba was from Syed community. The difference between them is like water and fire; it is like the difference between the sky and the earth. They are thousands of miles apart from each other. Tauseef was like a *jamun* fruit... Sheeba was like a *falsa* fruit... people are as sour as

Kakraunda . . . they were all surprised. How could she? What did she find worthy in him?

"Tauseef's silky voice . . . "

"What a wonderful singer!"

"What a beautiful smile!"

"What an eloquent speaker!"

If Sheeba is happy, everyone is happy; the whole world is happy. The most appropriate way is not to give a damn to the obdurate society. Without rhyme or reason . . . *Huh*!

Although, time and again, she kept struggling with the past but Tauseef's unconditional devotion would take her to the cloud nine. On the day she eloped with Tauseef, her mother kept calling her:

"Sheeba . . . Oh! Sheeba . . . "

Sheeba wasn't there to respond... Drenched in torrential rain, she flew away on her feet. Amma's voice was echoing: "These runaway girls . . . you see, are like moths. They fly out of nowhere and die dancing around the flame of lamp." They search for her at her friends' place. The whole city was ransacked, but they were not even able to find Sheeba's footprint. Sheeba was in Kolkata. Her brother who used to whip her; her cursing father, her quarrelsome sisters-in-law, and her grudging mother—they were all lamenting the destruction of their false pride. They all only had a wish; they all wanted to find her, atleast for the very last time. Her brothers were banging their heads. "Can someone bring her back one last time?"

She went to Sheeba's home recently to enquire about her family's condition. Throughout the visit, she was so proud of Sheeba and was continuously murmuring prayers for her: "Allah! Please do not send Sheeba back. Please don't send her back . . . "

Suddenly, Sheeba's number flashed on her cellphone's screen. Her heart began to pound! May no one knows that she is calling me! She switched off her phone and rushed out of their home. Sheeba's mother told her that Sheeba's phone was switched off.

Run . . . Run for your life . . .

While leaving, she had shown everyone their trueselves through her long letter. Today, she also did not hesitate while taking the same step. Why shall I tolerate anyone's rebuke? Tomorrow, if I meet a terrible death as Rani, who will cry for me? Ammi? Abba? Brother or sister-in-law? Neighbours? Or no one?

Why shall I sacrifice myself at the altar of their false pride? Why shall I offer my delicate-as-flower life? Why shall I not follow Sheeba's footstep and save my life? And save the dignity of love? Let me not disgrace my ancestors, who sacrificed themselves for loyalty. Shouldn't I bring honour to their name?

She heard grunting and squeaking sounds and opened her eyes. A monkey was sitting in front of her, and was scratching its thighs and underarms. It appeared to her that the monkey was teasing her with its strange postures. She felt disgusted and turned her face away. Then, gradually, the clamour and cry of her home started taking forcefully over her imagination. They might have read her long letter three to four times by now. Ammi would be beating her chest and Abba would be abusing her with his newly invented cuss-words. My brother must be banging his head in anger.

"We will eat her alive if we find her."

"Find her and cut her to pieces with a knife; put her in a gunny sack, and throw it in a river." Her aunt might have suggested:

Shhshhhssss.

May such a place be cursed where there are boundations on celebration of happiness, where one has to take permission even for breathing, where one needs application letters for everything! And every time my application gets rejected because I am a woman! What do I get there? ... Only the pain of being a woman!

Alas! ... a girl child.

As if I am not a woman but a scavenger!

I am eloping with a Hindu man.

There will be communal clashes between Hindus and Muslims.

How does it matter to me! They all are idiots. You can't force idiots to live like civilized human beings!

Hum ne Ghar chora hai ... rasmo ko toda hai

Hum door kahin jayenge, Nayi duniya basaenge

(We have left our homes ... we have broken the traditions/ We shall go somewhere far and start a new life).

Look! How the Gulmohar tree is smiling at us. As if it is showering its blessing upon us, hugging us close to its chest. Now, this city will be left behind... it will be left behind ... let it be ... let it be ... so be it.

Suddenly, a curtain fell on her eyes.

"Ouchhh!"

Her heartbeats began racing.

"Who is this … ?" Her teeth froze. Is it her brother? Or her father? The hands palming her eyes were tightened their grip. She was panting heavily; someone's lips were on her lips.

"Hey"

"Rohit"

"So late?"

The moon was smiling above them. "I have come. Will you come? Won't you?" She was holding Rohit's arm. Two veiled women passed. They were grumbling:

"Allah only knows where these run away girls disappear, they are never found back."

She was scared and hid behind Rohit.

"I told you to wear a burqa."

"What shall I do now … ?" She said. She accepted her mistake while embracing Rohit tightly.

"Nothing. Just cover your head and sit. And don't look towards the crowd."

He started dialling a number on his phone.

"This is Rohit speaking, Hafeeza. Yes, yes … Razia is with me. Do one thing: bring a burqa to the platform of the railway station. Be careful. No one should even get a clue. Do call me as soon as you reach here … "

"Haf… Haf… Rohit… " Razia heard everything with a gaping mouth. She was staring with her wide-opened eyes.

"What are you looking at … you have been foolish … fifty percent of smugglers in today's world are using burkha for their illegal activities … especially female smugglers … whatever, the case may be, but burqa is an extremely safe and successful item … "

Moon was gradually coming down, and the sky was, now, full of stars. There was still no information about the train.

The cellphone rang!

"Yes, Hafeeza speaking… towards the toilet… "

Hafeeza was coming from the right direction, taking long steps. She came near and looked at him: "here it is … wear it quickly. Your mother called me twice. The news is spreading. Be thankful and just run away… "

"Go to the bathroom."

After handing over the burqa, Hafeeza disappeared from our view. Before going, she bent and hummed in Rohit's right ear:

"*Rohit bhai . . . Hum hain Rahi pyar ke phir milenge chalte-chalte . . .* "

(Brother Rohit . . . we are co-travelers of in the path of love. Our paths will cross again!)

First published as "Neele Pankhonwali Ladkiyan." Translated from Hindi by Haris Qadeer.

37
There Once Was A Mouse

Malika Amar Shaikh

He was really little, smaller than a fist, and ordinary, like any other mouse. There was nothing exceptional about him except his small jewel -bright eyes and an extraordinary agility. Although he was so little, whenever she caught sight of him Raju's mother, the mistress of the house, let out a shriek and hop skip and jumped around the room. She was not half as nimble as him, of course. And because she couldn't match his speed, she would curse him loudly. Just as well the mouse didn't understand the language . . .

Raju's mother would keep yelling hysterically, "Get that mouse out of here at once . . . I am scared of him, he loots the grain sacks . . . If you can't, at least get a cat . . . " Raju's father would look around and quickly plant a kiss on her cheek. "Aga, you must have someone for company in the house . . . you'll get bored on your own, isn't it? And you think getting a cat will solve your problem? The cat will drink up all the milk when you are not looking. That will be an additional headache! Once you set up a home, some problems are to be expected. People will come and go . . . And he is such a tiny fellow, you are afraid for nothing."

The mouse would listen to all this quietly. His beady eyes would watch everything. Then, he would dart across and like a naughty child get up to all sorts of mischief . . . pull out the stuffing from the mattress, spill the wheat from the bin . . . he had taken Raju's older sister, Tai's new hairclip and hidden it in his den. The tantrum she threw, and the cushions that accompanied it, he dragged them away to his home. If he could laugh, he would have surely guffawed. He must have probably thought to himself I am not all that destructive, am I? These people crumple paper napkins at the table and make a mess . . . what's wrong if I nibble one end just to get a taste of it? There is a sack of grain in a corner of the storeroom. I am not

Malika Amar Shaikh, *There Once Was A Mouse* In: *The Silence That Speaks*. Edited by: Haris Qadeer, Oxford University Press. © Oxford University Press India 2022. DOI: 10.1093/oso/9780190132613.003.0038 taking all of it, am I? The whole sack I'm leaving for you. So, what happens if I keep a few grains for myself? These and many such thoughts must be going through his mind. It isn't as if a mouse doesn't have a mind. And when you have a mind, thoughts are bound to come.

Despite all the grumbling and complaining, the people in the house gradually got used to having the mouse around. Screaming and jumping about even if the mouse didn't go anywhere near her became a habit for Raju's mother. Finally, the family acknowledged his presence in the home. The shift happened unintentionally.

Raju's father began to leave grains of rice and scraps of fish from his plate near the mouse hole. Raju's mother would finish her chores and lie down, hoping to read the newspaper. But then, her sleep-heavy eyes would look around for the mouse, waiting to see his antics as he scampered hither and thither, stopping suddenly to survey his surroundings with his pebble like eyes, ears pricked up and body alert. She loved it when, fearful of her gaze, he would take refuge under the cupboard in the room. Sometimes, she was so overcome with affection that she would caress him with her eyes, but then, a combination of revulsion and a nameless fear would emerge , just like the mouse. Relationships are like that, very complex things. Even though some of them are distant and unexpressed, they are long-lasting. They don't break even if, say you want them to. And that is something everyone knows in the depths of their hearts.

The mouse couldn't have known this, because there is no evidence to show that animals contemplate upon relationships. Of course, some people will declare that many things in the world are accepted even if they are not proven. If that is what they believe, then so be it.

Early one morning, Baba received a letter. It was quite unexpected, and it left him very disturbed. The whole house gathered around him saying "What happened?" "What happened?" Holding his hand up Baba announced, "The good news is that Ajoba is coming. The other, slightly bothersome news is that a friend, a professor from Nagaland, is also coming. Dinesh, Raju's friend will be here at the same time." Happy that they were all coming, but anxious about the fate of the monthly budget . . . —Anyway, a private discussion on the matter was held between Aie and Baba.

That day, the mouse made sure he took fewer grains from the gunny sack. But he didn't decrease his quota of mischief. On the contrary, it was at its height. Familiarity, disregard, disrespect, all came into play. He broke the string of Tai's violin. Tai brought the house down … Once again, dire threats to get a cat were made, but the mouse either did not recognize the gravity of the threat or didn't know what a cat was … Who knows.

Brazenly and audaciously, he would crouch behind the pile of chadars, the covering sheets and when he felt people had forgotten all about him, he would appear before them, all innocent and guileless, but with an arch "catch me if you can" look. He would charge from here to there daring them to trap him. Immediately, the whole household would chase after him with broom, cardboard, anything they could lay their hands on. This game would go on for a while, much to Raju's delight. Baba would watch the proceedings with an indulgent half smile as he carried on with his work.

On a hot blazing afternoon, along the black, sweaty city streets came the unexpected guests. In a flurry of activity—welcomes, greetings, enquiries, excitement, bathwater arrangements, tea, snacks, introductions—all the elaborate rituals were completed.

It was too much for the tiny brain of the mouse to absorb. He was bewildered. He made a quick dash outside to see what was going on. Nobody took any notice of him. Disappointed at being ignored, he stopped outside his hole and wondered what was wrong with them. A little while ago, he had found a piece of potato bhajji near the table. As he crouched there munching on it, he had deliberately swiped his tail over Tai's foot. There was no reaction. Deeply dejected, he was scurrying back when he spied a piece of ribbon. Quickly he dragged it into his house. For a long while, he stood at the entrance peeping out to see what was going on. His little shell shaped ears twitched, his bright eyes dimmed with sadness, as he went back into his den. He felt a strange unease, he couldn't say why.

Then he caught sight of the ribbon. He delicately ran his hands over it. It was pure white with little red dots and small, very small pearly beads stitched on it. Hands … a very pretty ribbon indeed. As he gazed at it, he forgot the many people outside, the hustle bustle they created, their indifference to him … The ribbon became his sole preoccupation; it filled his whole world. Soon, the sparkle returned to his little eyes. Until now, he had never ventured beyond this house, had never felt the need to, but suddenly he felt he should take the ribbon and explore the world. But to step out of one's home, one's familiar surroundings, one's context, one needs to be in a particular state of mind … And at that moment, he did not think of that which lay outside this house—the street, the rushing traffic, the menacing miaow of the cat rubbing itself against the curve in the wall, the flying leap to escape it, none of these things came to his mind.

Even the thought, what shall I do with this ribbon, didn't occur to him. As if he knew deep inside how, why, for whom he had picked it up. A strange yet familiar entity which was felt but not seen took birth inside him … the outside world was not privy to its presence. He no longer felt so alone. He sat in his hole, quietly stroking the ribbon. Who knows if he was even in his den. Was he? Perhaps not.

As he was running his hands over the ribbon, a bead broke loose and rolled away. The mouse was startled. Nimbly he leapt out. But something was not quite right. Quite wrong, in fact. As he was chasing the bead, his tail came under the heel of one of the guests' shoes. The pain was excruciating, but somehow he managed to grab the bead in his mouth and drag his hurting tail back into his hole. He could hear everyone curse him. It was not unusual for them to abuse him, but today was different. They expressed their heartfelt commiserations for the newly arrived guest, as if the gentleman's shoe was injured by a mouse's tail. Even Baba uttered an embarrassed, "Sorry!" as if having a mouse with no manners or a sense of how to behave with guests was a crime of sorts.

But the mouse paid little heed to it. He had found the bead. Actually speaking, he was more pained because the ribbon's beauty had been marred by the loss of the bead, rather than by the injury to his tail. He sat in his house, morosely glancing from the ribbon to the detached bead.

All sorts of sounds were emerging from the house—loud laughter, raised voices, clattering vessels, clinking glasses … as the table was being laid with pretty porcelain plates and dishes, as tantalizing aromas swirled around. While all flavours were distinctive, they blended and mingled into a brand new one. Earlier the smells would be most tempting. The mouse would widen his eyes, then wiggle his ears and lifting his snout, sniff a few times, isolate each flavour from the mix and then draw it into his den. This was the spicy biryani, this, fried chicken … that has to be the smell of bhajjis … And this one? Must be halwa garnished with cardamom and almonds … or was puri and basundi? After gathering together all these flavours, he'd take a long deep breath and swallow the whole lot of smells. Then, with great agility and urgency, he'd bound into the kitchen … That day however, for the first time despite these casual invitations floating in the air along with the aromas … the bustle and the tumult, the uproar in the house, the mouse remained aloof. Mr. Undeer (the mouse) was in no way a part of it. Where earlier he would feel compelled to go outside to join the people and take his place beneath a chair, that day he didn't feel like leaving his hole. Nobody in the house noticed his absence. He kept looking at the ribbon. Who knows what he had been thinking—Was he convinced that it would suddenly come to life and stand before him? If that happened then what language would the ribbon speak to him in? Would the ribbon have small beady eyes like himself? What would the live ribbon eat? Such weird questions must have come to him.

Just like the waves of the ocean crash against a stone wall, break and disperse, all the aromas continued to float up to the mousehole, strike and dissipate. But Mr Undeer's sense of smell seemed to have become numb, as if some imaginary little mouse had chewed up that tiny stomach's appetite.

Dinner was finished. Again, the clatter of vessels, gurgle of water, burps of satisfaction, idle chatter … Never before had Undeer felt such a strong urge to like scream "Quiet!" … What came out of his throat was a pathetic squeak.

How much human beings can talk … how much noise they make … why don't they just get out, he thought when it occurred to him that it was their own house, and he was staying in their home. He must have felt genuinely ashamed at this ungrateful thought, being a member of their home and yet cursing them … How often had Baba chosen to disregard my pranks, Raju had played with me so innocently, Aai lovingly allowed me to steal peanuts and pieces of bhajji … Should I myself leave this place? Take the ribbon and go away, out of this den, out of the house? This house is also a den, albeit a big one … Mr. Undeer probably wasn't aware that no one in this world can escape from the den.

From one hole to another we go, every one of us. And the time between getting from one hole into another is the time between one inhalation and exhalation. The time between one poem and another. The interim between one experience and another, one relationship and the next. Between one human being and another.

When that which is unavoidable and inevitable becomes hateful and acceptable at the same time, one is being true to one's self, of living independently and handling the responsibility that comes with it, be it man or mouse. Whether it is right or wrong becomes inconsequential when one moves from one rat hole to another. To choose between being safe and taking a risk is a very tough call.

Mr. Undeer had become eager to get out of his hole. He felt that one kind of hunger had died and another was beginning to take its place. Actually, he was fed up. By the time this hunger was fed another would make its appearance. One that was quelled would be replaced by another... Where's the ribbon in all this? He ran his hands over the ribbon again. It calmed him. He ran his tail over the ribbon. The tail was hurting, but it felt good with the ribbon's touch. He put the ribbon aside, let out a long breath and stepped out of the hole ... as usual beneath the cupboard, along the wall, under the table, through the hall, from the bedroom to the kitchen. But the restlessness, the heavy heart, the loneliness and the painful tail hampered his movements. He realized it himself. Moreover, the house was cluttered with the bags and baggage of the guests.

He paused for while by the meat-safe to survey the scene. Human feet were still criss-crossing the kitchen floor. He couldn't see much from between the feet. A thought struck him, What if human beings were transparent and one could see through them! What fun it would be... He took cover under the fridge and waited. He was figuring out how he could jump from the base of the fridge onto the counter without causing more damage to his injured tail.

Finally, when all human traffic ceased, he took a big leap and landed on the counter. To his dismay, someone had left a pretty patterned brand new bone china cup there. It fell to the floor and shattered into a hundred pieces. Terrified, the mouse again took refuge under the fridge. Aai came into the kitchen screaming, followed by Tai and Baba. Aai raved and ranted against the mouse. She swished the broom firmly under the fridge. One of the long sticks poked his eye. He winced and moved further back, and back.

"Enough of this tolerating and indulging I am going to get a rat trap this time... too much of this creature's mischief have I put up with. Bai ga! The havoc he has caused! A 50-rupee cup, brand new! Just today, I took it out of the cupboard... If I get my hands... such a tiny little thing, but bai...!" Aai continued grumbling as she swept up the pieces.

More tears filled Mr. Undeer's eyes when he heard this rather than when the broom had pricked his eye. He let out a pitiful "chi" and fell silent. Just then, one of the guests came into the kitchen. "What happened, vahini?" he asked Aai solicitously which set her off on her litany of complaints about Mr Undeer. "Arrey! Is that all? Wait and see how I put an end to your troubles," he said cheerfully. Immediately, Aai protested, "Are you going to kill him or what? Oh no, no, don't! He is Ganapati's vehicle, after all, and we observe the Ganapati festival. No, we don't want the sin of..."

"Relax, vahini, I won't kill it. I will catch it and take it with me."

"To your place?"

"To my laboratory. I urgently needed a mouse for my experiment. This way my need will be fulfilled, and your problem will be solved. Besides, it is the rat's good fortune to be chosen to participate in this monumental research project. Three birds or one rat with one stone, eh?" he said with a hearty laugh. The others laughed too, but only half-heartedly.

Mr. Undeer, hiding under the counter was pleased ... Great! My wish is being fulfilled. This man, he won't kill me, will he? Be that as it may, at least I will get out of this hole. And take that ribbon with me too.

After that, Mr. Undeer feasted to his heart's content. Then, he packed some crumbs in the side of his mouth and ran to his den. He dropped those tasty titbits in front of the ribbon. A gentle breeze ruffled the ribbon slightly. To him, it was a sign of her appreciation. He felt like smiling. But mice can't smile, can they? He just felt good inside. Humans are strange, he thought. They can smile, but their eyes, their minds, their brains , and their hearts are heavy and sad.

Sounds of chatter, laughter, argument, applause drifted in. Gradually, they faded away. Darkness stole into the house with light feet and laid a heavy hand on eyelids. But Mr. Undeer could not sleep. Again, he reached out for the ribbon. Soft, delicate, fine ... He went into the kitchen. A exciting smell assailed him ... he followed it eagerly ... grabbed the scrap, and heard a snap. Something behind him had shut. He spun around. Terrified, he scrabbled around. He started yelling. The door remained shut. Looking for a way to escape he began gnawing at the thin wire bars. His teeth became sore but the wires didn't bend. Frantic, he ran thither and hither. In that cramped space. Sharp pointed nails bit into his feet. The metal sheet grazed his body. Beyond the wire walls was his familiar world, divided, barred, and striped. For a long time, he kept shouting, running ... then finally collapsed into a corner exhausted, gazing outside with dimmed forlorn eyes. The vessels on the counter, the door, his den, none of it was visible from where he was. For a moment, he felt—this is not much smaller than my hole, what difference does it make—this one or that one? May as well stay here ... these people aren't that heartless ... they will throw me some crumbs ... but then it registered and he was benumbed. There was a difference between this den and that one. Oh yes, there was. This den had no ribbon! He became desperate. Again, he started pacing up and down, again he tried to cut through the wires, he battered his body against the bars ... Soon he was bruised in body and spirit. He kept thinking of the ribbon. The round beads were just like his eyes, shiny, bright ... the smooth silky feel, the gentle fluttering; it was all his and yet he was here and the ribbon was there. I must go there, I must get out, he kept repeating to himself. Why am I held captive here? How did Aai-Baba allow it? Or are they beginning to get tired of me? How would the ribbon know all this? What if she suddenly came alive? What if she gets soiled? That fluttering, that gentle caress, will it all remain locked up in that hole?

Again, the desperate scrabbling, the struggle to break free continued till morning.

Aai was the first to wake up and when came in she screamed!

"Aga ba-eee, look! He's been caught ... "

"Oh, really, he is!"

"Very good. Stealing my ribbons!"

"Aai, release him, na ... "

"Don't worry, I will not kill it ... come with me to see for yourself if you like ... "

"He is Ganapati's vahan, his mount, kill him and it will be a sin ... "

"What sin! Jivo jivasya jivati – one living being is food for another – it's the law of nature!"

"But he's lived in this house for so long, such a tiny little life ... "

"Why all the pity and sympathy now? When he nibbled stealthily at food you made such a fuss ... besides he is not going to kill him ... let him go ... here, take him ... give me some tea, will you ... "

"Where are the biscuits?"

"Who's going for a bath first?"

"Where's the towel gone?"

"Aga, he hasn't got his tea yet..."

"Get lunch ready early ... I will bring some fish ... " and the day went on normally.

Mr. Undeer began to burrow furiously, squeaking, scampering about ... Aai, though she was so busy, did throw him a piece of pav bread ... He squeaked louder ... pitifully, mournfully ... But Aai didn't hear him. I don't want any bread, he whimpered, I don't want any bhajji, just give me the ribbon from my den ... put it here next to me ... I don't want the bead ... But no one understood him.

He was taken to the laboratory in a cloth bag. Carefully and very gently, he was released into the clean transparent glass house. Brightly lit, airy, spotless ... smooth floors and walls ... everything so clean so new ... Mr. Undeer was bewildered. Alarmed. He didn't know what to make of this experience, how to deal with it. This world—brand new, desolate, gleaming, unused ... a different den ... the old house, the sounds, the hustle the bustle, the disgust, the smells, the grains of rice kept secretly at the mouth of his den, and that ribbon!

None of that was present here. Only silence. What was going on? Why was it happening? For whom and for what? Mr. Undeer couldn't understand any of it. For good or ill, though he had nothing to do with it, he was going to be used. Just as everybody is, all the time.

Crushing that pristine silence were human feet ... People clad in white robes peered at him ... Mr. Undeer was still. His ears pricked up with a nameless fear ... his heart thudded, his eyes terror stricken, unblinking ... They shook their heads, talked among themselves for long ... not a breath, not a smell, not a colour did Mr. Undeer understand ... They lifted him out and put him under a large instrument. Mr. Undeer's senses had gone beyond fear ... Once again, a fleck of hope, of escape took root in his heart and circulated throughout his body. In the next instant, a tight grip ... a sharp pain ... he screamed ... he saw a needle withdrawn and put away. Again, he became fearful ... the clasp and then back in the glass cage. All this was dreadful for Mr. Undeer ... He wondered, are these the creature they call Cat, Cat? They grab hold of you in a second ... you feel your life is gone ... they hurt you a little, then they let you go ... But in that release is embedded the anticipation of the next torture ... and life hangs in waiting , wondering when and how the torment will happen again ...

Suddenly, Undeer caught sight of a piece of cheese in front of him. For a while, the sharp flavour enticed him into forgetting everything. He nibbled at the delicious cheese and suddenly like a thousand pinpricks a memory stung him—the memory of a fluttering white ribbon … The ribbon he had stolen and hidden away in his hole, now languishing there all by herself! If that ribbon came alive I would have given away half the cheese to her, he thought.

The next day, Undeer was taken out again, but he was less afraid. Again, he was placed under a huge microscope. He too looked up … a large single human eye … He peered at it. It wasn't a particularly beautiful eye. In fact, from behind the lens it looked quite ferocious …

Again, the needle sting. He let out gasp and felt better. Just then, another needle jabbed him … He shuddered … a tiny fire was ignited inside him and soon it spread through his entire body right to the claws and the tail, to the tips of his ears. His mouth became rough and dry … he writhed in near fatal agony …

"My goodness, it seems the dose was slightly excessive … "

"Anyway, let's wait till tomorrow and then see … the mouth has turned red … that's a new development … "

"Give him this to eat, and only this much … nothing else … watch him carefully … "

They departed. The fire continued to burn his insides … the smooth insensitive cage … its cold lifeless touch … the deafening silence … it was only him and this burning body of his … he dragged himself around … gradually the fire cooled … Undeer wondered, Will Aai-Baba-Tai- Raju come to visit me today? Or have they forgotten this troublesome creature? My ribbon, she doesn't know my suffering, what I am going through! Had she been here the pain would have been easier to bear. .

The day went by … just like this.

Again, the sound of boots … the terrifying wait for unbearable pain … today, the doctor's girlfriend was accompanying him. Doctor was eager to show her his magnificent experiment. He was making a note of the joy on her wheatish face. Blooming, vivacious, exuberant … she floated into the laboratory like a colourful vision …

Blinking rapidly, she entwined her fingers with the doctor's and kept gazing at him dreamily, lightly; she rested her head on his shoulder trustingly, her sinuous body arching like the ribbon had done. Her brown hair cascaded down her back. He looked indulgently, lovingly at her transparent face … Her eyes were sparkling like the beads on the ribbon. He couldn't resist the temptation … he kissed her cheek … abashed, she moved away smiling …

"See … my new experiment … "

"Hmm … "

"From tomorrow, I expect to see many changes … Then, I can prove it … Watch … you know … After such a long and arduous journey, I have finally reached the point of success … All because of you … if you hadn't been by my side … "

"If you are going to talk like this, I am going …"

"Oh no … look at the chemical in this. We are giving it small doses … these are the preliminary signs … the skin looks slightly scorched … as if burnt … look even the mouth … "

"eeeee … sh! So ugly!"

"No baby, he will slowly get better. And then this thesis, this research will be presented to the world, name … fame … success … money … you know I have even identified a bungalow …" They were overcome with thoughts of imminent joy … She bent down to look at the poor unfortunate creature …

Undeer also raised his bleak helpless eyes and suddenly shuddered. The girl's hair was also tied up in an identical ribbon! He moved back and further back …

She was saying something and laughing and the ribbon, with its beads trembled and shook … Undeer stared at the ribbon with tired but joyful eyes. He dragged himself on his tired haunches, with painful claws and injured tail, along the floor of the smooth glass case. He went round and round … his eyes fixed on the ribbon … It was tied firmly to the hair … its ends flapping about helplessly … Undeer couldn't help himself. He uttered a feeble "chee… Will you come again tomorrow? The day after? Every day, wearing this same ribbon?" With their backs to him the two of them were laughing, pure, genuine laughter, their hands locked in a tight clasp. Lost in a world of dreams of the future, like a pair of cooing pigeons … The ribbon was mute. Undeer was silent. No one understood his language. They did not and would not. Ever. This ribbon wasn't that one. But at least she reminded him of his ribbon and was nearby. In front of him.

Undeer sighed long and deep. Not because of an intimation of death but because of a nameless anguish. It made him dejected, helpless, troubled but even then … the hope … perhaps this girl will come again tomorrow wearing this ribbon, to see my half dead suffering self … That ribbon!

And Undeer, running his hands over his burnt mouth awaited the next wave of pain …

Translated from Marathi by Keerti Ramachandra.

38
People's Court

Sarwat Khan

"So many heirs of the distinguished family residing in the splendid mansion were killed. But no one whimpered. Do the women have hearts made of stone?" Kalu Ram, the tea vendor, whispered secretly to Dongar Gola, while handing him a glass of tea in the morning.

"Yes, brother! All the men in the family were killed. The son of the elder lord, Hukum, and the two sons of the second lord, Hakim, study in a college in Mumbai. Only they are safe." Dongar Gola, who was now old, replied coughing and spitting on the dusty ground.

"Oh! Brother!" First tell me, did they have any animosity with the rioters?"

"Why do you ask this?"

"Don't you know that the riots are aimed at killing only minority." Kalu Ram's tone was a little sad.

"There was no animosity, brother! They were coming back in their flashing cars from their factories located far from the city. All tall, pink and fair. They were mistaken for Muslim-*pathans* and killed."

"Didn't the mob pull down their pants to confirm? Did they?"

"No, they didn't. It all happened too fast and in confusion. They had set the vehicles on fire. They realized their mistake only when the half-burnt bodies started to get exposed."

"How were the bodies brought home?"

"The mob came to leave them. They just said, "It happened by mistake. Perform their last rituals." The bodies are just lying there since yesterday. The relatives from Rajasthan will arrive today and then the last rites will be performed."

"Why are they quiet since yesterday? No wailing? The widows of those men ... their hearts must have shattered into pieces." An astonished Kalu

Sarwat Khan, *People's Court* In: *The Silence That Speaks*. Edited by: Haris Qadeer, Oxford University Press.
© Oxford University Press India 2022. DOI: 10.1093/oso/9780190132613.003.0039

Ram asked. Dongar Gola was his friend. They always talked to each other frankly.

"Oh, you don't know these Rajputs! Their women don't cry over death. Even when their husbands die, they control their tears."

"Why so? They are also human beings. Women have weak hearts. They wail and beat their breasts most."

"Yes, the junior Rani was on the verge of tears but when the eldest, Kunwar Rani Sahiba eyeballed her; she had to stifle her cries with the help of her *aanchal*."

"Why don't they cry?"

"Because they strictly observe *purdah*. So that their wailing is not audible outside."

"But this is a modern world. They all go outside. There is no *purdah* now."

"Yes, you are right." Dongar said yawning, "there is another important reason. Crying is against their prestige, dignity, and honour."

"Why so?" Kalu Ram's curiosity was increasing.

"This is how it has always been in their community."

"Why has it been so? What kind of a practice is it?"

"Brother, their custom is like that."

"That is what I would like to know. How did it become a custom?"

"As a matter of fact, crying is supposed to be a sign of timidity and cowardice, and the community has a reputation of being brave or it tries to look brave. Demonstrating cowardice hurts their dignity. It is a common custom in this community in Rajasthan." Dongar Gola explained to Kalu Ram wisely, as he picked up a half-burnt matchstick from the stove and lit it for his *beedi*.

"Oh! This is the matter. But it is like mocking the dead."

"Think what you like."

"It is not necessary that everyone is stout-hearted."

"True! It is not necessary."

"And if they want to cry, then?"

"The elders of the family don't let them do it. They stuff some piece of cloth into their mouths."

"This is not fair."

"May be, it's not. But the customs have to be followed. There is something called shame and honour."

"What will happen now?" Kalu Ram expressed his concern.

"Yes, I am going to see if I can get women of the *Golijat* caste from somewhere."

"Who are these *Golijat*?" Kalu Ram asked again taking an empty glass from a customer.

Now Dongar Gola was annoyed. He sharply retorted. "*Arey*! I am also from the same caste. But I am not married. I did not get married. Otherwise, our caste has always been following this custom. When men die, our women wail for them, and do it appropriately. If they feel like crying, they just try and pretend to cry, wail, and shriek, pull their hair, tear their clothes. This mourning ceremony is called "*palla lena.*" The more effectively it is performed, the more satisfied are the hearts of the Rajput women. They feel happy that they (hired women) are worth their salt. This is why I didn't get married. I don't like these customs. On top of that Rajput men don't spare our women their lasciviousness. Brother! It is an extreme kind of helplessness." Dongar Gola's anger and irritation gradually turned into sighs.

"Is this caste found in all the cities of Rajasthan?"

"No. This caste came into existence under the slave tradition. Rajputs give their daughters *Golas* and *Golis* as their wedding gifts. They slave for them throughout their lives, serve them and if anyone dies, they mourn. But only *Golis* do. *Golas* don't." Now Dongar Gola was feeling annoyed with Kalu Ram's questions.

"How does your generation perpetuate?"

"You don't know this? I'll tell you later. It is late now. The sun has climbed higher in the sky. The task is difficult." Dongar Gola said as he threw the remaining *beedi* stub.

"No, No! First, answer my question. Come on! Take another cup of tea. You can leave after that." Kalu Ram poured into a glass what was left over from the tea he had made for another customer and spoke with such sympathy and concern that Dongar Gola could not help but take it and resume his story. "Look! They bring us as dowry and marry us off to each other. They keep us with them. This is how our people have been serving them for centuries. But now our caste has stopped doing this. There are very few *Golas* and *Golis* in Rajasthan. They have also started adding the titles such as Shekhawat, Jhala, Rathore, and Bhati to their names. They, now, keep their surnames after their masters. They have also got rid of the tradition of *Gola* and *Goli*. Now, anyone who is needy, may be called to weep and lament on a paid basis. This is how they follow the custom of *palla lena*." Dongar Gola finished talking quickly and left Kalu Ram in a state of bewilderment and shock. He rode his bicycle, started to peddle fast and disappeared in a distant neighbourhood.

The entire city was divided into two parts. One part had turned into a cemetery, the other busy in celebration and jubilation. The latter was taking pride in demonstrating to the former how humanity is shamed and disgraced. The massacre of Muslims was carried out in an organized way. The state and the police provided full cooperation.

The rioters first prowled in trucks in the Muslim neighbourhood with computerized lists raising provocative slogans, then the mobs of young men armed with inflammable items, dangerous ammunitions, spears, and tridents would come in trucks to join them. First, they would plunder the houses of rich Muslims, then they would fill gas into the houses from the gas cylinders carried in the trucks, and burn the entire family alive by throwing a lit matchstick in. They would rape women in public. They would kill fathers, uncles, and grandfathers in front of their children, throw children into fire in front of their mothers. Not only that, they would also rip open the bellies of pregnant women and take foetuses out to throw them into fire. When women and children would be terrified, the rioters would laugh and dance naked in front of them, and would catch any woman and rape her in public.

It has been several months since all this started in the city. It seemed as if the city had no protector, no god, no Ram, no Rahim. Half of the city was burning. The other half was busy burning it. Not only human, but animals too were extinct. There were only hollow bodies, and their monstrosity shamed the animal kingdom. Thinking about the situation in the city, Dongar Gola reached a locality that was destroyed by fire. It was totally deserted, not even a soul was there. It was all scorched, devastated, blackened, and scattered. He felt scared and took to his heels. He had tears in his eyes. He had never come across such a spectacle in his entire life. "O God! What has happened to my country?" He thought to himself and looked up at the sky. He kept peddling on half-heartedly. He finally reached a locality which was in a state of chaos. It was infested with mosquitoes, and was full of squalor and stench. Much more fetid smell was coming from of half-naked, small and shrunken human bodies

… youth wrapped in just a piece of cloth … desolations of yellow eyes and skins hanging in folds. Dongar Gola parked his bicycle near a dirty slush flowing out of the gutter, and started to look around with curiosity. A number of children and women surrounded him. "What is the matter? What are you looking for?"

"You will have to cry and wail. Will you come with me? No one will get less than one thousand rupees."

The women started to look at him as if he had come from another planet. But when Dongar Gola explained the entire matter to them, they happily agreed. Now they had no doubt in their minds. What could they lose now? Husbands, honour, dignity, wealth and possessions, or household - they had lost everything. They were now free from fear and dread. Now they could only see their half-naked starving children, old and sick parents, and many such things. The sum of one thousand rupees meant a lot to them in this state.

"Only five women are enough."

"Rabia, you go … "

"Noor Jahan, you too … I will also go. I am more in need of money. My child is suffering from fever since yesterday. I have to arrange for his medicines no matter how." Maimuna insisted.

"Okay. Fine. You can go … Don't be late." This is how five women decided among themselves and started to follow Dongar Gola in a state of curiosity and sorrow. Each one of them had hundreds of questions in their minds. They were wondering how it would be possible to feel the intensity of the pain and sorrow of people who were not related to them so much so that they could wail. However, the need for money gave them strength … Oh God! What times have befallen us! The hands that were always raised to give were today forced to take. No one knows when time and situation change. Someone please tell us, what was our crime? Why were we ruined in the name of religion, politics, and community? … For what and how long will they be dispossessed and ruined? What has happened to human beings? It is so difficult to understand. A flood of emotions had sealed their lips. All of them looked up at the sky together with sorrowful eyes. They saw tears in each other's eyes and tried to console each other by pressing each other's shoulders, holding hands, and patting each other. But they didn't shed tears. Tears had dried up long ago. Half their way was covered in this state.

"Walk fast ... walk fast ... cover your heads. Hide your faces." Dongar Gola had sympathy in his tone.

"Okay". They all followed.

"I will take you to a place in the mansion where you must sit and cry. You must know this much that this is the custom of the family. You don't have to bother about anything else." The women kept listening to Dongar's instructions and followed him. There was a bustle in the mansion. Three *Kunwars* had arrived from Mumbai. Other relatives from Jodhpur had also reached. Dongar was an old servant in the house and was familiar with the etiquettes of the family. He kept leading them from the threshold to *mardana* (men's quarter) to *zenana* (women's quarter).

On the way, he instructed the women how to perform the custom of *palla*. Initially, the women hesitated and then realized there was no way out. They covered their heads and faces with their veils and started to weep and wail. The eldest Kunwar Rani was taken aback as she saw them. She knitted her brows; she immediately sent for Dongar Gola. She said as he came, "Dongar! Whom have you fetched? You could find only these Muslim women in the entire city? You should have thought a little. Have you lost your mind?"

"My Lord! The entire city is under curfew. I couldn't go too far. I brought them from a nearby relief camp. I was helpless. So were they. *Huzoor*, my lord! Please make do with them." Dongar Gola stooped down, joined his hands, and spoke in a tone which made the eldest Kunwar Rani speechless. She realized that she should be satisfied with whatever was available in these critical circumstances. The level of sympathy and humility she sat down with was the same as her level of alacrity she had gotten up with. Her eyes met the questioning eyes of a few women. She quickly averted her eyes and focused her attention on the Muslim women. These women were performing *palla* and the six young widows of the family were choking in their unsuccessful attempt to control their tears. The elderly women of the family and some relatives started to take off their jewelry. They remover their bangles, from wrists to elbows, and from the elbows to arms. One of them took off the *haath phool*, the other took off *pag pan*, and another, *jod*. When the eldest maternal aunt took off junior Rani's big necklace, *aar*, a lot of things became visible! The neckline of her shirt was deep and the elderly women tried to cover her with her fine *aanchal* but their efforts remained futile. It was all ready to spill out, the bosom as well as the pain and the grief … on one side these customs were being practiced, on the other … those five women …

In the beginning their wailings were fake and then one of them remembered her father; another, her husband; another, her young brother; another, her innocent child; one cried at her helplessness, one at her children's hunger … at their being orphaned … at their future … at their situation … the tragedies … the community … humanity … and many other things unknown. It turned into a squall. This was required. All the family members were satisfied with the *palla*. But even after two hours the *palla* didn't stop. All the members from the family were shocked to see this unprecedented kind of lamentation and expression of grief that ever was demonstrated in their family … even their faithful *Golis* had never mourned in this manner … finally, all the relatives joined to consoled these *Golis*.

Since it was not possible for them to get ice, the dead bodies started to smell. So, they somehow managed to stop the *palla* and asked the mourners to leave after paying them a sum of one thousand rupees each. Rabia, Noor Jahan, Maimuna, Shakira, and Zakia came out of the mansion and with heavy steps started to head towards their relief camp while trying to handle their swollen eyes, scattered hair and unkempt *aanchals*.

They had hardly reached the second turn on the road … when …

A mob … found their swollen eyes intoxicated … their hair scattered dark clouds … and their disorderly *aanchal* … and the cold wind and the mob started to perform a play. The scene started to be enacted. The atmosphere was already conducive, the performance was smooth. Characters started to appear on the stage. Rabia, Maimuna, Zakia … with inflamed eyes … torn hair … tattered *aanchal* … the mob … saffron clad … trident … spears … and freshly minted notes … and the spectators …

Around eight to ten women who were returning after worshipping at the temple of the Mother-goddess on the opposite end of the turn … worship-plates in their hands, and sacred offerings of the goddess in them … were absorbed in watching the street play with surreptitious gaze … they watched the entire spectacle and their hearts overflowed with joy and enthusiasm. They raised the slogan, "Hail to the Mother-goddess!," and began to sing devotional songs for the Mother-goddess… breathing fire … women, men, human … all had disappeared from the play, stage, characters, plot and spectators … they had all become hollow bodies … epitomes of depravity … they had started to dance … the spectator-women … their love, loyalty, sacrifice, meditation … all the virtues had left their bodies, and were now dancing in the sky in form of a circle. And incarcerating the virtues are many Mother-goddesses … God knows how many other mother-goddesses!

All these mother-goddesses had confined the virtues and the souls of the spectator-women in the circle they had built. The insensitive and emotionless hollow bodies and empty flesh and bones were demonstrating hatred, contempt, and violence with such barbarity that would shame the souls of beasts and animals. The street play had come to an end in half an hour and so had … inflamed eyes … unkempt hair … and their *aanchals* … !

Now for these *aanchals* there was no *Goli* available to perform *palla*.

First published as "Lok Adalat." Translated from Urdu by Aysha Munira Rasheed.

Notes on the Authors

Sara Aboobacker (born 1936) is a Kannada fiction writer and a translator. Her stories depict the plight of Muslim women in Kerela and Karnataka. She has seven novels, four collection of short stories, and a collection of essays to her credit. Her novel *Chandragiriya Theeradalli* (1984) was translated in English as *Breaking Ties*. She has received various prestigious literary awards such as the Karnataka Sahitya Akademi Award, 1984; Anupama Niranjan Award, 1987; Rathnamma Heggade Mahila Sahitya Award, 1996, etc.

Mrs. K Ahmad was a Muslim woman author from colonial Bengal. Her story "Spartan Hriday" appeared in *Saogat*, a leading monthly Bengali journal edited by Mohammad Nasiruddin and Abdul Karim. The journal encouraged women authors to publish their writings in the journal.

Eli Ahmed (b. 1934) is a renowned short story writer, script-writer, director, lyricist, costume designer, actress, and a social activist from Assam. In 2017, she was awarded Padma Shri by the Government of India in recognition of her immense contribution to literature, art, and education. She was also honoured with the Sahitya Akademi Bal Sahitya Puraskar 2015 for her lifelong engagement with children's literature. She has been the editor, publisher, and proprietor of *Orani*, the only women's magazine in the north-east India, since 1970. She composed the lyrics for some of most popular Assamese films of yesteryears, namely, "Dr Bezbaruah," "Baruar Sansar," "Sonmaina," and "Sadari," besides being the script-writer, art director, and costume designer for these and many other Assamese films. Her short story collections, among many, include *Ankur, Ashirbador Borosun*, and *Ji Kotha Nohole Kowa.*

Semeen Ali is the author of four collections of poetry to her credit. *Broken Barriers* (Writers Workshop, 2008), *Rose & Ashes* (Writers Workshop, 2008), *Origins* (Poets Printery, South Africa, 2012), and *Transitions.* Her fourth book- *Transitions* published by (Writers Workshop, 2014). She reviews books for *The Book Review, Muse India,* and for Sahitya Akademi's *Indian Literature* and other leading Indian journals. She is the Fiction and the Poetry editor for Muse India. She has edited an anthology of English poetry written by women poets from New Delhi called *Dilli* (Poets Printery, South Africa, 2014). She has co-edited *40 under 40 – An anthology of post globalisation poetry* with poet Nabina Das (Poetrywala, Paperwall Media & Publishing Pvt. Ltd, 2016), and *A Map Called Home* (Kitaab, Singapore (2018) edited with poet and journalist Manik Sharma. Her forthcoming anthology includes *Of Dry Tongues and Brave Hearts* (co-edited with Reema Ahmad, Red River, 2021).

Malika Amar Shaikh (b. 1957) is a Marathi author and political activist. From 1974, after her marriage to Namdeo Dhasal, the firebrand Dalit Poet, she got closely involved with the Dalit Panther Movement. She has chronicled her relationship with her husband in her controversial memoir *I Want To Destroy Myself* (Mala Udhvasta Vhaychai). Her poetry collections include *Manuspanache Bhinga Badalya Nantar, Valucha Priyakar, Mahanagar*, and *Deharutu*.

Asma Anjum Khan teaches English at a college in Maharashtra. She has written for prestigious publications like *Arab News, DailyO, Siasat Daily*, among others. She runs an NGO called the Foundation of English and Ethical Learning (FEEL) and regularly writes on issues of gender inequality and social and cultural inequalities. Her writings focus on marginalisation of Muslim community in India.

Jeelani Bano (b. 1936) is an acclaimed Urdu author who was awarded Padma Shri by the Government of India for her contribution in the field of literature. She also received the Andhra Pradesh Sahitya Akademi Award in 1960, followed by the Soviet Land Nehru Award in 1985. She is the recipient of the Qaumi Haali Award from the Haryana Urdu Academy. She has 22 books to her credit. Her major works include *Aiwaan-e-Ghazal, Baarish-e-Sang, Roshni ki Minar*, and *Sach ke Siwa*.

Jamila Begum lived in Kolkatta. Her Urdu short story "Husnara Begham" appeared in December 1915 in the Urdu journal *Tehzeeb-e- Niswan*, which was founded by Mumtaz Ali (1860–1935) in 1898 in partnership with his wife Muhammadi Begham (1878–1908).

Seemin Hasan (b. 1960) is a professor of English, translator, and a folklorist. Her stories, articles, and poetry have been published in journals and magazines of international repute. Her major publications are *The Voice of Feeling: Myth and Mythology in Keats' Poetry* and *Folktales of UP Tribe*.

Hijab Imtiaz Ali (1908–1999) was a renowned Urdu author from an aristocratic family of the Princely state of Hyderabad, Deccan. She is considered to be among the pioneers of romanticism in Urdu. She has written short stories, novels, and diaries. She published *Meri Natamam Mohabbat* at the age of twelve. She has the distinction of being among the first women pilots in the Indian subcontinent. She has translated Louisa May Alcott's famous classic novel *Little Women* into Urdu.

Rashid Jahan (1905–1952) was a doctor and writer known for her short stories and plays. She was a prominent member of the Communist Party of India and one of the founders of the Progressive Writers Association. She is believed to have written around twenty-five to thirty short stories and fifteen to twenty plays.

Sulema Khatun Kajol is a short story writer, a poet, and a social worker from Garo Hills, Meghalaya. She retired as a schoolteacher, and has four collections of poetry to her credit. Her two important works are *Bakya Baan and Jharochhshash*.

Mariam Karim is a pedagogue of French Language and Literature, freelance editor, and an author. She was born in Lucknow and studied at Jawaharlal Nehru University and the Sorbonne in Paris. Her first novel, *My Little Boat* (Penguin India, 2003) was nominated for the IMPAC International Award 2005 and the Hutch Crossword Award. Her second novel, *The Street of Mists*, was longlisted for the Man Asian Prize 2009. Her play *The Betrayal of Selvamary* was shortlisted for the Hindu Metro Plus Playwright Award 2010. Her play, *Fractals Search for the Real*, was longlisted for the Hindu Metro Plus Playwright Award 2011. Her children's musical dealt with street children. She writes reviews and articles on literature and has contributed short stories to anthologies such as the *Siècle 21* (Paris), *South Asian Review* (University of Pittsburgh), and *Our Voice*, the *PEN International Women Writers Anthology*. She published her first book of folk and fairy tales for children under the title *Tales Old and New* (Harper Collins India, 1994). For more than eleven years, she wrote a Read Aloud page in *Parenting* magazine with her illustrations. She has published a number of children's books (Tulika Publishers, Chennai) and contributed to anthologies, available in several Indian languages.

Sarwat Khan is an Urdu author based in Rajasthan. She has seven books of fiction and criticism to her credit including famous her novel *Andhera Pag* (2005). She is one of the first Urdu writers to depict cultures and traditions of Rajasthan in fiction. She is also known for her strong and vocal female characters. She currently teaches Urdu in Government Meera Girls' College (PG), Udaipur, Rajasthan.

Tasneem Khan works as a senior subeditor of *Rajasthan Patrika*. She has several short stories to her credit. Her novel *Eh Mere Rehnuma* was published by Bhartiya Jananpith; It was also recommended for Navlekhan Award in 2015. Her story *Khwabo Mein Uljhi Barat* won Nilima Tickoo Award. Her recent publication includes *Dastan-e Hazrat* (2019), a compilation of nine short stories.

Asrafi Khatun was born in Burdwan, West Bengal. She is a professor of Bangla at Jamalpur College, and has twenty books to her credit. Her notable works are: *Akash Hote Cheyechhilam, 50 ti Golpo, Alo-Andharer Golpo, Anu Golpo, Ami Nari Tai* amongst others. She writes poems, short-stories, essays, and children's literature. She also edits a magazine for children called *Lal Pori Nil Pori*.

Kasema Khatun (b. 1951) hails from the Telipara village in the Dhubri district of Assam. She is a retired schoolteacher and a recipient of literary pension. She writes poetry in Assamese, Bangla, Hindi, English, and the *Goalparia Desi* dialect. She has authored thirteen collections of poetry, two collections of short stories, a novel, a collection of prose narratives, and a dictionary of the *Goalparia* dialect. She was honoured with the National Award for Teachers by the Government of India in the year 2002. She is also the recipient of the Bharatiya Dalit Sahitya Akademi Fellowship, Bhagwan Buddha Award, Michael Madhusudan Dutt Award, and Rohilla Puraskar.

Huma Kidwai is the author of the novel '*The Hussaini Alam House*,' published in 2012 by Zubaan, New Delhi. Her website www.humarkidwai.com carries her other writings like reviews of her novel, poetry, essays, travelogue, book reviews and other works. Her novel has been a part of the syllabus for Study in India Programme for foreign students in Hyderabad Central University and for women's studies, and at MA level in Tata Institute of Social Sciences. She has taught 'Literature as a resource for study of Muslim societies' for five years at Hyderabad Central University, as part of a new inter-disciplinary optional course, 'Sociology of Muslim Societies' to MA sociology class. She has also taught History of Islam and Sufism. She is interested in *Dakhni*, the language of the Deccan Plateau and has begun translation of literary works from Urdu to English. Interested in the Progressive Writers' Movement of Hyderabad and its impact on society. She asserts that her primary identity is that of an Atheist social observer, creative writer and traveller. Passionate about wildlife.

Moghal Mahmood was born in 1914 in her ancestral house Nawab-ki-Deorhi in Benares. She did her MA in Persian from Allahabad University in 1952. Most of her stories were set in Nawab-ki-Deorhi and published in the 1950s and 1960s in the literary journal *Kahani*. A collection of her stories for children, *Sunahle Pankh*, was published by Saraswati Press. In 1966, she established the Bal Bharti School in Benares and functioned as the principal till her death in 1993.

Zakia Mashadi is an acclaimed Urdu fiction writer and a translator. For a brief span of time, she worked at the Demographic Research Center. She has taught Psychology for six years at Loreto College. She has published four collections of short stories so far and has also published several books of translated fiction. Her major works include *Paray Chehre* (1984), *Naqsh-e-Natamam* (2008), and *Ye Jahan-Rang-e-Bu* (2013). She has also translated Urdu short stories of Jeelani Bano into English as *The Alien Home & Other Stories*.

Husn Tabassum Nihan (b. 1976) is a Hindi fiction writer and a poet. She has won many awards such as Samaj Ratan Samman, Saraswati Sahitya Samman, Mahadevi Varma Smriti Samman, and Kavya Bharti Samman. Her works include *Neele Pankhonwali Ladkiyan*, *Mausambhar Yaad*, and *Jab Hum Chaand Dekha Karte Thae*.

Mrs. Abdul Qadir was born in Jhelum (now in Pakistan) in 1898. A prolific author of short fiction, She wrote several anthologies of short stories beginning in 1940s. Described by Qurratulain Hyder as the "peerless writer of horror stories," her oeuvre traverses several other generic traits, such as speculative fiction, romances, melodramas, and even political/social commentaries. Her stories are often atmospheric, and play heavily on elaborate descriptions, detailed moods and evocative settings. She published her debut collection, *Lashon ka Shehr*, in around the year 1939 followed by another collection *Sada-e-Jaras was Digar Afsaane* in the same year.

Sami Rafiq is Professor of English at Aligarh Muslim University, Aligarh, India. She writes poetry and short Stories for which she has received several awards. She translates from Urdu into English and has been a regular contributor to the Inner Voice column (*Hindustan Times*) and has also contributed many humorous verses to Khushwant Singh's Malice Column. She has also published for Young World (*The Hindu*) and Friday Review (*The Hindu*). She has published more than a hundred articles, features, and stories in different national newspapers and magazines. Her translations have been published in *The Sunday Observer*, *Indian Literature* (Sahitya Akademi), and in *Neither Night Nor Day* (Harper Collins) besides others. Her works include an E-novel titled *The Small Town Woman* and *Aahung*, an English translation of Asrarul Haq Majaz's poetry.

Zahra Rai was born in 1917 in the same ancestral house as her sister, Moghal Mahmood. Between 1957 and 1977, her stories were regularly published in *Kahani*, *Kalpana*, and *Nayi Kahaniyan*, among other journals. She had an MA in Music from Allahabad University and remained an informal practitioner of Indian classical music all her life. She was the founder and principal of the Munshi Premchand Memorial School in Allahabad and continued to be involved in its activities till her death in 1993. She was married to the editor and publisher Sripat Rai, who was the elder son of Munshi Premchand.

Rokkiah Begum alias Rajathi Salma (born 1968) is a poet, novelist, columnist, and a social worker. Her novel *The Hours Past Midnight* was longlisted for the Man Asian Booker Prize. Her collection of poems includes *Oru Maalaiyum Innoru Maalaiyum* (2000) and *Pachchai Devathai* (2003). With her collections of poetry, she has pioneered a new genre of women's poetry in Tamil literature.

Tarannum Riyaz (1960–2021) was a noted Urdu fiction writer, poet, essayist, and a translator. She was a senior fellow of the Ministry of Culture, Government of India. She was a SAARC Literature Awardee for the year 2014. She authored more than fifteen books of fiction, criticism, and poetry. Her works have been translated in various Indian and foreign languages.

Razia Sajjad Zaheer (1917–1979) was born in Ajmer, Rajasthan. She was married to Sajjad Zaheer, an important Litterateur and one of the founders of the Progressive Writers Association. Her first novel *Sare Sham* (1953) deals with partition and communal riots. She published *Nuquush-e-Zindaan*, a compilation of her husband's letters that he wrote from the Rawalpindi prison. Her notable novels are *Suman*, *Kaante*, and *Allah Megh De*. Her short stories are collected under the titles *Zard Gulab* and *Allah De Bandah Le*.

Rokeya Sakhawat Hossain or Begum Rokeya (1880–1932) was feminist thinker, litterateur, educationist, social reformer, and a political activist from colonial India (present-day Bangladesh). She is widely regarded as a pioneer of women's liberation in South Asia. She played a crucial role in awakening women in general and Muslim women in particular. In 1911, she set up Sakhawat Memorial Girls' School, and in 1916, she founded the Muslim Women's Association, an organization that fought for women's education. Her major works are '*Sultana's Dream*', *Padmarag*, and *Motichur*.

Rubina Shabnam (b. 1971) is a poet, short story writer, translator, and an academician. She writes in Punjabi and Urdu. Currently, she is the Head of Department, Nawab Sher Mohammad Khan Institute of Advanced Studies in Urdu, Persian and Arabic, Punjabi University, Malerkotla, Punjab. She received State Shiromani Sahitkar award for her contribution to literature.

Shajahana is a poet and a short story writer; she writes in Telugu. Her first collection of poetry, *Nakab* deals with the issues gender discrimination, culture, and communal disharmony. Her writings majorly depict the agony of Muslim women in her society.

Nasira Sharma (born 1948) is a noted Hindi fiction writer. She has published ten novels and a number of short stories. Her famous works include *Parijat, Mere Priya Kahaniyaan, Ajnabi Jazira, Patthar Gali,* and *Aurat Ke Liye Aurat*. She was awarded Sahitya Academy Award for her novel *Parijat*.

Sheeba EK is a prolific writer from Kerala. She has published novels, short stories, and novelettes in Malayalam. She has won several prestigious awards including Ponkunnam Varkey Story Award, Sahithyashree Award, Suvarnarekha Award, Thulunadu Novel Award, Pravasi Shabdham Award, New Age Riyad Kamala Surayya Award, and many more. She has written novels such as *Dhuniya* (2013), *Manjanadikalude Suryan* (2017), *Rithu Marmarangal* (2012), short story collections such as *Y to K* (2004), *Neela Lohitham* (2013), *Kanalezhuthu* (2016), novelette such as *Vasanthathil Tharishakunna Poomaram* (2018), and a memoir titled *Azhichukalayanavathe aa Chilankagal*. She has also translated the following works into Malayalam: *Typhoon* (Qaisra Shahraz), *Saraswathi Park* (Anjali Joseph), *The Novice* (Thich Nhat Haan), and *Beyond the Veil* (Fatema Mernissi).

Begum Sufia Hossain was a Bengali Muslim author. Her story "Dear Naseem" appeared in *Saogat*, a leading monthly journal from Bengal.

Wajeda Tabassum (1935–2011) was a novelist, short story writer, poet, and a film lyricist. She has twenty-seven books in Urdu to her credit. She used Deccani Urdu dialect for her stories. Her stories appeared in various popular twentieth-century Urdu magazines such as *Shama* and *Beeswin Sadi*. Her short story "Uttran" was adapted into *Kamasutra: A Tale of Love* by Meera Nair. Her works include *Shahr-e-Mamnu, Teh Khana, Kaise Samjhaoon, Phul Khilne Do, Utran, Zakhme-e-Dil Aur Mahak*, and *Zar, Zan, Zamin*.

Noor Zaheer is a researcher and social activist. She is a recipient of the Times Fellowship for "The changing face of Theatre in Northern India" and the Senior Fellowship from Department of Culture for "Surviving on the edge" an analysis of the performing arts of the tribes of the north-western border of India. She has written the Delhi Hindi Academy Award winner *Mere Hisse ki Roshnai, Barh Uraiyye*, and *My God is a Woman*, and *Surkh Karawan ke Hamsafar*, a travelogue of Pakistan. Noor is at present working on the Buddhist Monasteries of Himachal Pradesh, documenting the oral traditions and the performing arts of the Lama tradition.

Annie Zaidi is the author of *Bread, Cement, Cactus: A Memoir of Belonging and Dislocation, Prelude to a Riot, Gulab, Love Stories # 1 to 14, Known Turf: Bantering with Bandits and Other True Tales*, and the co-author of *The Good Indian Girl*. A series of illustrated poems, *Crush*, was made in collaboration with artist Gynelle Alves. She is the editor of *Unbound: 2000 Years of Indian Women's Writing*, and *Equal Halves*. She received Tata Literature Live Award for fiction (2020) and the Nine Dots Prize (2019) and The Hindu Playwright Award (2018) for her play, *Untitled 1*. Her radio script 'Jam' was named regional (South Asia) winner for the BBC's International Playwriting Competition (2011). Her work has appeared in various anthologies and literary journals including *The Griffith Review, The Aleph Review, The Massachusetts Review, The Charles River Journal, The Missing Slate*, and *Out of Print*. She has also written and directed the documentary film, *In Her Words: The Journey of Indian Women*.

Ather Zia is a political anthropologist, poet, short fiction writer, and columnist. She is an Associate Professor in the Department of Anthropology and Gender Studies program at the University of Northern Colorado Greeley. Ather is the author of *Resisting Disappearances: Military Occupation and Women's Activism in Kashmir (June 2019)* which won the 2020 Gloria Anzaldua Honorable Mention award, 2021 Public Anthropologist Award and Advocate of the Year Award 2021. She has been featured in the Femilist 2021, a list of 100 women from the Global South working on critical issues. She is the co-editor of Can You Hear Kashmiri Women Speak (Women Unlimited 2020), *Resisting Occupation in Kashmir (Upenn 2018) and A Desolation called Peace (Harper Collins, May 2019)*. She has published a poetry collection "*The Frame*" (1999) and another collection is forthcoming. In 2013 Ather's ethnographic poetry on Kashmir has won an award from the Society for Humanistic Anthropology. She is the founder-editor of Kashmir Lit and is the co-founder of Critical Kashmir Studies Collective, an interdisciplinary network of scholars working on the Kashmir region.

BM Zuhara (b. 1952) is a renowned author from Kerala. She is the first Muslim women to have won the Kerala Sahitya Academy Award (2008). In 1992, she received Lalithambika Antharjanam Smaraka Visheshal Puraskaram. Her major novels are *Kinavu* (1990), *Mozhi* (1991), *Iruttu* (1994), *Nilavu* (1997), *Nizhal* (1999), *Aakashabhoomikalude Thakkol* (2008), *Prakashathinumel Prakasham* (2012).

Notes on the Translators

A Suneetha is a senior fellow at and coordinator of Anveshi Research Centre for Women's Studies. She is a political theorist who is invested in the questions of gender and minority. Her research interests include gender and violence, secularism, and the Muslim woman's question and Muslim politics in the Telugu region, more specifically of Hyderabad. She is part of the editorial team of bilingual Anveshi Broadsheet on Contemporary Politics. Along with MA Moid, she is working towards a book on Muslim politics.

Amit Julka likes to think that he can wear several hats. The formal one that he wears is that of a political scientist, where his work takes him to the intersection of international relations, South Asian studies, and popular culture. His research revolves around understanding the role of the masses' common-sense on international and domestic politics. He is also working on a co-authored book manuscript, tentatively titled *Past Perfect, Future Tense: The Evolution of Indian National Identity, 1950–2010*. However, he finds real joy as a student of Punjabi and Urdu literature. He is also the co-founder of the *Mitti Pao* podcast, a multilingual India-Pakistan collaboration that aims to blur the Radcliffe line.

Aysha Munira Rasheed is professor at the Department of English, Aligarh Muslim University, India. She has delivered talks and has participated in panel discussions on topics of social, cultural, and literary relevance in India, USA, Italy, and UK. She has been published by reputed publishers including Routledge, Wiley-Blackwell. and Sahitya Akademi. Her areas of interest include, but are not limited to, Postcolonial Studies, Comparative Literature, Translation Studies, and Gender Studies.

Ayshath Shamah Rahmath is a Language Instructor at Lakepark Residence KL, North Kuala Lumpur, Malaysia. She has earned her PhD in postcolonial literature at Universiti Kebangsaan Malaysia (National University of Malaysia). She has worked in several educational institutions, both in the public and private sectors, in Kerala, India. She has also worked with LILA Foundation for Translocal Initiatives, Delhi.

Arzuman Ara teaches English at the English and Foreign Languages University, Shillong. Her areas of interest are Partition literature, English Studies in India, Media Rights, and Language and Education. She has extensively published on various academic fields like Pedagogy, Film Studies, Narrative Cultures, Gender, and Postcolonialism. Her English translation of Imtiaz Mahmud's Bangla poetry. *Maxim*, has been published from Bangladesh. Her forthcoming work includes an English translation of Imtiaz Mahmud's poems, *Kalo Kautuk* (Black Humour).

B Mangalam is professor at the Department of English, Aryabhatta College, University of Delhi. Her research work pertains to gender and caste intersectionality in Tamil Dalit fiction. She has published critical editions of *Pride and Prejudice* (1999), *Paradise Lost*, Book 9 (2000), *The Balcony* (2001), *The Book of Vanci, Cilappatikaram* (2015), and Ilango Adigal's Silappadhikaram (2020), Worldview Publications.. She has published articles on translations and Dalit Studies in various journals and critical volumes. She translates from Tamil and Hindi into English.

Dhurjjati Sarma earned his MA (English) and MPhil (Comparative Indian Literature) from University of Delhi, and PhD degree in English Literature from the English and Foreign Languages University, Shillong. He is assistant professor at the Department of Modern Indian Languages and Literary Studies, Gauhati University, Assam. His areas of interest are literary criticism, literary history, comparative literature, and cultural studies, with special emphasis on Indian Literature.

Haris Qadeer teaches at the Department of English, University of Delhi. He has translated writings of Rokeya Sakhwat Hossain, Zafar Ali Khan, Krishn Chandra, Joginder Paul, Anis Rafi, Manto, and Tarannum Riyaz. He was a visiting fellow to the Department of English, Potsdam University, Germany (2019). He has coedited a special issue on Postcolonial World Literature, *Thesis Eleven* (SAGE). His forthcoming books include *Sultana's Sisters: Genre, Genre, and Genealogy in South Asian Muslim Women's Fiction* (Routledge, 2021) and *Medical Maldaies: Doctors, Patients, and Hospitals in Indian Fiction* (Niyogi Books, forthcoming).

Hina Nandrajog is Associate Professor at the Department of English, and currently serving as Officiating Principal, Vivekananda College, University of Delhi. After her M.Phil. in English from the University of Delhi, she completed her Ph.D. from Punjabi University, Patiala. She is an academic, scholar, critic, teacher, and translator, and has published more than fifty critical articles and translations. Her areas of interest are the Partition of India in 1947 from a historical and literary perspective, the idea of diversity and multi-linguality in India and translation. She translates from Punjabi and Hindi into English and has won several awards. Among these are Katha Prize for Translation in 1999 and 2001, and a Consolation Prize from Sahitya Akademi in 2007. She was on the panel of jury members for the Sahitya Akademi Translation Prize 2008 in Punjabi and has been a part of several translation projects for the National Book Trust, Sahitya Akademi, Centre for Development of Punjabi Language and Culture (Punjabi University), Punjabi Academy and the Centre for Academic Translation and Archiving (CATA), (University of Delhi & University Grants Commission). She has also been actively involved in creating e.content for the Institute of Life Long Learning, University of Delhi.

Jaideep Pandey is a doctoral fellow at the University of Michigan, Ann Arbor, US. His research is on early 20th-century Urdu periodicals for women. His interests lie at the intersection of Islam, gender, genre, and print culture. He has previously taught at

St. Stephen's College and completed an MPhil in Women's and Gender Studies from Ambedkar University, Delhi.

Jyotika Elhance is Associate Professor of English at Vivekananda College, University of Delhi. Her areas of interest are Translation Studies and Indian Literature. Her doctorate is on *Naturalism in the Novels of Stephen Crane*. One of her translated works has been awarded Consolation Prize in the *Golden Jubilee Literary Translation Competition* organized by Sahitya Akademi, New Delhi. She has to her credit the English translation of *Kasturi Mrig*, an award-winning compilation of Rajasthani short stories by Chetan Swami and *Eh Mere Rehnuma*, a novel shortlisted by Bhartiya Jnanpith in the '*navlekhan*' category by Tasneem Khan.

Kanupriya Dhingra researches on the History of the Book and Print Cultures, with a focus on Delhi (India), from an ethnographic perspective. She earned her doctorate under the Felix Scholarship Fund from SOAS, University of London in 2021, for the dissertation titled 'Daryaganj's Parallel Book History'. While writing her doctoral thesis on the parallel book markets and the *nayi-jaisi* books of Old Delhi, she delivered talks on her research at The University of Oxford, The British Library, The Institute of Historical Research and the Book and Print Initiative, School of Advanced Studies, London, University of Delhi, SOAS, Ambedkar University, and Jadavpur University. Her work, creative and academic, has been published by *Himāl SouthAsian*, *The Caravan*, *Scroll.in*, *Indian Literature*, *Guftgu*, *Indian Writers Forum*, among others. She is also contributing a chapter to the fourth volume of the *Book History in India* series. Currently, she teaches at the Jindal School of Languages and Literature, at O.P. Jindal Global University, Sonipat.

Keerti Ramachandra has been a teacher of English, a translator of long and short fiction and nonfiction from Marathi, Kannada, and Hindi and has edited over 75 books from all the leading publishers. She has won the Katha A K Ramanujan Award for translating from two languages, and her translation of a Marathi novel *A Dirge for the Damned* was shortlisted for the Crossword award in 2016. The following are among her Marathi translations: *A Dirge for the Dammed, and Mahanayak* (Vishwas Patil), *A Faceless Evening and Other Stories* (Gangadhar Gadgil's short stories), *The Song of Life and Other Stories* (Vijaya Rajadhyaksha), and *Of Closures and New Beginnings* (Saniya) Marathi. From Kannada, *Hindutva or Hind Swaraj* (UR Ananthamurty) with Vivek Shanbhag, and several short stories by Bolwar Mahamad Kunhi which have appeared in anthologies and magazines in India and abroad. From Urdu/Hindi, *A Dying Sun and other stories* (Joginder Paul) with Usha Nagpal, and several stories by Premchand in the Premchand collection. Three of her translations appeared in *Land Lust* (Joginder Paul). Presently, she is a visiting faculty at Mount Carmel College, Bangalore, where she teaches post graduate courses and communication skills.

Mohammed Afzal is assistant professor of English at Zakir Husain Delhi College, University of Delhi, India. His PhD thesis is a sociological study of the early Urdu novel with special reference to the emergence of the Muslim service class in late nineteenth-century colonial India. He has made many academic presentations on the Urdu novelist Deputy Nazir Ahmad in many international and national conferences, such as University of Wisconsin, Madison, USA, School of Oriental and African Studies, University of London, UK, University of Chicago, USA, University of Delhi, and Aligarh Muslim University, India. He is the author of the book *Relocating Jane Eyre: Religion and Politics in Victorian Britain* (2019).

Noor Zaheer is a researcher and social activist. She is a recipient of the Times Fellowship for "The Changing Face of Theatre in Northern India" and the Senior Fellowship from Department of Culture for "Surviving on the Edge" an analysis of the performing arts of the tribes of the north-western border of India. She has written the Delhi Hindi Academy Award winner *Mere Hisse ki Roshnai*, *Barh Uraiyye*, and *My God is a Woman*, both novels and *Surkh Karawan Ke Hamsafar*, a travelogue of Pakistan. Noor is at present working on the Buddhist Monasteries of Himachal Pradesh, documenting the oral traditions and the performing arts of the Lama tradition.

Sara Rai is the author of three collections of short stories and a novel in Hindi. She has translated, among other books, *Premchand's Kazaki and Other Marvellous Tales*, Hachette 2013 and (with Arvind Krishna Mehrotra) Vinod Kumar Shukla's *Blue is Like Blue* (Harper Collins, 2019). Johanna Hahn's German translation of her stories *Im Labyrinth*, published by Draupadi Verlag, Heidelberg, won the Coburg Rückert Prize 2019 and was also nominated for the Weltempfänger Prize, Frankfurt 2020. She is Zahra Rai's daughter and lives in Allahabad. She is currently working on a collection of autobiographical essays in English.

Semeen Ali is the author of four collections of poetry to her credit. *Broken Barriers* (Writers Workshop, 2008), *Rose & Ashes* (Writers Workshop, 2008), *Origins* (Poets Printery, South Africa, 2012), and *Transitions*. Her fourth book- *Transitions* published by (Writers Workshop, 2014). She reviews books for *The Book Review*, *Muse India*, and for Sahitya Akademi's *Indian Literature* and other leading Indian journals. She is the Fiction and the Poetry editor for Muse India. She has edited an anthology of English poetry written by women poets from New Delhi called *Dilli* (Poets Printery, South Africa, 2014). She has co-edited *40 under 40 – An anthology of post globalisation poetry* with poet Nabina Das (Poetrywala, Paperwall Media & Publishing Pvt. Ltd, 2016), and *A Map Called Home* (Kitaab, Singapore (2018)edited with poet and journalist Manik Sharma. Her forthcoming anthology includes *Of Dry Tongues and Brave Hearts* (co-edited with Reema Ahmad, Red River, 2021).

Somrita Ganguly is a poet and literary translator. She was affiliated with Brown University, USA, as a Fulbright Doctoral Research Fellow. She is the editor of *Quesadilla and Other Adventures: Food Poems* (Hawakal Publishers, 2019) and has translated Dinesh Chandra Chattopadhyay's *Firesongs* (BEE Books, 2019), Ashutosh Nadkar's *Shakuni* (Juggernaut Books, 2019), and Shankarlal Sengupta's *The Midnight Sun* (2018). She translates from Bengali and Hindi to English and was selected by the

National Centre for Writing, UK, as an emerging translator in 2016. She was invited as translator-in-residence at Cove Park, Scotland, in October 2017, and in December 2017, she was invited as poet-in-residence at Arcs of a Circle, Mumbai, an artistes' residency organized by the U.S. Consulate in Bombay. Her work has been showcased at the 2017 London Book Fair, and she has been published in *Asymptote*, *Words Without Borders*, *In Other Words*, and Trinity College Dublin's *Journal of Literary Translation*, among others. She has taught British literature to undergraduate and graduate students in Delhi and Calcutta and has presented research papers at various national and international conferences in India, Singapore, UK, and USA. She has fourteen academic publications to her credit and is a recipient of the Jawaharlal Nehru Memorial Fund Award (2013) and the Sarojini Dutta Memorial Prize (2011).

Tahira Naqvi is a Senior Language Lecturer, New York University, US. She is the author of two collections of short stories: *Atar of Roses* and *Dying in a Strange Country*. She is also known for her translations into English of several works of prominent author, Ismat Chughtai, as well as other well-known women writers of Urdu fiction. Her major works include *Vintage Chughtai: The Best of Her Stories*, *The Quilt and Other Stories*, *The Heart Breaks Free*, *The Wild One* (Women Unlimited/Kali for Women Press), and *My Friend, My Enemy: A Prose Anthology*. Ismat Chughtai (Kali for Women) *Cool, Sweet Water by Khadija Mastur* (Oxford University Press, Pakistan), *Quilt and Other Stories by Ismat Chughtai. A collection of short fiction* by Ismat Chughtai (Sheep Meadow Press, New York), *Another Lonely Voice: The Life and Works of Saadat Hasan Manto* (Vanguard Books Ltd., Pakistan), *Masooma* by Ismat Chughtai (Women Unlimited, India), *A Very Strange Man* by Ismat Chughtai (Women Unlimited, India), *The Crooked Line: Terhi Lakir* (The Feminist Press, New York, 2006). Currently, she is translating fictions by Hijab Imtiaz Ali.

Miraan Punjabi is a translator, freelance photographer, traveller, and an entrepreneur. He has translated short stories, poetry, articles, and essays which have been published in several Indian as well as international literary journals

Varsha Rao was born and raised across the length and breadth of the country and believes she has seen it all. After a short stint as an engineer, she realised her heart and mind belongs to the world of words. Six long years as a journalist, endless bylines and hundreds of interviews later, she's currently taking on the messy world of social media as a content producer in an Australian travel company. She's constantly dabbled in translation works alongside her grandfather who was a well-known writer in North Karnataka.

National Centre for Writing, UK, as an emerging translator in 2018. She was invited as translator-in-residence at Cove Park Scotland in October 2017, and in December 2017, she was invited as poet in-residence at [illegible] of a Circle, Mumbai, an artists' residency organized by the [illegible] Consulate in Bombay. Her work has been showcased at the 2017 London Book Fair and she has been published in *Asymptote*, *Words Without Borders*, *In Other Words*, and Trinity College Dublin's *Journal of Literary Translation*, among others. She has taught British literature to undergraduate and graduate students in Delhi and Calcutta and has presented research papers at various national and international conferences in India, Singapore, UK, and USA. She has fourteen academic publications to her credit and is a recipient of the Jawaharlal Nehru Memorial Fund Award (2013) and the Sarojini Dutta Memorial Prize (2011).

Tahira Naqvi is Senior Language Lecturer, New York University, US. [illegible]

day however, [illegible] first time despite these casual invitations floating in the air along with the aromas [illegible] the bustle and the [illegible] in the house [illegible] remained aloof. Mr Under [illegible] was in no way a part of it. Where earlier he would feel compelled to go outside to join the people and take his place beneath a chair that [illegible] like leaving his hole. Nobody in the house noticed him [illegible] kept looking at the ribbon. Who knows what he had been thinking. Was he convinced that it would suddenly come to life and stand before him? If that happened then what language would the ribbon speak to him in? Would the ribbon have small beady eyes like himself? [illegible] live [illegible]? Such weird questions must have [illegible]

[illegible] like the waves of the ocean [illegible]

[illegible]

[illegible] was hushed. Again [illegible] of satisfaction, idle chatter [illegible]. Never before had Under [illegible] urge to like scream "Quiet!" [illegible] squeak.

[illegible]

getting [illegible] and exhalation. The time between [illegible] between one experience and another [illegible]. Between one human being and another.

When that which is unavoidable [illegible] and acceptable at the same time [illegible]

[illegible] the hearing of his ear yet.

[illegible] I will bring some fish [illegible] and the day went on [illegible]

Mr. Under[illegible] began to burrow [illegible], squeaking, scampering about [illegible] and though she was so busy, did throw him a piece of bread [illegible] He squeaked louder [illegible] pitifully, mournfully [illegible] But Aai didn't [illegible] he whimpered, I don't want any bhajji, just give me the [illegible] from my pen [illegible] put it here next to me [illegible] I don't want the bread [illegible] But no one understood him.

He was [illegible] to the laboratory [illegible] Carefully and very gently he was [illegible] to the [illegible] transparent glass house [illegible] brightly lit [illegible]

[illegible]

[illegible] of his den and the ribbon [illegible]

[illegible] What was going on? Why [illegible]